James Morton was ~~~
marily involved in defence work. ~~~
*Gangland, Gangland Volume 2, Gangland Interna~~~
East End Gangland, Bent Coppers: a survey of police
corruption* and *Supergrasses and Informers*, a study of
the informer's role throughout history. James Morton has
also co-written *Nipper*, the story of a man who brought
the Krays to justice, *Mad Frank*, the autobiography of
the celebrated villain Frankie Fraser, and its sequel, *Mad
Frank and Friends*, and edited *The Barmaid's Tale*, the
story of the woman whose evidence secured the conviction
of Ronnie Kray.

Also by James Morton

NIPPER (co-author with Leonard Read)
GANGLAND
GANGLAND Volume II
GANGLAND INTERNATIONAL
EAST END GANGLAND
BENT COPPERS
MAD FRANK (co-author with Frankie Fraser)
MAD FRANK AND FRIENDS
SUPERGRASSES AND INFORMERS
THE BARMAID'S TALE (ed)

A CALENDAR
OF KILLING

James Morton

WARNER BOOKS

For Dock Bateson, with love.

A *Warner* Book

First published in Great Britain in 1997
by Little, Brown and Company
This edition published by Warner Books in 1997
Reprinted 2001

Copyright © James Morton 1997

The moral right of the author has been asserted.

All rights reserved.
No part of this publication may be reproduced,
stored in a retrieval system, or transmitted, in any
form or by any means, without the prior
permission in writing of the publisher, nor be
otherwise circulated in any form of binding or
cover other than that in which it is published and
without a similar condition including this
condition being imposed on the subsequent purchaser.

A CIP catalogue record for this book
is available from the British Library.

ISBN 0 7515 1842 5

Typeset by Palimpsest Book Production Limited,
Polmont, Stirlingshire
Printed and bound in Great Britain by
Clays Ltd, St Ives plc

Warner Books
A division of
Little, Brown and Company (UK)
Brettenham House
Lancaster Place
London WC2E 7EN
www.littlebrown.co.uk

Acknowledgements

My thanks are due, as always, to a number of people. In strictly alphabetical order they include Mickey Bailey, J.P. Bean, Lisa Crandon, Marie and Clifford Elmer, who have gone out of their way to send me the books I needed, Jonathan Goodman, Jean-Ann Hyslop, Jennifer Kavanagh, Rebecca Kerby, Paul Koreng, Dominique Harvie, Loretta Lay, Edda Tasiemka, Richard Whittington-Egan, Alice Wood, Camille Woolf, who has allowed me to browse through her shelves at Grey House Books, and to the *Globe and Mail*, the *Hayes and Harlington Gazette* and the staff at the Public Records Office at both Chancery Lane and Kew as well as various public library staff.

As always, the greatest thanks are due to Dock Bateson who, in addition to her usual support, has tirelessly searched out cases which would not otherwise have come to my attention.

Author's Note

Pin-pointing the moment of death is something of an inexact science. I have tried to ensure that the date given is the one when the killing definitely occurred, or when the victim was last seen, or when the body was found.

JANUARY

1 January, 1961

On the morning of 1 January 1961, Jean Sylvia Constable was found dead in the Great Dunmow, Essex flat of Wills Eugene Boshears, a staff sergeant in the American Air Force. Boshears, whose wife was in Scotland with her parents, and who had been drinking all day, met Jean Constable in a public house and returned to his flat with her and another man, Salt. They all fell asleep on a mattress in front of the fire. Salt woke at around 12.45 am and left.

'I went and lay down beside her and fell asleep,' Boshears is alleged to have said in a statement to the police. 'The next thing I remember something scratching me. I opened my eyes. Jean was lying there under me, and I had my hands round her throat. She was dead.' He then went on to say how he had started to cut her hair off and then had carried her body into the spare room and had gone back to sleep on the mattress. 'When I woke up I decided that it was a dream. I looked in the spare bedroom. Then I saw she really was dead.' He left the body in his flat until about 11.30 on the evening of 2 January when he wrapped it up and dumped it in a water-filled roadside ditch. He then burned most of her clothing but kept her wristwatch.

On 17 February 1961, despite the evidence of Professor Francis Camps as to the inherent improbability of his version of events, the jury accepted Boshears' story and he was acquitted after a retirement of one hour and fifty minutes. Legal experts agreed that on the facts it was murder or nothing. There could be no halfway house for a manslaughter verdict. In the House of Lords a few days later Lord Elgin, with his tongue wedged firmly in his cheek, suggested that in future a verdict of guilty but asleep should be allowed.

Staff Sergeant Boshears was given three days' leave after his acquittal so that he could be with his wife with whom he had become reconciled. Later he decided to enter a US military hospital for treatment. He was transferred to the US base in Montana and dismissed from the service in July 1961 under what were described as 'other than honourable conditions'. He was later killed in a car crash.

His was not the first case in which a killer had been acquitted after a sleepwalking defence. On 9 April 1878 Simon Fraser, a man who had persistently suffered from nightmares, killed his baby. He woke a neighbour to tell her how he had battered his baby to death. The jury did not even retire before they acquitted him.

In 1943 at Covington, Kentucky, 15-year-old Jo Anne Kiger killed her brother and father in a nightmare in which she dreamed there was an intruder. Her father, the local mayor, had fallen foul of racketeers and had a fear that his home would be attacked. He hid a gun in every room in the house and it was one of these that Jo Anne used. She was acquitted of murder on 16 December 1943.

Brian Lane, *The Encyclopaedia of Forensic Science*; E. Spencer Shew, *A Companion to Murder*; David Thurlow, *The Essex Triangle*; Leslie Watkins, *The Sleepwalk Killers*.

2 January, 1993

On 2 January 1993, businessman Donald Urquhart was shot three times in the head in Marylebone High Street, London W1. The millionaire property tycoon and owner of Elstree Golf Club lived in a block of flats off the High Street with his Thai girlfriend, Pat Lamspithone. They were on their way home after a meal in a public house, walking hand-in-hand, when a man in a white crash helmet walked up, pulled out a .32 pistol and shot Urquhart in the head. The man then jumped on a black Yamaha 250 motorcycle and disappeared. Urquhart's killing was said to have been worth £20,000 and, according to persistent newspaper reports, the assassin was said to be an ex-boxer who worked for a South London gang. In December 1994 hitman Graeme West was jailed for life and on 10 February 1995 his assistant Geoffrey Heath received a five-year sentence after pleading guilty to conspiracy to murder.

The police had been able to trace the bike. It was advertised in the 23 November 1992 issue of *Loot* magazine for £275 and had been sold for £200. A similar ten-year-old bike, also advertised in *Loot*, had been used by the killer of ex-boxer Roger 'The Growler' Wilson, then manager of an off-licence and also a jewellery fence. He had been shot in the head as he got out of his Mercedes in Kensington on 5 March 1992. The man whom West had paid to buy the motorcycle on this occasion was a police informer.

Heath, a bricklayer and cab driver from Maltby, Yorkshire had been paid £2,000 for a four-month surveillance on the property dealer, tapping his telephone, following him to Spain and spending up to five hours a day watching his flat in Bickenhall Mansions. One of West's employees, Terry Burr, led undercover police to trap him and he and Andrew Karn, a former soldier who turned informer and told the police that West had cut up the gun used and burned his clothing on his patio, were given places in safe houses. Karn, who admitted a string of unconnected offences including armed robbery, was sentenced to two years' imprisonment which meant, because of time served, his immediate release.

It seems West made a number of mistakes which led to his arrest. Calls to Urquhart's ex-directory number made from his mobile telephone were traced and he had been seen at Elstree Golf Club. His BMW was clamped near Urquhart's home and a parking ticket was put on a van he used whilst it was outside the flat. There was also evidence that within a matter of hours of the killing West was celebrating in a bar, punching a friend's arm and repeating, 'I've done it. I've done it.'

It was, said ex-Detective Superintendent Bill Scholes, nothing to do with drugs or money laundering but simply a straightforward business transaction which went wrong leaving one side bankrupt and nursing a big grievance. West was paid £20,000 for the hit. 'It does show how contract killing is on the increase. There is a pattern now in which bouncers progress to debt collectors and on to handing out single 'clumpings' for, say, £2,000 and finally becoming contract killers.'

The police were convinced they knew the identity of the contractor and two other middlemen, each of whom may have been paid a finder's commission for the killing. They believed the contractor to be on the Costa del Sol although other reports said that he was a solicitor who had gone to America. A nightclub owner and a Triad gang were also suspected of being involved in the killing. The Crown Prosecution Service had declined to proceed because of lack of evidence. 'I think that was a terrible decision,' said Mr Scholes.

Urquhart, who had risen from being a hod carrier to a millionaire, was said to be a ruthless businessman. Apart from owning the £9 million Elstree Golf Club he ran a fleet of expensive cars and loved wearing expensive jewellery. He never wore socks, a reminder, he said, of his humble upbringing. His brother Lovat Urquhart feared that because he had taken over Donald's affairs he too would be the subject of a contract killing. At the time of West's trial his body was still in the police mortuary and Lovat Urquhart was reported as saying it would remain there until the man who contracted the hit was convicted. As for Urquhart's millions it was reported that Heather Urquhart, aged 34 and living in a council house at Aldbury with five children, was claiming a share of the estate. Urquhart had previously denied he had a daughter.

3 January, 1980

Joy Adamson, the wildlife preservationist, famous for her best-selling book *Born Free*, the story of a lioness and her cubs, was stabbed to death on 3 January 1980 at the Shaba Game Reserve, 170 miles north of Nairobi. It was her habit to walk around the perimeter shortly before sunset but on this night her body was found with multiple stab wounds. At first it appeared she might have been killed by a wild animal but a postmortem showed stab wounds caused by a simi, a double-bladed knife.

A local herdsman, Paul Wakwaro Ekai, who had once worked with the Adamsons, was charged with the murder and convicted. Found guilty on 29 August 1981 he was saved from the death penalty because he claimed he was 18 years old. He was thought to have held a grievance over his dismissal by Mrs Adamson who had become increasingly distanced from her employees.

4 January, 1964

Sisters Joan and Jenny Murphy were attacked and robbed in The Small Profit Shop which they owned in Ballybough, Dublin on 4 January 1964. Jenny, aged 70, had been battered about the head and was dead on arrival at the hospital. Her younger sister, Joan, told of a man who had come into the shop with an iron bar, attacked them and then snatched £20 from the till.

The investigation got off to a bad start because it was believed that a lady in curlers had been the last person in the shop before the killer but this turned out not to have been the case. She was able to name several who had been in after her and who were able to say the sisters had been alive. One witness described a man of five feet six or five feet seven inches, in his twenties, of medium build, and it was this description which the police circulated. A stout but short young girl in a full-length red coat and a headscarf had been with him.

The murder was the first case in which the Irish police used an Identikit to try to trace suspects, and the description of the girl varied from being short and stout to having a slender, heart-shaped face. A nun reported that she had seen a couple, of whom the girl bore a striking resemblance to the picture. They had called at her convent and asked for money to get to Wexford. Eventually some 96 people were identified through the kit and most were checked and eliminated.

In the end it was not the Identikit which brought about the solution. About two months after the killing the Manchester police, worried about the safety of a Rita Malone, known to be living with two black men and whom they feared might be being held against her will, brought her to the station. There she mentioned the Irish case but, by the time the Garda arrived to question her, she had decided not to say anything. Later, under lengthy questioning, she agreed she had been present at the robbery but had taken no part. She told them her friend, Frank Murtagh, was now in Poole in Dorset. He was one of the suspects still to be eliminated. Almost immediately Murtagh wrote a short statement admitting his guilt. The robbery had been a spur of the moment crime. The couple had no money and had chanced on the shop. Murtagh had carried out the attacks and Rita Malone had stood there, incapable of responding to his urging to get the money.

Murtagh later made a statement from the dock denying the validity of his confession and denying he had been in The Small Profit Shop. His confession, his counsel said, was based on a pathetic desire to be known as the Ballybough Killer. Rita Malone was acquitted and Frank Murtagh was sentenced to life imprisonment. He was released in March 1986 and convicted of arson in December 1987, for which he received a seven-year sentence.

Terry Prone, *Irish Murders*.

5 January, 1967

The body of 33-year-old Angus Sibbett was found in the back seat of his Mark X Jaguar which was badly parked beneath a bridge at South Hetton, near Newcastle, at about 5.15 am, on 5 January 1967. A pit worker had seen there was someone in the vehicle, thought he was asleep and opened the door to wake him and tell him to move. In fact Sibbett had been shot at close range. Two days later Dennis Stafford, aged 23, and 29-year-old Michael Luvaglio, were charged with the murder. The case became a *cause célèbre* and has featured in many compilations of miscarriages of justice in the British legal system.

Sibbett, burly and bearded and handsome, had been a key figure in one of the biggest gambling set-ups in the country. His territory was in the north-east, at that time stuffed full of gaming machines which were then a major source of Underworld income. He had served his apprenticeship in London with one of the biggest gangs, and this connection lasted until his death. He was a larger than life character who had served in Korea, been a shoe salesman, run a Chinese restaurant and done 12 months for receiving before gravitating to Newcastle where he worked for Vince Landa, otherwise Vincente Luvaglio, who had set up Social Club Services Ltd, a company with many subsidiaries which installed gaming machines – then mainly the old-fashioned one-armed bandits – in clubs.

Dennis Stafford, one of the two men charged with the murder, had led what can most charitably be described as an interesting life. The good-looking, if also brilliantined and spiv-like, Stafford junior made his name in the Underworld as a high-class con man, burglar and prison escaper. At the Inner London Sessions on 26 July 1956 he had been sentenced to a seven-year sentence for breaking and entering and being in possession of a loaded revolver. He had pleaded guilty. Four months later he escaped over the wall, along with Anthony Hawkes, another con man. They went to Newcastle where they opened a wholesale cloth long-firm fraud, which they operated successfully until February 1957.

At Durham Assizes Stafford received an additional 18 months for the Newcastle long-firm. In 1965 he made his way back to Newcastle where he too joined the employment of Vince Landa, working as booking agent for the cabarets playing the clubs. He was now earning a basic £25 per week and could possibly double it with commission.

Landa, whose younger brother was Michael Luvaglio, the other defendant in the Sibbett killing, had at one time been in the multi-millionaire category, and had formerly been a police officer in the RAF before he had moved to the north-east and established a gambling empire.

Stafford was not lucky with informants in the north-east. Someone had tipped off the police about his long-firm in 1957. Now ten years later someone told the police that a damaged red E-type Jaguar was in a Sunderland garage to which it had been taken for repair.

One thing in what became an increasingly misty case was clear. Michael Luvaglio had driven the red E-type on 3 January. He had been to his brother's home in Majorca with his parents, Stafford and their respective girlfriends. Everyone had flown back to London and then all except Landa had flown up to Newcastle. Landa had stayed behind to see his accountant and then had returned to Majorca. On 4 January Luvaglio had telephoned his brother who told Stafford to use the E-type as his own car was in for repair.

The prosecution case against Stafford and Luvaglio ran as follows. The red E-type Jaguar had been in some sort of collision with the Mark X. It was common ground that Stafford and Luvaglio had arranged to meet Sibbett that night. They said he had not turned up for the meeting and whilst they waited at the Bird Cage Club, Stafford went outside to the Jaguar to get some duty-free cigarettes he had brought back from Majorca. He noticed that the E-type was damaged and drew it to the attention of a Matthew Dean, the acting doorman. There were tyre marks in the snow which suggested a vehicle had collided with the E-type and had then reversed away. Both men were well alibied by their girlfriends Pat Burgess and Selena Jones, the singer. Much of the prosecution case depended on the time of death and whether the defendants could have driven from the club, killed Sibbett, dumped his body and driven back within three-quarters of an hour.

The jury was out for three hours before returning a guilty verdict. The Court of Appeal was unsympathetic and although in March 1972 Reginald Maudling, the then Home Secretary, referred the matter back to that court for a rehearing of the appeal, there was no joy there. Luvaglio's parents stuck loyally by him, instructing Sir

David Napley, soon to be president of the Law Society, on their son's behalf. In his book Napley firmly maintained his belief in Luvaglio's innocence.

In January 1973 two men swore statements which were handed to *The People* alleging they had been offered £5,000 to kill Sibbett. George Shotton, a Newcastle car dealer, with a long criminal record including convictions for violence, said he had been approached by a man who seemed to be Italian in the Bird Cage Club. A second man, whose name was not given, said the man who approached him seemed to be Greek.

But, despite representations by MPs, lawyers, newspapers and by JUSTICE, Stafford and Luvaglio remained in prison. In October 1973 their appeal to the House of Lords was rejected. Both men were paroled in 1979 and the next year Stafford did neither of them a favour when in an exclusive interview with David Mertens in the *News of the World* on 7 September 1980, for a reported fee of £10,000, he confessed 'I did it.' He said he had committed the crime whilst Luvaglio was in bed. Once more he was out of favour with the Underworld and, to compound his problems, he was on the run for a drink-driving offence. He was also wanted in connection with some credit card frauds. Luvaglio was unavailable for comment. During his stay in prison he had obtained an Open University degree and since his release he had been working with handicapped children. Later he and Sir David Napley issued a statement pointing out discrepancies in Stafford's account.

Stafford backtracked quickly, telling readers of the *Sunday People* on 28 September that his confession was a lie and he had only made it for financial reasons and '. . . to prove how hypocritical the system is and how people will believe what they want to believe. We did not commit the murder and the evidence and the facts of the case remain as they were.' Earlier he had told the *Guardian* that Luvaglio had nothing to do with the shooting.

Landa's empire collapsed after the trial. It emerged that Sibbett had been organising thefts on a wholesale basis from the clubs which had rented machines from Coinamatic, a subsidiary of Social Club Services Ltd, to the tune of £1,600 a week.

David Lewis and Peter Hughman, *Most Unnatural: An Inquiry into the Stafford Case*; James Morton, *Gangland 2*; Sir David Napley, *Not Without Prejudice*; Bob Woffinden, *Miscarriages of Justice*.

6 January, 1931

At six o'clock on the morning of 6 January 1931 the body of 83-year-old Englishman John Drinan was found at the foot of the stairs of the Villa Marie-Renée, on the outskirts of Nice, in which he had a room.

He had arrived the month previously, accompanied by a middle-aged woman who spoke French with a foreign accent, and had paid the equivalent of £8 in advance for board and lodging. Drinan lived the life of a recluse for the three weeks he stayed in the boarding house. He received no letters, visits or telephone calls. He was profoundly deaf and communication was in French with questions written on a slate. He was regarded as eccentric, washing himself for two hours a day but not changing his shirt. The woman who brought him to the villa was never seen again.

When he was found he was unconscious and never recovered from the coma. A doctor certified he had died from a cerebral haemorrhage. After his death it was discovered he had left an estate of £230,000, most of which he had bequeathed to the Poor Boxes of the London Police Courts. He had also given his daughter an annuity of £300 a year.

As enquiries proceeded it transpired that Drinan, who had lived like a miser for many years, had disappeared for some months in late 1930 before reappearing at the hotel.

It was also discovered that his signature on a number of documents had been forged and a Joe Haiat, said to be a cotton broker from Manchester, had benefited to the tune of nearly £100,000.

Although the London solicitors Theodore Goddard conducted a wide-ranging enquiry and a young man was sentenced for forgery, no charges for murder were ever brought. Haiat had died in the meantime. The death of Drinan was one of any number of cases over the years where it appears the French police have not exerted themselves to enquire too closely into deaths in circumstances which could amount to murder.

Harry J. Greenwall, *They Were Murdered in France*.

7 January, 1973

On 7 January 1973 Mark Essex, a 23-year-old black man from Emporia, Kansas, who had been discharged from the United States Navy as a troublemaker, went to the Howard Johnson Motel in downtown New Orleans where he began a short reign of terror. Before leaving his flat he had decorated the walls with such slogans as 'Kill White Devil' and 'Kill White Pig'.

Armed with a .44 Magnum rifle, he parked and then ran down corridors starting fires and shooting any white guests whom he encountered. He took the keys from one black maid telling her not to worry as although the revolution was on, only whites were being killed that day. He wounded 16 people and killed seven. His victims included a honeymoon couple, Dr Robert Stegall and his wife, two hotel employees and three policemen before police machine gunners in a helicopter shot him dead as he defended his position on the motel roof from behind a stone blockhouse.

8 January, 1914

It is unusual for the hero of one killing to be charged with another. It happened to the unfortunate John Starchfield. On 27 September 1912 Stephen Titus, a 28-year-old Armenian tailor, walked into the bar of the Horseshoe Hotel in Tottenham Court Road near the junction with New Oxford Street and had a drink, smoked a cigarette and then opened fire, killing Esther Towers, the manageress. John Starchfield, who had a newspaper pitch outside the hotel, cut off his escape. On 11 November 1912 Titus was found guilty but insane and sent to Broadmoor. Starchfield received a £50 award and a £1-a-week pension from the Carnegie Hero Fund Trust.

The case had a tragic sequel. On the evening of 8 January 1914 the body of seven-year-old Willie Starchfield was found in a train at Shoreditch, north-east London. The train had left Chalk Farm at 4.33 pm and terminated at Broad Street. A boy who had apparently got on at Mildmay Park had noticed the body under the seat and called the guard.

Willie Starchfield, son of John, described as a mother's boy with long curly brown hair, hazel eyes and a missing tooth, who in a photograph looked rather like Little Lord Fauntleroy, had been strangled. The thin cord was still around his neck. His mother said she had sent Willie on an errand for their landlady, to change an advertisement for lodgings in a shop some 200 yards down the road. It was, it seemed, a complete mystery how he had ended up on the train. Two theories emerged. First that he had been murdered on the train, and alternatively that he had been murdered in the station lavatories and that his body had been carried on to the train. His teeth had been loosened and the medical evidence from Sir Bernard Spilsbury was that he had been killed between 2 and 3 pm.

John Starchfield, the Horseshoe shooting hero, estranged

from his wife, was questioned about his son's death. He produced an alibi witness, Thomas Stickley, a hotel porter, who shared lodgings with Starchfield and who said he had been with him in bed at 12.50 and 2.50 that day. This was not to imply an intimate relationship, something which would then have resulted in a substantial term of imprisonment, but rather an arrangement dictated by reasons of economy.

The waters were considerably muddied by Horatio Bottomley, the devious proprietor of the magazine *John Bull*. He put up £500 reward money for information leading to the conviction of the killer and, amongst others, out of the woodwork came John Moore to say he had seen Starchfield with his son. Others were also sure they had seen him at 3.30 pm in Endall Street, Covent Garden.

On 29 January John Starchfield was arrested and charged with his son's murder. On 3 February at the inquest a signalman gave evidence that, for a period of some ten seconds and from a distance of twenty-five yards, he had seen a man kneeling over a boy as a train passed by his box. The descriptions he gave tallied with those of the father and son. The inquest jury returned a finding of murder against John Starchfield who was committed for trial at the Old Bailey.

Meanwhile John Moore was found on his bed in his room in Tolmers Square behind Euston Station with one end of a gas tube in his mouth. The other end was attached to the stove. As soon as he was well enough he was charged with attempted suicide. He said he was being hounded for giving evidence.

On the second day of the hearing at the Old Bailey, Mr Justice Atkin stopped the case, saying to Sir Archibald Bodkin, prosecuting, that he did not consider 'the evidence of identity is sufficient in a case of life and death' and making critical remarks about the conduct of the coroner's inquest. Later commentators seem to have taken the view that Starchfield was fortunate in his judge but the likelihood is that the child met his death at the hands of an unidentified maniac.

Almost two years to the day after Willie's death, John Starchfield died from the effects of the injury he received in the shooting.

H. L. Adam, *Murder by Persons Unknown*; Douglas G. Browne and Tom Tullett, *Bernard Spilsbury, His Life and Cases*; E. Spencer Shew, *A Companion to Murder*.

9 January, 1995

Five feet one inch tall Susan Engel, known as 'Shortstop' by her husband, the six feet nine, 68-year-old Lowell, 17 years her senior, disappeared with him on 9 January 1995. The financial affairs of the mentally slow couple had been looked after by the Reverend James Castria of the Faith Gospel Church, Clifton, New Jersey. On 23 March the Reverend Jimmy turned what had been intended to be a Vigil of Hope into a memorial service for the pair whom he had married six years previously. 'What a friend we have in Jesus,' sang the congregation, led by the bespectacled balding parson.

It was perhaps the service which initially put Castria under suspicion. The police had not yet announced that they believed the couple dead. How could the pastor have known they were? Answer, said the police, because he had killed them. He had been embezzling money from Susan Engel's inheritance to supplement his $17,000 annual stipend.

The police reconstruction of the case was that he had gone with them to buy some property on a housing development in nearby Coolbaugh and he had lured them into the woods. First he had struck down Engel, who walked with a stick, with a tyre lever or iron bar and had then chased after Susan, killing her before returning to kill her husband.

Castria was never charged. He had been questioned by the police and on the morning of 28 March when he was due to return for further questioning he cleared all his belongings from the church, putting them in garbage bags. He then went to a Christian bookstore and purchased a 10-cent bookmark printed with the words of the Lord's Prayer before driving his rented car into a 10-feet-wide bridge wall in Mountain Lakes. His speed was estimated to be at least 80 mph.

10 January, 1953

At about 6 pm on 10 January 1953 Ronald Jones, a laboratory technician who lived in the fishing village of Laugharne near Carmarthen, was walking to collect his car from the village garage. As he passed the cottage of the 78-year-old Elizabeth Thomas, a retired schoolmistress, he heard screams and the old lady calling out to someone not to hurt her. He heard a name being shouted but was not sure what it was and went for the village police officer, Sergeant Morgan. On their return they found Miss Thomas lying in the doorway. Her head had been split with a heavy object, her right arm was fractured and she had been stabbed four times in the chest. She died of her injuries the next morning without regaining consciousness. Her neighbour, a Mrs Phillips, said, 'She had worked hard all her life. She was very independent and I don't suppose she owed a penny to anybody.'

Morgan, who had pulled down a window to get into the Thomas cottage, had previously looked through the keyhole. 'In the pale light reflected from the oil lamp I saw a person, wearing a light-coloured man's cap, in a bent position. I can't say whether this person was a man, woman or child.' When he had rattled the door of the cottage the lamp had been lowered.

No knife was ever found, but by her body was a heavy stick with hairs matted to it. The motive was possibly robbery and, if so, it may be that the robber was disturbed because under the mattress in the murdered woman's bedroom was found £200, enough at the time to buy a small cottage. A fingerprint expert said that it had not been tampered with.

The police fastened on to their suspect with some alacrity. He was a 46-year-old odd job man, George Roberts, who lived in the Ferry House in the village. Illiterate and a deaf mute, he had not learned to communicate in anything more than the most rudimentary sign language.

The Carmarthenshire police called in Scotland Yard and Detective Superintendent Reginald Spooner was sent to assist the local force. He was able to trace Miss Thomas's movements quite easily. About 5 pm she had gone to the sweet shop across the road to buy peppermints and had told the grocer's wife she was going home to have an egg for her tea. Roberts had been seen by another of Elizabeth Thomas's neighbours, a Miss Lewis. At about 4.30 pm he had called round to show her a pair of gloves he had bought and an hour later he had been seen by Phillips, the grocer, standing on the pavement near his shop. Other people put Roberts near Miss Thomas's cottage up to a quarter to six. They said he was wearing a macintosh and cap at the time.

So far as clues were concerned there had been far too many people in and out of the cottage for any to survive. There was a print of a Wellington boot but this had been blurred and a footprint in the back garden was not capable of being cast. There was, however, a trace of green distemper similar to that in Miss Thomas's cottage on Roberts's macintosh. A witness saw Roberts outside his front door at about 6.15 pm but all he could say was that the man was wearing Wellington boots. From then on Roberts was seen by a number of people up to about 6.40 pm.

With the help of his uncle, Roberts made a statement

that he had come home about 4.45 pm and then later that he had come home at 5.30 pm. The next day, with a deaf and dumb interpreter, he made a statement that at about 4.15 pm he had seen Miss Thomas on her doorstep and had waved to her. He said he had not been out after 5 pm. The police version of events was that he was then told he could go home but he did not leave the police station. In fact he stayed there for the next four days before he finally left.

On Sunday, 18 January Roberts arrived at the police station where he made a statement to Spooner without the benefit of an interpreter. Spooner had already carried out some simple tests on Roberts which had led him to believe that he was able to give intelligent answers to questions put to him. Now Roberts was shown two photographs of Miss Thomas's cottage. He then made a sign he wanted paper and a pencil and drew a sketch of the row of cottages. He drew a sketch of himself and pointing to the middle of the five cottages made thrusting motions.

'I showed him a knife and he nodded. He made a movement from that particular house in the middle, over its top, along the top of the two houses to the right and down by the side to the end of the house to where he had pictured himself. He then indicated walking along the road.'

Roberts was then taken along a path to the cliff edge where he stopped and made a cutting motion with his hand, drew his arm back and brought it over his head and made a throwing motion. The police officer with him, Detective Sergeant Millen, interpreted that as Roberts telling him he had thrown the knife into the sea. Roberts was then re-interviewed with two interpreters and, so Spooner believed, confessed to the murder.

At the magistrates' court during the committal proceedings the court interpreter failed to make Roberts understand the evidence of the first witness. Nevertheless, the magistrates committed Roberts for trial at the next Carmarthen Assizes.

He appeared there on 6 March 1953 in front of Mr Justice Devlin on the question of whether he was fit to plead to the charge. If he had been found unfit he would have been committed to a lunatic asylum. 'To insist on the issue being tried first might result in a grave injustice,' said Mr Justice Devlin, 'to detain as a criminal lunatic a man who might be quite innocent. I can find no authority which would prevent the defence, which wishes to test the prosecution's case on the general issue, from having the right to do so.' Evidence was given that Roberts had not spoken in 29 years and a jury found him mute by visitation of God.[1]

After the prosecution opened its case, the judge asked whether, if the statements were ruled inadmissible, there was any evidence on which a jury could convict. Counsel for the prosecution replied there was not. The next day Mr Justice Devlin ruled the confession inadmissible and told the jury, 'The evidence comes down to the fact that Roberts was seen before and afterwards and the fact that he previously had a knife in his possession. Those things are coupled with certain statements said to have been obtained from a man with whom conversation is almost impossible. You could never have been asked to convict on evidence of that sort.'

After his discharge, Roberts drew two pictures for reporters. One was a man with a spade and the other a man fishing from a rowing boat. The interpreter said these meant he was going back to work after having first taken a holiday.

There was much evidence which suggested that Roberts was not the killer. Before he 'confessed', it was thought a man named Harry might have been involved. When Jones heard a name being called out he was sure it was not 'Booda', the name by which Roberts was known in the village. He thought it was more likely 'Harry'. Secondly, this was another of those cases where there was no blood on or near the suspect. Could Roberts have gone home and wiped away from his clothes all the blood there must have been, without leaving any trace? Nor were

[1] The other verdict open to them was 'mute of malice'.

his fingerprints found on the piece of wood by the body. Why had the lamp been lowered? The totally deaf Roberts could not possibly have heard the policeman rattling the front door.

That leaves his apparent lies about the time he was in his own cottage and the 'confession'. It can never be known exactly what grasp Roberts had on the concept of time or indeed whether he was answering the questions put to him. As for the 'confession', he may just as easily have been recounting in his own way what he saw the actual killer do.

It has been suggested that Miss Thomas was the victim of Ronald Harries, another local man who was convicted of killing his aunt and uncle and hanged in April 1954.

In February 1975 Donald Lang, described as a 30-year-old illiterate deaf-mute, had his 1972 conviction overturned by the Illinois Appellate Court. He had been convicted of strangling Earlene Brown in a hotel room. The court held that it was constitutionally impossible to try Lang with whom neither family, lawyers nor four counsellors could communicate. In 1965 he had been found unfit to stand trial for killing another woman. In 1971 he had been acquitted after two key witnesses had died while he was in a state mental institution. His laywers had pressed for him to have the right to trial in the earlier case. Now he was placed in another mental institution.

Iain Adamson, *The Great Detective*; Rupert Furneaux, *Famous Criminal Cases 6*.

11 January, 1920

On 11 January 1920 a married farm labourer, Albert Burrows, killed his mistress Hannah Calladine (whom he called Nance) and her two children. Over thirty years younger than Burrows, she had 'married' him in 1918 and he had served a six-month sentence for bigamy as a result. When he left prison she took out bastardy proceedings against him for which, when he failed to pay, he received another 21 days in prison. Now Hannah Calladine moved into Burrows' cottage and the real Mrs Burrows moved out, in her turn instituting maintenance proceedings.

On the day of the murders Burrows, in arrears with his rent and with no way of paying his mistress or his wife's maintenance, took Hannah Calladine and her son, Ernest, on to the moors and probably strangled them before throwing their bodies down the airshaft of a disused coal mine at Symmondley Moor. Later he also murdered her daughter. He told a neighbour Nance had left to go and work in a bacon shop in a suburb of Manchester. He wrote to her sister asking for all her clothes to be sent to him and these he sold, together with her wedding ring. Mrs Burrows obtained a maintenance order in the sum of £1 but then returned to live with her husband.

For the next three years Burrows was able to keep up the pretence that Hannah Calladine was still alive by writing to her sister and sending her a picture of a little boy named Williamson, claiming that he was Ernest.

On 4 March 1923 four-year-old Thomas Wood, whom he had sexually assaulted, disappeared from his home and Burrows told the police he had been with the boy on the moors. He took the police to the same disused shaft down which he had thrown the other three bodies. Wood's body was also in the shaft.

Whilst awaiting trial Burrows tried to persuade a fellow prisoner to write a letter from Hannah Calladine saying that she was still alive. The man gave evidence for the prosecution. Burrows' defence, such as it was, suggested that Hannah Calladine had killed herself and her children whilst depressed. Because of the decomposition of the bodies it was impossible to ascertain how they had been killed. No evidence was called on his behalf and he was hanged on 8 August at Nottingham prison.

E. Spencer Shew, *A Second Companion to Murder*.

12 January, 1920

Nurse Florence Nightingale Shore was found on 12 January 1920 on the London to Hastings train. She had been on her way to visit friends in St Leonards. She had been badly beaten and her body propped up to look as though she was asleep. Indeed, some platelayers who had entered the carriage at Polegate, one of only two stops the train had made, saw her in the corner but paid no attention. Later it appeared that she was about to slip off the seat. It was then they noticed there was blood on her face and on the magazine open on her lap. Her smashed glasses were on the floor.

She was taken off the train at Bexhill and sent to the East Sussex Hospital where she died four days later. It was thought the blows to her head could have been caused by the butt of a revolver. No charges were ever brought.

13 January, 1919

On 13 January 1919 Lieutenant Colonel Norman Rutherford called at Sir Malcolm Seton's house in Clarendon Road, Hyde Park, asking to see Major Miles Seton who was visiting his cousin. Miles Seton and Rutherford went into the dining room and, some ten minutes later, Lady Seton heard gunshots, ran into the drawing room and found Miles lying on the threshold of the dining room with blood pouring from six wounds, and Rutherford holding a gun. 'I wish I had another bullet for myself,' he remarked. He helped lift the body onto the sofa and awaited the police. When they came he was allowed to write a note to his wife: 'I am sorry; an awful thing has happened. Seton is dead.'

Rutherford had known Miles Seton for some years and had coached him for a medical examination at Edinburgh. They became friends and during the First World War Seton was commissioned in the Australian medical corps. Rutherford was now a half-colonel in the Royal Army Medical Corps, married with six children. Seton would visit the Rutherford homes in Mill Hill and Carshalton. However, the Rutherford home was not a happy one. There was a history of lunacy in the colonel's family and he suffered violent swings in his temperament. Mrs Rutherford turned to the older Seton for advice. Things did not improve. Rutherford had been buried by a shell-burst in the war and after that his temper became the more uncontrollable. It is possible that he also became enamoured with a cousin who had joined the household as a companion. Mrs Rutherford wrote to her husband in France saying she was leaving him and asking him to give her a divorce.

It seems Rutherford wished to run a defence of justification. He wrongly believed Seton was the cause of the break-up of his marriage. With some difficulty his counsel,

Rigby Swift and Travers Humphreys, persuaded him that
if he failed in this he would be hanged. His defence to the
murder charge then was that he was insane. He was found
guilty but insane and sent to Broadmoor from where he
was released in 1930. The Rutherford divorce dragged
its way through the courts. Initially Mrs Rutherford
was granted a decree on the grounds of her husband's
adultery with his young cousin. In 1922 the House of
Lords rescinded the decree and substituted one of judicial
separation.

14 January, 1953

On 14 January 1953 George 'Daddy' Walker, a semi-
crippled junk dealer-cum-recluse, was found battered
to death at his 12-roomed house in Warbreck Road
near Aintree, Liverpool. It was the maniacal work of
unemployed labourer John Lawrence Todd who had hit
Walker 32 times with an axe. The motive was robbery.

After the death in 1944 of his wife Madam Pepper, a
dancing teacher, Walker, who had been a master tailor,
had lived in the house increasingly surrounded by junk.
When his dog would not stop howling neighbours went
to investigate and found his battered body. The axe had
been clumsily hidden in a chimney. Of his own accord
Todd went to the police to explain why he might have
been seen in the area but he was identified through a
watch stolen in the robbery which he had sold. He was
hanged at Walton jail on 19 May 1953.

15 January, 1947

The body of 22-year-old Elizabeth Short was found on a vacant lot on South Norton Avenue, a block east of Crenshaw Boulevard, Los Angeles, on 15 January 1947. Born in Medford, Massachusetts, she had run away from home in Boston to California to become a would-be bit-part actress, and certainly a part-time prostitute.

Over the years more than fifty people offered what the police thought were false confessions. Short was known in the bars and hotels as the Black Dahlia because of her jet-black hair and her predilection for wearing black clothing. On 10 January 1947 she was offered dinner by a salesman at the Los Angeles Biltmore, declined the invitation and at 10 pm went south on Olive towards Sixth. Her body, cut in half at the waist, was found five days later. The autopsy showed she had been tortured for two or three days, gagged and bound, possibly with wire, that she had been hung head downwards, alive, whilst she was stabbed and burned with cigarettes. Finally her throat had been cut from ear to ear. A rose tattooed on her thigh had been gouged out and the initials 'B D' had been carved on the other one. Every drop of blood had been drained from the body. Her hair had been shampooed and hennaed.

The first problem was identification. Fingerprints were taken and matched not because of a criminal record but because she had once been a clerk in the United States Post Office Exchange during the war. She had also been a waitress in Miami, a cocktail waitress in Chicago, had been found in the El Paseo Restaurant in Santa Barbara drinking as a minor and shipped back east. On the way she skipped from the train and returned to Santa Barbara where she became 'Cutie of the Week' at Camp Cooke. After several liaisons she met and probably became engaged to a Matthew Gordon Junior from Pueblo,

Colorado, an Air Force Major. He was killed in an air crash just after the war. Certainly his mother sent her a telegram of condolence.

Shortly after that she went to San Diego and stayed with the Frenches, a family in Bayview Terrace. She had spun them the sob story of a dead husband and baby son. She left on 8 January 1947 in a tan coupé with a red-haired man. She told Mrs French the man was an airline employee. From then on there were various sightings of the Black Dahlia in a number of bars and clubs and a former boyfriend received a letter saying she was planning to move to Chicago with a man named Jack. She also seems to have returned to San Diego where she was seen in a drive-in restaurant with a red-headed man.

One man, Robert 'Red' Manley, was arrested and questioned. An ex-Air Force Band saxophonist, he had been admitted to a psychiatric ward before being discharged from the service in 1945. He had been seen with Elizabeth Short and voluntarily submitted to a lie-detector test. This proved inconclusive and his wife alibied him for the day of Elizabeth's death. He was released without charge. Seven years later he was committed to another psychiatric hospital where he was once again questioned over the death of the Black Dahlia and again released after taking truth serum. Later he committed suicide.

On 21 January 1947 the city editor of the *Los Angeles Examiner* received a call giving details of the Black Dahlia's death and saying that he could expect to have some souvenirs of the killing. The caller said he would give himself up '. . . but I want to watch the cops chase me some more'.

Ten days after Short's body was found, an unsealed envelope containing her social security card, birth certificate and some personal papers was sent to the police. Accompanying them was a note made up of cuttings from the *Los Angeles Examiner* and other papers: 'HERE! is Dahlia's belongings . . . Letter to follow.'

There were over 50 confessions which the police thought to be false. Various people gave themselves up and were painstakingly eliminated from the enquiry. A number of copycat killings followed her death. The police came no nearer to a solution than to suggest the killer might be a sadist who had picked her up, a repulsed lesbian or someone from whom Short had attempted to extort money who had made the killing look like a sex offence. A number of commentators, including Captain Donahoe, in charge of the investigation, have suggested that because of the nature of the injuries and the spite with which they were inflicted the killing was done by a woman. One line of enquiry tended to show that Elizabeth Short had had a lesbian relationship which she had broken off just prior to her death. Medical evidence suggests that she was sexually malformed and unable to undertake full intercourse.

John Gilmore, in his recent book, has laid the blame for her killing at the door of a criminal, Jack A. Wilson, otherwise known as Arnold Smith. In later life he had become a transient and died when he set fire to himself in a rooming house. An even more recent book has Janice Knowlton writing that her father was the killer of the Black Dahlia.

John Gilmore, *Severed*; Richard and Molly Whittington-Egan, *The Bedside Book of Murder*; Janice Knowlton and Michael Newton, *My Daddy was the Black Dahlia Killer*.

16 January, 1961

Twelve-year-old Linda Smith disappeared from near a baker's shop in the High Street of Earls Colne, Essex, on 16 January 1961. She had been given 10 shillings to go and buy an evening paper from the paper shop and was last seen shortly after 5 pm.

Her body was found three days later near Polstead across the Suffolk border, some 10 miles from her home.

She had been strangled and although she had not been sexually assaulted the medical evidence was that she might well have been killed resisting an attack. Her parents were adamant that she was not a girl who would get into a car with a stranger and it was thought that her attacker was someone she knew.

There were heel marks near the body and on her coat were fragments of red lacquer paint and flour powder. A local baker was extensively questioned. Throughout he maintained that he had never, to his knowledge, seen Linda. On the back seat of his car were found traces of flour similar to that found on Linda's coat and also similar traces of the red paint.

When questioned on the specific items he said that he thought Linda might have sat in his car which he left unlocked – by no means an unusual thing to do in 1961 – and that as for the paint she might have picked up traces from the dump which he used and where she played. He was able to provide an alibi, saying he had been at home with his wife and his brother. The manager of the local butchery was able to say that he had seen the baker going home shortly after 4 pm.

The papers were sent to the Director of Public Prosecutions who refused to bring charges, and the girl's family endeavoured to launch a private prosecution against the baker. The magistrates refused to issue a summons, saying they did not believe there was a *prima facie* case.

Two days after their refusal the inquest was held. In the days before the Lord Lucan case a jury could name a person whom they believed to be the killer and there was much speculation that they would do so. Although warned that he need not give evidence and could decline to answer questions which might incriminate him, the baker decided to go into the witness box and, by all reports, gave a good account of himself and his movements. The jury retired for only 20 minutes before returning a verdict of murder by a person unknown.

David Thurlow, *The Essex Triangle.*

17 January, 1901

On 17 January 1901, a farmer, William Pearson, climbed into a third-class compartment on the London-bound train from Winchester. Already in the carriage was a Mrs Rhoda King, who was on her way to visit her sister, and George Henry Parker, a former marine. From Winchester the train was non-stop to Vauxhall, London and, as it neared Surbiton, Parker went to the lavatory, loaded the gun he habitually carried with him and, on his return, shot and killed Pearson. He then turned the gun in the direction of Mrs King and shot at her, grazing her cheek. She was not badly injured and asked, 'What have you done?' Parker replied he had done it for the money. Mrs King produced some coins but Parker then rifled the dead man's pockets.

He seems to have been totally inept for he then asked Mrs King what he should do with the gun and wondered out loud whether if he put it in Pearson's hand this would make it seem sufficiently like a suicide. Mrs King suggested he throw it out of the window. As the train ran into Surbiton station Parker jumped onto the platform. Mrs King gave the alarm and after a short chase Parker was captured in the South Metropolitan Gasworks.

His defence was one of temporary insanity induced by alcohol but he was convicted of murder and hanged on 19 March at Wandsworth prison by James and Thomas Billington. Before his death he admitted the murder had been to finance his liaison with the wife of a soldier.

There had been some sympathy for him after he wrote to the widow of William Pearson:

> I am writing these few lines to ask your forgiveness for the crime which I have done. I read an account of your husband's funeral in the paper. I am really and truly sorry and I feel for you and your late husband's

brothers. I purchased the revolver at Southampton
with the intention of shooting the girl whom I have
been going with and myself. She was unhappy at
home, and so was I. I shot your husband on the
spur of the moment. I never spoke to him in my
life. I would now only ask you to write me a few
lines and say that you have forgiven me for your
husband's death.

18 January, 1938

Henry Dobson found the body of his 67-year-old wife
Margaret on a cinder track about 50 yards from their
home, High Grange, Wolviston, County Durham, on the
morning of 18 January 1938. Mrs Dobson had been raped
and stabbed to death. The afternoon before she had set out
to walk to the nearby village and had not returned.

Henry Dobson had farmed his land for over 30 years.
Recently there had been bad blood between the Dobsons
and the Hoolhouse family in nearby Haveton Hill. At
1.15 am on 20 January the police arrested 20-year-old
Robert Hoolhouse. At one time his family had been
labourers on the Dobson farm but there had been allegations of polluted milk and they had been evicted from
their cottage. It was believed that Robert, in particular,
harboured a grudge against the Dobsons.

Robert Hoolhouse had been seen drinking in The Bell
public house at Newton Bewley between 1.45 and 2.45 pm
on the afternoon of the murder. He had met a friend at about
3.10 pm and they had cycled together to Wolviston. They
split up about 3.35 pm and Robert said he was going to visit
a girlfriend, Dorothy Lax, who lived with her aunt.

It was not clear at exactly what time Mrs Dobson
had been killed. Henry Dobson said she left home at
about 4.30 pm after having had a beef sandwich for tea.

However, a workman who brought a threshing machine shortly afterwards did not see her on the track. At 5.30 pm two men delivered some pigs and as they did so they saw a man in their headlights. They described him as aged about 30, wearing a smock and leggings. He dropped to the ground. Lying on the cinder track was a racing bicycle. They asked him if he was all right and he said he had been drinking and to leave him alone. A quarter of an hour later he and the bicycle were gone.

What was the evidence against Hoolhouse? There was motive; he was known to be in Wolviston, two minutes from the farm; he more or less matched the witnesses' description although he was younger; he owned a drop-handled racing bike and he had scratches on his face consistent with the type of marks often inflicted by the victim of a rapist. He explained these as having come from a fall off his bicycle. Blood of the same group as Mrs Dobson (and 42 per cent of the population) was found on his clothing. He said he had cut himself shaving. He refused to submit to a blood test.

In his favour was evidence from the pathologist that death had taken place before 4 pm. He could provide an alibi until 4.30 pm. After leaving Miss Lax he claimed to have cycled home for a wash and his tea before catching the bus to take his girlfriend to the pictures. There was no seminal staining. There was also a heel print on the ground locked under one from Mrs Dobson's boot. It was not that of Hoolhouse. There were no other prints which linked him to the scene.

At his trial at the March Assizes at Leeds, it was submitted he had no case to answer. The judge rejected this but in his summing-up told the jury: 'They [the prosecution] have got a number of things in regard to each one of which, when you test it, it amounts to no more than this, that it is quite consistent with this man having committed the murder; but it is consistent with him not having committed it.'

An acquittal was expected and his parents had a taxi waiting to take him home. After four hours the jury returned a verdict of guilty. His appeal failed and a reprieve was refused. He was hanged on 26 May 1938 at Durham prison.

PRO/DPP/1

19 January, 1990

London's best-known female armed robber, Linda Calvey, who boasted she was the original of one of the characters in the popular ITV series, *Widows*, eventually committed murder on 19 January 1990.

She had married Mickey Calvey in 1970 whilst he was in Wandsworth prison serving eight years for armed robbery. Mickey Calvey died on Saturday, 9 December 1978 in a shoot-out during an attempted robbery at Caters supermarket in Eltham, south-east London.

Linda earned her nickname of the Black Widow by shouting 'Murderer!' at the police officer who stood trial for the shooting. There had been some evidence Calvey had been shot in the back but the officer explained that this was the way he had been standing rather than that he had been shot whilst fleeing. He was acquitted and given a bravery award.

Shortly afterwards Linda became involved with robber Ronnie Cook, accompanying him on trips abroad, including one to Las Vegas in which it was said they spent £30,000 in just over a week. He lavished gifts on her – clothes from Harrods, jewellery, money, a car, even £4,000 for cosmetic surgery – but also forbade her to speak to other men and beat her savagely.

Three years later Cook was jailed for 16 years for his part in what was described as 'one of the most spectacular and well-planned robberies in the history of crime'. A hijacked mobile crane had been rammed into the back of a security vehicle containing almost £1 million near a school in Dulwich.

Calvey promised to wait for him and as a mark of her fidelity had *True Love Ron Cook* tattooed on her leg. But, it seems, she could not now give up the lifestyle to which she had grown accustomed. Almost certainly Cook had had money salted away and she began to spend it, taking up with one of his friends, Brian Thorogood, whom Cook had arranged to act as a 'minder' for him whilst he was inside. Thorogood left his wife, bought a house in Harold Wood, Essex, and moved in with Linda. Later he received 18 years for a post office robbery. Linda, who seems to have supplemented her income by being the armourer for various robbery teams, served three years of a five-year term for conspiracy to rob. That was the end of Thorogood but now Cook was due for release. What could she do?

Afraid that he would find out about both her infidelity and her dissipation of his money, she planned to kill him, offering a £10,000 contract. Finding no takers, she turned to Daniel Reece, a convicted rapist whose evidence had assisted the police convict David Lashley, the killer of Australian heiress, Janie Shepherd. Quite apart from the money, Reece too was enamoured of Calvey and agreed to do the job.

In theory Ron Cook had a cleaning job outside the prison but he spent his days out more agreeably. On 19 January 1990 Linda Calvey collected him from Maidstone prison and drove him to London whilst Reece, whom she had already collected from another prison, waited outside her flat. Cook brought in the milk and as he stood holding it Reece followed him in and shot him in the elbow. He could not, he later told police, bring himself to kill the man. Linda Calvey had no such qualms. She grabbed the gun from him, ordered Cook to kneel and then shot him in the head.

Reece took a train back to the West Country to continue his thirteen-year sentence for rape, buggery, and false imprisonment.

At first it seemed as though Calvey had been successful. The police appeared to accept her story that an unknown gunman had burst in and shot Cook whilst she cowered in a corner. Then it was discovered Reece had been with her over the weekend and had been her lover. It was curious he had not been mentioned in the statement. Under questioning Reece cracked first, telling all.

Reece, who was not notedly popular in prison following the evidence he gave against Lashley, thought twice about squealing again and withdrew his confession in court. Linda Calvey told the jury his confession was a fabrication. 'Ron meant everything to me,' she said. Found guilty she received a sentence of life imprisonment. Reece also received a life sentence for the murder.

In December 1995 the Divisional Court upheld a decision of the Criminal Injuries Compensation Board when they decided Mrs Cook was not entitled to compensation for the death of her husband.

James Morton, *Gangland*

20 January, 1992

Khalid Dad's car was seen parked outside the home of Majid Syed in Slough on the night of 20 January 1992. The 22-year-old Dad, who ran a supermarket with his two brothers, never returned home and the next day the caretaker of a primary school found a large bundle on the pavement outside the school. When he opened the pink candlewick bedspread it contained Dad's headless body, naked except for underpants and with washing line rope tying wrists and ankles. Shortly after 8 am that morning a car driving down the same road hit a bag which split open, and Dad's head rolled into the gutter. The postmortem showed he had been killed with a single blow. The body had a number of bruises which indicated Dad had been beaten with a blunt instrument before he died. He had then been beheaded, probably whilst in a kneeling position.

When the police searched Syed's house they found bloodstains on the walls and floor and in an upstairs loft Dad's bloodstained clothes, as well as bloodstained clothes of Syed and his 24-year-old son Moddessir Jafri. The weapon used was never found and the prosecution could not suggest a motive for the killing of Dad who used to deliver groceries to the Syed home.

The case against his other son, 21-year-old Kauser Jafri, was stopped at the end of the prosecution's evidence with the judge ruling there was not a case for him to answer. Moddessir Jafri, giving evidence, said he could not explain how Khalid Dad's bloodstained clothes came to be found in the loft. Jafri told the court that he was in bed when his stepmother telephoned him to say someone was banging on the door, threatening to kill them.

Both he and his father were convicted in September 1996 after three re-trials. They were sentenced to life imprisonment. At the earliest Mrs Fatima Syed, the second wife of Majid Syed, had been acquitted of conspiracy in the murder. Detective Superintendent Mike Cox believed that Dad had been having an affair with a close relation of the Syeds. On the other hand Khalid Dad's father said that it was a question of money. He believed his son had lent Syed several thousand pounds which could not be repaid.

21 January, 1978

Twenty-two-year-old Yvonne Pearson, who was killed in Bradford on 21 January 1978, was the seventh victim of Peter Sutcliffe, the Yorkshire Ripper. Most but not all of Sutcliffe's 13 victims were prostitutes whom he stabbed in what he described as his mission to clean up the streets.

The police investigation – which was the largest manhunt ever mounted by British police and in which 250,000 people were interviewed and 32,000 statements taken – into the deaths of 13 women, mostly from Leeds and Bradford, lasted from 30 October 1975 until 1981 and was not one of their most successful. Not only were they bedevilled by a hoax tape recording of a voice, purporting to be that of the killer, in a Wearside – as opposed to a Yorkshire – accent, but Sutcliffe had been questioned on three occasions and had slipped through the net.

The investigation finally ended on 2 January 1981 when uniformed officers became suspicious of a Rover car in which Sutcliffe was having sex with a prostitute. The car was parked in a dimly lit driveway at an office block in Sheffield and the registration plates were false. At first Sutcliffe gave his name as Peter Williams but later admitted his identity. He then asked to urinate and before being taken to the police station was allowed to do so in nearby bushes. Two days into his questioning the police searched the bushes and found a hammer and knife used in some of the murders.

Sutcliffe, who had worked as a grave digger, claimed that his mission to kill prostitutes had begun when he was working at Bingley municipal cemetery. The prosecution, led by the Attorney General Sir Peter Rawlinson, was prepared to accept Sutcliffe's claim that he heard voices and so allow a plea of not guilty to murder on the grounds of diminished responsibility. The trial judge would not allow this – partly it was said because of personal animosity to the Attorney General – and so Sir Peter had the unenviable task of cross-examining the witnesses whose evidence he had been prepared to accept some days earlier.

Sutcliffe was found guilty on 22 May 1982 of all 13 counts of murder and sentenced to life imprisonment. Whilst in prison and prison hospitals he has been repeatedly attacked by prisoners including Ronald Kray. Over the next decade Mrs Sonja Sutcliffe, his wife, mounted a series of successful actions for libel against a string of newspapers and magazines. It included a verdict against

Private Eye in the sum of £600,000, reduced on appeal to £60,000. Finally, however, a verdict in favour of the *News of the World* ended her run of success.

D.A. Yallop, *Deliver Us from Evil*; Gordon Burn, *Somebody's Husband, Somebody's Son*.

22 January, 1949

The body of 35-year-old Ernest Melville, a known homosexual, was found by some children about 75 yards from the Full Moon public house, on waste ground near Croft Street in the Swansea dock area, on the afternoon of 22 January 1949. It was thought he had been killed around 11 pm the previous evening.

Melville was of slight build and about five feet five inches in height, one of a family of three sons and three daughters. He had always been regarded as a girlish individual. During the evening he had been importuning men and indeed had made an indecent assault on one man.

He had been seen in various public houses in the company of two seamen, probably from the merchant navy, in their early twenties and wearing dark blue gabardine raincoats and dark blue peaked caps. One was thought to have some gold insignia on the badge. There were severe injuries to Melville's head, including fractures of his skull; there was evidence of gripping of the throat and the scrotum. The body was fully clothed and the trousers had been ripped down the inside seams from crotch to turn-ups. Some of the fly buttons were undone. Near the body was a plain brass brooch-type tie pin and an artificial tooth, as well as one white and two black buttons. None of these belonged to Melville.

Dr A. F. Sladden, who conducted the postmortem, believed the sequence of events had probably been that first Melville's testicles had been squeezed, after which he had been throttled into at least helplessness, if not unconsciousness. He had then been struck several blows under the chin and to the face, either with a fist or a stone.

The Master of the SS *Killurin*, which had docked at 10.40 pm on the evening of the killing, made a statement that to his knowledge none of his men left the ship that night but, if they did, it was certainly not before 11 pm. The police then turned their attention to other ships which had docked, but with no more successful result.

The Swansea police then called in Scotland Yard in the form of the chain-smoking Detective Inspector Reginald Spooner, who additionally conducted a trawl of men in the locality with any convictions for sexual offences.

The locals were certainly not forthcoming. They may have helped the Welsh police but they were certainly not going to assist strangers and people whom they considered as intruders. Spooner encountered considerable difficulties in his investigation. Whilst in Swansea he wrote to his wife, Myra:

> Don't know how long we shall be here – it's a very sticky job, one of the worst I've had. Not very much to go on and all sorts of unreliable information and rumours – and a dock area full of strange people and strangers. Apparently, they have never cleaned up a murder down here, so this may be the one! But we have not had any lucky breaks so far, so am looking forward to one or two, which might make all the difference.

He did not get the breaks. Spooner believed he had narrowed the suspects to two but that they were being sheltered by members of the community. No charges were made.

PRO/MEPO/3/3125; Iain Adamson, *The Great Detective*.

23 January, 1931

On the night of 23 January 1931 Louisa Maud Steele, a 19-year-old maid in the Andrews family, left their home at 72 Lee Road, Blackheath, to complete some errands in the village. Members of the family heard the door slam around 7.50 pm. It was not her night off and when she had not returned by 11 pm Mrs Andrews reported the matter to the police.

Louisa Steele's body was found the next morning near the Prince of Wales's pond, a haven for model yachtsmen. The body was naked except for one brown stocking with a broken suspender on her left leg. Nearby was a dark coat, a black dress with a linen collar and what was modestly described as a navy blue garment, probably a petticoat. In her left hand she was clutching the heel of her right shoe. Her other shoe was found some 20 yards away.

Sir Bernard Spilsbury who conducted the postmortem found that there were numerous injuries to her face and the right bone of her nose was fractured. She had, he thought, been attacked from behind and possibly strangled with tape coming from the neck of her dress. Her tongue had been bitten and there were bites on her breasts. Apart from that she had not been sexually molested. The facial injuries, he thought, had come from a kick whilst she was on the ground. He was not able to say whether she had been killed on the heath or in a house or car and her body subsequently dumped.

Louisa Steele, who came from a local family, was not thought to have had any boyfriends or admirers. There was a suggestion that a girl had been seen talking to a man with a twisted lip on a seat by the pond and she had called out, 'Come back, Jack.' It was never established whether this girl was Louisa and the only Jack she knew was eliminated from the enquiries. Two other girls went to local police stations to allege they had been assaulted on the night of Louisa's death. Appeals were made by the police and flashed on cinema screens in the locality. Three thousand statements were taken and over a thousand interviews held. An anonymous note was sent to the police saying 'Watch Lady Well Recreation Ground' but this proved to be a hoax. To the annoyance of the model boatmen it was suggested the pond should be drained for clues. The East Lewisham Women's Citizens' Association demanded adequate lighting on the heath.

In all probability the murderer was a man from a wealthy family who, shortly before the attack, had been released from a mental institution and of whom his family were said to be frightened. Two days after the attack he was questioned by the police but released. His family seems to have taken heed and had him recommitted to the institution. In his book *Great Unsolved Crimes*, ex-Superintendent Charles Cooper who investigated the case wrote: '. . . as my suspect had already been sent to a place where he would be unable to perpetrate any similar crimes we were never called upon to present it to a jury.' The place euphemistically referred to was Broadmoor.

Douglas G. Browne and Tom Tullett, *Bernard Spilsbury, His Life and Cases.*

24 January, 1907

William Whiteley, the founder of Britain's first department store in Queensway, was shot by his illegitimate son on 24 January 1907. Whiteley, who saw himself as the 'Universal Provider', ran his emporium with a rod of iron, dismissing his staff for the most trivial of reasons. His other fault was a corresponding weakness for the young female staff and, in November 1882, then aged 50, he became enamoured of Louisa Turner whom he set up in Greville Road, Kilburn. He was already involved with her sister, Emily, who lived in Hove with a George Rayner and for the next few years the two pairs became something of a *ménage à quatre*.

In about 1880 Emily had a son, Horace George Rayner, fathered by Whiteley. In 1889 Louisa had a son, Cecil Whiteley. In 1888 Whiteley and Louisa Turner ended their relationship and she later married. Horace Rayner married in 1901. He and his wife, and later children, lived in poverty in a series of cheap rooming houses with Horace Rayner telling anyone who would listen that he was the son of a prominent citizen and that he would soon be coming into an inheritance of £1,000.

On 23 January 1907 Horace bought a Colt Police Special and a box of bullets from a gunsmith and the next morning confronted his father in the store. He had tricked his way in by pretending he was a clerk to the solicitor Sir George Lewis who acted for Whiteley. The magnate, recognising blackmail when he saw it, suggested that Rayner should go abroad to the colonies and indicated that he had no intention of recognising him as his son. He then called an employee and asked him to send for the police.

Staff heard Rayner say, 'Is that your final word?' the reply, 'Yes,' and 'Then you are a dead man'. Rayner shot his father between the eyes and then turned the gun on himself. He shot himself in the eye and the bullet exited through the cheek. Rayner hovered between life and death until on 19 February he was well enough to be charged and remanded to the prison hospital at Brixton. In his pocket there was a letter he had written:

> To whom it may concern – William Whiteley is my father. He has brought upon himself and me a double fatality by reason of his own refusal of a request perfectly reasonable. RIP.

His trial in March 1907 lasted less than a day and, sentencing him to death, the Lord Chief Justice said,

'I cannot hold out to you the slightest hope that the sentence of the law will not be carried into effect, and I call upon you most earnestly to spend the time which may be allowed to you in earnest communication with your Maker.'

The Lord Chief Justice was wrong. Public sympathy, believing he was the victim of the greed and lust of his betters, was on the side of Rayner, and a series of petitions totalling over 200,000 signatories was mounted. The solicitor defending him suspended all other work and had to open other addresses for the petitions to be delivered. As the date of his execution drew nearer it was apparent to the Home Secretary that there would be a massive public outcry if the sentence was carried out. Rayner was reprieved but his immediate life was not a great deal happier. Whilst in prison he twice tried to commit suicide before being released in 1919. He died two years after his release.

S.T. Felstead, *Sir Richard Muir, The Memoirs of a Public Prosecutor*.

25 January, 1902

Charlotte Cheeseman, who worked in a cigar factory in Hoxton and whose body was found on Tottenham Marshes, was last seen alive on 25 January 1902. She had been walking out with 24-year-old George Woolfe and had every expectation that he would marry her. He had a different view of things and wrote to her saying he had met someone he liked better and that was the end of their relationship. 'I hope I shall never hear of you or see you again, as I am indeed thankful I have got rid of you so easily.' So far as he was concerned there was to be no question of blame being put on him if she found herself in 'a certain condition'. He also wrote to her employer saying she was untrustworthy. Poor Charlotte. In her turn she wrote in the time-honoured fashion of a young girl betrayed:

> Dear George, Don't be offended because I am writing this letter to you. Will you go out with me again as you know what you have done to me. I think it is a shame how you have treated me, but I will forget that and think of you all the more. You don't know how much I love you.

Woolfe kindly showed that letter to another man who was courting Charlotte Cheeseman and had the satisfaction of hearing that he would have nothing more to do with the girl. Instead she and Woolfe did go out again. They were seen in the Rosemary Branch, a public house in the Southgate Road, North London. The next morning her body was found by some young boys. The Tottenham Marshes were at that time a desolate place. Her nose had been broken and her face and hands were covered in blood. Woolfe had beaten her about the head with a chisel. His execution on 6 May 1902 was the last to take place at Newgate prison. Sir Richard Muir, who later prosecuted Crippen and who prosecuted Woolfe, remarked to his clerk:

> I am very glad I have had the opportunity of putting that young gentleman into the condemned cell. He will know what it is to suffer before the hangman comes for him.

S.T. Felstead, *Sir Richard Muir, The Memoirs of a Public Prosecutor*.

26 January, 1994

Forty-one-year-old Colin Middleton, described at the time of the killing as having smiling, laughing eyes, was jailed for life at Birmingham Crown Court on 16 February 1995 for the murder of his former manager, Terry Maidens, in front of his wife and young child. The murder, which at first had seemed to have all the hallmarks of a contract killing, took place after Middleton had been moved from night to day shifts, following claims that he had been terrorising other staff and refusing to carry out instructions. He was also reprimanded for kicking a door. He then stormed out of the factory, vowing never to return.

On 26 January 1994 Middleton went to Maidens' house where he was watching *Coronation Street* with his four-year-old son on his lap. The door was opened by Katherine Maidens who thought the caller was a man delivering pizzas, and Middleton pushed past her, went into the living room and shot his former manager at close range. He then fled to Scotland where he was found two months later. At the trial his defence was that he had gone to Maidens' house merely to punch him but he had tripped and the gun had gone off.

At his trial, the judge said, 'The evidence I have heard makes it plain to me that there will be a need for considerable care to be taken in assessing you over the next few years to establish the extent to which you need help.'

27 January, 1985

The body of 50-year-old Margaret Bennett, reported missing by her husband, Frank, on 27 January 1985, was not found for 10 years. Frank Bennett claimed he had last seen his wife three days earlier when they had had a row as he was leaving for work from their home in Field Terrace Road, Newmarket. The couple had what neighbours called a 'turbulent' relationship and Margaret, who had two sons by a previous marriage, was well known at a local women's refuge.

Frank Bennett was interviewed by the police after nationwide enquiries had failed to trace Margaret, but no evidence emerged that would have justified a full-scale search of the house. He told the police that by the time he returned home his wife had left, taking a suitcase of clothing and £25 in cash.

On 7 November 1988 Frank Bennett's body was found by the railway at Welwyn Garden City. He had walked in front of a train. He left no suicide note and the coroner returned an open verdict.

In 1993 the police received an anonymous tip-off and dug up the patio of the Bennetts' house. They found nothing. Then in July 1995 a builder checking the house for damp removed part of the fitted carpet in the downstairs front room and found that a section of the floorboards had been cut away and replaced. He decided to investigate further and in the soil underneath the boards found the remains of a body wrapped in polythene.

28 January, 1948

The body of Sylvia Styles was found early in the morning of 28 January 1948 in a walk known as Lovers' Lane near Syon Park, Isleworth, Middlesex. The 26-year-old former ARP warden had been strangled but no sexual assault had taken place nor had any of her property been stolen. There were signs that she had struggled and there was flesh under her fingernails.

A solitary woman with a passion for the cinema, she was not known to have any boyfriends but her colleagues at the factory where she worked said she had made arrangements to meet a man named Dan on the night of her death. One man gave evidence at her inquest, saying he had taken her to the cinema on the Sunday before her death. He had broken two subsequent engagements and was able to provide alibis for those dates. Another witness confirmed the 'Danny' story, saying that Miss Styles had told her she was going to meet a sailor of that name on 27 January. There was also some evidence that a man who had been with her on that evening had hitched a lorry ride north. A verdict of murder by person or persons unknown was returned.

29 January, 1943

When Bruno Ludke was questioned about the death of 51-year-old Frieda Rosner, found strangled on the outskirts of a village, Kopenick, near Berlin, on 29 January 1943, he tried to attack the police officer questioning him. Later he admitted that he had killed her but that, as a mental defective, he could not be convicted. Finally, he readily admitted to killing another 85 women, whom he mostly stabbed or strangled, throughout Germany from 1928 onwards. A subsequent investigation carried out over the next year showed that where it was possible to verify them, his confessions were true, but it may well be that there was a certain amount of ledger clearing by police forces.

Although Ludke sometimes stole their possessions the main reason for the attacks was rape. Born in 1909 he had a long history of sadism and theft. On one occasion, whilst working as a laundry delivery man, he ran down a woman with his horse-drawn van.

He never stood trial but this was partly because of the

embarrassment caused by the fact that a number of other men had been convicted of his crimes. He had already been sterilised following a sex attack and the realisation that he had a very low intelligence. Now he was placed in a hospital in Vienna where he was the subject of a number of Nazi-type experiments. He died on 8 April 1944 as a result of an injection administered during the course of one of them.

30 January, 1948

At 5.15 pm on 30 January 1948, the father of the Indian nation, the 78-year-old Mahatma Gandhi, who more than any other had brought about the end of British rule in India, was assassinated. He was shot in the chest and stomach, at a dawn prayer meeting in the garden of the Birla House, his New Delhi home. His killers, Nathuram Godse, a newspaper editor and member of a violently anti-Muslim organisation, Mahasabha, and Narayan Apte, were sentenced to death. Five other conspirators, including Nathuram Godse's brother, Gopal, were sentenced to life imprisonment.

The killing was a political one and followed the decision that the Indian Government should pay millions of dollars to Pakistan, as agreed by the two countries. It came at the time of a quarrel over partition when millions were crossing the border to live in the other country. Gandhi's aim had been to unite the country, whilst Godse feared peace would lead to a Muslim takeover. At his trial he said of Gandhi that he was 'a curse to India, a force of evil ... the masterbrain guiding the civil disobedience movement'. Godse and Apte were strangled to death on 15 November 1949.

After his release from prison, when he had served 17 years, Gopal Godse spoke only rarely to the press who largely boycotted the radical Hindu-revivalist family. In 1987 he did however give an interview in which he claimed, 'Considering the situation existing then, I still feel that our act was just the natural reaction . . . our act was justified because we were prepared to pay the price for the blood we shed with our own blood. We wanted to check the harm done and in order to do so if some blood is shed then it is justified.'

He went on to say that he was included late in the conspiracy which had originally intended that Gandhi be kidnapped rather than killed. 'But the alternative was not possible because it would require manpower which we did not have. So the shortest and easiest way out was to do away with him. We didn't expect any support and we didn't wait for any. We were there to sacrifice ourselves for the betterment of the nation and remove the hurdle in its path.'

Some short time before he died, Gandhi had said, 'I do not want to die . . . of creeping paralysis of my faculties . . . a defeated man. An assassin's bullet may put an end to my life. I would welcome it.'

31 January, 1969

Gail Miller, a nurse living in Saskatoon, Canada, was raped and stabbed to death on 31 January 1969. A year to the day later, 17-year-old David Milgaard was convicted of her murder and sentenced to life imprisonment. Her partially unclothed body was found in an alleyway in the snow. She had been stabbed 11 times, five times in the back. There were also some 15 small nicks in her neck. Four days after the discovery of the body police found two small clumps of frozen yellowish liquid in the snow near where it was found. One contained semen which, the prosecution said, could be linked to Milgaard.

Over 20 years later the Supreme Court of Canada held that the Minister of Justice set aside the conviction and direct a new trial. The court went on to say that if there was a retrial and Milgaard be convicted then consideration should still be given to a conditional pardon. It was not prepared to go the whole way and rule that Milgaard was innocent.

Early in the morning of 31 January 1969 Milgaard and his friends Nichol (Nicky) John and Ronald Wilson drove from Regina to Saskatoon. Some time about 7 am that morning they stopped a woman walking by their car to ask for directions and shortly after that the car became stuck. Wilson and Milgaard went off in separate directions to get some help and Nichol John stayed with the car. Wilson was back before Milgaard.

A little later Nichol John found a woman's compact in the car after they left Saskatoon. Milgaard seized it and threw it out of the window. Albert Cadrain, to whom the trio had later given a lift, said he saw blood on Milgaard's pants and shirt. Cadrain was later to receive C$2,000 reward. It was he who first brought Milgaard to the attention of the police. When details of the killing were shown on television two men awaiting trial for armed robbery gave evidence that damaged Milgaard. He was alleged in court to have picked up a pillow and re-enacted the crime saying, 'I killed her.'

He was convicted after an 11-hour retirement by the jury and sentenced to prison. During the first 10 years in prison he managed to escape twice; once in 1980 when he was on the run for several months and obtained work in Toronto.

In January 1990 an allegation was made that Larry Fisher, formerly of Saskatoon and then in prison for rape and attempted murder had, in fact, been Gail Miller's killer. Interviewed, Fisher's wife repeated a story she had told to the police 10 years earlier that her husband had been out on the night of the murder and then when, in temper, she accused him of the crime, the colour had drained from his face. Fisher had been convicted of rape and assault in 1971. He was released on parole in 1980 but returned to prison for attacking another woman. Interviewed on television he denied any involvement in the Miller killing.

By the middle of 1990 Cadrain said that his questioning by the police had been 'hell and mental torture'. Ronald Wilson denied seeing blood on Milgaard's clothes or seeing him with a knife. An official investigation was ordered.

Giving judgement, the Chief Justice said:

> While there is some evidence which implicates Milgaard in the murder of Gail Miller, the fresh evidence presented to us, particularly as to the locations and the pattern of sexual assaults committed by Fisher, could well affect a jury's assessment of the guilt or innocence of Milgaard.

The court added that its decision should not be taken as a finding of guilt against Fisher. Milgaard was released.

Carl Karp, *When Justice Fails*.

FEBRUARY

1 February, 1974

A psychology student at the State University, Lynda Ann Healy, the first victim of the serial killer Ted Bundy, went missing from her rented accommodation in Seattle on 1 February 1974. She shared a basement apartment with four other young women.

The bedclothes were found to be heavily bloodstained. Probably Bundy came in through an unlocked door and knocked her unconscious before kidnapping her. Prior to this, he had attacked another young woman in her apartment, thrusting a rod into her vagina and causing severe internal injuries.

After Lynda Healy's disappearance in February 1974 girls went missing on a regular basis in the states of Oregon, Washington, Utah and Colorado. Between then and April 1975 attacks on 18 girls can be traced to Bundy. Later in 1974 he attacked Carol DaRonch when, posing as a policeman, he approached her in the centre of Salt Lake City and persuaded her to get in his car. He drove her to a quiet street but she survived the attack and managed to escape. He was arrested the following year on 16 August 1975 in Utah when a police officer became suspicious of his car in which hair was found which matched that of Caryn Campbell, one of the girls who had disappeared in Utah. He was extradited to Colorado and escaped from prison on 7 June 1977 but was quickly recaptured. He remained in custody until 30 December that year when, by climbing through the ceiling of his cell, he again escaped.

Now using the name of Chris Hagen, he fled to Florida where he attacked six more young women between 15 January and 14 February 1978 when he was arrested, again by chance, in a stolen car near Pensacola Airport. Two of his victims survived.

At first Bundy denied any involvement in the killings, claiming the police had made a terrible mistake. However, a wax impression of his teeth matched those on the buttocks of Lisa Levy, killed on 15 January 1978.

Bundy, a handsome man with abundant charm, had been awarded a scholarship in Chinese studies at Stanford, obtained a BSc in psychology and, for a time, was an assistant director of the local Seattle crime commission. He moved to Utah where he studied law at the University. During the time he was with the Seattle crime commission he worked with Ann Rule who later wrote *The Stranger Beside Me*, on which Bundy collaborated. She was to say that he fitted no criminal type pattern.

Bundy was seen by one psychiatrist as being '. . . a man who has no problems, or is smart enough, or clever enough, to appear close to the edge of "normal".' He himself claimed, 'Sometimes I feel like a vampire.' It was his opinion that very few killers responded to voices and visions but the majority were intelligent people who could make rational decisions so far as their crimes were concerned. The problem for law agencies was, he believed, that the serial killer would continue until stopped and that he would become more proficient at killing as time went by. Bundy may not always have been consistent because on another occasion he said that an entity resided within him and gradually took over his conscious mind.

It is not clear how many women he did kill. At one time he admitted to over a hundred but later withdrew that confession. After a series of appeals which lasted some 10 years he was electrocuted on 24 January 1989. Outside

the prison a huge crowd cheered the announcement of
his death.

Elliott Leyton, *Hunting Humans*; Ann Rule, *The Stranger
Beside Me*.

2 February, 1964

Ever since the era of Jack the Ripper, London has buzzed
with the *frisson* that there is another serial killer in its
midst. In the 1920s the unnamed killer of Louisa Steele
was described as a second Ripper; Cummings-Hay, the
murderer during the Second World War, was another.
After that war there was a spate of killings of prostitutes in
Soho but attempts to link them together failed. They were
probably not sex killings but carried out for professional
reasons.

However, there has been one genuine candidate for
the title of the second Ripper. His identity, known to
the police, has never been released. His work is known
as 'the Jack the Stripper murders'. The soubriquet is a
double entendre: the killer worked in a paint stripping
business and many of his victims were found naked. The
first victim was 30-year-old prostitute Hannah Tailford,
who also called herself Anne Taylor and Teresa Bell, and
whose body was found on 2 February 1964 in the Thames
near Hammersmith Bridge. Her clothes were missing but
her stockings were still around her ankles. She had facial
bruising and her pants were stuffed in her mouth.

She had last been seen leaving her home in West
Norwood, south London a week earlier and at first it was
thought that she might have been killed by a former client
to stop her attempts at blackmail. She was a known party-
goer and in the flat she kept in Victoria she had studio
lighting equipment and a camera. Her diary was missing.

Curiously, despite the fact that a second death had occurred by that time, the entry in the police records [MEPO/20/10] regarding Hannah Tailford shows that by 3 June 1964 Tailford's death was not being treated as a crime. 'The Hammersmith Corner returned an open verdict, there being no evidence to show how the deceased came by her death. In view of this and the *lack of evidence* to show that the victim was murdered, this is no longer recorded as a crime.'

The second body was found in the Thames, this time at Duke's Meadow on 8 April. Irene Lockwood had been strangled and again the police thought she might have been blackmailing her former clients. Irene Lockwood had provided the alibi for a man accused, a year earlier, of murdering another prostitute, Vicki Pender. Both women were involved in blue movies.

The body of the third victim, Helen Barthelemy, was found on 24 April a little way from the river, in a driveway near Swincombe Avenue, Brentford. Four of her teeth were missing and a dark ring around her waist indicated that her pants had been removed after she died. She had traces of paint spray on her body which made the police think her body might have been kept in a paint strip shop before being dumped. Traces of spermatozoa in her mouth suggested she had either been orally raped or that she had performed fellatio before she died. Now it appeared that if one man was responsible for the murders the blackmail theory was wrong.

The next day the police must have thought their Sundays had all come at once when Kenneth Archibald, a caretaker, walked into Notting Hill police station and confessed to killing Irene Lockwood. He was able to give a detailed statement of his movements with the woman, saying, 'I must have lost my temper and put my hands around her throat. She could not scream. I then proceeded to take her clothes off and rolled her into the river. I took her clothes home and burned them.' It was apparent, however, that he was not involved with the murders of either Tailford or Barthelemy.

Archibald was charged and indicted for Lockwood's murder. His trial began at the Old Bailey on 19 June and four days later the jury retired for only 40 minutes before returning a verdict of Not Guilty. Afterwards, Archibald told reporters that he had confessed only because he was fed up. He was upset because he was being questioned about a break-in at the club where he worked and had drunk six pints of beer before he walked into the police station.

Superintendent John Du Rose who headed the investigation later wrote, 'We had no reason to believe that Archibald had anything to do with the murder but he had to be charged and a jury had to decide the case because he had repeated his false confession twice before retracting it.'

Coincidentally, whilst Archibald was in custody the murders stopped. The police later believed that this was due to the extensive coverage the case had received and that prostitutes were being more careful in their choice of clients. The next murder came on 14 July when Mary Fleming, a mother of two, was found in a sitting position near a garage in Berrymead Road, Chiswick, west London. She too was naked and her denture was missing. Again there was sperm in her mouth and traces of spray on her body. She also fell into the height range of the dead women. None was more than five feet three inches tall.

On 25 November the body of yet another diminutive prostitute, Margaret McGowan, was discovered on a pile of rubble in a car park in Hornton Street near Kensington High Street. Again spots of paint covered her body and she had a tooth missing. She had disappeared on 23 October. The last of the killings was discovered on 16 February 1965 when the body of Bridie O'Hara was found behind a store-shed off Westfield Road, Acton.

There was little doubt that the killings were all the work of one man. Apart from their lack of height all the prostitutes worked the Bayswater–Kensington beat, all were suffocated whilst clothed and all were kept in a store before their bodies were left to be found. All were found in or near the Thames.

The paint on the bodies was traced to a covered transformer near to a paint-spray shop on the Heron Factory Estate in Acton. Matters did not end there, however. There were over seven thousand people working on the estate. Then in June 1965 a married man living in south London killed himself, leaving a note to the effect that he was unable to stand the strain any longer. The killings ceased and the police believed that this man was in fact Jack the Stripper. His name has never been made public but journalist Brian McConnell claimed that he was an ex-policeman who was a heavy drinker. Despite his grotesque sexual tastes and a lifetime obsession with prostitutes he had married and had returned to drink only when refused a transfer to the plain-clothes division. He had then left the force.

The unsolved murders of two other women were at one time thought to be the work of Jack the Stripper. Elizabeth Figg was found dead in June 1959 and Gwyneth Rees, who had strong east London connections, was found dead in November 1963. In the case of Gwyneth Rees it is almost certain she died following an abortion. As for Elizabeth Figg her death was rather outside the time span of the Stripper's operations.

Brian McConnell, *Found Naked and Dead*; John Du Rose, *Murder was my Business*; Leonard Read, *Nipper*.

3 February, 1943

One of the major players in the Chicago Crime Syndicate was long suspected of the murder of cocktail waitress, sometimes described as dice-girl, Estelle Carey on 3 February 1943. Marshall Joseph Caifano was the brother of Leonard 'Fats' or 'Fat Lennie' Caifano who was killed a decade later whilst trying to kidnap Theodore Roe, who ran much of the numbers racket in Chicago. Marshall Caifano was himself picked up for questioning but Roe was unable, or more probably unwilling, to make an identification. This reticence did him little good. He was killed within a matter of weeks.

Estelle Carey had the misfortune to be the girlfriend of Nick 'Dean' Circella who at the time was serving a 10-year sentence following his conviction in the Willie Bioff movie-extortion case. Apart from blackmailing producers over labour relations, Bioff had forced cinema owners in Hollywood to use two projectionists, resulting in a substantial payoff to himself.

It was feared that, like Bioff, Circella might turn informer in a deal to secure his early release and, with the intention of showing him the folly of such behaviour, Estelle Carey was tied to a chair in her apartment, tortured and then set alight after having petrol poured over her. The only witness, and one who survived, was her poodle, found cowering in a corner.

A principal suspect for Carey's murder, Caifano was convicted of extortion in 1964 and served a 10-year sentence. In 1977 his victim, oil tycoon Raymond J. Ryan, was killed when his car was bombed in Evansville, Indiana. Caifano, who legally changed his name to John Marshall, was convicted of interstate transportation of stolen securities following a raid in 1968 at Chicago's O'Hare airport. He was sentenced to concurrent terms of 20 years' imprisonment and released in 1991.

J.R. Nash, *World Encyclopedia of Organised Crime*.

4 February, 1984

In October 1987 the former Toronto Maple Leaf, New York Islander and Buffalo Sabre left-winger, as well as member of a host of minor-league hockey teams, Brian 'Spinner' Spencer, stood trial for murder in Florida. The prosecution said that he had kidnapped and killed a 32-year-old real estate salesman, Michael James Dalfo, who had been pistol-whipped and shot twice in the head. Dalfo's body had been found near PGA Boulevard, west of the Florida Turnpike at West Palm Beach, on 4 February 1984.

Spencer had not been arrested until November 1986 when a former call girl, Diane Delena, was once more interviewed by the police. This time, in return for immunity from prosecution, she said that her part-time boyfriend, Spencer, had kidnapped and killed Dalfo as a result of Dalfo's treatment of her on a call-out.

Diane Delena's version of the story, which comprised more or less the whole of the prosecution's case, was that she worked for an agency called Fantacee Island Escorts and around 11 pm had gone to estate agent Dalfo's condominium. He had been drinking and taking cocaine during the evening and when Diane arrived, he was wearing nothing more than a black cache-sex. He wanted her to give him oral sex but he could not sustain an erection. When she wanted to leave he offered her a cheque payable to cash which she refused. Delena telephoned the agency to say she was leaving but he tried to detain her. She ran out of Dalfo's home and drove to her own where she took another call-out. On the way she noticed Spencer's truck at a bar, called in and told him of the fright she had had with Dalfo.

After she had been with the second client she returned to the trailer she shared with Spencer. It was there he called her and insisted she took him to Dalfo's condo.

Reluctantly she did so and Dalfo came out to the car. Spencer asked him to get in and they drove off. According to Delena, Spencer made her get out of the car, then drove away a short distance. Dalfo had been saying he would call his lawyer. When Spencer returned, according to Delena he was alone and said to her that Dalfo would not be calling his lawyer now.

The defence was able to show that the escort agency had been involved in some serious crime in the West Palm Beach area. The owners had made threats against other clients who had caused trouble to their girls. As far as Spencer was concerned, there was no reason for him to have shot Dalfo. True, he had a bad temper but there was no doubt he could easily have beaten the man up. He had no qualms about Delena acting as a prostitute. Indeed, it appears when she wanted a second man for a trick she called on his services. Nor, apart from giving her a scare, was Dalfo much of a threat to her. The defence was that Delena knew much more than she was telling the police and the court and that Spencer was the fall-guy.

The jury acquitted Spencer after a little over an hour's retirement. It did not help him much. Shortly before midnight on 2 June 1988 he was shot and killed in Riviera Beach. According to Greg Cook, the man who was with him, they had been going to buy some cigarettes from an all-night drugstore when they were the victims of a petty hold-up. Cook's arms were scorched; Spencer was shot in the heart.

The title of the book and the film written and made about Spencer's tragic life – early in his career his father was shot dead after trying to persuade a television station to show one of his son's hockey games – comes from a 10-minute penalty handed out in an ice-hockey game for extremely bad behaviour.

Martin O'Malley, *Gross Misconduct*.

5 February, 1966

The body of Cork prostitute Peggy Flynn was found at
Sandycove Point, Dalkey, Dublin on the morning of 5
February 1966. It was the day of her 49th birthday and,
according to reports, she looked every day of her age.
She had been strangled with a scarf and one of her own
nylon stockings. One report said she had also consumed
enough alcohol before her death to have died of alcohol
poisoning. This was not quite accurate. Certainly she
had been drinking and indeed had been given a room
in the neighbourhood to sober up but death was due to
strangulation. Because of the lack of salt water in her
lungs it was thought she had been killed elsewhere and
her body moved.

Despite the case being featured on Telefis Eireann's
Garda Patrol programme it was a year and a half before
an arrest was made. A witness was able to describe a
woman who could have been Peggy Flynn being picked
up by a man in a white Triumph Herald motor car with
black flashing on the side. From then on it was a matter
of sifting through the owners of this type of car. One was
a young man who had become a cadet in the British Army.
Inspector John J. Moore of the Garda and Superintendent
Leonard 'Nipper' Read, who was to use the case to mask
his concurrent investigations into the Kray twins, saw
the young man in the Royal Victoria Hospital, Netley,
near Southampton. He had, it appears, already made a
'confession' to his girlfriend, saying that he had killed a
'bloody old woman' and had decided to tell all before his
marriage.

He had told the psychiatric department at the hospital
that he had killed Peggy Flynn because she had demanded
more money than the small amount he had agreed to
pay her. When questioned by the police there were
inconsistencies in his story and the officers were by

no means convinced that the young man had not made the confession after reading reports of the case in the newspapers. But confession there was, and he was charged and returned to Ireland to face his trial.

He appeared on 20 March 1968 at the Central Criminal Court, Dublin where the defence case was that the young man had a disordered personality of the kind which led him to confess to crimes he had not committed. The jury took four and a half hours to acquit him.

Terry Prone, *Irish Murders*; Leonard Read, *Nipper*.

6 February, 1938

John Stanley Phillips, a 21-year-old graduate of Selwyn College, Cambridge, and studying for the ministry at Oxford, murdered pantry-boy Harold Matthews on 6 February 1938. The boy's naked body, which had suffered severe injuries, both before and after death, was found on the roof of Wycliffe College. Phillips immediately admitted his guilt to the Chief Constable of Oxford, saying that no one had helped him. The only question was whether Phillips was sane and Norman Birkett for the defence argued that he was a schizophrenic and for him the concept of right and wrong did not exist.

Dr Henry Yellowlees agreed, saying that, in his opinion, Phillips was indeed a schizophrenic: '. . . he was comparable with a child who has been brought from his solitary play to listen to the polite conversation of grown-ups in a drawing room. He was slightly bored. He was simply not in the least interested, and slightly peevish.'

As might be expected the Brixton medical officer giving evidence for the prosecution did not agree, although he was forced by Norman Birkett to accept that Phillips was 'not a person of normal mind'. At the time doctors and lawyers had even greater differences of opinion on what constituted insanity and Mr Justice Asquith, summing up, said:

> What insanity would justify a verdict of 'Guilty but Insane'? Abnormality is not enough, nor, even, is certifiable insanity necessarily enough. There have been cases where a man has been convicted and the conviction has been upheld by the Court of Criminal Appeal, although every one of the medical witnesses said he would be willing to certify him insane in the ordinary sense.

Mercifully, the jury disregarded him and took only a few minutes to return a 'Guilty but Insane' verdict. Phillips was detained during His Majesty's Pleasure.

7 February, 1996

Glenda Hoskins, a 45-year-old accountant, was last seen alive at 8.30 am on Wednesday, 7 February 1996 when she took her children to school. Later that day her daughter was unable to gain access to their flat overlooking the Port Solent marina near Portsmouth. She contacted her father and with her younger brother made unsuccessful efforts throughout the evening to get into the flat. Finally the police broke into the flat at about midnight and found Mrs Hoskins's body. She had been suffocated and badly beaten. Her white Ford Escort Cabriolet was missing. It was later found abandoned in Plaistow, east London.

The police linked her death with a savage attack on Ann Fidler, a 43-year-old who ran an escort agency and had been left for dead at her home in Eastleigh, Hampshire, on 27 December 1995. She suffered brain damage after being hit with a bottle and stabbed.

The police took the unusual step of naming the man

whom they wished to interview. He was thought to have gone abroad, possibly to Belgium. In July 1996 a man was arrested in France and extradition proceedings were commenced.

8 February, 1995

On the morning of 8 February 1995 the body of Barry Trigwell, a private investigator, was found in his three-bedroomed rented house in Fowey Close, Walmley, Sutton Coldfield, a well-to-do Birmingham suburb. His severely beaten body, wearing only trousers, was in a half-filled bath. It seemed he had been beaten by a blunt object and had sustained severe fractures to his skull and face.

Trigwell had bought a Nationwide Investigations franchise and, based in Birmingham, worked with two other detectives. Unusually he was not listed in the professional directories and was thought to have carried out much of his work in Hong Kong and the Middle East. Known as Barry the Bastard by his colleagues, who regarded the short stocky man as fearless, he particularly enjoyed snatching children back from abroad. As a result he had made many enemies. One of his former colleagues thought that, at the time of his death, he may have been investigating money laundering.

He had been killed after he returned home from an Indian restaurant some time after 7 pm on the previous evening. His body was found by a colleague who came the next morning to drive him to work – Trigwell was disqualified from driving.

On 26 February 1995 an article in the *Sunday Times* reported that a gang of South African mercenaries was operating in the contract killing market at a price of £20,000 a hit. It was suggested that Trigwell's killing might have been one of their efforts.

In fact the contractor was Trigwell's wife, Ethel Anne – something she denied throughout her trial. In July 1996 the Birmingham Crown Court was told how she had stood to gain in the region of £380,000 in the event of her husband's death. She had, according to the prosecution, discussed the possibility of the death of her husband with a Johannesburg nightclub owner when she visited the country in January 1995. Two men were subsequently recruited and flew to England. According to the prosecution she supplied them with a key to her husband's house and £300 in expenses which she left at the Clover Hotel in Sutton Coldfield where they were staying. The receptionist was suspicious that the package might contain drugs and had it opened, found it to be innocent and resealed it. It was only when the news of Trigwell's death became known that she recalled the woman, whom she identified as Mrs Trigwell, as having left the packet. Mrs Trigwell had an alibi for the killing. She was back in South Africa, where she dined on the night of Trigwell's death with her lover. She was arrested when she returned to England to attend her husband's inquest. On 25 July 1996 she was sentenced to life imprisonment for what the trial judge called a 'cold, calculated and chilling' murder.

The two killers and the nightclub owner are thought to be in South Africa from which there is no extradition treaty. Mrs Trigwell's son by a previous marriage had died with gunshot wounds to the head. He had inherited a substantial sum of money shortly before his death. Both he and his father died within a short time of each other.

9 February, 1942

The body of chemist's assistant Evelyn Hamilton was found in an air-raid shelter early on the morning of 9

February 1942. She had been strangled by, it appeared, a left-handed killer, and her scarf had been wrapped tightly over her throat and nose. The following night the body of Evelyn Oatley was found in her flat in Soho. The former Windmill girl had been strangled but additionally her body had been mutilated with a tin opener. On 13 February the body of Margaret Lowe was found in what she euphemistically called her 'office' in Gosfield Street. One of her stockings had been used as a ligature and once again the body had been mutilated. Another body, that of Doris Jouannet who worked as Doris Robson, was found the same night. She was the wife of a hotel manager and had been attacked in her Paddington flat. She had been strangled and the body slashed.

On the same night a Mrs Heywood was pushed into a shop doorway in Piccadilly and partially strangled. A passer-by scared off her attacker who fled, leaving behind his RAF gas mask. He did strike once more and attacked a Kathleen King whom he had taken in a taxi back to her flat in Paddington. She screamed and alerted the neighbours. This time he left behind his RAF belt. Both it and the mask carried the number 525987 and it was only a matter of time before he was traced. Twenty-eight-year-old Gordon Frederick Cummins was arrested and charged. His fingerprints matched those left at the various flats. Evelyn Oatley's cigarette case was found in his room.

Cummins, known as 'The Duke' to his RAF companions, came from a good family and was well educated. He had however been dismissed from a number of jobs on the grounds of unreliability and dishonesty. In 1936 he married the private secretary of a theatrical producer. He was said to speak with a phoney Oxford accent and claimed the right to use 'Honourable' on the grounds that he was the illegitimate son of a peer. He was hanged at Wandsworth prison on 25 June 1942.

It is probable that he killed at least two other women. The partially clad body of 19-year-old Maple Church was found by some children playing in a bombed-out house at

225 Hampstead Road, London on Monday, 12 October
1941. She had been strangled. Her shoes were later found
in the basement. Friends had seen her in the company of
a soldier and she had said she was engaged. About 10
pm the evening before, she had seen a girlfriend onto a
train at Charing Cross and it was thought she had been
picked up by her killer as she waited for a bus home.
She was not mutilated but neither was Cummins's first
accepted victim. He is also suspected of killing Edith
Humphries who was bludgeoned to death at her home
in Gloucester Crescent, Regent's Park, less than a mile
from Cummins's billet.

10 February, 1995

Josie O'Dwyer, a 39-year-old lesbian from Highbury,
north London, changed her plea to guilty as the judge,
Nina Lowry, in her last trial at the Old Bailey, was preparing to send the jury out on 11 October 1995. Leaping
to her feet and shouting, 'I want to change my plea, I killed
him', O'Dwyer admitted murdering 39-year-old council
worker Peter Sutherland on 10 February 1995.

Throughout the trial, during which she had an epileptic
fit, O'Dwyer had maintained that she had killed Mr
Sutherland in self-defence as he tried to rape her when
she had gone to his house in Pyrland Road to discuss
letting one of his rooms to a friend. She claimed he had
lunged at her breast saying she needed 'a good man'. The
prosecution claimed that although neighbours had heard
the sound of furniture being overturned they had heard no
shouts. 'If there was an attempted rape, why no shouting?'
asked Orlando Pownall for the Crown.

After the killing, in which she struck Sutherland nine
blows on the head with a plank, some from behind,
she fled to Cornwall to see members of her family. She

later gave herself up. Sutherland's body was found nine days later.

O'Dwyer, who was sentenced to life imprisonment, is regarded as one of Britain's toughest women prisoners. She has boasted of attacking Myra Hindley, the Moors murderess, when they were in prison together in Holloway in the 1970s. She has also spoken of stabbing her probation officer with a paper knife.

11 February, 1962

Toronto police officer Fred Nash was killed by small-time criminal Ronald Turpin on 11 February 1962.

The body of Lorne Gibson, who was thought to have been killed by gambling competitors, had previously been found in a car in O'Keefe Lane which runs along the east side of Yonge, north of Dundas in Toronto, and Turpin was suspected. He and his girlfriend, Lilian White, had hidden out over Christmas, and now returned to downtown Toronto where Turpin had undertaken some work to finance a move to Northern Ontario. It was unfortunate that when Turpin was stopped it was by Fred Nash.

At the time the Toronto Morality Squad was a unit of uniformed police operating in plain clothes. Nash had been a very good, very effective morality officer, but he had just been transferred into uniform because he had been overly aggressive in an investigation. He knew every petty criminal in downtown Toronto.

If it had been almost any other officer Turpin could have tried to pass himself off under another name but Nash knew him by sight and that is why he was killed. Other officers on the scene shot Turpin in the arms.

An officer who was with Turpin afterwards recalls, 'I had worked with Nash. After he was shot, and when Turpin was in custody but in hospital, it was decided that he should not be guarded by officers from downtown Toronto. He never showed any remorse. He never even spoke to us.'

Turpin was hanged in a back-to-back double hanging in Toronto's Don jail on 10 December 1962. His companion was Arthur Lucas, a Detroit pimp, convicted on doubtful evidence of a gang murder. They were the last men to be executed in Canada. They were buried in Toronto's West End cemetery under markers 415 and 416.

12 February, 1976

The film actor Sal Mineo was killed on 12 February 1976. He was stabbed in the heart whilst in the car port of his West Hollywood home. Mineo had been nominated as best supporting actor for his part in the 1953 James Dean film, *Rebel without a Cause* and also for his part in *Exodus* seven years later.

Now neighbours heard calls of 'Help me, please' and found him lying on his side. He had been stabbed with a heavy-bladed knife. Despite an attempt at mouth-to-mouth resuscitation he died. His car keys and wallet had been left with him.

Witnesses saw a man drive off in what was thought to be a yellow Toyota. Twenty-one-year-old Lionel Williams then bragged to his girlfriend that he had killed the actor when he saw a telecast of the attack. She did not report his possible confession to the police but, when he was in prison in Michigan on a charge of passing a bad cheque, he again told an inmate that he had killed Sal Mineo. The inmate, mindful of the benefits of co-operation with the authorities, reported the conversation and on investigation it appeared that the yellow Toyota closely resembled the Dodge Colt which Williams owned at the time of the incident.

Williams was recognised through a tattoo on his arm and the owner of a shop gave evidence that he had sold a knife to Williams which could have caused the wounds to Mineo. Williams was sentenced to 50 years in prison after being found guilty of second-degree murder and 10 counts of robbery.

13 February, 1901

Bessie Taylor died on 13 February 1901. Her death was attributed to 'exhaustion from vomiting and diarrhoea'. She had been poisoned by, and was the second victim of, her Polish husband, Severin Antoniovitch Klososki, rather better known as George Chapman.

Bessie Taylor had been a barmaid at the Prince of Wales public house in Bartholomew Square off the City Road of which Chapman was the landlord. She had answered an advertisement after Chapman's first English 'wife', Mary Spink, had died on Christmas Day 1897. Officially her cause of death was consumption but she too had suffered from severe vomiting attacks. Bessie Taylor probably became Mrs Chapman in 1899 and the next year Chapman gave up the lease of the Prince of Wales and took over The Grapes in Bishop's Stortford. Whilst there Bessie had to go into hospital and, it seems, Chapman treated her badly, once threatening her with a revolver. They moved again to the Monument Tavern in Union Street near London Bridge.

After her death Bessie Taylor was succeeded by Maud Marsh who soon began to suffer in the same way as her predecessors. For a time she returned to her parents but when she went back to Chapman he had moved again, this time to The Crown, also in Union Street. Her ill health continued and after both she and the nurse had drunk a glass of brandy and soda which resulted in vomiting,

Maud's parents became suspicious and called in a doctor. It was too late however to save Maud. She died on 22 October 1902. An autopsy was performed and arsenic was discovered. Chapman was arrested on 25 October 1902 and prosecuted by Sir Edward Carson. The jury retired for only 11 minutes. Chapman was hanged at Wandsworth prison on 7 April 1903. He was in a state of collapse and had to be supported by warders on his way to the gallows where he was hanged by William and John Billington.

It has never been clear why Chapman should have poisoned his wives. There was certainly no question of inheriting a fortune or of insurance money. He was born in Kolo, Poland, and was apprenticed to a surgeon. He failed his examinations and for a time travelled the country as a barber-surgeon. After a period working in a hospital and in the Russian army he came to England, probably in 1888. He had married a woman in Poland and for a time she, Chapman and a Lucy Baderski formed a *ménage à trois*. Chapman and Lucy Baderski had two children and when they parted she retained custody of the children.

Chapman has long been a favourite candidate for the identity of Jack the Ripper. In support of this theory is his training as a surgeon, his appearance and that he was in and around Whitechapel at the time of the killings. He had been investigated at the time of the Whitechapel killings and Chief Inspector Abberline was said to have favoured Chapman as the Ripper. Against the theory, however, is that with Chapman still in the East End the killings stopped. Nor is it common for killers to totally change their *modus operandi*, in Chapman's case from ripper to poisoner. There is an unsubstantiated story that he had decapitated a woman in Poland. This would certainly fit more with his Ripper image than that of a calculating poisoner.

H.L. Adam (ed), *The Trial of George Chapman*; Donald Rumbelow, *The Complete Jack the Ripper*.

14 February, 1984

On 14 February 1984 London's gangland had what the
papers later described as its own St Valentine's Day Mas-
sacre. Dave Elmore and Jimmy 'The Wad' Waddington
left The Hope pub in Barking together and disappeared.
Their Vauxhall car was found a week later, unlocked and
abandoned, near Barking railway station.

A year later bar steward David Maxwell stood trial for
the murder of the two men. David Reader was accused of
providing the transport to take away the bodies from the
Kaleli Restaurant, Station Road, Barking, and the police
wished to interview his brother Ronald Reader who was
abroad.

The prosecution claimed that the killing had resulted
from a long-standing feud dating back to 1976 between
David Maxwell and Elmore over an attack on Maxwell's
brother Mickie who had been hit on the head with an axe.
Waddington's killing, said the Crown, resulted from the
misfortune of his being in the restaurant with Elmore.

Maxwell was alleged to have arrived carrying a sword
which he pointed at Elmore saying, 'Down boy or I kill,
kill.' It was then suggested that Ronald Reader had struck
Elmore with blows from a double-handed sword he was
carrying. William Denny QC for the prosecution said that
the bound and gagged Elmore, knowing his end was near,
recited the Lord's Prayer. When he reached the line 'Thy
will be done' he was interrupted by one of his attackers
who said, 'You're dead right, son.' Elmore broke off his
prayers to apologise to Waddington for getting him into
this trouble. The bodies of Elmore and Waddington have
never been found.

Maxwell was acquitted, as was David Reader. 'They
[Scotland Yard] told witnesses what to say – but the
jury believed me,' said Maxwell as he left the court
in triumph. Ronald Reader returned from Spain and

was also acquitted of the charges. No further arrests were made.

A sequel occurred in November 1985 when two skulls were thrown into the entrance of Harold Hill police station in Essex. Winifred Waddington commented sadly, 'I wanted to have him found in one piece but it looks like it could be him.'

15 February, 1952

Eighteen-year-old May Thompson, who wore thick spectacles and was described in the newspapers as 'not pretty', was murdered at her home in the then tiny village of Low Spennymoor, County Durham, on 15 February 1952, the day King George VI was buried. After spells as a domestic servant and nursemaid she had turned to work in a radio factory. She was not known to have a boyfriend and her nights were spent knitting. On the day of her death she collected her pay packet, amounting to £8, and left the factory with a friend, Veronica Alderson. They went to the local post office store and Veronica bought a wedding present for a friend. May returned to her home where she lived with her father. A salesman saw her when he delivered the week's groceries. May then told her father she was going to give the two-up, two-down house a good clean and he went off to the local public house to be out of her way. He reached the pub at 5.40 pm. The landlady recalled him as being her first customer.

May Thompson's friend Ellen Kipling had dinner with her every Friday and went and knocked on 32 William Street at about 7 pm. There was no reply, nor was there half an hour later although she heard the radio playing. At 7.45 pm she went in. May was lying in the kitchen. She had been stabbed 36 times in the back, chest and arms, probably with a double-edged knife. From bruising on her face it appears she tried to fight off her attacker. No weapon was found and her father did not know if a knife was missing from the kitchen. Her pay packet was untouched in a vase on the mantelpiece. No attempt had been made to rape her.

A boy said he had seen a young man put something in his saddlebag as he cycled away from the Thompsons' around the time May was in the house alone, but of course at that time of year it was dark. Other children said they heard screams.

A fortnight after the killing the *Sunday Pictorial* postulated that May might have been killed in revenge or that she had a secret life, and invited their readers to 'SEND YOUR THEORY'. A prize of £10 was to be awarded to the best solution and there would be three runner-up prizes of £5 each. To make the whole thing respectable, letters would be sent on to the officer in charge of the case, Detective Superintendent Richard Hall. 'I shall be glad to read letters you pass on to me if they offer any hope of a solution to this mystery,' he told the newspaper.

Some weeks later the police in Middlesborough received an anonymous call suggesting that a George Patterson was the killer. The caller gave no more details of the killing, nor did he leave a telephone number. No arrests were made.

16 February, 1949

Malcolm Frederick Roach, a 34-year-old painter and decorator of 79 Coopers Lane, east London, was charged with the murder of his wife, Rose, on 16 February 1949. They were boarders at number 79 where the landlady was Lilian Grace Fox, Rose's aunt.

There had been difficulties in the wartime marriage. Roach was serving in the Canadian Air Force when he met Rose who was working in the NAAFI. He was very jealous and used to take her to work and wait for her at the end of the day. She used to aggravate matters by going out with friends. Her aunt described her as 'a silly girl'.

The Roaches had returned to Canada for a period after the war where Roach complained she was associating with other men and shot himself in the chest.

On the day of the murder Rose said that she was going to live on her own at the hospital where she was now working. In temper, Roach struck her with an exercise dumbbell and then strangled her with a silk stocking. He then walked into Leyton police station and when asked his business told the station sergeant, 'I am a Canadian. You will be looking for me presently, I have killed my wife.'

Roach then made a full confession, saying, 'I don't know what made me do it, I loved her very much.' Mrs Roach had been going out with a Frank Smith who, when interviewed by the police, said that no intimacy had taken place but that he was hoping she would obtain a divorce.

At his trial Roach endeavoured to establish serious provocation by reason of his wife's affairs. The jury returned a verdict of Guilty but added a strong recommendation of mercy. Roach's appeal was dismissed but he was reprieved.

17 February, 1980

The body of Mary Carol Maher was found in a dumping area behind the airport at Daytona Beach, Florida, on 17 February 1980. She had been stabbed repeatedly but was fully dressed and there were no signs of a sexual attack. She had been laid out neatly with her arms at her sides and the body was partly covered. The ensuing investigation was one of the first to use the psychological profile. Mary Maher, a local swimming star, had been in the habit of hitching lifts and had vanished towards the end of January.

Nearly two months later a prostitute complained she had been attacked by a potential client. She could not give the details of the cause of the quarrel but it had led to slashes to her body, including a cut on her thigh requiring 27 stitches. She was able to describe the attacker as a man with glasses and a moustache and the car he drove as a red Gremlin with tinted windows. She was also able to say she thought he was a repeat customer and that he lived near Derbyshire apartments.

Gerald Stano fitted the picture. There had been a number of allegations against him for attacks on prostitutes, usually hitchhikers, and he had a car of the correct description. He was arrested and questioned by Detective Sergeant Paul Crowe who made a study of Stano's movements. If he was telling the truth he would pull his chair to the desk or lean forward. When he was not he would push away from the desk and cross his legs. Under questioning Stano eventually admitted killing Mary Maher when she fought off his attack. Later he would go on to confess to the murder of another prostitute, Toni Van Haddocks. Her body had been found covered in branches torn from trees in the locality, and Crowe, using his knowledge of Stano's body movements, obtained an admission to that killing. Stano, for the present, denied the murder of any other prostitutes but little by little – although he changed his 'signals' the new ones were as readable – he confessed to killing 34 women in both New Jersey, where he lived until 1973, and Florida.

Stano had been fostered as a child and was deemed to be 'unadoptable' by psychiatrists. He had never been able to form any bond and, although himself compulsively neat, he had married a woman who was absolutely the reverse. He also suffered from the shame of small genitalia.

In September 1981 he received sentences totalling 75 years when he admitted six murders, including Maher and Toni Van Haddocks. He was later sentenced to death for other killings.

Colin Wilson, *Written in Blood*.

18 February, 1989

Police informer Alan 'Chalky' White disappeared on 18 February 1989. He was last seen walking to the off-licence in Minchington, Gloucestershire, to buy some lager. Three months later his body, wrapped in a blue tarpaulin, was spotted by a family at the Cotswold Water Park near Cirencester. He had been stabbed in the heart.

White, who had several minor convictions, had been due to give evidence against a Danny Gardiner with whom, so he said, he had robbed a petrol station in Stroud in 1986, netting £4,800. White, who had a drug problem, had declined the police offer of a new identity. He was given a 'panic button' to use if he felt threatened but most nights he could be found in the local Crown public house. After White's death the case against Danny Gardiner collapsed and he went abroad.

With the help of Interpol the police conducted inquiries in Egypt – where Gardiner was wrongly reported to have died in Cairo – France, Spain, Morocco and Israel. On 4 January 1991 Gardiner flew back voluntarily from Tel Aviv. He had been found there working in a tourist hotel after apparently entering the country under a false name. Gardiner was later convicted of White's murder. Another man was acquitted.

James Morton, *Gangland 2*.

19 February, 1952

The naked body of Norman Edward Rickard, a 38-year-old civil servant working at the Admiralty and a well-known homosexual, who had been reported missing four days earlier, was found in a cupboard at 264A Elgin Avenue, west London on 19 February 1952. He had been strangled with his dressing gown cord. The next day Alan John Vigar, another known homosexual who was a dresser at the ABC television studios at Teddington, was found by his landlady, Olive Molyneaux, dead in his bed in his dismal bedsitter in St George's Drive, Pimlico. His hands had been tied and he too had been strangled with his dressing gown cord.

The police said they wished to interview an Irishman, based in Glasgow, with known sadistic tendencies. They discovered a reel of film in Rickard's room which they hoped would provide helpful clues. It contained 32 shots of 10 men. The film however yielded nothing useful.

Three days later the *Sunday Pictorial* carried a front page story about Patrick Lambert, a 32-year-old chef and a regular churchgoer. He had met a young man at Piccadilly Tube Station when he had been asked for a match and had agreed to put him up for the night. He told crime reporter Norman Lucas that they had talked for some time and he had dozed off in his chair, only to awake to find the man squeezing his throat. He became unconscious and when he came round the man had gone 'with my wallet containing about £2 and my churchman's blue diary'.

It was not until Lambert read the description in the newspapers of the Irishman the police wished to interview that he associated his attacker, whom he knew as Johnny, with the other murders and he told the newspaper. By and large the newspapers were not sympathetic to the plight of the men. Rickard was castigated for exchanging his

pinstripe suit for 'light blue American-style jeans, a red
and white check shirt, thin leather gloves and no hat' for
his evenings out. 'These are twilight murders ... Two
men, if you can call Norman Rickard and Alan Vigar
men, lived in the twilight world of the homosexual and
they died in the garrotter's noose,' said the *News of the
World*.

Although it is possible that a police officer had actually
seen Vigar's killer – an officer was standing near his flat
when he passed with a man described as about five feet
ten inches tall, with 'classic' features and fair hair – they
made little progress with their inquiry.

Later, Detective Superintendent Cornish commented:
'We just came up against a wall of silence. People either
evaded us or didn't tell us what they knew. We had no
real leads. We have a theory and all I can say is that there
is a connection with high society.'

In 1971 The *People* offered £5,000 reward, part of a
£50,000 total being offered for the solution to a number
of killings. It was not called upon to pay up.

20 February, 1960

On 20 February 1960 nine-year-old Iris Dawkins was
stabbed 30 times in Mayfield Park, Southampton. It was
believed she was killed for a toy gun she was carrying
which her killer wanted. There had been no sexual assault
but many of the wounds had been inflicted after death.
She had been playing in the park and when she had not
returned for tea her family went in search of her.

At the end of March a 10-year-old boy was charged
with her killing. He was alleged to have confessed to his
mother.

Questioned by the police the boy told them they were
playing chase. 'When she fell over I fell on top of her and

I think the knife went into her shoulder when I fell on her. Only a little though.' He added, 'I think it might have gone into her more than once but very rare.' Asked what he meant by this he said, 'I think I might have stuck it into her more than once. I cannot remember now. She was lying down, her eyes were open and she was breathing normally. I thought she was playing. I said, "Cheerio, I am going now."'

The next day the boy's story changed four times, ending with a denial that he had ever seen her. The knife was never found. The judge ruled that the questioning was inadmissible under the Judge's Rules.

At his trial the boy said he was watching ITV's Saturday afternoon wrestling programme and had seen two men fall out of the ring during their bout. From tapes held by the company it could be shown that this occurred at 4.18 pm and the likelihood was that Iris's death happened not before 6 pm. He was acquitted on 13 July 1960.

In November 1969 Sir Norman Skelhorn, who had defended the boy and who was now the Director of Public Prosecutions, was given further information and decided to prosecute Keith William Ridley for the offence. He had been 13 at the time of the killing.

Ridley had recently been seen by an off-duty policeman exercising his dog and then loitering by some houses. He was carrying a sheath knife and, when questioned, at first claimed he was planning to rob someone. Then he admitted he had come out with the intention of killing someone, adding, 'I killed someone in Mayfield Park about 10 years ago. Her name was Iris Dawkins.' He went on to say he had seen some younger children playing and had forced her into the bushes before stabbing her. The officer who had questioned the 10-year-old boy now said that he personally had never believed the first boy to be the killer but that the matter had been taken out of his hands. On 27 March 1970 Ridley was found guilty of the murder and detained during Her Majesty's Pleasure.

It was apparently the only recorded case in Great

Britain in which the sole evidence was a confession by a man that he had committed a murder as a child.

21 February, 1994

Until he allegedly killed waitress Irma Horvath on 21 February 1994, maintenance worker Julio C. Rodriguez had only a $35 fine for a traffic offence on his criminal record. By the time he was arrested for that murder he was also alleged to have killed his sister-in-law Josephina Garcia and wounded her 11-year-old daughter Yelitza Mulera.

According to the prosecution, at about 9 am on the day of the murder Rodriguez, who worked with the murdered girl at the University Club of Hartford, saw Horvath arrive for work. She changed from her street clothes into her black and white uniform and reported to The Deli Room on the third floor, to prepare sandwiches for the members' lunches. Rodriguez began setting up the Blue Room for an evening banquet.

Horvath was discovered missing at about half past nine in the morning and a search was organised. The police looked in the Blue Room and also an attic-type storage area but with no success. After the club dinner at about 10.30 that evening police dogs found Horvath's naked body stuffed behind a ventilation duct in the storeroom. She had been stabbed with a fork, beaten and strangled with the cord of a hairdryer.

Rodriguez continued to work at the club and when interviewed by the police described his relationship with Horvath as friendly. After the club's regular closure in February he did not return to work, telling the manager that he had found a new job.

On 6 April the new chef at the club found Rodriguez's bloodstained pants in the basement. DNA tests were able to match blood on them with Horvath's. As they were preparing to serve warrants to search Rodriguez and obtain blood and hair samples from him they were called to Freeman Street where Rodriguez had once lived. There they found the body of Garcia. Rodriguez was spotted in the South City Café on Franklin Avenue and arrested.

He allegedly admitted killing Horvath, saying that he had got 'upset' but could not say why. At first he said that she had given him the 'come-on', but medical evidence showed that her clothes had been ripped and there was blood on the stairs to the attic, indicating she had been forced to go there. Rodriguez also told the police he had been having blackouts.

Before the hearing of Rodriguez's case Irma Horvath's family filed a civil suit claiming $15,000 plus punitive damages against the Club, alleging that it had received prior complaints that Rodriguez had assaulted and harassed female staff at the Club but the management had done nothing about it. The claim also alleged that there had been an unjustifiable delay in reporting the disappearance of the waitress to the police. The allegations were described as 'absolutely false and insulting' by one of the directors. The trial has not yet taken place.

22 February, 1933

Michael Malloy, whose only claim to fame was the manner of his death, was murdered on 22 February 1933 in an insurance swindle. A Bronx saloon owner, Tony Marino, together with his chief barman Joe Murphy and two others, chose Malloy, a semi-derelict, to be the victim of their second swindle. The first had been Betty Carlsen the previous year.

In Carlsen's case they had plied this relatively attractive young woman with drink and arranged for her to have a room in a nearby lodging house. Willing to please her benefactors she signed papers which she understood were to propose Marino as mayor. In fact she signed an insurance policy application for $800 in his favour. Rendered completely drunk she was left in her room naked, with cold water poured on her and the window open. She died from what the coroner certified as pneumonia brought on by alcoholism.

Malloy was a much tougher character altogether. He too was picked off the streets and over a period of time plied with drink. His life was insured for $3,500 under a double-indemnity clause but Marino's aim was to recoup only $1,750 and so avoid suspicion. Malloy steadily resisted their efforts to get him to drink himself to death. He appeared to flourish on the free and excess alcohol. Next he was given what was probably antifreeze mixed in liquor. He collapsed but, in apparent good health, re-emerged from his room at the back of the bar within an hour. He was fed an increasingly strong quantity of antifreeze, together with horse liniment mixed with rat poison, but it appears to have had no effect on the man's iron constitution. According to the stories he was next fed with oysters poisoned with raw alcohol, again to no effect. Various other efforts were made to dispose of him. He too was left naked, but this time in a Claremont park. He survived after being found by the police and given a new set of clothes.

Other attempts on his life included throwing him from a cab, and an effort was made to find a professional hit man. Unfortunately the latter appears to have wanted $500, now well beyond the means of the conspirators. Finally he was gassed on 22 February 1933. Again Marino and his fellow conspirators were able to obtain a certificate stating that Malloy had died from pneumonia. Unfortunately, they had involved too many people this time, including the cab driver and the thwarted hit man, who began to complain about not being paid for their work.

Marino and the others were executed in the summer of 1934 at Sing Sing prison.

23 February, 1957

Eleven-year-old Moira Anderson disappeared whilst on an errand on Saturday, 23 February 1957. She left her home in Eglinton Street, Coatbridge in Lanarkshire – now almost a Glasgow suburb – on a day of heavy snow and a driving wind. She was due to meet her cousins, with whom she was going to the cinema, at about 4.30 pm and had arrived at her grandmother's house where they were to meet in plenty of time. Her grandmother asked her to go down to the Co-op on the corner, about two hundred yards away, to get some margarine. She never arrived and has never been seen again. The cousins left for the cinema on their own, thinking she would meet them there, and her grandmother thought she must have met up with her cousins. When by nine o'clock she had not returned the alarm was raised.

A lorry driver said he had seen a girl who resembled Moira at Ferrybridge near Doncaster the following day but eventually this girl was traced. Then on 25 February a Greenock woman gave the police a description of a girl which included details not released by the police.

There was considerable political pressure placed on the police. How could an 11-year-old disappear in a street in her home town near a bus stop where it was found 11 people had been queuing that afternoon? They opened their files to private detectives and psychics but no one had any success. Some new evidence came to light in 1962 and the police took their inquiries well outside the Coatbridge area but once more nothing came of their efforts.

On a number of occasions in 1994 the police interviewed a pensioner regarding the case but no arrest was made.

24 February, 1958

Alan Godfrey Johnson was stabbed to death on 24 February 1958 in a fight between rival gangs at Woodward Hall, Barking, Essex. There had been trouble between local youths and a gang from Canning Town in previous weeks and at the dance a group of men who had been in the local public house went around the dance floor asking each person if they came from Canning Town. If they replied 'yes', as Johnson did, they were attacked. Johnson was stabbed in the heart, the stomach and back.

Terence Cooney, a 19-year-old, was arrested the next day and when questioned said, 'I didn't know he was dead until this morning. I am ashamed to say I used a knife on him. He assaulted me first. I didn't mean to kill him. Can I tell you what happened?'

According to the prosecution evidence, he had told two girls that he was going to the dance hall to 'have' some of the Canning Town boys. He had bought a knife for a shilling in the Fanshaw public house and later went to the dance hall. There he saw groups of youths fighting, and indeed the fight spilled over to the pavement where a full-scale affray with bottles, bicycle chains and bars took place. Cooney joined in and fought Johnson who was getting the better of him. Cooney pulled out the knife he had bought and stabbed Johnson.

Cooney's version was slightly different. He admitted fighting with Johnson and, knowing the reputation the Canning Town boys had for carrying knives, when he saw him put his hand in his pocket he drew his own knife. He stabbed Johnson only once in the stomach. Cooney, defended by Malcolm Morris QC, who had defended Timothy Evans, received a life sentence. The all-male jury had retired for only 20 minutes.

Indirectly, the Cooney–Johnson case had a significant effect on the abolition of capital punishment. Shortly afterwards Ronald Marwood stabbed a police officer who was trying to break up a dance hall fight and was hanged. There was considerable agitation that the death penalty had been carried out in one case and not the other.

25 February, 1924

On 25 February 1924 the body of 11-year-old Vera Hilda Emma Hoad was found in a field near the mental hospital at Greylingwell, near Chichester, Sussex. She had been raped and there was considerable bruising to the vagina but no signs of internal semen. There was, however, 'an abundant amount on her bloomers'.

At first the police had a variety of suspects, including one youth who had an obsession with Vera. He was eliminated when his parents gave him an alibi. Based on the fact that there had been no signs of a struggle until she had reached the field and her music case was still with her, there was a theory that she knew her assailant. There was also speculation that at first she might have been agreeable to some form of sexual activity – her right hand was ungloved – but that ultimately she had been raped and then strangled to prevent her identifying her attacker. There were barracks close by and it was next thought that a soldier might have committed the crime. The police believed the man's penis might have been damaged in the attack. One hundred and fifty men were paraded and inspected without arrests being made.

The probablity is that she was killed by Earl(e) Leonard Nelson, also known as Earle Ferrell and Virgil Wilson, who was hanged in Winnipeg, Canada, on 13 January 1928. He was suspected of the deaths of over 20 women in the United States and Canada, in cities as far apart as San Francisco, Detroit, Kansas City, Philadelphia, Buffalo and

Portland. One of his *modus operandi* was to gain entry into their homes on the pretext of looking for lodgings and then rape and strangle them. He was finally arrested after killing Emily Patterson in Winnipeg on 9 June 1927. Among his possessions were found clippings of the killing of Vera Hoad and also of another young girl, Nellie Clarke. The death of 11-year-old Nellie Clarke on 10 January 1925 occurred at a time when Nelson was in Liverpool waiting for a passage back to America. She had been to a concert for war orphans and had then, in the early evening, been sent on an errand by her mother. Her body was found the next morning propped against a telegraph pole.

Nelson, a man with a receding hairline, protruding lips and huge hands, was nicknamed by writers The Gorilla Murderer. He was born in Philadelphia in 1892 or 1897 (dates vary). His mother contracted venereal disease from his father when Nelson was a baby and he was brought up by a religious aunt who hoped her nephew would train for the Baptist ministry. His first conviction was in 1918 when he was sent to the Napa State Hospital for the Insane for attempted rape. He escaped and commenced his killing spree. Although he normally killed older women he had murdered a 14-year-old flower seller, Lola Cowan, the day before he strangled a Mrs Patterson. Unfortunately, Lola Cowan had called at his lodgings and had been 'strangled, stripped and raped'. He was convicted for the latter killing after an unsuccessful plea of insanity was offered on his behalf.

The British authorities hoped that there might be a stay of execution to enable him to be questioned over the English murders, but none was given. On the scaffold, he is reported to have said, as a number of others have offered similar words, 'I am innocent. I stand innocent before God and man. I forgive those who have wronged me and ask forgiveness for those I have injured. God have mercy!'

Brian Lane and Wilfred Gregg, *The Encyclopedia of Serial*

Killers; Jay Robert Nash, *World Encyclopedia of 20th Century Murder*.

26 February, 1989

Terence Brown from Port Talbot, Wales has the doubtful distinction of killing two of his girlfriends on the same day, 26 February, albeit six years apart. In 1989 he strangled Mary Button at the flat they shared in Weymouth, Dorset, and then stabbed her 10 times. He went on the run and eventually gave himself up. He said that he had blacked out when he killed her. Convicted of murder and jailed for life at Swansea Crown Court, his conviction was quashed by the Court of Appeal who substituted a manslaughter conviction coupled with a sentence of eight years. There had, it appears, been a distant relationship between a juror and a police officer which had not been disclosed.

After his release in 1993 Brown moved to Newberry Road, Weymouth where he met 38-year-old Tina Doyle, also from Port Talbot. Despite warnings from the Button family and Tina Doyle's sister, Patricia, who had known Brown in Port Talbot, they began living together but, following an argument, he strangled her also. He left her body on the floor in the sitting room where it was discovered a fortnight later.

In his defence Brown said that he had nothing to do with Tina Doyle's murder but when he found her body he simply ran, thinking that no one would believe him.

Sentencing Brown, Mrs Justice Ebsworth said, 'You are quite incapable of keeping your hands to yourself, particularly when you are in drink. I recommend that you are not released until it can be certain that you are safe.'

27 February, 1995

Russian-born 16-year-old Vladimir Polevi shot dead six
people near Paris on 27 February 1995. His victims
were his stepmother, his timber-merchant father, his
grandparents and two visiting friends. The only survivor
was his two-year-old stepsister who had been christened
earlier in the day and who was found weeping by the side
of her mother's body. She had been in bed upstairs when
her brother began to kill the family. He later telephoned
the police and told them the family had been murdered
by burglars.

At first the police thought that the killings had been part
of a gangland feud between the Russian Mafia but they
then realised that the boy's story was false. He had been
quarrelling with his family, particularly his stepmother.
The shootings began as his parents were drinking tea. 'I
just could not stand my stepmother,' he finally told the
police. 'That led to constant rows with my father.'

He took guns from his father's collection housed in a
glass cabinet and used a different gun on each of his
victims.

28 February, 1905

Jane Stanford, the widow of the Californian senator
Leland Stanford, founder of the University, was found
dead in her room at what is now the Sheraton Moana
Surfrider Hotel in Waikiki on 28 February 1905. The
coroner's jury returned a verdict that she had been the
victim of 'strychnine poisoning introduced into a bottle
of bicarbonate of soda with felonious intent'. The hotel,

however, insisted she had died of heart failure – which of course, strictly speaking, she had. No one was ever charged.

29 February, 1984

A body was found on 29 February 1984 in Wast Water, Cumbria, the deepest lake in England. Wrapped in carpet and polystyrene and weighted with a kerbstone, it was identified partly through a wedding ring bearing the inscription *Margaret 15.11.63. Peter*.

The body was discovered quite by chance because police divers were looking for that of another woman, a missing French student, Véronique Marr. Margaret was Margaret Hogg who had disappeared from the family home in Mead Road, Cranleigh in 1976. Peter, her airline pilot husband, had reported her missing, saying he thought she had gone off with another man.

Peter Hogg had been something of a hero when in 1974 the airline for which he was then working went out of business. He was in Halifax, Nova Scotia with 400 passengers under threat that the aeroplane, a Lockheed Tristar, would be impounded. In the early hours of the morning he daringly took off. He said it had been his first duty to get his passengers home.

On 5 March 1984 he was charged with the murder of his wife. A great deal of sympathy was engendered for Peter Hogg when it emerged that his wife had a string of lovers. 'She ate men for breakfast,' one of her former neighbours told a newspaper.

At the Old Bailey on 8 March 1985 Hogg was found guilty of manslaughter. He had strangled his wife during a fierce quarrel before driving to Wast Water and dumping her body in 100 feet of water after rowing a dinghy past Tiffers Rock. He had then established himself an alibi.

He had been a trifle unlucky. Had he rowed another 50 yards or so he would have encountered the deepest part of the lake and the body might never have been found. He received a sentence of four years' imprisonment and was released on 25 June 1986.

The body of Véronique Marr was recovered in May 1985. She had fallen some 300 feet whilst walking on the fells above Wast Water.

Jonathan Goodman, *Modern Murder File*.

MARCH

1 March, 1994

Colin Hickman, a 55-year-old solicitor who specialised in civil litigation in Coventry, was stabbed more than 10 times in the head and chest after he opened the front door of his home during the evening of 1 March 1994. The bell had been rung persistently until he had answered it.

His partner, Vera Phillips-Griffiths, a chemistry teacher in Leamington Spa, who was speaking on the telephone, ran downstairs as the attacker was raining blows with a stiletto-type knife. The man, heavily bloodstained, ran off into the night.

On 12 March 1995, 33-year-old Timothy Carlton Caines of Moseley, Birmingham was charged with Colin Hickman's murder. He was jailed for life. The motive had apparently been to prevent Mr Hickman from blowing the whistle on a series of fraudulent deals.

2 March, 1934

Mavis Agnes Rowland was murdered by her father on 2 March 1934. She was then aged two. He was convicted and sentenced to death before being reprieved.

Her killer, Walter Rowland, stood trial a second time
for murder when he was charged with the murder of
Manchester prostitute Olive Balchin. There was no doubt
as to his guilt in the killing of his daughter. There were
considerable doubts over the verdict in the Balchin case.

On 20 October 1946 the 40-year-old Olive Balchin was
found battered to death on a bomb site in Manchester.
A bloodstained hammer had been left by her body. The
evidence against the 39-year-old Walter Rowland was
forensic, as well as identification by witnesses, including
one, Edward MacDonald, who said he had sold the hammer to Rowland on the day of the murder. There were
also traces of hair which could have been that of Olive
Balchin. There was human blood on Rowland's shoe but
it was impossible to type it. There was no blood on his
shirt, however, nor were his fingerprints on the hammer.
On his arrest in a local hostel he had asked, 'You don't
want me for the murder of that woman, do you?'

He pleaded not guilty but was convicted. Whilst awaiting his own trial, a prisoner in Liverpool, David John
Ware, confessed to the murder of Olive Balchin and the
confession was a principal ground of Rowland's appeal.

The Court of Appeal, however, was dismissive about
the idea of calling Ware to give evidence. 'It is not an
unusual thing for all sorts of confessions to be made by
people who have nothing to do with a crime,' said the
Lord Chief Justice. He also commented that questions
had to be asked about Ware's mental state. If anyone
was to re-examine the case then it was for the Home
Secretary who had infinitely more resources. As he was
taken down Rowland shouted, 'I am an innocent man.
This is the grossest injustice which has ever occurred in an
English court. Why did you not have in court the man who
confessed to the crime? I am not having justice because of
my past. I am innocent before God.'

J.C. Jolly KC was appointed to head an inquiry which
acted fast. He interviewed both Ware and Edward
MacDonald from whom Rowland was said to have

bought the hammer used to kill Balchin. An identification parade was held at which MacDonald failed to pick out Ware. In turn Ware withdrew his confession and it was decided that he had garnered most of his information from reading newspaper cuttings about the killing. Something which particularly told against the confession being genuine was that he gave the name of the dead woman as Balshaw. That was the name which had initially appeared in the papers. Rowland's appeal was dismissed on 10 February. On 22 February 1947 Ware made a final statement saying that his confession had been compiled from reading newspapers and from information gleaned from conversations with other prisoners. On 25 February Jolly filed his report and immediately the Home Secretary announced that there were no grounds for interfering with the verdict. Rowland was hanged on 27 February. He had occupied the same cell on his conviction for the murder of his daughter before his reprieve. He had been released from that sentence in 1940. It was to this he referred when he mentioned his past.

In November 1951 Ware appeared at Bristol Assizes charged with attempted murder. He told the police, 'I have killed a woman. I keep having an urge to hit women on the head.' He was found guilty and sent to a mental hospital.

Considerable debate has raged over the correctness of the verdict in the Rowland case, with experts lined up on both sides of the fence.

Henry Cecil, *The Trial of Walter Rowland*; Bob Woffinden, *Miscarriages of Justice*.

3 March, 1922

Jack Hewett, a 15-year-old farmhand, was convicted of the murder on 3 March 1922 of Sarah Blake, a 55-year-old widow, at the Crown and Anchor public house, Gallowstree Common near Henley-on-Thames. She was found the next morning, beaten and hacked. Her neck was cut to her spine and there were more than 60 wounds on her head, face, neck and hands.

She had been seen alive the previous evening at around 6.30 pm and Sir Bernard Spilsbury, the pathologist, was of the opinion she had been killed shortly after that.

The case aroused a good deal of local indignation and, as is sometimes the case, it was the murderer who came forward with an offer of help. He had been the last person known to have seen her alive. Questioned closely he made what amounted to a full confession, blaming the killing on the influence of the cinema. At the trial he endeavoured to withdraw his confession on the grounds that his parents had not been present.

Hewett was well known to Mrs Blake. In the previous January she had found him in her pub cellar and, in the hearing of a policeman, she had told him the next time she would prosecute him if she caught him thieving.

From the point of view of the police the case was a complicated one. In the pub was nearly £500 in bonds, along with deposit books, and they were not sure that the motive for the murder had been robbery, but instead, it might have been a private quarrel. Whilst in custody for a burglary a petty criminal, Robert Alfred Shepherd, also confessed to the murder and was charged. He had blood on his coat which eventually turned out to be rabbits' blood. Shepherd retracted his confession and was discharged. A second suspect was another convicted man, whose brother positively declared that he was the murderer. The police were able to prove that this was not the case.

In addition to the series of confessions Hewett had made, the knife which killed Mrs Blake had been positively identified as belonging to him and he could not account for its disappearance. The judge said the gist of the defence was that four police officers had committed wilful perjury.

PRO/MEPO/3/1571; Douglas G. Browne and Tom Tullett, *Bernard Spilsbury, His Life and Cases*.

4 March, 1933

At about 9.30 am on 4 March 1933 Elizabeth Mary Standley was visited by her nephew, 31-year-old Jack Samuel Puttnam, at her home at 13 Blackstock Road, Finsbury Park, north London. He left about an hour later. At 12.25 pm her body was found by a lodger. She had been struck on the head, stabbed through the heart and there were signs that an attempt had been made to strangle her. The quarrel was over the sum of £35 said to be owed by her husband to Puttnam. On 2 May 1933 he was found guilty of murder and sentenced to death. His appeal was dismissed on 22 May.

MEPO/20/3.

5 March, 1984

On 5 March 1984 Elizabeth Kenyon, a 23-year-old schoolteacher from Coral Gables, Florida, who had won

the Miss Florida pageant two years earlier, disappeared
from a South Dade petrol station. She was never seen
again. Later an attendant identified a photograph of
Australian Christopher Wheeler as the man who had
been with her. Wheeler had arrived in Florida after being
arrested for his part in a gang rape in Australia.

Elizabeth Kenyon was the second victim of a killing
spree which the 39-year-old builder, who ran the Sawtel
Construction Company in Boynton Beach, carried out
over a seven-week period. During that time, in which
he kidnapped 12 women, he was chased from Florida
to California and back East, always one step ahead of
the police who monitored his progress from his use of
his credit cards.

Regarded as mildly charming and a successful and
flamboyant businessman, Wheeler had picked up his
first victim, Rosario Gonzalez, at the Miami Grand Prix
a week earlier – he drove in minor motor car races. He
had known Elizabeth Kenyon for about two years and
he had, by accounts, fallen in love with her. She had told
him she regarded him as no more than an older brother.

On 15 March Colleen Osborn, aged 15, disappeared at
Daytona Beach and three days later, at Cocoa, Wheeler
picked up Theresa Ferguson. Her body was found four
days later. She had been strangled. On 20 March he
abducted Linda Grober in a Tallahassee mall, after telling
her that he was a fashion photographer. He beat her,
raped her and sealed her eyes with glue before she
managed to escape. She was later able to identify him.

He then moved West, picking up, raping, torturing
and murdering women in Oklahoma City, and then in
Newton, Kansas and Colorado before he moved down
to Arizona, Nevada, on to California, back to Arizona
and up to Indiana, on to New York and New Hampshire
before, in Boston, he picked up a woman whose car had
broken down. She became suspicious and jumped out of
the car. He drove to Colebrook, eight miles from the
Canadian border, where he was seen by the police as
he was filling his car with petrol. A struggle followed

during which he shot a policeman and then himself. In
all, including those who disappeared, he had killed nine
women.

6 March, 1952

Mahmood Mattan, a 28-year-old Somali seaman, was
hanged at Cardiff prison in September 1952 for the
murder, on 6 March of that year, of a Jewish shop
owner, Lily Volpert, who had an outfitters' in Bute
Street in the notorious Tiger Bay district of the city. The
murder occurred not long after there had been anti-black
rioting in the area. Mattan's Welsh wife Laura had been
the subject of racial abuse, being called 'a black man's
whore' by neighbours.

The case against Mattan was slight, based on circumstantial evidence and the word of a notorious informer
who came forward once a reward of £200 was posted.
The informer said she had seen Mattan with a roll of
money shortly after the killing in which £100 was stolen.
The other key witness claimed that Mattan had been seen
coming out of Miss Volpert's shop around the time of
the murder. This witness, who himself had convictions
for violence, had said a number of other black men were
near the shop at the time. Mattan gave an alibi that he
was with his wife, Laura, a mile away from the shop at
the time.

In 1995 a witness, who was aged 12 when the murder
took place, came forward to say that she saw a black man
with a moustache go into Miss Volpert's shop at the time
of the murder. She said she later attended a confrontation
with Mattan and had said that he was not the man she
had seen. Although strictly, at the time, the prosecution
was required, on request, to pass names and addresses
of witnesses from whom statements had been taken but

whom it did not intend to call, this was by no means always done.

Following this evidence Mrs Mattan and her sons were petitioning for a posthumous pardon for Mahmood Mattan.

7 March, 1966

The end of the Richardson gang who ruled south London in the early 1960s came, quite by chance, with the unrelated death on 7 March 1966 of the small-time Kray hanger-on Richard 'Dickie' Hart. He was shot in a fight in the Catford nightclub, Mr Smith and the Witchdoctors. 'Mad' Frank Fraser, a Richardson associate, stood trial for his killing but was acquitted.

The club, owned by a Manchester businessman, was at the time under the protection of the Hayward brothers, who had interests in clubs and businesses in south London. According to Fraser a deal was struck that he and Eddie Richardson would mind the club in return for a percentage of the profits and the opportunity to install some of their fruit machines.

On the night they took over no one had explained the new arrangement to the Haywards and at about three in the morning the quarrel over control of the club broke out.

According to Frank Fraser, at first it was a fair fight between Eddie Richardson and Peter Hennessey when Hart began firing at random. The police allegation was that Fraser shot Hart, possibly after taking the gun from him. Certainly he, Fraser, was shot in the thigh. Hart died a few hours later in hospital.

Fraser received five years for the affray, as did Eddie Richardson. Whilst they were awaiting trial a number of small-time villains complained to the police that they had been beaten up by Fraser and both the Richardson brothers over debts and lost money. At what was called the Torture Trial in 1967 Mr Justice Lawton sentenced Charlie Richardson to 25 years, Eddie to a further 10 and Fraser to the same sentence, to run consecutively to the five years he was already serving.

In their book *Our Story*, the Kray Twins claim that the death of George Cornell two nights later was a reprisal for that of Hart.

Frank Fraser, *Mad Frank;* Reg and Ron Kray, *Our Story*.

8 March, 1963

Mr Justice Simon Kuper was shot dead at his home on Sixth Street, Lower Houghton, Johannesburg on 8 March 1963. At about 9 pm that night the judge went outside with his daughter, Ruth, to say goodbye to an uncle and aunt who had been visiting them. Ruth Kuper stayed outside for a short time and whilst on the veranda heard a slight movement in bushes to the side but thought nothing of it. She returned to the house and into her father's study. He was reading, literally a sitting target, and she was at the telephone when a shot was fired through the window. Kuper was killed with a single bullet to the forehead. The killer then had the presence of mind, and the time, to retrieve the spent cartridge case.

Kuper did not die instantly and, for a little while, tried to speak and write. The word he tried to utter and write seems to have begun with the letter P but it was impossible to be sure what he said and because his hand was unsteady he wrote other letters on top of the initial. In a seven-hour operation efforts were made without success to extract the bullet and the judge died 12 days later. The firearm was of a common type.

Two theories were advanced. First, that the judge had been trying to write the word Poqo, the name of an illegal terrorist organisation. However, a search of the judicial calendar showed he had not presided over any trials of Poqo terrorists which might have led to reprisals. The second theory revolved around a young man who, some two months before the murder, had called at the judge's house demanding to speak to him. He had been told that any communication must be through a lawyer. The young man had, apparently, a number of convictions relating to stolen vehicles. Over the next six months arrests were made in connection with the killing but they did not lead to charges.

Benjamin Bennett, *Some Don't Hang*.

9 March, 1952

In February 1952 Arnold Schuster, a 24-year-old Brooklyn clothing salesman, had the misfortune to see the legendary bank robber Willie Sutton, then on the FBI's list of 10 most wanted criminals, on a New York subway and gave the police information which led to Sutton's capture. He compounded his misfortune by giving radio and television interviews, so becoming a minor and temporary celebrity. In Andy Warhol's words he had his 15 minutes of fame. It lasted until 9 March when he was found dead on the street where he lived. He had been shot in each eye and twice in the groin. The execution was ordered by gang leader Albert Anastasia, after he had seen the pictures of Schuster on television, on the grounds that he could not stand informants. The contract was almost certainly carried out by Frederick J. Tenuto, at the time also on the

FBI's list. Tenuto was himself later killed on the orders of Anastasia.

As for Sutton, he was appalled by the murder of Schuster, realising that the backlash would mean a longer sentence for him. He received a term of 60 years to life but was released in 1969. He died in retirement in Florida in 1980 after writing his autobiography. Anastasia was shot in the barber's chair at the Park Sheraton Hotel in New York on 25 October 1957.

Peter Maas, *The Valachi Papers*.

10 March, 1919

On 10 March 1919, Iorlando Jordano, aged 69, heard screams from the Cortimiglia household across the street in a New Orleans suburb. He and his son went over to find Rosie Cortimiglia holding Mary, her two-year-old daughter, dead in her arms. She had also been hit and her husband, Charles, lay on the floor. She accused Jordano and his son Frank of being the attackers, even though before he died Charles Cortimiglia said they were nothing like the men. Mary's death was one in the series of attacks attributed to the Axeman of New Orleans, as indeed was that of her father.

A decade earlier there had been a spate of axe murders of Italian grocers, including Tony Schiambra and his wife. It was thought that they had been protection money murders by members of the Italian Black Hand who had had a strong presence in New Orleans for the previous 40 years.

The so-called Axeman killings recommenced when on 24 May 1918 Joseph Maggio, an Italian grocer living in New Orleans, and his wife were attacked in their room in the house they shared with his brothers, Jake and

Andrew. Jake Maggio had heard noises and together with his brother Andrew had gone to Joe's room to find Mrs Maggio lying in a pool of blood with her head almost severed, and Joe with his throat cut. Entry had been gained to the house by removing a panel in the back door. The safe door in Joe Maggio's room was open but he had been sleeping with a quantity of money beneath his pillow which was untouched. The police were inclined to believe that the safe door had been opened to fool them into believing the motive was robbery. A bloodstained axe was on the steps to the backyard, as was a cut-throat razor. Both surviving brothers were arrested but were later released.

On 28 June 1918 another grocery shop owner, Louis Besumer, was found by a delivery man. He had been attacked, as had the *soi-disant* Mrs Besumer, Harriet Lowe. This time both survived, she to accuse Besumer whom, for good measure, she alleged was a German spy. He was arrested and she then withdrew her allegations. Later, in hospital and seriously ill, she accused Besumer once more and then died. He was charged with her murder.

It was fortunate for Besumer that, the same night, the Axeman struck again. Edward Sneider returned home to his pregnant wife to find her covered in blood. She had been asleep, she said, and had awoken to find a man with an axe standing over her. Attacks came swiftly after this. The next victim was a barber, Joseph Romano. His nieces, who slept in the next room, heard noises and saw a dark man, tall and heavy-set, with a hat, standing by Romano's bed with an axe. Again a panel on the back door had been cut to provide access. The last attack that year was on 30 August when a man named Nick Asunto scared off a man he described as heavily built and carrying an axe.

In April 1919 Louis Besumer was acquitted of killing Harriet Lowe. The Jordanos however had not been so fortunate. Against all odds they were convicted. Frank was sentenced to death and his father to life imprisonment.

There was another attack on 10 August and subsequent

ones occurred at the beginning of September. Although the victims were injured they survived.

On 27 October another grocer, Mike Pepitone, was killed in his bedroom. His wife, who had been sleeping in an adjoining room, heard noises and ran in to find his blood splashed on the wall. Again entry had been gained by removing a door panel, and a bloodstained axe was on the back porch. It was the last of the killings. Curiously, in 1909 Pepitone's father, Pietro, had refused to pay protection to Paul di Cristina who operated Black Hand activities in New Orleans and had shot and killed Cristina. He was released after serving six years of a 20-year sentence for manslaughter.

Meanwhile, the Jordanos kept up their appeals against their convictions until, on 7 December 1920, Rosie Cortimiglia went to the offices of the *Times-Picayune* to confess that she had made up her story against the Jordanos because she had hated them. They were released.

Shortly before this there had been an incident in Los Angeles when the widow of Mike Pepitone shot and killed Joseph Mumfre, whom she alleged was the Axeman. The dates fitted because when there had been a lull in the killings Mumfre had been in prison and he certainly had been in the New Orleans area at the times of the killings. However, there was no hard evidence against him.

Mrs Pepitone pleaded justifiable homicide and was sentenced to 10 years' imprisonment but was released after just three. Possibly both the 1911 killings and those at the end of the First World War were Mafia extortion operations, but, against this proposition, not all were carried out against Italians. There may have been an element of the copycat in that there was more than one Axeman. What is certain is that with the death of Mumfre the killing stopped.

John Canning (ed), *Unsolved Murders and Mysteries*.

11 March, 1991

Drug dealer and adopted son of the powerful south-east London family the Arifs, Ahmet Abdullah, known as Turkish Abbi, who had quarrelled with other powerful south-east London interests, was shot in the William Hill betting shop in Bagshot Street, Walworth on 11 March 1991. He was hit in the back after pleading with his attackers not to kill him. He then tried to use another customer as a shield and managed to escape from the shop before he was shot again. Brothers Tony and Patrick Brindle were charged with Abdullah's murder and stood trial at the Old Bailey in a case where witnesses gave evidence from behind screens and were identified only by number. Two other witnesses vanished and one committed suicide. The prosecution evidence was that before he died Abdullah had told two friends that the Brindle brothers were his killers.

In his defence Tony Brindle said he had not been in the betting shop but had been playing cards and drinking in The Bell public house in East Street, Walworth. He also said that he did not know Abdullah from Adam. Patrick Brindle did not give evidence. After their acquittal on 16 May 1992 Grace Brindle, their mother, told how the boys helped old ladies across the road and how they had wept when their pet budgie had died. The police said the enquiry was closed.

In the meantime a third brother, David, had been shot and killed whilst drinking in The Bell. Life did not go well for the Brindles over the next few years. In 1995 Tony Brindle was ambushed and shot in a south London street but the police were on hand and arrests were made. Another brother, George, had survived being shot from a passing van earlier in the year. No arrests were made on that occasion.

12 March, 1976

Janise Gamble, together with her husband John, and William Nicholls, were stopped by Detective Sergeant Allan Harrison on 12 March 1976 as they were fleeing from a credit union robbery in Calgary, Alberta. The officer made Gamble and Nicholls put their guns on the roof of the car but, so the court was told, Mrs Gamble did something in the car to distract the officer who was shot dead. Gamble died in the ensuing shoot-out and Mrs Gamble and Nicholls were tried for capital murder. She was amongst the first people convicted of first-degree murder after Alberta abolished the death penalty but, according to the Alberta Appeal Court, she should have been tried under the law existing at the time of the crime. She received a life sentence without the eligibility to apply for parole until she had served 25 years.

On 8 December 1988 the Supreme Court of Canada ruled she had been convicted under the wrong law and had she been properly charged she might have been eligible for parole after 10 years. Hers was a story of frustration and error. Although she applied for a writ of *habeus corpus* for her release in 1976 her first problem was that she was in prison in Ontario and not Alberta. The court ruled that to deny Mrs Gamble her constitutional right because of a prosecution error was 'completely unacceptable'.

13 March, 1949

Forty-six-year-old newspaper warehouseman Leonard Jack Thomas stood trial twice for his attack on his wife, Florence Ethel Lavinia. They had been living apart for some time when on 13 March 1949 he called on her and stabbed her 13 times with a jackknife. He had accused her of seeing another man and when she denied this asked her to return to him. She had refused saying she was quite happy where she was with her daughter.

Thomas was charged with attempted murder and on 2 May he was sentenced to seven years' imprisonment. Within a matter of weeks Mrs Thomas died from her injuries and Thomas was charged again, this time with her murder. He pleaded not guilty and also raised the old defence of *autrefois convict*. In other words he had been convicted of the offence once and should not be put at risk a second time. This plea was rejected by both the jury and later the Court of Criminal Appeal.

Thomas was left with a plea of not guilty on the facts. He told the court his wife had left him because he would not take up dancing. When he did so and obtained a proficiency medal after two months she called him an old fool. 'My mind became a complete blank until I found myself holding a knife and my wife lying on the floor.'

The jury returned a verdict of guilty after 30 minutes, adding a strong recommendation for mercy. Thomas's appeal was dismissed on 30 August but, after receiving a petition signed by 12,000 people, the Home Secretary advised the King to grant a reprieve.

The Criminal Justice Act 1988 amended the law so that now it is the judge and not the jury who decides on the issue of *autrefois convict* and the similar but slightly more usual plea of *autrefois acquit*.

Richard Harrison, *Criminal Calendar*.

14 March, 1936

As he left for work in his tool merchant's shop on 14 March 1936, Oswald Fisher Walker, aged 68, told his wife he would be late home because he had to see a man about a saw bench. Walker had apparently dealt with this man before. When he had not returned by 10.30 pm his wife called the police. Walker's body was found at the rear of his shop at 29/31 George Street, Hull where he ran quite a substantial business. He had been robbed and battered to death, probably from behind. He had been the subject of repeated blows, probably with a claw hammer, and there were injuries to the skull and to his jaw. He had also been partially strangled. He was wearing his overcoat as if ready to leave the shop.

Walker was regarded as a very mean man, giving to Methodist charities but paying his staff less than the going rate. He had also quarrelled with members of his family from a prior marriage and considerable time was spent by the police eliminating them from their enquiries. Even then, with a reward of £100 on offer for Walker's killer, the police were deluged with suggestions and potential names. One man made a statement amounting to a confession but enquiries disproved it.

Anonymous letters repeatedly suggested a Hull man was responsible for the murder but enquiries showed they were written by his deserted wife. An exercise book of hers with pages torn out matched those on which the letters were written and the ink matched that from a bottle taken from the woman's house.

Then Mrs Walker received a letter from a soldier in India:

Just a few lines to tell you how sorry to hear about your husband because I know he was a free-hearted fellow and would not see anybody down and out. I know the chap who done that terrible thing I read in the paper and I am willing to tell you where he is and what he look like for the sum of £60 for telling you, and do not let the Police know about it. Well I hope that you will agreed with my confession

Yours
Truly
Friend

When interviewed the soldier was able to give little help, telling of a man he had met in prison who had made what might be self-incriminating remarks. Consideration was given to prosecuting the soldier for blackmail when his regiment returned to England. In the event Mrs Walker was thought to be too frail to give evidence.

Over a thousand pages of statements were taken and, although searches for the claw hammer continued for weeks, it was never found. The best theory was that Walker was killed by the man who came about the saw bench. He was described as being in his late thirties, five feet eight inches tall, clean-shaven, with dark hair, unkempt dirty hands, and dressed in working-class clothing.

PRO/MEPO/3/796.

15 March, 1996

Late in the evening of 15 March 1996, teenager Mark Fyke, in Daytona Beach, Florida for the traditional Spring Break, was shot dead with a bullet in the back of his neck moments after making a telephone call back home to his mother in Belleville, Ontario. The police maintained that he was the victim of a bungled robbery; Mark's wallet was by his body on the pavement outside the hotel where he was staying.

Two days later, 18-year-old Donald Shoup waved down a police vehicle and gave himself up saying he was wanted in connection with the murder. Initially it was thought that he was the gunman amidst a number of youths who waylaid Fyke but his answers were confused and contradictory.

The prosecution then alleged that a 17-year-old John O'Neal Rainey was the youth who fired the gun and were demanding the death penalty in his case. Early psychological reports showed that Donald Shoup was now confused, anxious and non-responsive, to such an extent that he would be unable to assist his lawyer.

Fyke was the second tourist to be killed in a month in Florida. In February a Dutch tourist was shot in another attempted robbery, this time in Miami.

16 March, 1974

Nineteen-year-old Rhodesian Simon Kerr, a promising schoolboy cricketer who had played a few games for the Gloucestershire second eleven, went to a party given on 16 March 1974 by two nurses at their flat in North Road, Bristol. In the basement of the house lived 24-year-old Desmond Carroll who was also at the party. Kerr had too much to drink and Carroll allowed him to sleep it off in his flat. Then, as Carroll later told the police:

> He was under the bedclothes and he didn't see me come in. I got the knife from the cupboard. I saw the terrible fear on his face. I stabbed him in the back about three times.
>
> While I was stabbing him he was shouting for

help. Nobody heard because of the noise of the party. I put a hand over his mouth to stop him shouting. I stabbed him in the heart three times and I stamped on the knife.

He took about 15 minutes to die. He was as hard as concrete. It's easy to get a knife out, but not to put it in. It was so pleasant I feel I could do it again. I have no regrets. I feel better now.

At his trial in October 1974 at Bristol Crown Court Carroll was convicted of murder and sentenced to life imprisonment.

John Scott, *Caught in Court*.

17 March, 1941

Although Private Walter Clifford Burridge shot and killed Provost Sergeant Major Samuel Victor Sims in Crete on 17 March 1941 it was nearly five years before he stood trial for the murder.

That day the Welsh Regiment had taken over the Paragoria camp, and defaulters, of whom Burridge was one, were required to dig the latrines. He failed to appear for defaulters' parade and was found during the afternoon, drunk, in a local wine shop.

Burridge was arrested for drunkenness at about 5.15 pm. He had an argument with CSM Shellard and Corporal McCullough and was sent to another tent. Sims took McCullough's place at the report table. This was when he was shot. Fired from some distance the bullet entered the left shoulder and ruptured a main blood vessel.

According to the evidence, in the second tent Burridge sat down for a little while and then got hold of a rifle with fixed bayonet which was standing up against the centre tent pole. He threw a tin of bully beef to the ground and twice lunged at it with the bayonet, piercing it the second time. He then said, 'That's what I'm going to do to Corporal McCullough', the man who had arrested him. Another soldier, Percival Rees, said, 'I won't see that done.' Burridge said, 'You will.'

Burridge had a bad temper in drink. Whilst in India he had hit one guard on the head with a boot whilst also trying to hit another with an Indian club. According to Rees he was afraid of Burridge after this, and that afternoon Burridge more or less robbed him of two rounds of ammunition. Rees said, 'Give it back to me and don't be a bloody fool.' Burridge replied, 'Sit down, keep quiet and be wise.' Rees says he thought that Burridge would in time give him back the ammunition and so he started to write up his report. Burridge took the rifle and aimed and fired. Rees then took the rifle away from him. Burridge said, 'Who did I shoot?'

A soldier, Ralph Scott, was sent to assist in the arrest of Burridge. 'I said, "Come out here, Burridge, you have shot Sims." He said, "It's all right, Scott. I can take it." I said, "Look what you've done, you've killed a bloody good man." He said, "I'm sorry it was him."'

A summary of evidence was taken in front of Burridge in late March 1941 and it was directed that he should be court-martialled for murder. However, the Germans then overran Crete and Burridge was amongst those captured.

Burridge was sent to Silesia and twice he tried to escape. He was repatriated on 21 April 1945 and was on release leave in Eltham when the papers relating to the killing were retrieved and considered. He could not be tried by a court martial as the offence had occurred over three years previously. As a result he appeared at the Old Bailey at the January Sessions in 1946 where he was represented by Thomas Edie and Victor Durand.

His defence was that he could not remember anything from 11 am to 7.30 pm on the day of the killing, blaming the event on a local drink, 'gracia'.

Possibly because of the length of time between the incident and the trial, and because of his imprisonment in Silesia, Burridge was fortunate. The jury returned a verdict of manslaughter and on 15 January 1946 he was sentenced to a term of five years' imprisonment. Mr Justice Oliver told him, 'The jury have very mercifully returned a verdict of manslaughter on the clearest evidence of murder. You are a dangerous and violent man and have on three occasions assaulted your officers.'

PRO/MEPO/3/2307.

18 March, 1910

On 18 March 1910 John Innes Nisbet, a colliery wages clerk, was found dead, shot through the head, when the 10.27 am slow train from Newcastle arrived at Alnmouth station. Nisbet's wages satchel containing £370 was missing. He had left Newcastle station with another man who had left the train at Morpeth paying an excess fare. The man was 43-year-old bookmaker's commission agent John Alexander Dickman. There was some paper on the floor of the compartment. The Nisbet murder was the sixth murder on a British train.

Questioned by the police Dickman admitted he had been on the train but his answers did not match those of the witnesses and, on his subsequent arrest when his house was searched, a pair of bloodstained trousers and £17 in gold sovereigns were found. He explained the blood on the trousers as coming from a nosebleed and the coins as part of his commission. At an identification parade Percival Hall, a colleague of Nisbet's, picked out Dickman. Later it was learned that before attending the parade he had caught a glimpse of the defendant.

At his trial on 4 July 1910 at Newcastle Assizes the

evidence against Dickman, a married man with two children, was almost wholly circumstantial. The missing satchel was found down a mine shaft at the Isabella pit near Morpeth where Dickman had left the train; he had been losing heavily at the races and was in debt to moneylenders. He was identified as Nisbet's travelling companion by Nisbet's wife and another man. Dickman had bought a gun through a newspaper advertisement. There was some evidence that when he handed the excess fare to the ticket collector he had kept his other hand out of sight. The implication was that he was carrying the satchel in this hand and endeavouring to conceal it. There was, however, a problem for the prosecution. The scientific evidence was that Nisbet had been killed with a total of five shots with bullets of two different calibres. This suggested a two-man robbery.

Despite his protestations of innocence, telling the jury, 'I declare to all men, I am innocent', Dickman was convicted. A public outcry ensued and a petition got up for a reprieve which was signed by five members of the jury. It did not assist Dickman. He was hanged at Newcastle prison on 10 August 1910. A crowd of some fifteen hundred people gathered outside the gates on the morning of his execution.

It is thought likely that the conviction was indeed a correct one. It appears that Dickman had used smaller bullets wrapped in paper as well as bullets of the correct size for his revolver.

There is an unsupported theory that Dickman was also responsible for the Luard killing of 24 August 1908. Caroline Mary Luard, the wife of Major General Charles Luard, was found shot dead in a summerhouse near their home in Ightham Knoll, Kent. The motive appeared to be robbery and four rings had been taken from her fingers. There was some evidence that Dickman had forged a cheque sent by Mrs Luard in response to an advertisement he had placed asking for financial help. Her husband later committed suicide.

19 March, 1949

George Kelly had had a long life of petty crime before he killed Leonard Thomas in Liverpool. His first conviction was at the age of 10 when he was discharged under the Probation Act for breaking and entering. It was the first of a long list of convictions he acquired before he joined the Royal Navy, from which he deserted five times. In 1943 he was sentenced to nine months' imprisonment for assault. In 1945 he received a sentence for what is now termed 'dishonest handling' and, in the same year, three years' penal servitude for desertion, along with a year's hard labour.

On his release he worked in a café, as a street trader and as a barker for an escapologist. Then he took up pimping and ran a small string of prostitutes. His gang was by today's standards a pretty pathetic affair. His henchman was Charles Connolly, also a Royal Naval deserter and, after the war, a one-time railway porter. Connolly was a capable amateur boxer who was always looking for a street fight. The pair had two girls working for them.

One of the girls in the Kelly milieu was Jackie Dickson who may well have had tuberculosis and who was befriended by Jimmy Northam. Northam was known as Stuttie from a speech impediment suffered as a result of an accident in the war, during a part of which he had been involved in a gang which rolled servicemen. Dickson had married a sailor who had deserted her immediately after the wedding. She was summoned by Kelly and the party was joined in the public house by Marjorie Dawson, known as Norwegian Marjorie.

Kelly, it seems, put up a number of propositions including the waylaying of a taxi driver known to be a police informer, a shopbreaking expedition and the robbing of the funfair in New Brighton.

It seems to have been Connolly who originally suggested the theft of the takings from the Cameo Cinema in Wavertree. It was agreed that a gun would be needed to frighten the manager and one was produced without difficulty by Kelly. Norwegian Marjorie told him to put it away in case it was seen by other people in the pub but Kelly calmly loaded it. There was some discussion about a disguise and Dawson was made to hand over a small green apron for Kelly to use as a mask whilst Northam surrendered his overcoat.

The next evening, 19 March 1949, Kelly and Connolly went to the cinema. Connolly remained outside whilst a little after 9 pm Kelly climbed the stairs to the office and demanded the takings from the manager, Leonard Thomas. Thomas refused to hand over the takings and Kelly shot both him and Leonard Catterall, the assistant manager. Then he panicked and dropped the bag of money he had snatched. On his way out he was seen by Patrick Griffin, the cinema fireman.

Connolly was long gone by the time Kelly reappeared. He had left at the sound of the first shot. Kelly then started to build himself an alibi, going into the Leigh Arms and buying a drink for a James Currie, a man whom he hardly knew. Currie would later give evidence that Kelly seemed nervous and out of breath. He asked him what was the matter and whether he had been in a fight. Kelly agreed he had. Connolly had gone off separately to join his wife and sisters in a local dance hall.

The next day the papers were full of the news and Connolly, a very frightened man, said he was going to leave the country, something for which Kelly roundly denounced him. He also threatened Stuttie Northam and Jackie Dickson with a 'seeing to' from his brothers if they should open their mouths. Shortly after this Norwegian Marjorie committed suicide.

A month after the murders Northam and Dickson decided to write to the police. Northam, helped by the girl, printed the anonymous letter which told of plans for the robbery.

The letter continued to the effect that the writer could give more details of the murder if the police put an advertisement in the local newspaper offering immunity from prosecution. Eventually the police did place a notice in the personal column of the *Liverpool Echo:* 'Letter received. Promise definitely given.' But by this time Northam and Dickson had disappeared in the direction of Manchester.

The one outstanding recollection Griffin, the cinema fireman, had of the gunman was of his dark eyebrows, a feature of Kelly's face, and even before the letter detective Herbert Balmer had pulled Kelly in for questioning but his alibi stuck. His girlfriend Doris O'Malley swore that before he went to the Leigh Arms he had been with her in another pub, the Coach and Horses.

Balmer eventually heard the story that Jackie Dickson had been involved and after a huge search over the north of England she was retrieved from Manchester. So was Northam but it was not until six months after the robbery that he gave up the names of Kelly and Connolly.

When they, in turn, were arrested, they denied knowing each other and Kelly said, 'I never had a gun in my life. I don't know how to handle or fire one . . .'

There really wasn't much evidence against Kelly and certainly less against Connolly: an identification witness against the former and the tainted evidence of Dickson and Northam against both. The prosecution had, however, a serving prisoner, Robert Graham, doing six months for receiving stolen property. He bolstered the case with the evidence that Kelly had told him of the 60 witnesses he had in the Leigh Arms to give him an alibi. Connolly had also allegedly made a confession to the robbery to Graham.

Connolly's alibi was broken. He said he had been at a dance hall from about 8.20 in the evening and that his wife had joined him 20 minutes later. He also said he had entered a rumba competition and his wife, two of his sisters and their friends all put him in the dance hall before the murder was committed. The Master of Ceremonies, however, was sure that Connolly had not arrived until after the pubs closed. He remembered the man specifically because he had been wearing his hat on the dance floor and had been asked to remove it.

Even so the jury was unconvinced. After the 13-day trial, at that time the longest in an English court, they disagreed, were sent out again and failed to reach a verdict after another four hours. This time the prosecution had the idea of trying the men separately and the retrial was fixed for a week later. One of the reasons for the urgency was that Jackie Dickson was said to be suffering from a fatal and progressive disease.

This time Kelly was found guilty of murder – a decision with which the judge heartily concurred – with the jury retiring for only 55 minutes. Miss Heilbron took the case to the Court of Criminal Appeal with a novel if ultimately unsuccessful point. She argued that because there was a juryman who had a felony conviction the trial was a nullity and the conviction should be quashed. It was not an argument which appealed to Lord Goddard, the Lord Chief Justice. Kelly was hanged on 28 March 1950 at Walton prison. No evidence on the murder charge was offered against Connolly in his separate retrial and he pleaded guilty to the robbery of the £50 takings and was sentenced to ten years' imprisonment.

Norman Lucas, *Britain's Gangland*; James Morton, *Gangland 2*.

20 March, 1995

On 20 March 1995 Tokyo was sent into hysteria. Sarin nerve gases were released into the crowded underground system, killing 12 people and injuring a further 5,000. The leader of the right-wing Aum Supreme Truth cult, Shoko Asahara, was charged with ordering the attack, together with 170 members of his sect who themselves faced allegations ranging from perjury to mass murder. Asahara was also charged with the murder of a lawyer, Tsutsumi Sakamoto, who opposed the cult, his wife Satoko and one-year-old son, Tatsuhiko, who disappeared on 4 November 1989, a notary public who tried to prevent his sister from giving money to the cult, and at least one follower. Sakamoto had led a campaign against Aum which he believed was dangerously out of control. He had mounted his campaign following accounts of parents who had tried to retrieve their children from the cult and former members who wanted the return of property they had given. His body and those of his family were found in three separate mountain areas. Twenty-six thousand people attended a funeral service for the family on 22 October 1995.

In all Asahara faces 23 counts of murder. Part of the evidence against the leader came from two cult members, and the bodies of the lawyer and his family were discovered as a result of their information.

The trial may well last Shoko Asahara's lifetime. In Japan cases are heard a day or two at a time rather than straight through. The conviction rate in Japan is a staggering 99.8 per cent and, in a system where there is no jury but three assessors whose judicial future is dependent upon what are seen as correct results, the prosecution has a right of appeal against an acquittal. A defendant may be tried up to three times for the same offence.

21 March, 1980

Angelo Bruno, of the Philadelphia-based Mafia family, described himself as a commission salesman and was regarded, despite his control of illegal gambling and loan-sharking, as something of a peacemaker. At the age of 69 he was killed after leaving the Cous restaurant in

Philadelphia on 21 March 1980. Two men fired shotguns, killing him and wounding John Stanfa, his bodyguard. Bruno, who was one of the old-time leaders, had held out against Mob involvement with drugs and truck hijacking, and had recently appeared before the New Jersey State Commission of Investigation. Although arrested 13 times his only prison sentence was when he received two and a half years for refusing to testify in an inquiry into corruption in Atlantic City.

His contract killing was said to have been worth $250,000 and undertaken by 'Mad Dog' Joe Sullivan. It followed on the killing of the New York Mafioso Carmine Galante on 12 July 1979 and was said to have been necessary for a review of the ownership of Atlantic City gambling concessions. Another reason advanced for the killing was Bruno's refusal to enter the lucrative drug trade.

Bruno had particular connections with England. His representative was said to be Albert Dimes, a member of the Sabinis, the pre-war London Underworld gang, and later the right-hand man to Billy Hill who controlled Soho and the West End in the 1950s. In 1966 Bruno had visited England on a gambling junket but in reality to see whether gaming machines could be installed in various clubs. He had decided not to involve himself in things British, believing the operations were hopelessly old-fashioned.

John Stanfa received seven years' imprisonment for failing to testify to a Grand Jury over the killing of his employer. In the 1990s, on the conviction of Nicky Scarfo, the then current Don, Stanfa, rather against the odds, gained control of the Bruno family enterprises but in 1995 he was convicted of extortion and conspiracy. The ownership of the South Philadelphia mobs allegedly passed to Ralph Nardine. No one was charged with Bruno's murder.

Donald Frankos, *Contract Killer*; Joseph Salerno and Stephen J. Rivele, *The Plumber*.

22 March, 1915

At around 6 am on 22 March 1915 at West Shelby, New York, the bodies of farm owner Charles Phelps and his housekeeper, Margaret Wolcott, were discovered by Phelps's semi-illiterate immigrant farmhand, Charles Stielow. They had been shot to death. Stielow walked through the snow to the cottage of his brother-in-law Nelson Green who then went to inform the sheriff Chester Bartlett. When a doctor arrived he removed three .22 bullets from the body of Phelps. When questioned both Stielow and Green initially denied they owned any firearms at all.

They were questioned at length and eventually Green, thought to be even more educationally challenged than his brother-in-law, broke down and confessed that Stielow had once owned a revolver, a rifle and a shotgun. All were .22-calibre weapons. After more questioning he confessed that both he and Stielow had killed Phelps.

In turn Stielow was questioned and was offered the opportunity of seeing his wife and going home if he confessed. It took two days before he admitted to the murder. Robbery was the motive and he said he and Green had been interrupted by Phelps and then the housekeeper, whom they shot and left dying in the snow. Stielow refused to sign the confession and retracted it in court.

In one of the earliest ballistic cases in America a *soi-disant* expert, Dr Albert Hamilton, claimed that Stielow's weapon had in the muzzle an abnormal scratch which showed up on the bullets found in Phelps's body. Stielow was unfortunate. His case was the first murder trial handled by his lawyer, David A. White. White's inexperience was compounded by the fact that there was no money to secure the services of an expert who might be able to contradict Hamilton. On 23 July 1915 Stielow was convicted and sentenced to electrocution in Sing Sing.

His fortunes now took a turn for the better. He fell under the patronage of the Humanitarian Cult of New York who uncovered two tramps, King and O'Connell, who had been in West Shelby on the night of the murder and who had been heard discussing it before the facts were made public.

King made a voluntary confession to the trial judge but later retracted it and it was not until 1917 that an independent commission was appointed to examine the case. A detective on the New York police force gave evidence which exposed Hamilton as a charlatan. When Stielow's guns were fired the bullets were covered in dirt. No scratches were found to match that purportedly found by Hamilton. Stielow was pardoned and once more King confessed. He was fortunate – the Grand Jury of Orleans County refused to indict him.

Jurgen Thorwald, *The Marks of Cain*.

23 March, 1994

One of the most entertaining conspiracy theories of recent years was exploded in early January 1996. It ran that on 23 March 1994 a Mexican federal agent, Martin Antonio Guteirrez Cantu, had assassinated a presidential candidate in a shooting in Tijuana and had then himself been killed.

Luis Donaldo Colosio, presidential candidate of the long-ruling Institutional Revolutionary Party, was undoubtedly killed at a rally on 23 March. There is a videotape of the shooting in which an old pistol is held to the head of Señor Colosio but the tape blurs before showing who pulled the trigger.

The conspiracy theory ran that Señor Cantu fled after pulling the trigger and was then killed some hours later in a garage and his body buried under a false name. Better was to come. There was then an impersonation of the deceased agent by a 24-year-old vagrant, Mario Aburto Martinez, who was forced by the conspirators to act out the role of agent.

Originally, Martinez confessed to the killing and was portrayed by the prosecutors as a sole, crazed gunman. He received a 45-year sentence. There was however widespread disbelief in this theory. Few believed that Martinez had acted alone. In 1995 a second man was arrested and, at the time of writing, is awaiting trial on what is generally considered weak evidence.

The detailed conspiracy theory came following the work of a private investigator, Humberto Lopez Mejia, and was published in a number of Mexican newspapers in December 1995. It collapsed when, on 3 January 1996, the supposedly dead Señor Cantu appeared at a press conference in Mexico City. Far from being buried in Tijuana he had been on his honeymoon when the Mejia theory was published and so had been unable to refute the allegations earlier.

Matters were further complicated by the withdrawal by Martinez of his confession. He told his lawyer that he did not kill Colosio. He had simply been at the rally when he had been grabbed by agents and substituted for the real killer.

24 March, 1989

On Good Friday, 24 March 1989, 19-year-old Tracey Illman was stabbed to death in her bedsit in the Old Kent Road, London. She had been living with Bruce Santus and they had a four-month-old son, Jeremy. They had known each other for the previous three years. He worked as a porter at the Chelsea Hotel in Knightsbridge. During the last weeks of Tracey's pregnancy Santus had begun an affair with Carol Ann McDonald who worked as a nanny.

The case for the prosecution against Santus was based on the evidence of Carol McDonald, who gave evidence for the Crown. It was that Santus had become tired of Tracey and the baby and wanted to get rid of his long-time girlfriend. Santus's workmates did not agree. They said that he was inordinately proud of the baby and that the affair with McDonald had ended. She agreed that he had put an end to the relationship in February and had not told her of his new address. She hired a private detective to find him on the pretext that she was pregnant by him. She was not.

According to her evidence she gave Santus an ultimatum. He must decide between her and Tracey and he agreed he would do so by Good Friday. This, according to McDonald, was in the hearing of one of Santus's workmates, something which the man denied.

On the Good Friday, McDonald, on her evidence, met Santus at 10.15 am and he drove her in a large red car to the bedsit in the Old Kent Road. He was wearing a boiler suit she had never seen before. She believed he intended to tell Tracey that he was going to leave her and when he did in fact do this there was an argument. According to McDonald, Santus lost control and attacked Tracey, stabbing her. She tried to intervene and was slightly cut herself. She had tried to bind Tracey's throat to stop the bleeding but had then run away, called a taxi and had gone back to Knightsbridge. In all Tracey was stabbed nearly 20 times and had her jugular and carotid artery cut. There must have been a great deal of blood.

The taxi driver remembered Carol McDonald, first, because he had originally not intended to work that Good Friday and, secondly, because she paid with a £50 note, giving him a substantial part as a tip. He had picked her up between 11 and 11.30 am. This put the killing as before that time. Santus's alibi was that he had been working at the hotel and the jury had to decide whether there was time for him to go to the Old Kent Road, commit the murder, get back, clean himself and his shoes up, get rid of the boiler suit and be back at work as though nothing had happened. He had certainly left the hotel to deliver a package to the Rembrandt Hotel and there was evidence that he had borrowed a friend's maroon Mercedes to do so. Could he have gone to the Old Kent Road and back and delivered the parcel in, say, 45 minutes to an hour?

There was evidence from the head porter at the Chelsea that he had checked at the Rembrandt to see if the parcel had been delivered and it had been.

Carol McDonald returned to Scotland and meanwhile the police searched her room. She was a compulsive note maker and there was one note which read 'knives, clothes peg, plaster tape, Polo mints, rope, gloves, towel . . .' It appears it had been her intention to suffocate Tracey and then make it look as though she had choked on a mint which would have been pushed down her throat with a chopstick.

According to McDonald the notes had been prepared at the instigation and dictation of Santus. One, she said, had actually been written by Santus but a handwriting expert said that it had been written by McDonald. No weapon which could match the wounds was found, there was no matching blood found, even on the Mercedes, to connect Santus, nor was there any scientific evidence that McDonald had actually been in the Mercedes.

Tracey's body was found at 10.30 in the evening by Santus. The baby was unhurt, as was the dog. When questioned by the police he told lies, trying to conceal his affair. He insisted, for example, that he had walked to the Rembrandt. One reason for that lie was that he did not wish to admit to driving without insurance or a licence. McDonald was brought back from Scotland and Santus was arrested at his mother's home in Sussex. According to the arresting officer he said, 'It's my mum, did you not see her, did you see what I done to her.' He took a photograph from his pocket and said, 'Look, that's my mum, look at her there, now look at her, I've done that.' He then started to cry and said, 'I killed her, I killed Tracey.' He went on to admit he stabbed her but he did not know why.

In evidence he denied he had made the admissions. He was convicted by a ten to two majority and Carol McDonald was sentenced to four years for her part in the matter.

Santus's appeal was heard on 21 May 1991 when the court considered whether the conviction was unsafe. The court thought he could easily have left Tracey rather than murder her. He was likely to be the number one suspect and killing Tracey would deprive Jeremy, of whom he was immensely proud, of a mother. Nor was there any independent evidence that he had any great depth of feeling for McDonald. The evidence was that McDonald was doing the pursuing. The court also took the view that the alibi, which was really prosecution evidence, was a very strong one. It was not, according to McDonald's evidence, a planned murder so how did he manage to do everything in a maximum of an hour? There were no bloodstains which could be held against him whereas bloodstained clothes of Carol McDonald had been found partially burned. She had tried to set light to them at her workplace in Knightsbridge.

As for the remarks said to be made by Santus to the police when leaving his mother's, the Lord Chief Justice commented that whatever the rights and wrongs of those statements the court took the view the conviction was unsafe. Then Lord Lane went on to criticise the Crown Prosecution Service for accepting Carol McDonald's plea of not guilty to murder at such an early stage. '. . . once that decision is made to accept that plea from McDonald, much of what some might think is the function of the jury is automatically pre-empted. There on the court record before the trial starts is "McDonald on count 2, murder, Not Guilty by order of the court". As to that we say no more.'

25 March, 1992

Thirty-nine-year-old Daphne Pertwee shot her husband
Roger and then their three-month-old son, Henry, on 25
March 1992 at their home in Kincardine O'Neil, Deeside.
She had left friends in the living room to go to kill her
antique dealer husband as he slept. She went back to her
friends and told them, 'I just shot them both.' The gun
had been fired at a range of between nine and eighteen
inches. Later she told the police, 'I shot my husband and
baby because I could not cope. I had very bad depression.'
She had first been admitted to hospital for treatment in
1977 when she had received a course of electro-convulsive
treatment. After Henry's birth on 29 December 1991 she
was treated at the Royal Cornhill Hospital, Aberdeen
after being diagnosed as suffering from schizo-affective
psychosis. She felt inadequate and a failure as a mother
and wife and had intended to kill herself. She was ordered
to be detained in the Royal Cornhill after she admitted
culpable homicide.

   The killing had a sequel when in May 1994 a settlement
was reached over Roger Pertwee's estate. Under the
Forfeiture Act 1982 a Scottish High Court judge has
the power to modify the rule that a person may not make
a profit from crime and Mrs Pertwee had petitioned for a
share in the baby Henry's estate, said to be worth around
£110,000. He had survived his father by a few minutes
and therefore inherited the estate. Had Mrs Pertwee not
killed Henry she would have been the inheritor.

   Her claim was opposed by Roger Pertwee's sister, Jane
Hall, and his father, Harold Pertwee. The case, listed for a
two-day hearing, was settled on undisclosed terms before
the hearing began.

26 March, 1948

William George Silver, a nightwatchman aged 74 years, employed by the ABC, was attacked on the night of 26 March 1948. He was found at the Savoy Cinema in Teddington at 7.45 am the next day and died in the West Middlesex Hospital later that evening. He had been struck with considerable violence with something like a truncheon.

He had gone the previous evening to watch the cinema programme and then stay on as watchman. He was wearing a pair of black lace-up boots. The next morning staff discovered the manager's office had been ransacked and at the top of the stairs leading from the balcony to the circle Silver was found bound and gagged. His black boots were missing. The safe in the manager's office had been tampered with, as had a wardrobe in which the manager kept his evening suit. Fingerprints were taken and those on the wardrobe door, a fire hose branch and fire nozzle matched the prints of Norris Andrew Megaw.

Megaw had been employed as a fitter's mate doing work on the cinema and he had got to know Silver quite well. According to his statement to the police, he was short of money and he and a friend went to the cinema and got in because one of the main doors had been left open. They then met Silver who asked how they had got in and asked them to leave. Megaw decided to try again and he prepared a rubber tubing from a vacuum cleaner into which he put a solid iron pipe. He went to the cinema on a number of occasions before he could bring himself to carry out the robbery. He was going through the manager's office when he heard snoring and went and found Silver. He woke him and pulled him to a sitting position before he hit him. Silver got to his feet, shouting 'Police!' and Megaw struck him twice more. He then bound and gagged him.

Megaw said he had taken off his shoes and left them in the letter room. After he had carried Silver into the circle he saw Silver's black boots which were in much better condition than his own worn brown shoes so he put them on before going back to collect his own pair.

Megaw gave himself up on 27 March 1948 at Camberwell police station. At the trial at the Old Bailey on 10 May 1948 he pleaded guilty and was sentenced to death. The sentence was commuted to penal servitude for life.

The matter did not quite end there. An Arthur Chapple, a newspaper reporter in Wakefield, wrote in June 1951 to Chief Inspector Reginald Spooner suggesting that another man had been involved in the robbery.

Spooner knew Chapple because he, Spooner, had been the army officer in the case in which Chapple had received a sentence of 15 years' imprisonment for voluntarily aiding the enemy whilst a prisoner of war. Chapple had met Megaw in Wakefield prison before he, Chapple, was released on 9 December 1950.

Megaw had never mentioned a second man being present at the robbery in his detailed statement nor in a letter written to his wife. Nevertheless investigations were resumed and Megaw was re-interviewed and denied that anyone else had been involved. He said he had spoken to Chapple whilst in prison and had discussed his case. Chapple, he said, had suggested that someone might have been with him but Megaw had neither admitted nor denied it.

A note from Superintendent Capstick suggested that the information might have been given for publicity purposes.

MEPO/3/3000.

27 March, 1905

The body of Thomas Farrow, who ran a chandler's shop not far from the river in Deptford, south-east London, was found early on the morning of 27 March 1905. His wife, Ann, who was found with him, died four days later in hospital. Both had serious head injuries. The shop had been ransacked, the cash box broken open and the contents stolen. A milkman had seen two men lurking around the shop.

The science of fingerprinting was still in its early stages but a thumbprint was lifted from an ashtray and was found to match neither those of the Farrows nor a police officer who admitted handling it. Two black silk masks were found discarded in the shop. They had been made from Mrs Farrow's stockings and the police reasoned that they had been worn by the robbers because they were known to the Farrows.

A trawl of local criminals threw up a pair of brothers, 20-year-old Albert Stratton and Alfred, his elder by two years. Under police questioning Hannah Cromarty, the mistress of Alfred, admitted that on the night before the murder she had been with her lover. There had been a knocking in the early hours after which he had told her to say that he had been with her until 9 am. He had then left. She went on to tell the police that Alfred had destroyed a coat during the week. He had also dyed his brown shoes black.

On 2 April a police officer, learning that Alfred was drinking in a local public house, went in and arrested him. Melville McNaughten, then the Commissioner of Police, ordered that his fingerprints be taken. The thumbprint was found to contain 11 matching points with Alfred's right thumb. His brother was arrested later in Stepney. The evidence regarding fingerprints was crucial. Giving evidence Inspector Collins of the Fingerprinting Branch said that there were now around 85,000 sets on file. The evidence was denounced by H.G. Rooth, defending Alfred Stratton, who said it 'savoured more of the French courts than of English justice'. This was a reference to the technique of Bertonillage, a science of measuring parts of the body which for a time held sway on the Continent. However, to demonstrate the soundness of the technique, Sir Richard Muir, prosecuting, asked Collins to finger-print the jurors. Each juror could now see that although there were minor discrepancies when fingerprints were taken the basic patterns remained the same.

The trial judge, Mr Justice Channell, was by no means convinced that there could be no two people with matching prints: '. . . there is at any rate an extraordinary amount of resemblance between the two marks, and therefore to a certain extent it is corroborative evidence in regard to Alfred Stratton.' The jury returned a verdict of guilty in two hours and, with each brother blaming the other, they were hanged at Wandsworth prison by John Billington on 23 May.

Fingerprinting had been used as early as 1858 when a British magistrate in India, William Herschel, used it to prevent pensioners claiming benefits twice over, but his idea never gained widespread recognition. In May 1901 Edward Henry, formerly an Inspector General of the Nepal police, was appointed Assistant Commissioner at Scotland Yard and founded the Central Fingerprint Branch. Fingerprinting did not gain acceptance in America until 1928. It is now the practice in British courts to require 16 resembling points before the evidence is adduced. In America some States will accept as few as nine points.

S.T. Felstead, *Sir Richard Muir, The Memoirs of a Public Prosecutor*; Jurgen Thorwald, *The Marks of Cain*.

28 March, 1994

On 28 March 1994 Stephen James Wilkinson burst into a classroom at Hall Garth Comprehensive School in Middlesborough and stabbed 12-year-old Nikki Conroy to death.

Armed with a replica handgun, which he had placed at the head of another pupil, he forced the teacher to leave the class. He then barricaded the door and stabbed Nikki as well as two other girls, Michelle Reeve and Emma Winter, making them kneel in a corner and telling them, 'You are going to pay for what you have done to me.' The deputy headmaster Chris Bielby and another teacher, David Elland, rushed into the room and overpowered Wilkinson but they were too late to save Nikki who had wounds to her lungs, heart and liver.

Wilkinson, who believed his *alter ego* to be Wilson Jinks, an anagram of his name, told the police he remembered nothing of the incident and pleaded not guilty to murder but guilty to manslaughter on the grounds of diminished responsibility. The prosecution did not accept the plea and, because of local feeling, the trial was heard away from the area at Leeds Crown Court in December 1995.

In Wilkinson's possession the police found a six-page document, 'Thoughts/Confessions', dated January 1994 in which he wrote:

> Wilson Jinks wants to destroy me. If I let him gain ascendance he will also slaughter the lambs . . . This confession may read like that of a lunatic but I can assure you I am quite sane. In truth I wish only to convey to the world my absolute hatred of it. In doing so I shall steal the lives of society's weakest members; those most vulnerable and those most treasured.

The trial was suddenly halted when on 14 December Mrs Justice Smith formally directed the jury to return a verdict of guilty of manslaughter on the grounds of diminished responsibility. Four psychiatrists had agreed that Wilkinson was severely mentally ill on the day of the killing. The judge told the jury that two of the psychiatrists described Wilkinson's condition as paranoid schizophrenia and the others the similar condition of paranoid psychosis. 'They all agreed this was a severe mental illness which started in his late teens and had affected his life ever since.'

Wilkinson was sentenced to be detained in hospital without a time limit.

29 March, 1966

Agnes Standing, the wife of Chief Inspector James Standing, was found dead at Forest Side, Chingford on 29 March 1966. She had been strangled and suffocated. A piece of tissue had been rammed down her throat.

That evening her husband, together with a number of other police officers, had been at a dinner in the Windmill Public House at Leyton. Mr Standing had telephoned his wife, asking her to join them, shortly before 10 pm but, although she was seen getting off a bus near the public house, she never arrived.

The death caused a considerable scandal amongst the police. Seven cars belonging to officers were brought to the police station for forensic tests and amnesties were offered to police officers who might have been able to give information but who were not acting in accordance with their schedules on the night of her death.

One of the suggestions made was that Mrs Standing was a sexually promiscuous woman who, meeting a police officer on the way to the Windmill, had gone off with him, and that her death had been part of sexual by-play. It was an allegation vehemently denied by her husband at the inquest. Mr Standing said:

> I merely wanted to say a few words in the defence of her character and name which has been so maligned in the local press by the exaggerated and distorted reports of her social life to give a picture that she was a frequenter of dog tracks, bingo halls, public houses and Chinese restaurants which has given so much grief and distress – in addition to the death – to our family as to almost disunite us.

It was thought that Mrs Standing was killed by a police officer whom she knew and whom she had met by chance on the night of her death. He later emigrated. No one was ever charged with her murder.

30 March, 1913

Winifred Mary Mitchell, a 24-year-old cook, was last seen alive on 30 March 1913. She had fallen for 29-year-old William Walter Burton, an odd job man and rabbit killer for the local squire. Burton had a wife five years older than he, who was the local village postmistress in Gussage St Michael, Dorset, and a young child. Very much a ladies' man, he took on the task of seducing Mitchell who had come to work at the manor house, but she would only agree to his demands if he left his wife and they went to Canada. He appears to have made some effort to raise the money and put together £5, but before they emigrated he had grown tired of the young woman whom he believed to be pregnant. When he suggested ending the relationship, Winifred threatened to tell Burton's wife. He then told the girl he would leave with her and that she should tell her friends she was going to London.

Just over a month later, on 2 May, Winifred's body was found in a shallow grave. Children had come across it whilst picking primroses. She had been shot from behind. Almost certainly the grave had been dug in advance. Burton had arranged to meet Mitchell on 29 March but at the last minute she had been unable to keep the appointment.

Burton was convicted before Mr Justice Ridley at Dorchester Assizes. On 24 June 1913 he became the last man to be hanged at Dorchester prison.

31 March, 1995

Twenty-three-year-old Texan Superstar, queen of Tejano music, a blend of European and Mexican-based polkas, Selena Quintanilla was shot in the back at the Days Inn, Corpus Christi, Texas motel room of 34-year-old Yolanda Saldivar, on Friday, 31 March 1995. Quintanilla, who had been a singer since the age of 10, had gone to the motel room to collect the financial records of her employee Saldivar, who was president of her fan club. In the weeks before her death she had come to believe that Saldivar was stealing from her £5-million-a-year enterprises including the Selena Fan Club and 'Selena Etc', a fashion boutique in San Antonio. Saldivar had once described Quintanilla as being her 'inspiration'. 'I felt she had an obsession toward Selena. I felt she was unbalanced,' said Selena's father, Abraham Quintanilla.

Selena was shot through the shoulder, with the bullet piercing an artery. She struggled to the motel lobby where she collapsed, and died after being taken to hospital. After the shooting Ms Saldivar went to the parking lot and threatened suicide. She surrendered to the police about nine and a half hours later.

The evidence was that on 11 March Ms Saldivar had put down a $100 deposit on a .38-calibre five-shot revolver at the 'A Place to Shoot' store in San Antonio. She collected it two days later, returned it two days after that and finally bought the weapon on 26 March. She was convicted and sentenced to life imprisonment.

After Selena Quintanilla's death 30,000 people filed past her coffin.

A film has now been made of her life.

APRIL

1 April, 1989

Nineteen-year-old Robert Earl Jines of Indianapolis, who had been staying in a mountain top cabin in rural north-west Alabama with his girlfriend, Bobbie Lee Harrell, aged 20, disappeared on 1 April 1989. His skeletal remains were found almost five years later on 11 March 1994, some 200 yards from a cabin owned by Frank T. Potts of Lakeland, Florida. He had received two blows to the skull, one of which had been fatal.

Jines had been on the run at the time of his disappearance. Bobbie Lee Harrell told the court at the trial of Frank T. Potts, who was charged with Jines's murder, that they had met Potts after coming to Florida in 1988. Jines took up paving work and Potts was a friend of his boss.

By early March 1989 the police had traced Jines to Florida. He was wanted in Indiana over motoring and fraudulent cheque charges. When Jines told Potts that he was afraid of a jail sentence in Indiana he offered the pair the use of a cabin in Alabama until matters died down.

According to Harrell, who took her two children along with them, the first few days were peaceful but then Potts began asking her for kisses and hugs. On one occasion whilst they were sitting outside Potts asked her for a kiss and when Jines complained he was told to keep his mouth shut.

On 1 April Jines and Potts and a third man, Harvey

Wilson Taylor, left to repair a pick-up truck. Jines never returned. Later Potts flashed a note in front of Harrell. According to her evidence she was not allowed to read it properly and she could not say if it was in Jines's handwriting. Potts also told her that Jines had tired of her and had bought a car to go to California. After Jines had disappeared Potts climbed into bed with her but she told him she wanted some water. When he got up to get it for her she got out of bed as well. A few days later she managed to telephone her father who, much to Potts's annoyance, came to collect her and the children. A few weeks later she reported that Jines had disappeared.

Harrell's testimony was backed by Donald Barnes whose uncle was Taylor, the third man on the mountain. He told the court that Potts had spoken of an argument with someone named Bobby J. over a girl and that he, Potts, had 'terminated the problem'. It was a conversation bitterly challenged by Potts who said, 'I'm probably as dumb as a skunk but I've got enough sense to not tell anyone I killed somebody.' In his turn, Taylor said that although he was not with Potts when Jines had been killed he had helped to bury his body. In 1994 he had pointed out the grave to investigating officers.

The authorities were convinced not only that Potts had killed Jines but that he was a serial killer. His mountain top home was effectively taken apart and at one point four navigation satellites were used to pinpoint excavation sites on the land. Although thousands of pieces of children's clothing, animal bones and buried trash were uncovered there was no evidence to support the belief. At the time of his trial, which began on 10 April 1995, Potts was serving a life sentence in Florida. He had been convicted in December 1994 of a sexual assault on a 10-year-old girl of whose grandparents he was a friend. He had already served a six-year sentence following a conviction in 1982 for a lewd assault on an 11-year-old girl.

Reportedly offered a plea bargain – he was to plead guilty to the kidnapping of an Alabama wildlife officer in 1992 in exchange for the dropping of the Jines murder charge – Potts has consistently maintained his innocence and has asked for, and been refused, a lie detector test. His defence in the Jines case was that it was Taylor who did the killing, with robbery as a motive.

Potts was convicted in April 1995 without the authorities having been able to uncover a shred of evidence against him in relation to other killings. However, they remained convinced of his guilt. 'Potts is a demon in my opinion,' Polk sheriff's detective Paul Schaill told the *Tampa Tribune*. 'He's as evil as they come.' The police maintain he is the prime suspect for the October 1981 rape and killing of a 13-year-old girl whose body was thrown from an overpass and found on the pavement of Interstate 4. The police also question the circumstances of the disappearance of Potts's brother-in-law, Arthur J. Zechman Junior near his property in 1978. Potts maintains that he, Zechman and three others went to Alabama but his brother-in-law disappeared on his way up the mountain. He is also suspected in the case of the disappearance of 19-year-old Felicity Renae Dry who disappeared in Marshall County, Alabama in 1993. A photograph of her found in his cabin was identified by her mother.

Potts, who read a statement proclaiming his innocence before being ordered to serve a life sentence beginning after his present one, will be eligible for parole for the sex assault when he is 75. He will then be starting his life sentence for the Jines killing.

In September 1995 Gerald Lydell Voyles and Grady Lee Wilson, who were charged with the 1981 deaths of two men, Onton Jimmy Crumley and Thomas Eldridge Chambers near Polk City, maintained that the real killer was Potts who had told a cellmate the men had been shot by him over a drugs deal. They also said Potts had confessed to the murder of Zechman and the rape and killing of Linda Patterson Slaten of Lakeland. Potts had told his cellmate she had been killed because she knew of his involvement in the deaths of Crumley and Chambers. They claimed Potts had confessed to the killing of yet two

more people whose bodies were buried on his Alabama
property. Based on this information they asked they be
given bail pending their trials for which the prosecution
was seeking the death penalty. Their request was denied.
'I want some bodies found in the ground in Alabama,' said
Judge J. Tim Strickland. 'When they find some bodies in
the ground, I will begin to be a believer.'

2 April, 1993

Thirty-nine-year-old Barbara Meller Jensen, a German
tourist in Miami on 2 April 1993, lost her way from the
airport to her hotel and with it her life. She was attacked
by three men who deliberately bumped her car. When she
got out to inspect the damage they snatched her purse and
she was knocked down and run over as they fled in their
car. She fell underneath the Cadillac's rear tyre and her
skull was crushed. About 16 hours after Barbara Jensen
died a 57-year-old secretary had her handbag stolen at a
car wash in the vicinity.

Herman Perry, a juvenile justice officer, saw the theft
at the car wash, followed the getaway car and called
the police. When the police stopped the suspects they
still had the handbag with them. In their car a police
officer found a label and put it in the secretary's handbag
before returning it to the secretary. When she heard of
the killing of Mrs Jensen she 'ran to my purse, opened
the coin section and, lo and behold, I saw the name of
the person they had mentioned on the news, along with
a Berlin address'.

According to the police the two suspects, Leroy Rogers
and Anthony Williams, admitted feeling a bump as they
drove away after robbing Barbara Jensen. 'I never looked
back,' said Rogers in his statement, ''cause from my
knowledge I already knew ... a human being lying

there.' Williams said it looked as though she had been dragged by the car.

On 4 July 1995 Williams and Rogers were convicted of first-degree murder and sentenced to mandatory life imprisonment. They will each have to serve 25 years. Rogers received a further 15 years on a robbery count and Williams an additional 30 as a violent habitual offender. He will be able to apply for parole when he is 66, his partner a year earlier. The third man denied being in the car and proceedings could only be brought against him if either Rogers or Williams would agree to give evidence. They would not.

Mr Perry and the secretary shared a reward of $100,000. Rogers's mother was not happy with the sentencing. 'It's all tourism. Money talks,' she said. 'My son didn't do it. They could get him for robbery, but not life in prison.'

After Barbara Jensen's death, the German Government drew up guidelines for its citizens visiting Florida. They included not stopping for strangers and avoiding central Miami and Miami Beach after dark. Later, after a series of incidents in Florida involving the robbery and murder of tourists, including the death of Mahmet Bahar from Turkey, killed after a traffic dispute on 17 September 1993, and the case of Uwe-Wilhelm Rakebrand who, in the same month, was also shot after receiving a traffic bump, it was arranged that hire-cars in the State should have number plates which made them indistinguishable from local ones. Tourists have the opportunity of renting high-tech cars with electronic mapping systems and at Miami International Airport they can watch a police video of safety tips which include advising against pulling over to look at maps on dark streets.

3 April, 1989

Yury Gomez almost burned to death on 3 April 1989 at the Leisure Investments amusement arcade which stood on the corner of Gerrard Street and Wardour Street in London's Chinatown. In fact he survived to name his would-be killer. Fellow employees were not so fortunate.

When an employee of the company came to unlock the premises at 8 o'clock that morning he noticed a smell of burning, overlaid with chemicals. The small office safe had been ransacked, coins were scattered over the floor. The majority of the takings were kept locked in a room secured by a steel door beside the stairs. The employee heard noises and went to unlock the door. There he found Gomez, the relief manager, his clothing in rags, his face and body irretrievably burned. 'Victor,' he said. 'It was Victor who did it.' Victor was Victor Castigador, a Filipino who worked as a security guard in the arcade.

When the police arrived they found two security guards dead, as well as the 26-year-old cashier, Debbie Alvarez, who was still alive. All four had been bound, doused with an inflammable liquid, set alight and locked in the safe room. The guards had been asphyxiated.

Two days later the police arrested Castigador at a flat in Bow. He had in his possession £480 of the £8,685 stolen. The police later arrested 19-year-old Calvin Nelson, Allison Woodside, aged 20, Paul Clinton and Karen Dunn, both aged 17. All were charged with murder. Paul Clinton was homeless at the time and had been offered a bed by Castigador, Karen Dunn was Clinton's girlfriend, and Clinton's cousin Calvin Nelson and his girlfriend Allison Woodside also used Castigador's flat from time to time as a crash pad.

Castigador had set up the robbery really by way of

revenge. His complaints were against the general manager, Tony Doroudy, whom he believed was promoting
people over his head and failing to pay promised bonuses.
At one time Castigador had worked at the company's
Oxford Street arcade where he had broken the jaw of a
client he thought to be troublesome. Doroudy transferred
him to the Gerrard Street premises – by no means a
promotion.

Castigador had come to England in 1985. He had, he
said, been an assassin for the Filipino Government but had
become burned-out and when he met an Englishwoman,
Jacqueline Haddon, decided to retire, marry her and settle
down in England. The couple married within a week of his
arrival on 10 August 1985. At first they lived in Sussex but
the marriage was not a success and Castigador moved to
London.

The catalyst for the murders was Castigador's suspen-
sion by Tony Doroudy for failing to turn up for work.
Castigador believed he had arranged for his absence with
a duty manager and when he was told to come in to collect
his P45 he planned his reprisal.

He forced his workmates into the vault, and made them
kneel against a wall. He then gathered rubbish which
he piled in the vault, poured white spirit over, threw
lighted matches onto it and fastened the door, locking
his colleagues inside.

At his trial the judge said, '. . . you condemned to
agonising death your workmates who had done you no
harm (and) proceeded to execute that sentence without
one shred of pity or mercy.'

Castigador was sentenced to life imprisonment with a
recommendation that he serve not less than 25 years.
Allison Woodside and Karen Dunn were found guilty
of robbery and given 42 and 36 months respectively.
Found guilty of murder, Paul Clinton was ordered to be
detained during Her Majesty's pleasure. Calvin Nelson
received a term of life imprisonment with eight years to
run concurrently for the robbery.

4 April, 1936

The body of 54-year-old prostitute Beatrice Vilna Sutton was found in her flat at Elmhurst Mansions, Clapham, south-west London on 4 April 1936. She was naked and had been suffocated with two pillows. She was the second victim of Frederick Herbert Charles Field. Once before he had literally got away with murder.

Norma Upchurch, a prostitute also known as Laverick, had been found dead on 2 October 1931 in an empty shop in New Compton Street, Soho. Her clothes were awry and her handbag was missing. Her body was discovered when Douglas Bartrum, the manager of a firm of sign contractors, and Field, one of his employees, broke open a wooden door at the rear of the shop to gain access to remove some signs.

There were a number of suspects for the murder of this 20-year-old girl, who had been placed in care at the age of 16 and who from time to time had tried to break out of her life of prostitution. The first was a man called Peter Webb who, so Field said, had worn plus fours, and who had obtained the keys of the shop from Field several days earlier, showing him what appeared to be an authority from the estate agents for whom the sign was being erected. Webb had never returned the keys to him. At Richmond Police Station Field had identified Webb as the man who had taken the keys, something hotly denied by Webb. The second suspect was a former England cricketer who had been the last person to see Upchurch alive. He had spent the night of 28 September with her. The third person was a sailor from Chatham Barracks who considered himself engaged to her. The fourth was Field himself.

Field was a married man who lived in Sutton. He had spent six years in the RAF and had been discharged with a good character. The police were not happy with his story, particularly when he identified Webb who turned out to have an unshakeable alibi. The coroner, Ingleby Oddie, told the jury that whilst they might disbelieve Field's story altogether, that did not necessarily make him a murderer.

The jury followed the coroner's implicit instructions and returned a verdict of wilful murder by some person unknown. There the matter rested for some two years until, in July 1933, Field walked into a newspaper office and confessed. The paper had guaranteed his defence costs in 1931 if the jury had named him in returning the verdict of wilful murder. This is by no means as odd as it sounds. There was no such thing as legal aid in those days. Indeed it was about the only way a defendant could obtain the services of first-class counsel on a murder charge. The implicit agreement was that, in the event of a conviction, the defendant would leave a death cell confession to be printed in the appropriate Sunday paper the week after he was hanged. It was not something which, in this case, appealed to the trial judge, Mr Justice Swift.

Field's story was now that he had met Norah Upchurch near the Hippodrome on the corner of Leicester Square, had gone with her to the shop but that, although she had agreed to fellate him, she would not lie on the floor with him. In a rage he had strangled her.

He had then taken the Underground back to Morden. He said he had thrown her handbag in a water-filled ditch near Sutton bypass. Why had he suddenly confessed? First, he wanted money to send his wife back to her family in Cardiff. Secondly, he had, he believed, committed the perfect murder. He had outwitted the police and the coroner but now his mates at work would not believe him. The newspaper sent a reporter and photographer to the ditch but it was dry and there was no handbag.

On trial at the Old Bailey he now denied he had killed Upchurch, saying that he wanted to clear his name as he had been offered a job in Ceylon on a tea plantation and when it had been learned he was involved in the Upchurch murder enquiry the offer had been withdrawn. Apart from commenting that to confess to murder was a peculiar way of proving his innocence Mr Justice Swift was impressed and summed up with what amounted to a direction to the jury to acquit.

In 1936, now a deserter from the RAF, which he had rejoined, and on a charge of larceny, Field confessed to the murder of Beatrice Sutton. 'I went to her place and done her in, and, as you might say, put myself on the spot.'

Again, at the trial he withdrew his confession, but this time the investigating officer had obtained detailed descriptions from Field about the contents of the flat and the injuries to the woman, so negating Field's story of hearing a quarrel and seeing a man leaving the flat. He had, he said, been sleeping the past few nights under the stairs and had only gone into the flat when he saw the door was open. The jury took only 20 minutes to convict him and he was hanged on 30 June 1936.

Julian Symons, *A Reasonable Doubt*.

5 April, 1986

Anthony Connolly, who had been unemployed, was found dead in a disused railway shed on 5 April 1986. He had been strangled and there were bite marks on the body.

Originally from Newcastle he had been living with his friend, Simon Walder, on the Cowley Estate, Brixton. At first mortuary staff, fearing that Connolly might be AIDS infected, refused to allow a postmortem to proceed and it was two weeks before the examination took place.

There had been another recent killing of a homosexual. On 15 March the mutilated body of James Burns, known in the area as a 'leather man', had been found by vagrants in a disused basement in Warwick Road, Earl's Court, but for a time the murders were not firmly linked together by the police.

However, on 8 May another attack took place. David Cole, aged 30, was coming out of the Market Tavern at Nine Elms when he was approached by a man and invited to go to a lorry park in New Covent Garden. There the man attacked him and tried to strangle him with a silk sock. Cole managed to get away and contacted the Gay Switchboard, an information and crisis line. He later contacted the police. The attacks were now linked and the police took Cole on a tour of pubs and clubs frequented by homosexuals in the hope that he could pick out his attacker.

They were fortunate. Cole made an identification within four hours. The man he pointed out was Michael Lupo who at first denied the attack but then later admitted it, as well as the murders of Connolly and Burns. The sock with which he had tried to strangle Cole had come from Harrods.

Lupo also went on to admit to the murder of a vagrant on 18 April. Shortly after Lupo had left the gay rendezvous Heaven he had been approached for a cigarette and he had strangled the man. On this occasion there had been no sexual involvement. He also admitted to the killing of Damien McCluskey, a hospital porter, who had disappeared on 24 April. Initially the police had wrongly thought his disappearance related to an involvement with the IRA. His body was found in a basement in Earl's Court.

Lupo, a 34-year-old Italian from Bologna, was the son of a bricklayer. He developed his homosexual practices during his period of national service in the army. He came to England in his early twenties in 1977, acquiring a conviction for gross indecency in March 1977. He was fined £40. He probably trained as a hairdresser and, a most personable young man, soon developed contacts in the retail fashion world working first for Yves St Laurent and then a fashionable Knightsbridge boutique. He had left this job in 1984 and from then on took a series of less well-paid jobs.

By night, however, he was earning good money. As Rudi the Sado-Masochist, working as a prostitute and frequenting the gay bars and clubs of central and west London, he was charging up to £100 a session in his home in South Kensington which he had fitted out as a torture chamber. He boasted that he had had over four thousand lovers, both male and female. Shortly before the killings he proposed to a girl he met when he went riding in Hyde Park.

His first killing came shortly after he was diagnosed as having full-blown AIDS and one theory is that the killings, for which Lupo showed no remorse, were a revenge on the homosexual community. There was, however, another side to him. He was well liked in society and at the time of his arrest he was living in Chelsea, looking after an elderly Italian lady. He died in prison of the AIDS virus in early 1995.

Tim Tate and Ray Wyre, *Murder Squad*.

6 April, 1934

By the time they killed Constable Calvin Campbell in Commerce, north-east Oklahoma, on 6 April 1934, Clyde Barrow and Bonnie Parker had only seven weeks to live. Campbell and the Chief of Miami [Oklahoma] police, Percy Boyd, were shot as they approached the Barrow car parked in a country road. The pair had been seen in Commerce when they were spotted in town just before dawn and again around 9 am. They were seen to leave the town at about midday and drive towards Miami. It had been raining heavily and the roads were like quagmires. Outside Commerce Barrow stuck in a mudbank and he and Henry Methvin who was with them tried to hijack a passing car. They were unsuccessful and the motorist reported the incident when he reached Miami.

Boyd and Campbell drove out to the scene where by now Barrow had freed the car. Seeing the police approach he tried to drive away but once more stuck in the mud. As the police approached he shot them twice. A passing truck driver was then made to hook up his truck to the car to haul it out of the mud. Campbell died, whilst Boyd was wounded in the head and then taken hostage for 24 hours as Barrow, Parker and Methvin drove into Kansas. The officer was released in Fort Scott.

After his release Boyd was able to give a good deal of information about the trio and Barrow and Parker were tracked through Texas and into Louisiana where on 23 May they were killed in an ambush outside Arcadia. It is estimated that thirty thousand people trooped past Barrow's coffin as it lay in the funeral parlour and forty thousand visited that of Bonnie Parker.

Between them Barrow and Parker killed between nine and thirteen people as they toured the Depression States, robbing banks and small stores. They had met when Barrow went to Dallas in January 1930 to see a friend who had broken her arm in a fall on icy steps. Parker was staying with her. When he was imprisoned for a burglary in Waco, Texas, Parker passed him a gun which enabled him to escape. He was recaptured and served 20 months on the prison farm at Eastham, known for its brutality, before he was pardoned. From then, apart from a sentence of three months served by Bonnie Parker for the theft of a car, they were inseparable. Together with Barrow's elder brother, Buck, his wife Blanche, and a number of other robbers they toured the Depression-hit States robbing banks. Their relationship was an odd one. Barrow is thought to have been homosexual and Parker nymphomaniac. At least one of the men with whom they worked was the sexual partner of both.

Buck Barrow was killed and Blanche Barrow was wounded by a posse in Dexter, Iowa, whilst the gang was hiding in the deserted fairgrounds in July 1933. Later Blanche Barrow served 15 years for her part in the robberies and Methvin was sentenced to death for the killing of Campbell. He was reprieved on the grounds that the shots had been fired by Barrow and paroled after 10 years. He ran a restaurant in Minden, Louisiana until after the Second World War. He was killed when he was struck by a freight train.

E.R. Milner, *The Lives and Times of Bonnie & Clyde*; John Treherne, *The Strange History of Bonnie and Clyde*.

7 April, 1964

Two minor criminals, Peter Anthony Allen and Gwynne Owen Evans, young dairymen from Preston, Lancashire, were executed on 13 August 1964 for the murder of John Alan West on 7 April that year. They were the last men to be hanged in England.

The murder had been committed in the drab mining town of Workington. West, who worked for the local laundry, lived in a semi-detached house in Seaton, one of the suburbs. He was killed – hit by a poker and stabbed – in a robbery which went wrong and in which Evans left behind his macintosh together with a Royal Life Saving Society medallion bearing his name and initials.

Apparently Evans had known West for around five years. At the time of the murder Evans had been living with Allen and his family and they were behind with the rent and rates. They had also been on a small crime spree together, committing a series of shop-breakings and other thefts for which they were fined by Preston Borough Magistrates. It seems they committed their murder, in part, to pay their £10 fines. Evans told Allen that West had money lying around and they drove to Workington. Evans went in to see West in the early hours of the morning and in turn he let Allen in about 3 am. Each blamed the other for hitting West with an iron bar and the jury convicted both after a retirement of three and a quarter hours. It cannot have helped the men's case when it was revealed that Mrs Allen had been 'more than a landlady' to Evans.

Their appeals and applications for a reprieve were refused. The letters signing their death warrants were sent on Tuesday 11 August, the Permanent Under-Secretary of State at the Home Office saying, 'It seems kinder to let the prisoners go on hoping until the last possible moment.' Allen was hanged at Walton, Liverpool and Evans at Strangeways, Manchester. At the last meeting Allen had with his wife he 'went berserk, really berserk. He was strong, you know, and the glass in there, they say it's supposed to be bullet-proof, but he smashed it. He went berserk', said Mary Allen.

Elwyn Jones, *The Last Two to Hang*.

8 April, 1972

It was not until February 1995 that the circumstances surrounding the death of Roderick Mayes at The Boulevard, Weston-Super-Mare were revealed. His mother Joy Mayes had worked as a waitress and cleaner to educate her sons. Sean went to Trinity College, Cambridge and Roderick to college in Weston. She had always feared that her 23-year-old son Roderick would kill himself with his continued use of LSD. On 8 April 1972, to prevent what she believed would be a long and painful death, she dissolved a handful of sleeping pills in a mug of cocoa as he lay in bed. After he became unconscious she then fractured his skull with an iron bootscraper and cut his throat.

Some days later she told her son Sean and her father, Commander Thomas Thompson OBE, what she had done. Sean, a member of the rock band Fumble, had been on tour in Switzerland when his brother was killed. On his return he said he wanted his brother to have a decent burial and he and his grandfather helped take the body which she had hidden under the bed, wrapped it in a candlewick bedspread and plastic sheeting and placed it in a shallow grave in the back garden. Friends were told that Roderick had gone to live with hippies.

Commander Thompson died in 1975 aged 83 and Mrs Mayes in 1992. It was not until Sean, himself dying of AIDS, told the police what had happened that his brother's body was discovered. Because of the plastic sheet it was well preserved and dental records were able to confirm the identity. Death had resulted from the blows to the head and the coroner recorded a verdict of unlawful killing. No charges were brought against Sean Mayes. It was not regarded as being in the public interest to prosecute him.

The Commander had left a diary with entries which would appear to relate to the killing. On 12 April he wrote 'Terrific operation' which was believed to relate to the burial. Another entry said 'Such a relief with R and friends not popping in and out.'

9 April, 1986

The body of Nancy Emms was found on 9 April 1986, laid out as if for burial in her basement room in Wandsworth. The 48-year-old widow had been sexually assaulted and strangled. She was the first identified victim of Keith Erskine, the so-called Stockwell Strangler.

Other killings followed in quick succession: 68-year-old Jane Cockett on 9 June, 84-year-old Valentine Gleim and his friend 94-year-old Zbigniew Strabava on 28 June. Both men had been strangled and Gleim had been sexually assaulted. On 8 July William Carman, in his eighties, was found with his hands crossed over his chest and his bedclothes neatly tucked up. On 20 July William Downes was killed in south London and two days later Florence Tisdall was murdered in Putney.

Palm prints found on a wall and gate at the home of William Downes were matched to 24-year-old Keith Erskine, a semi-vagrant burglar of little ability. He had been in and out of the prison system and, with the mental capacity of an 11-year-old, he had been sent to schools for maladjusted children.

He was arrested when he went to collect his social security cheque in Southwark. Questioned by the police, at first he said he did not remember killing anyone but later he described how he suffocated his victims. He was charged with seven murders and one attempted murder, and was identified by the victim who survived. Erskine was sentenced to life imprisonment with a recommendation that he serve at least 40 years.

In 1996 it was reported that whilst in Broadmoor Erskine had saved Peter Sutcliffe, the Yorkshire Ripper, from an attack by another inmate who said that he resented being in the same place as sex offenders.

10 April, 1995

The killer of Janet Brown smashed through a patio window of her remote, 18th-century home Hall Farm, Radnadge near High Wycombe, Buckinghamshire. He

appears then to have been disturbed by Mrs Brown, the
wife of a research scientist who was in Switzerland at the
time. Her naked, handcuffed and gagged body was found
on 10 April 1995 by a builder called in to undertake
roofing repairs. Her head had been repeatedly battered.
She had probably sustained 10 blows from some sort of
a bar. The keys to the handcuffs were found under her
body. The television and video had been unplugged but
nothing had been stolen.

A reward of £10,000 produced no result and the belief
is that this was not a professional killing but rather
one committed by someone who knew the locality and
possibly Mrs Brown.

11 April, 1994

After drinking in a public house on 11 April 1994,
23-year-old Milton Wheeler, who had fallen out with
his opposite neighbours, an elderly and devout Hindu
couple, Madhavi and Raliat Ambasna aged 82 and 72
respectively, rang the doorbell of their flat in Hounslow,
Middlesex. Mrs Ambasna answered and was promptly
attacked by Wheeler with a Stanley knife. Her semi-
crippled husband came to her aid and in turn he was
attacked. Both were repeatedly stabbed. Their bodies were
sexually mutilated and Wheeler made off with jewellery
and cash.

That evening, when he went to buy some fish and chips,
he met two teenage girls who were sheltering from a gang
of youths. When he left the shop they followed him,
hoping he would protect them. He invited them to shelter
in a friend's flat and when they were inside locked the door
and raped the 14-year-old whilst the elder girl watched.
He then forced them to commit a sexual act with each
other. At knifepoint he took them back to his girlfriend's

flat, and later marched them naked across the corridor into the Ambasnas' flat, tying them up and making them lie on the beds there. He then bit them so hard that he left identifiable teethmarks. The 14-year-old girl managed to wriggle free and summon help.

Wheeler's plea of manslaughter on the ground of diminished responsibility was accepted at the Old Bailey on 27 February 1995. The next day the court heard that Wheeler had been convicted of attempted rape in 1988 and as a child he had been abused by both his father and brother. His father, Russell Gainford, a coalman, had served 15 years for murdering 79-year-old Gladys Bryant. The court was told that he had slashed his diminutive victim across the throat. Wheeler's elder brother also had convictions for a sexual offence.

In an exclusive interview with *Today* newspaper Gainford said, 'I don't know how or why but there seems to be a sort of bizarre competitive spirit in them [his sons] in which they seem to want to outdo me and each other. I know some people will say Milton has a rotten element in his genes and that he was bound to kill. I can't argue with that.'

12 April, 1932

The inquiry by the Bedfordshire Constabulary into the murder of Ruby Keen, found strangled with her own scarf on 12 April 1932 at The Firs near her home at Leighton Buzzard, was complicated by the fact that two police officers, one the girl's fiancé, were involved in the case. The other officer was a suspect. Scotland Yard was called in and Chief Inspector Barker who had arrested Frederick Browne, one of the killers of PC Gutteridge, eight years or so earlier, took charge of the investigation.

Ruby Keen was a good-looking girl of 23 who worked

in a factory in Dunstable. Although engaged to a police constable she was quite prepared to go out with other men including the second constable and a Leslie Stone. When he was questioned Stone admitted he had been out drinking with Ruby that evening but said he had left her outside the Stag Hotel at about 10.15 pm.

There had been no sexual attack on Ruby Keen but she had first been hit on the jaw before being strangled and Barker believed she had been trying to protect herself from rape when she died. Although attempts had been made to clean it, the forensic scientist, Sir Bernard Spilsbury, found traces of sand in Stone's new blue serge suit. It was identical to the soil at The Firs. Silk from Ruby's dress matched threads on Stone's jacket.

Stone was unable to explain how the girl's clothing had been torn from her body. He did admit he had been with her at The Firs and said he had quarrelled with the girl who had struck him. 'I caught hold of her scarf, I think, and pulled it. I think I knotted it again after that. I was in a kind of a rage.'

The jury sent in a question to Lord Hewart. 'If as a result of an intention to commit a rape a girl is killed – although there was no intention to kill her – is a man guilty of murder?' Hewart answered this tersely: 'Yes, undoubtedly.' The Court of Appeal held the answer to be a perfectly adequate one. Stone was hanged on 13 August 1932. Before the trial Ruby Keen's fiancé was, perhaps unfairly, required to resign. His colleague, who was also the recipient of Miss Keen's affections, was dismissed.

E. Spencer Shew, *A Companion to Murder*; Douglas G. Browne and Tom Tullett, *Bernard Spilsbury, His Life and Cases*.

13 April, 1905

The police opened an airtight trunk in a warehouse at Kensal Rise on 13 April 1905. In it were the bodies of Beatrice Maud Devereux and her twin sons Lawrence Rowland and Evelyn Lancelot. They had been poisoned with salts of morphine. The police had been alerted by Mrs Devereux's mother, Mrs Gregory.

Arthur Devereux, a chemist's assistant from Hastings, had deposited the trunk in the warehouse three months earlier. His defence to a charge of murder was that he kept the poison on his writing desk in case he ever felt the need to commit suicide rather than face starvation. He returned home one day in January to find the poison missing and his family dead. He concluded that his wife, with whom he was on particularly bad terms, had done away with herself and her sons. Because of the bad relations he had with his mother-in-law, Mrs Gregory, he feared she would blame him for their deaths and so he built the trunk and coated it with glue mixed with boric acid to prevent the smell of decomposition escaping. He then took the remaining child of the family, Stanley, and went to live in another part of London where Mrs Gregory traced them. She was not satisfied with his explanation that they had left him and went to Scotland Yard. Meanwhile Devereux had moved to Coventry. When questioned by the police his opening remark was, 'You have made a mistake. I don't know anything about a tin trunk!'

His defence at the Central Criminal Court in July 1905 was complicated by the evidence of a clergyman who suggested mental instability on the part of Devereux. He had, for a time, posed as an American millionaire in Malvern. He had also passed himself off as a widower before the bodies were found. There was medical evidence that he was a man of weak intellect but it did him no good.

He was hanged by Henry Pierrepoint at Pentonville prison on 15 August 1905.

14 April, 1953

Louisa Merrifield, aged 46, and her 70-year-old husband Albert were charged with the murder of Sarah Ricketts who died on 14 April 1953. They had been employed for little over a month as live-in housekeepers for the elderly widow who lived in a three-roomed bungalow in Devonshire Road, North Shore, Blackpool. They had led a fairly rackety life and over the preceding 20 years they had undertaken various caretaking and domestic jobs in the Blackpool area. By this time all their worldly possessions could be packed into five suitcases.

On 24 March Mrs Merrifield went to a local firm of solicitors with instructions to them to draw Mrs Ricketts' will in her favour. Shortly afterwards she was back at the solicitors. Now she and Albert were to share equally. Mrs Ricketts signed her will, and with it her death warrant, on 31 March. Mrs Merrifield was ecstatic, telling people that she had been left the bungalow. She began to make enquiries about raising a mortgage and starting a nursing home. However, she clearly began to worry about counter-attacks from Mrs Ricketts' relatives for she tried to persuade a Dr Yule to examine her employer to confirm her testamentary capacity. Mrs Ricketts sent him away.

On 12 April Mrs Merrifield rather prematurely announced the death of her employer, telling a friend she had to lay the old lady out. She was not, she said, quite dead but it would not be long. The next day she called on another doctor, Dr Wood, to see Mrs Ricketts and he found her to be in good health. On 14 April at 2 pm she called in Dr Wood again. Mrs Ricketts was dead.

Neither of the doctors would sign a death certificate and Dr Yule called the police. The postmortem showed that Sarah Ricketts had been poisoned by phosphorus, used in rat poison. A spoon was found in her handbag but tests showed it had been cleaned. The prosecution would later make the point that if Mrs Ricketts' death had been by accident or suicide there would have been no need to clean the spoon. Mrs Merrifield was arrested and a fortnight later so was her husband.

Medical evidence for the defence was that, far from being poisoned, she had died from necrosis of the liver; the phosphorus had not had time to act. Mrs Merrifield, a short and dumpy woman, was confident of an acquittal, telling her fellow remand prisoners that she would not be coming back. Each night her hair was curled by other prisoners. However, she made a poor showing in the witness box. Her evidence was a mixture of sentiment and coarse language and she was convicted. The jury could not agree about her husband and the Attorney General decided not to seek a retrial.

Mrs Merrifield, convicted because of her boasting, was hanged on 18 September 1953. Albert continued to live in the bungalow, fighting a legal battle for some three years when he received one-sixth of the value of the property in return for leaving. He then appeared in a sideshow on Blackpool's Golden Mile, living in a caravan and being billed as 'The Murderess's Husband'. He appears not to have regretted the passing of his wife. He told crime writer Richard Whittington-Egan that 'The old bugger would have had me next'. He died, aged 80, on 24 June 1962.

15 April, 1920

One of the great trials in American criminal and social history followed the killing on 15 April 1920 of Frederick

Permenter, the paymaster of a shoe factory in South Braintree, Massachusetts, and Alessandro Bernardelli, his guard, when the payroll of $15,776 was stolen. There had been a similar attack in nearby Bridgewater on the White Shoe factory on the morning of 24 December 1919.

At about 3.05 pm Permenter and Bernardelli were shot as they carried the money in two metal boxes across the street. Two strangers snatched the money and jumped into a car in which three others were waiting. Bernardelli died on the street. Parmenter survived for some 14 hours. One bullet had penetrated his vena cava, the largest vein in the body. When it was extracted it was marked with a white cross. A bullet from the lung of Bernardelli which had slightly flattened as it hit the hipbone was marked with III in Roman numerals. All the cartridges found were manufactured by either Peters, Remington or Winchester.

It was a time of great social unrest. The Wobblies, the Industrial Workers of the World, were at their height, struggling for proper pay and working conditions. It was also a period of anarchy of which the central tenet was that social justice could only be achieved by the violent overthrow of government. Bombs had been sent to senators and millionaires such as John D. Rockefeller. On 7 November 1919 a bomb had exploded in front of the Washington home of the Attorney General, A. Mitchell Palmer. The Government struck back; arrests and deportations were plentiful.

Two days after the robbery, on 17 April, an abandoned Buick was found in a wooded area of Massachusetts. It fitted the description of the car used in the hold-up. The police learned that an Italian named Boda had been seen in the Buick. Watch was kept on a garage where he kept an overland car. When the police swooped Boda and a companion escaped on a motorcycle. Boda would eventually reach the safety of Italy. The two who were caught were Nicola Sacco and Bartolomeo Vanzetti.

Unfortunately for them they denied they knew Boda. Sacco was carrying a loaded .32 Colt automatic and

in his pockets were 23 .32 cartridges manufactured by
the firms of Peters, Remington and Winchester. Vanzetti
had a .38 Harrington & Richardson revolver with five
cartridges and four shotgun cases. Both lied consistently
throughout their first interviews.

At the time of his arrest Sacco, who had been born in
southern Italy on 22 April 1892 and had come to the
United States in 1908, was working in a shoe factory.
Vanzetti, born on 11 June 1888 near Turin, had been a
pastry-cook before coming to America after his mother
died, also in 1908. He had a cart from which he sold
fish. There is no doubt that both were active in anarchist
circles but Sacco had a cast-iron alibi for the Bridgewater
robbery. Vanzetti was picked out and charged. They
were both charged with robbery and murder following
the South Braintree pay snatch.

The trial of Vanzetti began in June 1920 and of the
pair for murder in May 1921. As is often the case, the
trial was muddied by politics. They might have done
better to have simply run their defence on the basis of
mistaken identity. Instead the anarchists supporting them
saw the trial as an opportunity to 'unmask the criminal
nature of the American Government'. A radical lawyer
from California, Fred H. Moore, was brought in for the
defence.

It is now accepted that whether or not Sacco and
Vanzetti were actually guilty the prosecution evidence
was flawed and fabricated and at best the trial judge
Webster Thayer may not have been wholly impartial.
He was later admonished for making rash public – at
his golf club – comments after the trial. The prosecution's
ballistics expert Captain William Proctor claimed that the
bullet marked III had been fired by Sacco's Colt. He had
previously tried to push a bullet through the pistol and
had failed to do so saying it was not necessary. A second
expert said that he was inclined to believe III had come
from the Colt. Two witnesses called for the defence said
that III could never have been fired. Both the defence
experts had years of expertise in armaments. Neither of

the prosecution experts could distinguish between types of weapons.

On 14 July the jury retired and after five hours convicted both men. Moore, the defence lawyer, continued to challenge the convictions and lost two motions for a retrial. Unfortunately he then latched on to Dr Albert Hamilton who had previously been discredited in the case of Charles Stielow (see 22 March). In his efforts to clear his clients and establish himself as the finest ballistics expert of the time Dr Hamilton tried to switch the exhibit with a gun he had brought into court. He was seen by the judge. A motion for a new trial was refused.

Sacco and Vanzetti died in the electric chair on 23 August 1927. Sacco cried, 'Long live anarchy!' Vanzetti said, 'I am an innocent man.' The executions were marked by worldwide demonstrations. Socialist and Communist newspapers appeared with black borders; millions paraded through city streets. Meanwhile Judge Webster Thayer's home had been fire-bombed and his wife and maid injured.

In 1961 two experts re-examined Sacco's gun and were convinced that bullet III had come from it.

The best view of the case, and the one of newspaper editor Carlo Tresca, who did so much to help the defence of his fellow anarchists, was that Sacco was guilty and Vanzetti was not. One thing is certain and it is that at the time of their arrest these men of peace, as they portrayed themselves, were armed to the teeth, something they were never able to explain satisfactorily. Of course that does not mean they were guilty of the robberies and murders. In any event they were both pardoned in 1977 by Governor Dukakis.

It has been suggested that the South Braintree robbery was staged by the Morelli gang. On 18 November 1925, Celestino Maderios, already on death row for another murder, confessed to the crime but declined to name his colleagues. His confession was rejected and he was executed on 23 August 1927, the same night as Sacco and Vanzetti. According to Mafia defector Vinnie Teresa,

Frank Morelli told him in the 1950s, 'We whacked them out, we killed those guys in the robbery. Those two greaseballs took it on the chin.'

Vincent Teresa and T. C. Renner, *My Life in the Mafia*; Jurgen Thorwald, *The Marks of Cain*.

16 April, 1984

The fire occurred in Glasgow at 2 am on 16 April 1984, the night, as many of the witnesses recalled over the years, Tommy Cooper the comedian died on television. As a result of the fire, Christine Halleron, Anthony Doyle aged 14, Mark Halleron aged 18 months, James Doyle junior, Andrew Doyle and James Doyle died. Stephen Doyle jumped with his dog from a window, Lilian Doyle was rescued from a window ledge. Daniel Doyle survived when he managed to get his head out of a broken window and so avoided inhaling the gases.

There were two possible eyewitnesses to the fire-raisers. One, John Whitefield, described four young fellows aged 15 to 16 running past him, and another said he thought he might recognise the men involved. Neither was asked to stand on an identification parade.

At first the police considered whether the fire might have been started because of the Doyle brothers' work in the nightclubs where they were thought to have upset punters. However, slowly but surely they hardened on the theory that it was to do with the Glasgow ice-cream wars, the struggle which had been going on throughout the early 1980s between rival groups of mobile ice-cream salesmen. They came to this conclusion in part because as Andrew Doyle lay in the ambulance in Bankend Street he said to a police officer, 'I told you the bastards would torch me. If this is because of the ice-cream hassle I'll get the bastards.' Apparently, on an earlier occasion he had said to the same policeman, 'Look, they've battered me, shot me, all I'm waiting on now is the petrol bomb.' The officer duly reported the second conversation to a superior.

The first man arrested who confessed was Joe Grainger who admitted that he, Thomas Campbell and others had been keeping clock, or lookout, whilst Joseph Steele and others actually started the fire. He retracted his evidence at the trial and as a result served five years for his pains and perjury. He appealed successfully to the European Court of Human Rights which ruled that he had not had a fair trial, but the Scottish Office took no action. The second plank of evidence on which the prosecution would base its case was that of Billy Love who said he had been in the Netherfield bar when Thomas Campbell had asked for volunteers to firebomb the Doyle household. Steele had been with them.

The other evidence against Steele and Campbell amounted to little more than one sentence of verbal admissions. Campbell was alleged to have said that he intended the fire only to be a frightener whilst Steele had said it wasn't he who had lit the match. A further piece of supporting evidence was the finding of a map in a briefcase belonging to Campbell which circled Bankend Street and marked the Doyle flat with a cross. Steele and Campbell's defence lawyers point out there was no need for their clients to have such a map. They both lived in the area and knew it like the backs of their hands. Steele's alibi was that he was home in bed with the 'flu. His mother was his witness. Campbell said he had been watching a video with his wife, Liz. Both men were convicted. Campbell received a life sentence with a recommendation that he serve at least 20 years. Steele's sentence carried no recommendation.

After the trial the press had a field day. After all, here were two men both of whose families had been involved in heavy gang crime in Glasgow for years. There were suggestions that instead of raspberry ripple in the ice-cream cones there had been heroin at £10 a bag, something which had not been mentioned at the trial. It is a claim which Campbell fervently denies. The fighting between Fifti Ices and Marchetti did not end with the convictions. There were even allegations, again denied, that Campbell was controlling things from his cell.

Since the trial there have been persistent attempts to reopen the case. Billy Love has from time to time changed his story back and forth. In the latest version, made to a BBC journalist in 1993 on his release from Dartmoor, he said, 'I couldn't even ask Thomas Campbell or Joe Steele to forgive me for what they've been through. I know I've shortened their lives.' Campbell said he would neither shave nor cut his hair until his release. Filmed in Barlinnie prison he spoke bitterly of the Serious Crime Squad which he called the Serious Fit-Up Squad. 'They're called in to assess of all villains in the area who has the least defence. Then if they've no alibi or only one witness they'll do.' Steele escaped three times, once glueing himself to the railings at Buckingham Palace. On his last escape on 25 May 1993 he spoke to a BBC reporter, saying that although he was now nearly eligible for parole he would not apply. 'Only guilty men take parole.' He surrendered by climbing a scaffolding tower in front of the prison, staying there for an hour to be filmed by the press.

It was thought the chances of either Campbell or Steele winning their hoped-for retrial were slim. Two of the senior officers in the case were dead. One committed suicide shortly after the case. All they could hope for was a pardon or that the case would be referred back to the Court of Appeal. One of the defence counsel in the case who referred to the evidence brought against the men as 'rotten to the core' is now an Appeal Court judge and the men and their supporters hope he will somehow intervene on their behalf. One difficulty regarding Love's retraction is, as a Scots lawyer put it, 'Technically it is not what the Appeal Court would base any decision on. They have said before they will not entertain an appeal merely because a witness changes his story.'

Then in December 1996 the men were released on bail pending an appeal and this encouraging sign seemed to indicate their appeals would be allowed. This was not the case. The Court said there was not a reasonable explanation for the change in Love's evidence and no independent support. Their appeals were dated 10 February 1998 and they were returned to prison.

Douglas Skelton and L. Brownlie, *Frightener*.

17 April, 1958

Shortly after midnight on the night of 17 April 1958 a call was made to Scotland Yard from a telephone box in the London area: 'You had better get this down right first time. I am not going to repeat it. We broke into a mill house near Chelmsford and tied an old lady up. You had better release her.'

The Essex police were alerted but, by the time they found her, 83-year-old Susan Southgate was dead. She had been bound and gagged with electric flex and was sitting in her favourite leather armchair in her cottage in Writtle, near Chelmsford.

She was known locally as a wealthy lady who would pay bills from a roll of £50 notes and, living alone, was an easy target. The thieves had however missed £5,000 in coins.

There were some clues. Found in the house were a chisel and two reels of insulating tape stamped with the words FOOTPRINT, ENGLAND. There had been a sighting of a black Humber saloon at about 10.45 pm that night. A dark-haired man had also been seen in the village on consecutive nights during the week. He was described as having nicotined fingers and black oily hair. He had called in the Cock and Bell, the village public house, and had a couple of beers each evening that week, but he had not been seen since the Thursday.

The gang who attacked Susan Southgate was also suspected of another tie-up robbery, that of an elderly farmer who lived about 15 miles away. No one was ever charged with the killing.

18 April, 1991

The killing by David Teed of Dawn Chwartacki in her basement flat in Abbotsford, British Columbia on 18 April 1991 was itself unremarkable – two months later he confessed to bludgeoning her to death and in November was sentenced to life imprisonment for first-degree murder.

What was more interesting was that whilst he was in custody he told prison guards on 9 July he 'was guilty of two murders' and wanted to get them off his chest. When he was questioned by police officers he said the other victim was a Dr Carolyn Warrick whose body had been found in the underground car park of a luxury high-rise condominium at Bay Street, Toronto on 27 January that year.

In a later interview he gave fairly graphic details of how he killed her in the presence of two other men. He had met her at the lift and had smashed her head into the wall. Once he had done this the other men ran away. By this time Thomas Clancey and Craig Kimberley had been arrested for the murder.

Teed, who said he had been very drunk at the time, described how he '. . . kicked her at least a hundred times on the head. Her jaw was on the other side of her head . . . I can't believe no one saw me because I was there three, four, maybe five minutes stomping on her throat as hard as I could. I heard bones breaking like sticks.'

It was decided not to charge him but to call him as a Crown witness at the preliminary hearings against Clancey and Kimberley. Teed then gave a variety of versions of the murder. He said he had committed the murder or that he might have done it, that he had learned all the details from the police and a friend, and finally that he had been a witness and Clancey was the killer. On Christmas Day 1991 he hanged himself in his cell.

At the trial of Clancey and Kimberley in 1995 the trial judge, Mr Justice Watt, refused a defence application to have the confession and other related remarks made by Teed put before the jury who never heard that he had confessed.

The prosecution's case was that Dr Warrick had been held down and stamped on after she had fought off a handbag snatch. The bruising patterns on her body were said to be consistent with two types of footwear. The reason for the attack was said to be the men's cocaine habit.

Much of the evidence against the men came from Todd Vermillion, Clancey's AIDS-stricken lover. He told the trial he was with Clancey and Kimberley before and after the killing of Dr Warrick but had stayed outside whilst the pair went into the car park to steal from cars. Vermillion told the court that Clancey had returned from the building with a woman's purse – Dr Warrick's was never recovered – and said he had 'bitch slapped' the owner and knocked her silly. Kimberley agreed with much of Vermillion's evidence, saying that they had indeed separated and when Clancey had come from the building holding the purse he said, 'You don't want to see what's happened. Let's get out of here.'

Clancey had told the police he was not in Toronto at the time of the killing but gave several explanations of his whereabouts. At the trial he did not give evidence but in effect called an alibi. Both Clancey and Kimberley were found guilty.

An appeal was being lodged on the grounds that the judge should not have excluded the Teed evidence. There is a handwritten note on the Matsui police file regarding Teed's potential evidence. Teed wrote, 'If you stand back and let those two innocent guys go down, you're as guilty as I am.'

19 April, 1973

On 19 April 1973 a body was recovered from Shoreham Harbour, Sussex. Its legs had been tied to weights. It was that of Clive Olive, a one-time member of the Mad Dogs Chapter of the Hell's Angels (Brighton). The Mad Dogs did not have bikes of their own and were the equivalent of a sort of beagle pack. Olive had been reported missing a few weeks earlier on 2 March.

Olive had been killed because in September 1972 he had raped Karen Fielding [not her real name] on her 16th birthday. She later became Brian 'Angus' Moore's girlfriend and when he asked if she had her white wings, meaning virginity, she told him that she had been raped in Olive's bedroom whilst his mother was out. 'He seemed unable to put it out of his mind,' she told the court. On 27 February 1973 Moore told Karen that Olive had to be killed.

Together with his brother-in-law Albert Dorn, whose wife Christine was also in the van, Moore had gone in search of Olive. A fight had broken out and Moore had hit Olive with a truncheon and then thrown him into the harbour where he had drowned. There was no suggestion that Christine Dorn had participated in the beating.

Moore's defence at the trial was that of diminished responsibility. He had taken LSD in such quantities and over such a period of time that his brain might have been damaged. Albert and Christine Dorn's defence was that Moore was in such a frightful rage that they feared for their safety if they did not go with him. The men were convicted of murder and sentenced to life imprisonment. Mr Justice Thesiger said he doubted that the Home Secretary would ever release Moore.

Christine was convicted of manslaughter and sentenced to 10 years' imprisonment. Her conviction was quashed on appeal. The trial judge had told the jury that they could convict her if they found that, believing Clive Olive to be dead, she had encouraged or assisted the others in the disposal of the body. The Court of Appeal said it was apparent that she had not helped in this way.

Jim Marshall, *The True Story of the Ollie Murder.*

20 April, 1907

Richard Brinkley had no intention of killing Richard Beck and his wife on 20 April 1907. Unfortunately his victims drank from the wrong bottle at the wrong time. Brinkley, a jobbing carpenter, had embarked on a long-term plan to ensure himself a modest fortune. He made friends with Johanna Maria Blume, a German widow, who lived with her daughter in her own house in Fulham. She also had capital of £800. He arranged that the widow should make a will in his favour. His problem was having it signed.

To overcome this he proposed a seaside trip and asked if Mrs Blume wished to put her name down for it. He folded the will so that she would sign without seeing the contents. The witnesses to the will, including a Mr Parker, he deceived in a similar way. Two days later Mrs Blume died and, at the inquest, the coroner recorded a verdict of death by natural causes from a cerebral haemorrhage.

On the face of it Brinkley was now in possession of a valid will. Indeed when he presented it to Mrs Blume's daughter she acknowledged that it appeared to be in order. She had the sense, however, to consult a solicitor who entered a caveat. Brinkley now had problems. If the witnesses could be found and shown to have signed the will in error his plans would be undone. He decided to kill them too, beginning with Mr Parker.

On 20 April he went to Parker's lodgings in Croydon on the grounds that he had come to buy a bulldog Parker had for sale. He was solicitous of Parker's health for he left a bottle of oatmeal stout for him. Parker's landlord, Richard Beck, saw it on the table and he, his wife and daughter decided to drink it. His daughter sipped, Mrs Beck did not like the taste and spat it into the fire. Beck swallowed. All three collapsed and Beck and his wife died in convulsions. Their daughter survived. 'Well, I'm sugared,' said Brinkley when he was arrested. 'That's very awkward, isn't it?' Tests after the exhumation of Mrs Blume's body proved negative.

Brinkley was convicted at Lewes Assizes and hanged at Wandsworth prison by Henry Pierrepoint on 13 August 1907.

21 April, 1934

The body of eight-year-old Helen Priestly was found at about 5 am on 21 April 1934 in a sack in the hallway of 61 Urquhart Road, Aberdeen where she lived with her parents on the first floor of a tenement building immediately above Jeannie Donald and her husband, Alexander. The day before, she had come home from school for her lunch and was sent to buy a loaf of bread at the Co-operative shop about a hundred yards away. There is no doubt she bought the bread because the shop had a sales slip. She was never seen alive again.

When she did not return her mother started making enquiries, including asking Jeannie Donald, the daughter of the upstairs neighbour, if she had seen Helen. Jeannie said she had not.

Medical evidence showed that Helen had been sexually interfered with but had not been raped and it was thought that the interference had been carried out with the intention of making the attack appear to be sexual. Although she had been strangled the medical opinion was that the further injuries, inflicted whilst Helen was alive, had made her sick and this had choked her. In the sack were a number of cinders and there was a cinder in her mouth. Through an examination of the contents of her stomach, the meat and potatoes she had eaten around 12.30 pm, the time of her death was put at around 2 pm.

On 25 April the police spent some 13 hours at the Donalds' flat. Mrs Donald said she knew nothing of the death and that after getting some eggs and vegetables at the corner shop she had ironed a number of dresses for her daughter during the afternoon. Mr Donald said he had been at his barber shop. About nine in the evening the police found some stains in a cupboard which could have been blood. When the Donalds were finally arrested they were driven to the police station through a hostile crowd. They were known to have been on bad terms with the Priestlys. The next day a closer examination of the stains showed they were not blood.

Alexander Donald was released about six weeks later on 11 June after the police were unable to break his alibi. Mrs Donald's alibi was less than watertight and it was thought that she had perhaps been describing her visit to the corner shop on another occasion. Sir Sydney Smith, the eminent pathologist, was called in by the Crown and was able to establish a series of pieces of forensic evidence, including blood and hair samples which were found in the sack. The latter matched Mrs Donald's artificial wave.

Because of local ill-feeling Mrs Donald's trial was moved to Edinburgh where the case for the Crown was that Mrs Donald had killed Helen after 'previously evincing malice and ill-will toward her'. There was not much evidence to support this latter claim although Helen had apparently called Mrs Donald 'Coconut' and had been playing the children's game of Knock Down Ginger, ringing the doorbell and running away when she passed the Donalds' flat. Indeed the judge withdrew that part of the allegation from the jury.

Sir Sydney Smith's reconstruction of the case was that Helen had probably made a remark to Mrs Donald to which she took offence. She then grabbed and shook the child who fell, as she thought, dead. She had deliberately molested the child to divert attention away from herself, shoving some instrument into the girl's vagina. The child was not dead and the pain caused her to recover consciousness. She vomited and inhaled some of that vomit. Mrs Donald then strangled Helen and death could have come either from the strangulation or the inhalation.

Mrs Donald's defence was that she knew nothing about the death and she did not give evidence. The opportunity to plead guilty to culpable homicide – roughly the equivalent of manslaughter – was put to her and she declined it. She appears to have maintained a passive indifference to the trial until she collapsed when the verdict of guilty was returned after a retirement by the jury of only 18 minutes. On 6 August, a week before the date set for her execution, she was reprieved and the sentence commuted to one of life imprisonment. She was released on licence on 26 June 1944.

E. Spencer Shew, *A Companion to Murder*; Sir Sydney Smith, *Mostly Murder*.

22 April, 1977

Ian Rosenberg and his friend Joan Lipson, the estranged wife of a Toronto department store executive, were shot in the head in her bedroom, gangland style, at about 2 am on 22 April 1977. Almost a year later 25-year-old James Edward Bass was put on trial for the double killing.

The Crown's case was that the pair had been shot to silence them in relation to the killing of Edmonton teenager Chrystal Van Huuksloot, who had disappeared in Toronto during Thanksgiving weekend 1976. The 18-year-old had come East to try to obtain bail for her boyfriend who had been charged with a drugs offence. She had failed and was in possession of $3,500 in a money belt when she was last seen, driving with Bass away from Rosenberg's apartment.

Bass's defence was that he had been running hashish for Rosenberg the weekend of the killing – driving on his behalf to Barrie – and the jury accepted his explanation. After his acquittal he remained in custody for his own protection. On 24 September 1979 he was sentenced to nine months' imprisonment for the drug-running of hashish he had admitted during his earlier trial.

Had Bass taken the protection of the Canada Evidence Act at the murder trial it would have prevented a charge being brought against him for the drug dealing offence. 'As far as I am concerned, it's a unique case,' said Federal prosecutor Christopher Amerasinghe.

It is more likely that the killing took place because Rosenberg, who worked for Toronto gang leader Paul Viola, had become increasingly unreliable and his death had been ordered in consequence.

James Dubro, *Mob Rule*.

23 April, 1991

On 23 April 1991 at about 7.15 am, 26-year-old Ricardo Thomas and 22-year-old Lisa Johnson were discovered on couches at her home in south-west Philadelphia. Both had been shot in the head. Almost certainly Thomas had been asleep when he was killed. Lisa Johnson survived.

About noon that day, Shawn T. Walker, aged 20, walked into the Eastern Pennsylvania Psychiatric Institute to say he had shot two people that morning. He told doctors that after the shootings he had gone to a relative's medical chest and drunk peroxide and taken 20 pills.

He had also thought about cutting his wrists but had stopped after making a small scratch. His car had been found parked near Ms Johnson's flat.

Walker was the ex-boyfriend of Ms Johnson who had obtained a protection order against him. Thomas, a family friend, often spent the night at her apartment as a protection against Walker.

According to Walker's version of events he had spent the previous day having sex with a willing Johnson and playing with their children. In the evening Johnson had told him she had another boyfriend and not to call any more. At 3.30 am he had gone to her flat, pushed the door open, fought with Thomas and shot him. He then shot his former girlfriend.

Walker was convicted and sentenced to death by lethal injection. Whereas most American States would seek life imprisonment in what would be seen as a domestic killing, it is the practice in Philadelphia to seek the death penalty. 'It was a cold-bloodedly going from one person to another, planned for when the victims were almost defenceless,' said District Attorney Lynne Abraham.

24 April, 1990

Overall, the gang members who carried out the Great Train Robbery of 1963 have not made a great success of their subsequent lives. Apart from renewing swingeing prison sentences many found their share of the haul dissipated and stolen from them whilst on the run or inside. A number have returned to prison on drug dealing or other charges. However, after Charlie Wilson's release from prison in 1978 – he was the last of the Great Train Robbers to be freed – for a time, he led something of a charmed life, at least so far as the courts were concerned. In 1982 he had been one of seven men charged in a £2 million VAT fraud involving the melting down of gold Krugerrands valued at £16 million. Charges against him were dropped when the jury had disagreed twice and he paid a £400,000 penalty to Customs and Excise. In 1984 he spent four months in custody awaiting trial for the alleged armed robbery of a security van. He was freed amidst allegations of police corruption.

On 24 April 1990, however, his luck came to an end when he was shot dead beside his swimming pool at his home in Marbella, Spain. He had been hosing down the pool area in the early evening when his wife, Patricia, answered a knock on the door. A man with a south London accent asked for her husband. She fetched Charlie and he and the young man went off together.

Initially it was reported that Wilson had been killed with a single karate blow but the autopsy showed he had been shot in the side of the neck and the bullet had lodged there. As the shot passed through the larynx it would have caused heavy bleeding and as he inhaled blood he would have been unable to cry out.

The inquest was told that, although there was no direct evidence to link him with drug dealing, there was much circumstantial evidence, such as his lifestyle and his visits to Morocco.

A verdict that he had been shot by persons unknown was recorded. Solicitors acting for the Wilson family issued a statement after the inquest strongly denying any involvement by Wilson in drug dealing.

In a convoluted way his death is said to be linked to that of Paul Adkins. A James Rose had pleaded guilty to drug offences at Chelmsford Crown Court in January 1990, naming Adkins as the leader of the gang. Apparently he had been authorised to say this by Wilson and it was something which, not surprisingly, upset Adkins who had then ordered the execution of Wilson. There was, however, no suggestion that any of Wilson's friends had killed Adkins by way of reprisal. It was an entirely separate matter.

On 28 September 1990, the night of his death, Adkins

had met two Colombians in the Nightwatch bar of the American Hotel in Amsterdam. He had been the middle-man in selling parcels of stolen emeralds in Amsterdam. He had been approached by a Sean O'Neil and several successful runs had been carried out. Then one of the parcels had been stolen from O'Neil and the Colombians wanted their money as a matter of urgency. Adkins persuaded O'Neil to attend a meeting to explain in person what had happened.

According to O'Neil he had gone to the Nightwatch bar and had seen Adkins with the Colombians. Adkins gestured to O'Neil to continue walking. O'Neil had then heard eight gunshots and had run out of the hotel. He had not known Adkins was dead until he read the papers the next day.[1]

In May 1995 the Spanish police were seeking the extradition of Danny Roff who was thought to have been the lookout man in the Wilson killing. On 10 February 1996 he was shot four times in the Passport Club in New Cross, south-east London when a gunman sprayed the crowded bar with bullets. At the time of the Wilson killing he was on the run from a 13-year sentence for robbery. He was later held in Holland and returned to England. After the shooting in the Passport Club Roff was thought to be paralysed for life but, for a time, was able to drive his Mercedes. A senior detective is reported to have said, 'It looks like the debt has finally been collected for Charlie.' (The *Sun*, 13 February 1996.) On 24 March 1997 his attackers made no mistake. He was shot dead in the driveway of his home in Bromley.

---

[1]The evidence of this was given by a Customs and Excise officer. In 1991 O'Neil was acquitted at Isleworth Crown Court of charges relating to £10 million-worth of cocaine. Three Colombian co-accused were sentenced to terms of up to 18 years' imprisonment. Now, although he had previously made a statement, O'Neil could not be found to give evidence in person at Adkins' inquest.

25 April, 1935

On 25 April 1935 a tiger shark which had been captured a week earlier and was then swimming in an
aquarium at Coogee Beach, Sydney, suddenly regurgitated an arm on which was tattooed a pair of boxers.
The limb was eventually identified as belonging to
an ex-boxer, ex-bookie, bankrupt builder and billiard
hall operator, 40-year-old James Smith, who had been
missing for a fortnight. He had been on vacation from
his work with a Sydney boatbuilder, Reg Holmes, and
had rented a cottage with a well-known criminal,
Patrick Brady.

At first it was thought that Smith had committed
suicide. There was no clear evidence that the arm had
been either bitten or cut off and the theory went that
he had roped a weight around himself and jumped into
the sea from a boat. No one could be found who had
seen him go out in a boat and the line of enquiry
changed. Now it was thought that he had gone to a
seaside cottage with another man. A barman identified
Brady as drinking with Smith on the day he was last
seen, 9 April. The cottage was searched and found to
be spotlessly clean but the estate agent who had let the
premises said that he thought a large tin trunk had been
replaced by a smaller one.

Brady was interviewed and denied killing Smith, implicating the employer, Holmes, in forgery dealings. Holmes,
when questioned, denied knowing Brady and also challenged him face to face. Now Brady said that Smith had
left the cottage on 9 April with two men, one of whom was
Holmes. Three days after the police interviews, and after a
high-speed chase in a speedboat around Sydney harbour,
Holmes was arrested and found to have a gunshot wound
in the head. The police believed it was a suicide attempt
but Holmes claimed an attempt had been made to kill

him. Now he said that Brady had indeed killed Smith
and disposed of the body. Holmes was taken under guard
to Sydney hospital where he remained for four days. An
inquest was held into Smith's death and 39 witnesses were
called before an application was made to the Supreme
Court to stay the proceedings on the grounds that there
was no body. The Court agreed.

Brady was now charged with Smith's murder, for which
Holmes would have been a prime witness had he not been
found shot dead in his car, so giving some credence to
his story that he had been shot previously. The car was
parked under the Sydney Harbour Bridge in Dawes Park
and it was thought he had been killed by his passenger at
the moment a train passed overhead. Two men charged
with Holmes's killing were acquitted, as was Brady of
the murder of Smith. His counsel argued that since there
was no body it was impossible to be sure that Smith was
dead.[1] There is no doubt they were involved together
in drug dealing. All were acquitted. Brady died in a
veterans' hospital in 1965, maintaining his innocence and
suggesting the arm had bullet wounds, although how he
could know was never made clear by him. The better view
of the case is that whilst he was a talented forger he was
never a murderer. On 30 October 1952 Holmes's widow
died in a blaze which destroyed her house. The cause was
never discovered.

The English pathologist, Sir Sydney Smith, who was
holidaying in Australia at the time and who was invited
to look at the arm, concluded that James Smith had been
killed and his body placed in a tin trunk. He believed
that the arm would not fit into the trunk and so it
was roped to the outside. The trunk was dumped at
sea but the arm worked loose and was swallowed by
the shark. The beast died in captivity and on dissection
was found to have no other pieces of body in its stomach,

---

[1]At one time it was thought that in law there could be no conviction
for murder without a body. However, over the past century there have
been a number of cases where no body has been found but which have,
nevertheless, resulted in a conviction.

something which undoubtedly supported the pathologist's theory.

Alan Sharpe, *Crimes that Shocked Australia*; Sir Sydney Smith, *Mostly Murder*.

26 April, 1991

The body of prostitute Cherie Payseur was found on 26 April 1991. She was one of up to 20 prostitutes, most of them drug abusers, whom a warehouse clerk, William Lester Suff, was found guilty of killing, in and around Riverside, Southern California between 1989 and 1991. Most of his victims were strangled but some were also stabbed and sexually mutilated. He then dressed some of the bodies in his clothes and dumped them in the citrus groves and along lonely roads in rural Riverside County.

Known as the Lake Elsinore Killer, Suff was arrested in January 1992 when he was seen pulling up next to a suspected prostitute and then making an illegal U-turn as he drove away. At the time of his arrest he was in violation of his parole in Texas where he had served 10 years of a 70-year sentence for the killing, along with his wife Teryl Rose, of his two-month-old daughter. Initially he was remanded for extradition to Texas. Later his van was examined and forensically linked to two murders: that of Catherine McDonald, his 17th victim, killed on 13 December 1991, and Eleanor Casares, the last. Her body had been found in an orange grove on 23 December 1991.

Like many serial murderers who kill within the vicinity of their homes, Suff, a 41-year-old stock clerk at the time of his arrest, was never a suspect for the killings. A co-worker said of him, 'He was a friendly nerd who was always buying little gifts and doing things to help people.'

Suff wept as the verdicts of guilty were announced on 19 July 1995. 'I'd be upset too, if I was on my way to the gas chamber,' the Deputy District Attorney, Paul Zellerbach, said sympathetically.

He remains on Death Row as his appeals wind their way through the courts.

Brian Lane and Wilfred Gregg, *The Encyclopedia of Serial Killers*.

27 April, 1993

On 27 April 1993 Gary Pettitt and Jean Larkin were abducted and killed by the Mullen brothers from Liverpool; he because of an interest in drugs and she because she was in the wrong place at the wrong time. Jean Larkin, who ran a company selling window blinds, and her boyfriend Gary Pettitt, who ran an enterprise selling drugs, left their flat in Aigburth, Lancashire, in a hurry. The television was left on and her dog, Bruff, unfed. Pettitt had had a call to a meeting in a McDonald's in Markey Street, Chorley, some 25 miles away and Jean Larkin went with him. They appear to have kept the rendezvous because a van marked 'Calypso Blinds' was seen in the neighbourhood. It was found on 6 May at Manchester airport. Records showed it had been there since 1.55 am on 28 April.

On 1 June the police began digging in woods at Coppull, three miles outside Chorley. Some jewellery belonging to the couple was found, as was burned clothing. Pettitt's dentist identified a bridge and teeth embedded in a piece of jawbone. Seven brass shotgun cartridge cases, four of which had been fired from a gun borrowed by Francis Mullen, known as Frank, 'to shoot rabbits', were found near the scene. On 27 April the Mullen brothers had left the home of a couple with whom they were staying, dressed in camouflage outfits, returning at 11.30 pm. Both were sweating profusely and were said to be psyched up. There was no suggestion, said the police, that Miss Larkin had been anything other than an innocent bystander in what appears to have been an Ecstasy drugs deal which went wrong. On 4 October 1994 31-year-old Francis Mullen and his brother James, six years younger, were convicted of killing Pettitt and Jean Larkin. They were sentenced to life imprisonment with a recommendation that they serve not less than 20 years.

28 April, 1919

When Henry Perry, otherwise known as Beckett, returned from the First World War he was allowed to stay with Walter and Alice Cornish – she was a sister of Perry's stepfather – at their home in Stukeley Road, Forest Gate, London. After a few weeks a quarrel developed and Perry was asked to leave. Shortly after lunch on 28 April 1919 he was passing the house and Mrs Cornish invited him in. Another argument developed.

In his statement to the police Perry had this to say:

> She [Mrs Cornish] gave me two or three rough words . . . I lost my temper and knocked her down with the kitchen poker, and carried her into the shed at the bottom of the garden. She was not dead, but unconscious. I hit her with a pickaxe and then went back into the house, got a carving fork from the drawer, and stabbed her in the throat.

Perry had also cut off Mrs Cornish's finger to get her wedding ring. He then went on to say that he had hidden the body under some rubbish and waited in the house until the five-year-old daughter, Marie, returned from school.

I hit her on the head with a hammer in the passage. She fell down and I struck her again, then picked her up and threw her in the cellar. Soon afterwards, Alice [the 14-year-old daughter] came in from school. I let her in. She went into the kitchen. I struck her on the head with a hammer. She fell down, and I then hit her on the throat with an axe, and carried her into the cellar.

His fourth victim was Walter Cornish.

I waited until Mr Cornish came in from work. He said to me, 'What game are you having? I am going to hand you over to the police.'

Cornish clearly did not realise his family had been slaughtered for, according to Perry, he turned his back '. . . and I hit him on the head with the same axe'. Cornish managed to escape into the street calling out 'that soldier'. He died two days later.

The only defence open to Perry was one of insanity and at the Old Bailey trial Sir Robert Armstrong-Jones was called. He said Perry had told him of being blown up during his war campaign and, captured by Turks, he had been subjected to the bastinado, an unpleasant form of torture involving beating the soles of the feet. He had been 'put up' to murdering the Cornish family by voices. The Brixton prison doctor had the opinion that, whilst Perry was of low intelligence, he was not defective. Mr Justice Darling, passing sentence, said that he had never tried a case in which the circumstances of the crime were more horrible. Perry was hanged at Pentonville prison on 10 July 1919.

MEPO/3/262A.

29 April, 1947

On 29 April 1947 a robbery took place at Jay's, a jeweller's near what used to be the Scala Theatre in Charlotte Street, London W1. The raid was a failure from the start. The staff was held at gunpoint but one member managed to press the burglar alarm. When a director of the firm, Ernest Stock, leaped over the counter and shut the safe door, he was rewarded with a blow from a revolver. Seventy-year-old Bertram Keates threw a stool at one of the gang and a shot was fired in return. By now the raid was clearly in difficulties and the men ran into the street to their car. Because a lorry was blocking the street the three men involved could not reach their getaway car and instead ran off down the street waving their guns.

Two public-spirited passers-by attempted to stop the thieves. They were almost caught at the scene when a surveyor, Charles Grimshaw, who was in the street, tackled them. He was fortunate to escape with his life. A motorcyclist, 34-year-old father of six Alec de Antiquis, was not so fortunate. He was shot when he attempted to block the thieves' path by stalling his motorcycle. As he lay dying in the gutter he said, 'I tried to stop them . . . I did my best.'

The robbers turned out to be Harry Jenkins, his friend Christopher James Geraghty, and 17-year-old Terence Peter Rolt. They were traced through a massive police hunt led by Robert Fabian, the legendary 'Fabian of the Yard'. A raincoat was found in a room in a building in nearby Tottenham Court Road. In turn that was traced to a shop in Deptford where it was identified as having been sold to Jenkins's brother-in-law.

Jenkins, with a record of assaults on the police, and known by his associates as 'The King of Borstal', had been released only six days earlier. He was brought in for questioning. Now he told the police the coat looked like his but that he would say nothing more. His friend, Christopher Geraghty, who had twice escaped from a Borstal with Jenkins, was also picked up. His story was that he had been in bed with an attack of boils. He was released. Rolt was also known as a friend of Jenkins. He too had been ill in bed at the time of the raid and he too was released. Jenkins was also allowed to go after 27 witnesses on an identification parade had failed to pick him out.

The next day, however, Fabian had Jenkins in again. This time he told Fabian that he had lent his raincoat to a man in Southend. The man, William Wilson, was eventually found and admitted to a robbery in Queensway, west London, with Jenkins and Geraghty. After that they had all gone to Southend where he, Wilson, had tricked the others out of their money. He admitted casing the premises in Charlotte Street but denied being on the raid. That, he said, was down to Jenkins and the others. He later received five years for the Queensway robbery.

A loaded .45 revolver was then found in the mud at Wapping and ballistic tests showed it was the one which had been fired in Jay's. Jenkins's parents-in-law lived only a quarter of a mile from where the gun was found. Geraghty was the first to be arrested. He made a confession naming Rolt but refused to put Jenkins in the frame. Rolt was next to be pulled in and he too confessed but this time he named Jenkins. The so-called King of Borstal was arrested within hours.

The whole story came out in dribs and drabs. The bungling of the raid appears to have been largely the fault of Rolt. He had been told to wait for his colleagues outside the jeweller's but instead blundered in, leaving the others to follow. It was Geraghty who shot de Antiquis as they fled from the scene. Neither Geraghty nor Rolt gave evidence but Jenkins gave an alibi, calling a number of witnesses. His story was not accepted. He and Geraghty were hanged on 19 September 1947.

Rolt was ordered to be detained during His Majesty's pleasure.

When it came to it the Jenkins family had been fortunate that on an earlier occasion both Harry and an older brother, Thomas, had escaped the hangman (see 8 December).

Robert Fabian, *Fabian of the Yard*; Robert Higgins, *In the Name of the Law*.

30 April, 1942

Sam Dashwood, aged 22, and George Silverosa, a year older, were convicted of the murder of pawnbroker Leonard Moules on Thursday, 30 April 1942 at his shop in Hackney Road, east London.

The two ex-Borstal boys had met in a café in Bethnal Green and had agreed to do a job together. Moules was selected by chance as the victim when they were passing his shop. They waited outside as he put up the shutters just after 1 pm. It was early closing day.

They followed him back into the shop and battered him into unconsciousness, probably with the butt of a pistol. A palm print belonging to Silverosa, a machinist, was found on the left-hand side of Moules's safe, and a soldier recalled seeing men he knew as George and Sam handling a gun in the café. Moules survived for nine days. Silverosa was questioned first and he, whilst admitting his involvement, blamed Dashwood for the actual killing. When he was arrested Dashwood claimed that it was Silverosa who had been struggling with the pawnbroker.

At his trial Dashwood decided to defend himself, sacking the great barrister Sergeant Sullivan – Sergeant was roughly the equivalent of a Queen's Counsel – objecting to anything being said by his counsel in his defence. Both he and Silverosa were found guilty – neither had given evidence.

It was the first case of a conviction resulting from a palm, as opposed to finger, print. They were hanged at Pentonville on 10 September 1942.

MAY

1 May, 1920

West African-born Arthur Andrew Clement Goslett was hanged on 27 July 1920 for the murder of Evelyn Goslett on 1 May of that year. She was probably the bigamous, rather than the first, Mrs Goslett because her husband had contracted a number of marriages over the years.

Goslett had come to England in 1914, working in a Government aircraft factory and obtaining a comfortable flat in north-west London. During the First World War he obtained a commission in the Royal Naval Air Service.

In 1919, under the name of Godfrey, he courted a young woman, Daisy Holt, shortly afterwards admitting the existence of Evelyn. He must have been a man with considerable personal charm because he was then able to persuade Miss Holt to masquerade as the widow of his brother, Percy, and come to live with him and Evelyn. In 1919 Daisy became pregnant and Evelyn was told of the real relationship. She appears to have accepted this and perhaps encouraged Goslett to 'marry' Daisy Holt. Incredibly he seems to have 'married' yet again in 1920 – possibly twice.

On 1 May 1920 Evelyn was taken by Goslett to look at a house he was thinking of renting in Hendon. As they walked by the River Brent he hit her with a tyre lever and threw her in.

Despite his unsuccessful efforts to implicate Daisy and

a suggestion by Sir Henry Curtis-Bennett that injuries sustained in an aeroplane accident in 1913 might have led to mental disturbance, Goslett was found guilty at the Old Bailey.

2 May, 1942

In his confession to the murder of 40-year-old domestic Ivy McLeod in Victoria Avenue East, Melbourne on 2 May 1942, American serviceman Edward Joseph Leonski said:

> It was a funny looking bag. I reached over and felt it. It was very soft. We talked about something. She stepped back into the doorway and I grabbed her. I grabbed her by the neck. I changed the position of my hands so that my hands were at her throat and I choked her.

He had met her whilst she was waiting for a tram to take her home and they had chatted for a few minutes before he attacked her. Five days later he met Pauline Thompson in a café, went on a drinking spree with her and offered to take her home because of the murderer on the loose.

> She was singing in my ear. It sounded as if she was singing for me. She had a nice voice. We turned a corner. There was nobody around. I just heard her voice. Then we came to the steps. They were long steps. I grabbed her. I don't know why. I grabbed her around the neck. She stopped singing. I said: 'Keep singing, keep singing.' She fell down. I got mad and then tore at her. I tore her apart.

His third victim was Gladys Hosking who worked at the School of Chemistry at Melbourne University. It was raining and he asked if he could share her umbrella.

> She had a lovely voice. I wanted that voice. She was leaving to go to her house. I did not want her to go. I grabbed her by the throat, I choked her. I choked her. She did not even make a sound.

He was caught when he stripped off in a woman's flat when she was making him coffee. She ordered him out and called the police. The American Army camp was put on parade and a guard who had seen a soldier return drunk and dishevelled on the night of Gladys Hosking's murder identified Leonski.

Immensely strong, a keen weightlifter and thought to be something of a mother's boy, Leonski had long had a drinking problem. Before his call-up after Pearl Harbour he had been acquitted of rape at his home town, San Antonio. He appears to have accepted the death sentence cheerfully enough. It is said that on the day before his execution he sang 'It's a lovely day tomorrow'.

Alan Sharpe, *Crimes that shocked Australia*.

3 May, 1948

Twenty-five-year-old Rex Francis Farran was killed by mistake on 3 May 1948. He opened a parcel sent to his brother Captain Roy Farran at his parents' home at Codall, Wolverhampton. His brother was away in Scotland at the time staying with friends.

Inside the parcel was an omnibus edition of Shakespeare's plays but the book had been hollowed out

and filled with explosives. The explosion blew out the
windows of the house and Farran died in hospital from
his injuries. The killing was almost certainly the work of
the Israeli terrorist Stern Gang. Earlier in the year Captain
Farran had been acquitted at a court martial in Jerusalem
of the murder of a Jewish man, Alexander Rubowitz.
Since then his life had been threatened on a number of
occasions by the gang which had sworn to follow him
'to the end of the world'.

The 16-year-old Rubowitz had left his home at about
6 pm on 6 May 1947. Two hours later he was walking
down the street when he was grabbed by a man wearing an
army shirt and slacks and bundled into a car. Rubowitz,
who had delivered leaflets for the Stern Gang, was never
seen again.

The man who chased Rubowitz dropped a hat. On the
inside band was written FAR-AN.

Farran, who had a stunning war record, had been
seconded to act with the Palestine police and was regarded
as having applied the rules of procedure and arrest when
they conveniently fitted and not otherwise. He was not a
popular man with the local population.

He had, however, an alibi for the Rubowitz disappearance. Disguised as an Arab he had been dining with two
Arab friends in another part of the city. For the time being
he was confined to his home whilst the case was being
investigated.

Under the pretext that he needed clean linen he obtained
permission to leave his house and, shortly before an order
was issued placing him under close arrest, he drove to the
army camp in a stolen Ford V8 with false number plates.
He did not go in but members of his squad came out.
He told them that both he and they were likely to be
arrested and asked if they wanted to flee with him to
Syria from where they might be able to bargain with
the British Government. Two went with him and they
reached Damascus through a mixture of bluff and driving
through the control posts. Farran then drove on to Aleppo
in the hope that he could get to Greece with which there

was no extradition treaty. There his superior officer in the Palestine police caught up with him and persuaded him to return. He was put under arrest in the Allenby barracks.

Faced with mounting hostility in the press he escaped again, jumping a bar in the officer's mess, climbing a wall and disappearing. One of his escorting officers was dismissed and another retired. Now the Stern Gang wanted him back. They began to eliminate his friends. One was killed and another badly wounded before Farran, hiding in the desert, heard what was going on. On 29 June he surrendered to the barracks. He was put in a cell and charged with the murder of Rubowitz.

In conditions of great security W. A. Fearnley-Whittingstall and J. R. Bickford-Smith were flown in to defend him, paid for by a defence fund of fellow officers the night before the court martial which opened on 1 October 1947.

Although the hat was identified it does not seem to have troubled the court and no witnesses had picked out Farran. There was however the question of certain entries in Farran's diary which had been seized. It was argued that these represented notes for his defence and a submission that, as such, they were inadmissible was upheld. Colonel Bernard Fergusson, who later became Governor General of New Zealand, refused to give evidence of a conversation he had with Farran.

On the second day Fearnley-Whittingstall submitted there was no case to answer and Melford Stevenson, who later defended Ruth Ellis and went on to be the High Court judge who tried the Krays, appearing as Judge Advocate, told the court there was no evidence on which they could presume Rubowitz was dead. Farran was discharged. Tel Aviv was plastered with leaflets: 'Farran's time will come. We will go after him until the end of the world.'

After his brother's death Farran contemplated standing for Parliament as a Tory candidate but at the nomination meeting stood down. Later he emigrated to Canada and began a newspaper, the *North Hill News* in Calgary. By 1962 it had a circulation of 17,000. Farran was elected an Alderman of Calgary in 1959. He later became a Member of Parliament and Solicitor General.

Roy Farran, *Operation Tombola*.

4 May, 1929

George Armstrong, the 65-year-old homosexual manager of a Manchester clothing store, was found beaten to death on 4 May 1929. His attacker, 30-year-old George Fratson, was arrested shortly afterwards in a brothel in Preston. Questioned by the police he made a total of 15 contradictory statements. The last was, however, a confession. At his trial he retracted his confession, saying he made it only because he was despondent and wished to die. He was convicted at Manchester Assizes on 9 July 1929 and sentenced to death but reprieved on 9 August.

After his trial it was revealed that a cardboard collar-box in the shop was stained with blood and had a finger or palm print which matched neither Fratson nor Armstrong. His case came before the full five-member Court of Criminal Appeal when Inspector Battley gave evidence that he leaned towards the view that the impression had been made by the hand of a police sergeant who had visited the premises in the course of the investigation. A second ground of appeal was that the Crown knew that a raincoat belonging to Fratson and sold by him shortly after the murder showed no traces of blood. The Court of Appeal would have nothing of either point. The finger or palm print was purely negative and 'could not be important except on the unproved assumption that nobody other than the appellant was concerned in the commission of the crime'. In fact, in his confession Fratson had said another man had taken part. As for the raincoat, there was no evidence that Fratson was wearing it at the time of the murder. The court also found there were some 'unexpected and very striking corroborations of the appellant's own statements which could not leave any reasonable doubt of his guilt'. Whilst serving his sentence he became insane and was committed to Broadmoor.

The case did not end there. On 18 July 1934 Walter Prince, who had been found guilty of murdering 21-year-old Harriet Shaw, confessed to the murder of Armstrong. He too was sentenced to death but later sent to Broadmoor. Fratson's conviction was never overturned.

The case has similarity with that of Walter Rowland, convicted of the murder of Olive Balchin (see 2 March), and, so far as repetitive questioning is concerned, of Stephen Miller, convicted in 1989 of the murder of Lynette White. In Rowland's case a David Ware confessed to the killing but was not believed. Ware later attacked a woman and was committed to Broadmoor. Rowland was hanged. As for Miller, the Court of Appeal held that his questioning had been oppressive, and quashed the conviction.

5 May, 1954

The unhappy distinction of being the only test cricketer hanged for murder falls to the West Indian fast bowler Leslie George Hylton who, on 5 May 1954, shot and killed his wife, Lurline.

He had played a limited amount of test cricket, including the first two matches of the West Indies' tour of England in 1939. After that he continued to play cricket until 1950. After the 1939 tour he worked as a foreman in the Rehabilitation Department of the Jamaican Civil Service. In 1942 he married Lurline Rose, who was nine years younger than he and whose father was a police inspector. Their intention was to live permanently in the United States where Lurline had worked as a dress designer. In April 1953 she went to America in the hope that Hylton could obtain permission to join her. If not she would return in April 1954.

On 17 April Hylton received an anonymous letter suggesting that Lurline had been having an affair with a Roy Francis and was supplying him with money. He telegraphed her to return home at once. They spoke on the telephone and she wrote to him that she had not been having an affair but her family had known Francis for the better part of 25 years. She came home on Sunday 2 May. Meanwhile Hylton had purchased 15 rounds of ammunition for his gun.

On her return the matter was thrashed out and as a newspaper wrote: 'The matter was settled in true matrimonial form.' It was not, however, the end of things. Lurline was still in communication with Francis and Hylton intercepted a letter. A further quarrel broke out in which, according to Hylton, his wife pulled her nightdress up to her waist, saying, 'I am Roy's.' At his trial his evidence was that he said he was her husband and she replied that she would shoot him if he stood in her way. She grabbed the gun from the windowsill and pointed it at him. It did not go off and in turn he wrestled with her. He became dizzy and found there was blood all over the place. He then, he told the court, tried to commit suicide but missed with two bullets.

The medical evidence was that seven bullets had hit Lurline, including one which Hylton said he had used to try to kill himself. He was convicted by the all-male jury who added a recommendation of mercy after a 90-minute retirement. His appeal was dismissed, as was his application to the Privy Council. He was hanged on 17 May 1955.

John Scott, *Caught in Court.*

6 May, 1932

At 2.45 pm on 6 May 1932 the writer Claude Farerre autographed one of his books for a large, clean-shaven Russian, Pavel Gorguloff who, earlier that month, had completed his own, subsequently unpublished 636-page book, *The Story of a Cossack*. Attending the signing by one of France's most popular authors in the Salomon de Rothschild Hall in the Rue Berryer off the Avenue de Friedland, was the President of the Republic of France, Paul Doumer, then aged 75.

On Doumer's arrival, despite efforts by Farerre who fought with the Russian, Gorguloff shot the President. Farerre was hit in the arm by the last of the four bullets fired. The first went wild and the second and third hit the President who died the following morning. He never knew he had been assassinated, believing, in his delirium, that his stay in hospital was due to a motor accident.

Gorguloff told the examining magistrate he had killed Doumer because the French should have driven the Bolsheh-viks from Russia. Doumer had been the third on his list of intended assassinations. Previously he had earmarked Hindenburg and Masaryk but had abandoned his efforts.

During his trial it emerged that Gorguloff had also been known as Brade and as Mengol, under which latter name he had supervised the shooting of 200 people in Rostov during the Bolshevik uprising. Gorguloff first railed at the doctors who declared him insane and then at those who did not. He was sentenced to death on 27 July. During his time in prison his writing apparently became increasingly mystical and, as well he might, he urged against the taking of any human life. He was executed on 14 September. It is recorded that because of his height, strength, and particularly the dimensions of his neck, there were problems with the guillotine.

Rayner Heppenstall, *Bluebeard and After*.

7 May, 1970

David Knight, whose brother Ronnie, at one time married
to the actress Barbara Windsor, owned the Artists and
Recreation Club off the Charing Cross Road, was stabbed
to death by Tony Zomparelli. Earlier in the year he had
been badly beaten in a fight in Islington with a Johnny
Isaacs. On 7 May 1970, when he was out of hospital,
Ronnie took him round to the Latin Quarter nightclub
off Leicester Square to see Isaacs to whom he, Ronnie,
had already given a retaliatory beating. He also took with
him his brother Johnny and David's friend Billy Hickson
who had, it seems, been the cause of the original fight. As
Ronnie Knight put it in his book, *Black Knight*, 'I wanted
they should say sorry to my David, promise him that it
was all a big mistake. Then everything would be squared.
Then I could forget it. It would be forgotten.'

According to Knight, Isaacs was not there and whilst
he was making his peace with Billy Stayton, Hickson
attacked Stayton. In the ensuing fight Tony Zomparelli,
run-around man for Albert Dimes and bouncer for the
Latin Quarter, stabbed David Knight twice in the chest.
He died on the operating table.

Three weeks later Zomparelli, who had fled to Italy,
returned and gave himself up. He claimed that the Knight
contingent had walked into the club and violence had
erupted. He had grabbed a knife to defend himself when
two men attacked him. Looking back to the case of Tony
'Baby Face' Mancini, who in 1940 stabbed a man in a fight
in very similar circumstances and was hanged, he seems
fortunate that he was only convicted of manslaughter for
which he received a sentence of four years. To rub salt

into Ronnie Knight's emotional wounds he, his brother
Johnny and Hickson were charged with making an affray.
Hickson was given a suspended sentence. The jury disagreed in the case of the brothers and the next day the
prosecution offered no evidence. The witnesses had either
gone abroad or declined to give evidence a second time.

The police version of why the fight took place does not
quite match the account of Ronnie Knight. According to
them the Latin Quarter had been paying protection to
David Knight. (See also 4 September.)

Ronnie Knight with Barrie Tracey, *Black Knight*.

8 May, 1920

On 8 May 1920 a black Cadillac pulled up on the corner
of East 9th Street and Hamilton Avenue, Cleveland, Ohio.
Three men got out. An argument developed, a shot was
fired and one staggered into the doorway of a garage. The
other two men fled leaving the Cadillac behind them. It
belonged to William H. McGannon, the first chief justice
of Cleveland's Municipal Court – the equivalent of an
English Magistrates' Court – a man expected to be the
next Democratic candidate for Mayor. McGannon was
easy to recognise: he was always well dressed, stood over
six feet tall and weighed around 17 stone. Shortly after
the shooting two police officers saw him in downtown
Cleveland near Public Square on Superior Avenue.

Harold Kagy, a motorcar dealer-cum-mechanic, was
the victim. When he was first interviewed by the police
he named his attacker as John Joyce, a bondsman and
saloon owner. It was a story he maintained until his death
on 23 May. Reluctantly he named Judge McGannon as
the third man in the car. In what amounted to, but was not
technically, a dying declaration, Kagy said that Joyce had

asked him to take him to a place near Hamilton Avenue. When they arrived there and got out of the car he asked to be taken to another place. When Kagy refused Joyce had apparently said, 'Well I have a way of making people do what I want.'

Not surprisingly, Joyce had a different version of events although he too was unhappy about putting the judge in the car. His version was that the argument was between Kagy and the third man over a stolen motor car. The third man had shot Kagy when he had turned away. It was not a story which lasted long. Faced with a murder charge Joyce then named the judge as the shootist. His version of the affair now ran to the effect that he had been in Ferguson's Saloon when, around 11 pm, the judge and Kagy came in. Joyce knew the judge but not Kagy and the judge introduced them. Joyce maintained everyone was well drunk and he the worst for wear. The judge invited Joyce to come downtown with them. Although Joyce was dozing during the journey he picked up enough of the conversation to know that the judge and Kagy were arguing over money. When Joyce got out he went to be sick and whilst vomiting against a lamppost he heard a shot.

The judge had been questioned almost immediately after his car had been found. He maintained that he had got out of the car before it was parked at the corner where Kagy was shot. Kagy had been doing work on the judge's car and about 8 pm they met up and went for a drive to see how the car was functioning. They stopped at a bar and the judge had a mouthful or two of brandy. From then on it was soft drinks until they met Joyce, who seemed to be drunk, in Ferguson's. For no clear reason they had gone to Ferguson's office where the judge saw a revolver on the desk. The next time he looked it had disappeared. Joyce had been standing by the desk. There had been no stops for further drinks and although there had been an argument over money he had got out at Euclid Avenue and East 9th, offered Kagy $11 and then caught a Euclid Avenue tramcar.

This story had problems. There were a number of eyewitnesses who identified McGannon, including several who knew him well. Nevertheless Joyce was tried for murder in November 1920 and acquitted. Nine days later McGannon was indicted for second-degree murder. This time a nurse, Mary Neely, who had had a relationship with him for a decade and a half, gave evidence which put him at the scene of the murder. McGannon called sufficient alibi witnesses to instil some sort of doubt and after 53 unresolving ballots the jury was discharged. At the retrial Ms Neely retracted her evidence, saying the good judge was not guilty. He was acquitted. Now charges of perjury were brought against him. He served 19 months of a one- to ten-year sentence. He returned to his wife who had stood by him throughout the troubles and, disbarred, worked as a law clerk. He died in 1928 of a heart attack whilst getting on a streetcar.

Albert Borowitz, *The Judge's Black Cadillac.*

9 May, 1993

The body of Tiffany Bresciani was found in the boot of landscape gardener Joel Rifkin's pick-up truck when he was stopped for a traffic violation in Nassau County, Long Island on 28 June 1993. He then told the police that he had killed another 16 women, mostly prostitutes, by strangling them whilst having sex and dumping their bodies in graves and the waterways of New York.

One of the women was Leah Evans of Brooklyn whose body had been found on 9 May 1993 in the brush near County Road 51 in Northampton at the east end of Long Island. Some of her belongings were found in Rifkin's home.

He received a 27 years to life sentence for the murder

of Tiffany Bresciani after pleading not guilty on the basis of insanity and that, as a schizophrenic, he could not tell the difference between right and wrong.

On 24 August 1995, after the failure of a series of legal manoeuvres to exclude his confession on the grounds that he had not been read his rights, and with jury selection about to start in the Evans trial, Rifkin surprised everyone by pleading guilty. Previously he had indicated he would run another medical defence showing that, as an adopted child, he had suffered irreparable psychological harm. During his time in prison he had been examined by two psychiatrists, a psychologist and a neuro-surgeon. The court had ruled against defence motions that he should have further evaluation.

10 May, 1995

The bodies of the three children of Joy Senior were found stabbed to death on 10 May 1995 in the three-bedroom council house where they lived with their mother in Bury St Edmunds, Suffolk. The boy, Clinton, aged three, had defensive wounds to his hands indicating he had tried to put up a fight. Joy Senior then tried a number of ways in which to kill herself. She filled the house with gas, then crashed her car, slashed her wrists and throat and finally staggered into a pond where she drowned.

Until the tragedy there had been few signs that Joy Senior was sufficiently unbalanced to behave in this way. There were regular visits from the children's father; they were always immaculately turned out; Joy participated in their school activities and was part of the baby-sitting support network. Before the murders she had been out playing football with her family.

She had at one time been an active member of the Seventh Day Adventist Church and shortly before her death had returned to the church for advice. She did not reveal to the pastor, however, that she felt threatened by outside forces.

By November 1994 she had developed an acute paranoid psychosis and believed that she was responsible for the failure of her boyfriend to win the National Lottery. She believed she had ruined his psychic powers. After the first draw her relationship with salesman Sean Sutherland changed. In her diary she had written: 'God help me, Sean was protecting me, but since he went to Hades, I have no one to protect me. I have to pray to God to keep my mind straight.'

On the night of the death of the children Joy Senior had been upset and Mr Sutherland had been sufficiently worried to stay with her until after midnight. He then went home and was called at 5 am by her brother. He went to the home and found the children upstairs. A verdict of unlawful killing was recorded in respect of the children and an open verdict on Joy Senior.

11 May, 1995

A triple murder-suicide on 11 May 1995 ended the activities of the D-Mac Crew, a small-time, wannabe gang in the unlikely town of Appleton, Wisconsin. The police analysis of the killings was that Shane Gray agreed or was elected to shoot his friends Danny Gregurich and Mitch Weller in the head with a .25 pistol. He then shot himself. The killings followed the death on 2 May of Jermaine 'Jazz' Gray, an associate of the Crew, who had originally come from Milwaukee.

At first the townspeople believed that a gang war had broken out in the area known as Happy Valley. Then, given that Jermaine Gray was black, it was feared that the killings had been racially motivated.

The D-Mac Crew, named after a juvenile head of the gang who was subsequently charged with conspiracy in Jermaine's murder, dealt in drugs. Jermaine owed them about $250 for drugs and apparently mocked their gang aspirations. A vote was taken and five to nothing it was decided that Jermaine must be killed. The other juvenile, known as 'Joker' or 'Nig', tried to back out and was beaten for his pains.

There may have been some racial context to the killing. After Jermaine was lured to a cabin in Oconto County belonging to Danny Gregurich's grandfather with promises of cheap guns and marijuana, where he was choked, beaten and stabbed, one of the gang announced: 'Niggerboy is dead.'

Jermaine's body was first hidden under the porch of the cabin. It was then taken to a silo, 150 miles away in Langdale County, where it was burned and buried. Gregurich's grandfather became suspicious when Danny arrived at the farm, and alerted his family. It seems the boys dreaded the prospect of prison, where gang rape would have been a likely extra in their daily routine, and so they arranged the suicide pact. Their bodies were found in Danny's Mercury Lynx in a park in Grand Chute, Appleton. Danny was behind the wheel with Shane in the passenger seat and Mitch in the back.

In November 1996 18-year-old Derek Barnstaple, said to be the leader of the D-Mac crew, was sentenced to 45 years in prison for masterminding the murder. He had pleaded no contest to conspiracy to commit first degree intentional homicide and mutilating a corpse.

12 May, 1935

Mrs Louisa Baguley, the first victim of Dorothea Nancy Waddingham, who ran an unlicensed nursing home in Nottingham, died on 12 May 1935. She was aged 89 and

had been bedridden for some time. It was certified by Dr
George Manfield that cardiac muscular degeneration had
been the cause of death. Nurse Waddingham, who had a
long history of convictions for theft and petty fraud, told
the doctor that she had eaten too many chocolates. Her
daughter Ada had rewritten her will some six days earlier
leaving Waddingham £1,600 on condition that she would
care for both her and her mother until their deaths. They
had been in the home since January, sent by the County
Nursing Association, and were the only patients. During
that time Waddingham and her lover Joseph Sullivan, who
assisted in running the home, had continually raised the
fees, suggesting an alternative of the workhouse if their
patients could not meet them.

The second victim on 11 September was Ada Baguley
who suffered from creeping paralysis and was grossly
obese. She had been visited by a friend the previous day
and had been in good spirits. Her cause of death was certified to be cerebral haemorrhage, based not on any examination but on what the unqualified Nurse Waddingham
had told the doctor. Now Mrs Waddingham produced a
letter dated 29 August apparently written by Ada Baguley
saying that she wished to be cremated and 'my last wish
is that my relatives shall not know of my death'. The
letter was forwarded to the Nottingham Crematorium.
There it was noticed that all but the signature was in
the handwriting of Sullivan who had also witnessed it. A
postmortem was ordered. It revealed the body contained
over five grains of morphine, and an examination on
Louisa Baguley revealed a like dosage.

So far as Waddingham was concerned the inquest was
a disaster. Despite being warned she need not do so, she
gave evidence. Sullivan had more sense. Warned that he
need not do so he said, 'I don't think it is necessary.' The
coroner's jury returned a verdict that Ada had been murdered by Waddingham and Sullivan. They were put on
trial eight days later. In those days it was usual to charge
only one murder in an indictment. The case was heard by
Mr Justice Goddard who later became the much-feared

Lord Chief Justice. The evidence against Waddingham was formidable. She maintained that the morphine had been administered on the instructions of Dr Manfield. He said that he had never prescribed it but in February 1935 he had done so for another patient, a Mrs Kemp. So far as Ada Baguley was concerned her paralysis was such that he would not have expected her to die for some years.

The trial of Sullivan had been stopped by Goddard who ruled there was no case to answer. 'It seems to me,' he told Norman Birkett prosecuting, 'that it amounts to no more than that the prisoner Sullivan may have been concerned with the matter. Not that he must have been.' There was, however, evidence that on the day before she died Nurse Waddingham had fed Ada two large meals. Summing up to the jury Goddard commented, 'Can you as men of common sense think that anybody in their senses would give a woman suffering from such sharp abdominal pains that morphia had to be given her three nights, two helpings of pork, baked potatoes and fruit pie?'

The jury, when returning a verdict of guilty, made a recommendation for mercy. This was possibly based on the fact that Waddingham's husband had died from cancer and she had five children. The youngest, by Sullivan, was only four months old. Goddard's eldest daughter, Pamela, who was in court throughout the case described Waddingham as 'a poor cringing little creature; she looked a bit mental, frankly'. After he had passed the death sentence and was driven to his lodgings hundreds of angry women shouted abuse at Goddard.

Waddingham was hanged on 16 April 1936 at Winson Green prison, Birmingham. She was the last woman to be hanged in Britain for nearly 20 years. Poisoners were not usually regarded with much sympathy by the Home Secretary. Some two years earlier Ethel Major, who had poisoned her husband with strychnine, had also been recommended for mercy and she too had been hanged.

As the trial judge, Goddard would have had an influence on any decision that Waddingham should have been reprieved. His daughter said:

The fact that she was a woman affected him very much. In only one sense it made no difference to him that he was pronouncing sentence of death on a woman instead of on a man because, whatever people may say, I know he hated pronouncing the death sentence anyway. I remember the atmosphere in the house: a kind of pall.

Later in 1949, when giving evidence to the Royal Commission on Capital Punishment, Goddard said he saw 'no reason why a woman convicted of murder should not hang equally with the men'.

Fenton Bresler, *Lord Goddard*; H. Montgomery Hyde, *Norman Birkett*.

13 May, 1992

In April 1995 the Court of Appeal (Criminal Division) reserved judgment on the appeal of 62-year-old Sheila Bowler, convicted in 1993 of the murder of her elderly and incapacitated aunt, Florence Jackson, 89, who could walk only with the aid of a Zimmer frame. The ground of her appeal, and a difficult one to substantiate in English law, was that she had not been properly represented by the counsel at her trial at Hove Crown Court. The facts of the case were, in themselves, unusual. Opinion was polarised, with Sheila Bowler's supporters believing a gross miscarriage of justice had occurred and her opponents that she had carried out a cruel but nearly perfect murder.

On 13 May 1992 Mrs Bowler, an active member of a number of charitable organisations, collected the diminutive Florence Jackson from a residential home at Winchelsea. It had been arranged that she should spend a few days with her niece in Rye. Mrs Bowler did not take the direct route home but, instead, went to see friends in Bexhill.

At about 10 pm she knocked on the door of a house at Winchelsea Hill and told the occupants, Mr and Mrs Soan, that her front tyre had deflated and that she needed to telephone for help. She had, she said, an elderly relative in the car. At 10.21 pm the call to the car service company went through and she and the Soans walked back the quarter of a mile to her T-registration Audi car. Aunt Flo was missing.

Despite an intensive search which included the use of a helicopter her body was not found until the next morning in the river Brede. According to the pathologist there were signs of bruising to her upper arms, showing she had been gripped tightly, and mild bruising to her face, something which was described as 'encouragement blows'.

The prosecution case was simply that the drive to see friends had merely been a deception so that Mrs Bowler could kill her aunt under the cover of darkness. There was, said the prosecution, no way that Mrs Jackson could have walked unaided from the car. She did not even have her Zimmer with her. The police allege that Mrs Bowler parked at a pumping station on Station Road and then dragged her elderly relative out of the car. This explained the grip marks on Mrs Jackson's arms. Mrs Bowler threw her aunt into the river and then later let down her own tyre. The motive, it was alleged, was money. Mrs Jackson owned a small flat which Sheila Bowler would have inherited had there been anything left after payment of £1,000 a month nursing home bills. Mrs Bowler was not popular with the nursing home staff. She was regarded as overbearing and by one senior member as untrustworthy.

Mrs Bowler's supporters claim she had no need of money. She had a large mortgage-free house, her husband had died leaving her a pension and she was still earning around £13,000 a year as a music teacher. The children of the family were grown up.

Nor could it have been a killing caused by a fit of frustration or temper with an elderly lady. The whole plan had been carefully set up, said the Crown. Mrs Bowler made no admissions to the police and there was no forensic evidence such as fibres which could point to her guilt.

At the trial there was evidence that the tyre was indeed faulty. One of the problems Mrs Bowler faced was that of witnesses who said she had been walking away from an empty car. However, it is possible that with such a small lady as Mrs Jackson in the front seat, at a glance the car would appear to be empty. In any event the evening light was gone. The trial judge left the case to the jury on the basis that if Mrs Bowler did not kill her aunt then who did? She was convicted and jailed for life with a recommendation that she serve at least 12 years.

The appeal in April 1995 raised the possibility that, despite the belief that she was unable to walk, Aunt Flo could have left the car on her own. Research has shown that elderly people are quite capable of surprising their carers with the physical effort they are able to make, seemingly inexplicably. One line of thought is that Aunt Flo became upset and frightened about being left on her own and wandered from the car, slipping into the river.

On 5 May 1995 the Court of Appeal rejected Mrs Bowler's appeal. Far from her being badly defended, her counsel was, they said, to be congratulated for destroying so many planks of the prosecution's case. He later received damages for libel and the trial judge an apology for unfounded criticism from the BBC.

A television programme then pointed out flaws in the case and finally, in 1998, Mrs Bowler's ordeal ended when the Court of Appeal ordered a retrial. She was acquitted by a jury at the Old Bailey on 5 February 1998.

14 May, 1968

Maxwell Garvie, a Justice of the Peace and influential in
the Scottish National Party, who farmed 300 acres near
the village of Laurencekirk, Kincardineshire, was battered
and shot dead on 14 May 1968.

He had married Sheila Watson who had been a housekeeper at Balmoral and was regarded as one of the
most beautiful girls in the neighbourhood. They had
three children and a life in which they were leaders
of the community. Then, it seems, he began to change.
He bought an aeroplane from which he 'buzzed' local
fishermen and farmers, developed a penchant for drugs,
acquired a black girlfriend in London, as well as having
close personal friendships with both men and women. He
also set up a nudist colony on his estate. Sheila Garvie
swopped her tweeds for sunglasses and a black leather
mini-skirt.

Garvie, on another tack altogether, decided to form
the Stonehaven branch of the Scottish National Party.
There he met 22-year-old Brian Tevendale who had
been discharged from the army as being unsuitable and
undesirable, and who affected the dress of the Hitler
Youth Movement with brown shirt, leather jacket and
jackboots. Garvie made it clear he wished Tevendale
to sleep with his wife. Soon he and his sister, Trudy
Birse, the wife of a police officer, began to visit the
farm regularly for mixed foursomes. Then unfortunately
Sheila Garvie fell in love with Tevendale. The now-jealous
Garvie hired men to give him a beating as a warning-off
and the mixed foursomes stopped but Sheila Garvie and
Tevendale continued their relationship.

On 14 May 1968 Garvie went to a Scottish National
Party meeting. When he returned he and his wife had some
drinks and then went to bed. After he had fallen asleep, so
the prosecution alleged, Mrs Garvie told Tevendale who

was hiding in the house. He first knocked out Garvie with the butt of a rifle and then shot him through a pillow. His body was taken to Lauriston Castle and left in an underground tunnel. When Mrs Garvie was asked about her husband she said he had gone away. For three months Tevendale and Sheila Garvie continued a very public romance including, according to Tevendale's later account of things in the *News of the World* on 26 April 1981, having sex naked on outcrops of rocks.

Sheila Garvie was questioned by her mother about Garvie and what would happen when he returned. 'He won't be back,' said her daughter and Mrs Edith Watson went to the police. Tevendale was questioned and soon confessed, implicating his mistress. The trial at Aberdeen was something of a sensation. When Garvie's yellowing skull was produced as an exhibit one juror fainted.

Despite the efforts of Sheila Garvie's counsel to suggest she had nothing to do with the killing both were found guilty of Garvie's murder and were sentenced to life imprisonment. According to some reports, at the time of his death Garvie was already a dying man; he had ruined his liver with a combination of drink and drugs. A £50,000 insurance policy was paid out to a trust fund for the children.

Sheila Garvie was released after 10 years' imprisonment. She married again twice, the first marriage lasting only 10 months. Tevendale was released after 12 years.

Jonathan Goodman, *Modern Murder File*; Paul Harris, *The Garvie Trial*; George Saunders, *Casebook of the Bizarre*.

15 May, 1962

The bodies of two young burglars, Billy McCarthy and Jimmy Miraglia, were found on 15 May 1962 in the boot of a car dumped on the south-west side of Chicago. Both had been badly beaten and their throats had been cut.

Although no charges were ever brought over the murders, it emerged that the pair had robbed and shot three businessmen in Elmwood Park, a smart suburb in Chicago favoured as home for the top figures in the world of organised crime. As a result the area was a no-go one for the rank-and-file criminal.

Worse, so far as McCarthy and Miraglia were concerned, was the fact that they were in debt to the loan-shark and major enforcer Sam De Stefano. Miraglia disappeared on 2 May 1962 and from his injuries it would appear his head was placed in a vice to persuade him to disclose the whereabouts of McCarthy. His throat was then cut. McCarthy was more fortunate: he seems to have been killed without first being tortured.

Born in 1909 De Stefano had been a prominent enforcer, rapist and murderer working for the Chicago gang of Sam Giancana who ordered De Stefano to kill his own brother Mike, a drug dealer, something with which he complied without question. De Stefano was shot to death outside his home in 1973. At the time he was awaiting trial for the torture-murder of another gangster, Leo Foreman.

William F. Roemer, *The Enforcer*.

16 May, 1966

The body of John Whyte was discovered in a ditch near Nantwich in Cheshire on 16 May 1966. A man with a record of housebreaking and theft, he had been shot in the head and chest and his body dumped.

He was known to have hired a Morris 1100 in Shepherd's Bush, London at the end of March and there were reported sightings of the car in London on 3 May and again at a caravan site in Skegness where a man and woman had been seen giving it a thorough clean. The car turned up again with a woman driving it in Doncaster on 6 June and was finally seen on waste ground in London on 8 June. It had been set on fire in an effort to cover bloodstains.

Two of John Whyte's associates were 47-year-old William John Clarke, a man with a long criminal record who had been flogged for mutiny whilst in the Navy – he had also been sent to Broadmoor for slashing a fellow prisoner with a broken bottle – and his 40-year-old girlfriend, Nancy Patricia Hughes. The three of them had been involved in the post office book frauds which predated cheque card frauds and were prevalent at the time. The method was stealing savings books from both post offices and individuals and then touring the country making withdrawals. Given that there was a maximum of £30 which could be withdrawn from a book, even though individual withdrawals were, by today's standards, tiny, if done in sufficient bulk they could produce a substantial income.

Clarke and Hughes were interviewed and Clarke indicated that he could say nothing because his own life was at risk. Both he and Hughes were then sentenced at the Old Bailey to long terms of imprisonment for more post office offences. He received 10 years, reduced on appeal to seven. She received two.

Whilst they were in custody the police learned that at
a house in Morley, Leeds, Clarke had fired a gun into
the ceiling. Ballistics experts showed a match between
that bullet and one extracted from Whyte's body. At
Chester Assizes Clarke received a life sentence afer being
convicted of murder on a 10 to 2 majority. Hughes,
convicted as an accessory after the fact, received three
years. The quarrel had been over the proceeds of the
thefts.

17 May, 1956

On 15 May 1956 and then two nights later on 17 May, the
Buchra and then the *Windmill* houseboats were burned
at East Creek, an estuary on the Thames which separates
Canvey Island from South Benfleet, Essex. In the second
of the fires Reggie and Colin, the twin sons of Violet
Lavinia Wright, were burned to death. Mrs Wright had
managed to escape. The case is a good example of the
rumour and counter-rumour which can spread around a
small town.

Mrs Wright had been married to William Clark, an
employee of Benfleet Urban District Council. There had
been three children of the marriage. She had then lived
with a Mr Wright and together they had purchased a
houseboat, the *Buchra*. After his death in April, she then
met another local man by whom she had the twins. Later
she had met a local businessman, William Smith, with
whom she hoped to emigrate to Australia. Mr Smith
was at the time living with his wife and two grown-up
daughters.

The rumours began immediately and were to the effect
that Mrs Wright had fired the houseboats herself. She
had, after all, the reasoning went, owned one and had
been staying on the other which belonged to a friend,

Grace Richardson, when they burned. Mr Smith, who had visited her in hospital, issued a strong denial on her behalf:

> I have been hounded, persecuted, pursued by these lies. The people who are spreading these wicked lies about me are the very people whom the police should consider their number one suspects.

Mr Smith added on his own behalf:

> Malicious persons with a motive for their cruelty are trying to apportion some blame to her in connection with the fire aboard the *Windmill* and the fire, some two days earlier, in her houseboat, the *Buchra*. This fantastic suggestion has been believed by some people despite its absurdity. In the first fire she lost her craft. In the second she lost her two children, of whom she was intensely fond. And she very nearly lost her life. Both she and I have told the police of our suspicions as to who the fire-raisers were. I say 'were' because undoubtedly more than one person was concerned.

He also explained that he had first met Mrs Wright when he employed her at a Canvey Island café he owned.

Now the Vicar of Canvey, the Reverend David Cullen, entered the scene, complaining that there were a couple of bad eggs in the community and also that a number of couples in his parish were living in sin. This brought the wrath of the Chamber of Commerce on his cassock. The leaders felt that the vicar's remarks were damaging to the business interests of the community.

By now, at best, Mrs Wright was being castigated for not doing more to save her children.

On 26 June she was arrested and charged with the murder of her sons. What was more surprising to the community was that Mrs Richardson was also charged with the murder. The thinking of the Director of Public

Prosecutions and the police was revealed at the magistrates' court when, a fortnight later, the committal proceedings began. It went along the lines that Mrs Wright had moved in with the Richardsons on the *Windmill* after Mr Wright's death in April. Accommodation in one bedroom was shared by Mrs Richardson, her 18-year-old daughter Ann, a granddaughter and the twins of whom there was no doubt Mrs Richardson was enormously fond. In a second bedroom were two Richardson sons. Mrs Wright slept alone in another part of the boat. Mr Richardson, a seaman, only came home at weekends.

On 12 May Mrs Richardson told Mrs Wright that her husband did not want Mrs Wright staying any longer. The next day Mrs Wright said she must get rid of the *Buchra* and after the boat had burned, so the Crown alleged, persuaded Mrs Richardson to buy a gallon of paraffin to burn the *Windmill*. The aim was to make Mrs Wright homeless so that she could go with Mr Smith to Australia. He had, said the Crown, been unwilling to go with the twins. Their deaths would be a convenient way of settling matters. The Crown maintained that on the day of the fire the Richardsons and the Wrights had packed a number of clothes, including those of the twins, in preparation.

This story was hardly credible in view of the affection Mrs Richardson had for the boys. She had been more than willing to adopt the children if Mrs Wright did go to Australia.

The boat went up in the early hours of 17 May. Mrs Richardson's daughter threw her baby on to the bank and safety. The two teenage boys followed through a bedroom window, then Ann clambered out followed by Mrs Wright who, it was alleged, was delayed because she was trying to bring a basket of clothing with her. She was followed by Mrs Richardson who was burned in the fire.

According to Ann Richardson it was Mrs Wright who had awakened her on 15 May saying that her boat was on fire. She did not, she said, appear particularly distressed.

Most damagingly she said that in the *Windmill* fire Mrs Wright had failed to open a window which would have provided an escape and that she was actually standing on the bed on Colin's feet. After Mrs Wright escaped she spent some time looking for her handbag. Any tears had been saved until the arrival of the police.

The magistrates declined to commit Mrs Richardson – whose hair had turned from black to grey in the weeks after the fire – for trial and she left court to great applause. The decision may have satisfied the public. It did not satisfy the Director who, unusually but perfectly lawfully, sought a Bill of Indictment to have her tried along with Mrs Wright whom the magistrates had committed.

Meanwhile, anonymous and malicious letters were circulated detailing the alleged misdeeds of Mrs Wright, whom it was said had gone out with a rich lover immediately after the death of her husband. As a result of this and also persistent rumours that Mr Wright had died in peculiar circumstances, his body was exhumed. On that score at least Mrs Wright was exonerated. He had died of natural causes. However, the vicar, David Cullen, had been on the receiving end of abusive letters and calls following his denunciation of the community's morality. He was found dead, gassed in his vestry.

On Wednesday 7 November, Mrs Richardson's ordeal was over. Mr Justice Hilberry said that there was no evidence that she had known the boat was to be fired and that there was evidence she was devoted to the twins and had tried to get one of the boys out. The Crown agreed with this which made it somewhat surprising that they had persisted with the murder charge a second time.

When Mrs Wright gave evidence she denied any intimacy with Mr Smith, who did not give evidence. Her relationship with him had been that of father and daughter. As far as she was concerned there was never any talk of going to Australia. She had not stepped on Colin's foot but on the edge of the bunk to try to escape. She thought the twins were already out of the boat. She accepted in cross-examination that she had obtained a passport in

December 1954 and it had been sent to Mr Smith care of a bank. She had also written him a letter which, the prosecution alleged, was compromising to her story.

In court, she was asked:

> —Did you say in the letter, 'No matter how you have deceived me I will always love you, and if you ever come home I will be waiting because deep in my heart I still cannot believe you could do such a despicable thing to me'? [Smith had at the time gone to Australia.]
> —Yes.
> —Is that a father's love?
> —Yes.
> —Did you also say in the letter, 'It is hard for me to write this letter, darling, because I love you with all my heart. Take care of yourself, because we were meant for each other. There is only one love for everyone, and you are mine . . . Nothing will ever kill my love for you'?
> —Nothing in that letter was meant at all.

On 13 November Mrs Wright was found not guilty of murder but guilty of manslaughter. 'I am innocent. I didn't do it,' she told the court. She was sentenced to three years' imprisonment. Mr Justice Hilberry told her, 'You did nothing whatsoever to save either of those children but you took successful steps to save yourself.' Outside the court Mr Smith said he would wait for Mrs Wright. 'Everything I have here is for Vicki.'

Laurence Wilkinson, *Behind the Face of Crime*.

18 May, 1954

On 18 May 1954 the handsome, six feet two inches tall former Irish Guardsman Nathan Goldberg, whose service career had been finished when he suffered a slipped disc, shot and injured two men and killed a third, William Gibbons, 54, at Gascoyne Road, Hackney. Goldberg then went to the late-night film at the Leicester Square Cinema and, seen on leaving, jumped into a taxi cab and shot himself whilst being driven down the Strand.

Goldberg, who had suffered from mental instability and had petitioned the Queen for compensation for his illness, had spent time in a mental ward at Banstead Hospital, Surrey. Three days earlier he had been granted a firearms licence. 'There are some who fill me with hate to be reckoned with first,' he had written. He carried a list of 14 people whom he intended to shoot, including ones who had, in his opinion, spoken harshly to children of whom he was fond. The day before the killing he had withdrawn all his savings.

19 May, 1941

Lionel Rupert Watson, who had bigamously married Phyllis Elizabeth Croker and by whom he had an 18-month-old daughter, Eileen Alice, poisoned both with prussic acid on 19 May 1941. He buried their bodies in the garden of his house in Greenford, Middlesex. Five days later the digging was noticed by neighbours and the police uncovered the bodies. Watson claimed that he had come home and found both his wife and daughter dead but had not reported the matter because he feared, since his was a bigamous union, no one would believe in his innocence.

He was convicted and hanged at Pentonville prison on 12 November 1941.

20 May, 1979

On 20 May 1979 Helen Smith, a 23-year-old English nurse, died after attending an illegal drinks party thrown by an expatriate English surgeon, Richard Arnot, and his wife in Jeddah, Saudi Arabia. The initial statement by the Foreign Office was that she had fallen some 70 feet from a balcony. Also found dead was a young Dutch sea captain, Johannes Otten. His body was impaled on railings. The version of the matter given at the inquest was that Helen Smith and Otten had, whilst drunk, attempted to have sexual intercourse on the balcony and had fallen over. The guard railing around the balcony was, however, an extremely high one and the postmortem evidence did not appear to confirm a fall from a considerable height. There was a deep indentation in Otten's forehead but the severe damage to be expected in such a fall was missing. Arnot, his wife and seven guests were later imprisoned for alcohol offences.

Helen Smith's father, Ron, has never accepted the Home Office statement and has spent many years and thousands of pounds in an attempt to prove his daughter was murdered. There was some medical evidence to show she had been sexually assaulted and considerable evidence to negate the suggestion she had fallen from a height of 70 feet. One pathologist, Professor Dalgaard, gave his opinion that the maximum Helen Smith could have fallen, if she fell at all, was 10 feet. There was also a lesion which tended to show Helen Smith had been dead before her fall from the balcony. Ron Smith was eventually successful in obtaining an inquest for his daughter which was heard in Leeds on 18 November 1992. The Arnots' marriage had by this time been dissolved and Mrs Arnot was living in America and he in Australia. He attended the inquest whilst she declined to do so. The jury, whilst accepting she had fallen from the balcony, returned an open verdict.

Apart from the problems with the medical evidence, there are many questions which are unanswered about the death of Helen Smith. The first is why she and Mrs Arnot were the only women at the party. The second is the disappearance of Otten's trousers, although his passport and other belongings were found in the road. It was suggested the trousers had been taken by a vagrant. His spectacles and shoes were in the flat. Although Helen Smith had taken her camera to the party no film was found in it, and another guest who had taken photographs found that when the film was taken for development it had suffered from double exposure.

G. Wilson and David Harnson, *Inquest: Helen Smith the Whole Truth*.

21 May, 1995

On 21 May 1995 Peter Horrod battered his 60-year-old disabled wife, Brenda, with a hammer, cut her throat and then suffocated her. Then aged 62, he had just been released from Northgate psychiatric hospital in Great Yarmouth, Norfolk. He had taken an overdose but, although he had already spent two periods in hospital, it had not been felt necessary to readmit him. He was sent home in a taxi at 2.30 am. A female volunteer carer, who was in the flat because of her concern for the couple, woke up and saw the killing. She opened the door and saw Horrod holding a pillow, covered in blood, over his wife's face. She pressed the alarm button for the ambulance.

Horrod had been totally devoted to his wife whom
he had nursed since she suffered from a brain tumour
in 1988. His counsel, David Stokes, told the court:
'Those who care for seriously disabled relatives are the
stuff of which saints are made. But it requires a tough
constitution, both physical and mental. It was too much
for Mr Horrod's frail mind.'

His plea to manslaughter was accepted and he was
ordered to be detained under the Mental Health Act. The
chief executive of Anglian Harbours Trust, which ran the
hospital, said that an internal review had found no faults
but 'with the benefit of hindsight, this man should never
have been allowed home, but the psychiatric service is
unpredictable'.

22 May, 1924

One of the greatest defences of the American lawyer
Clarence Darrow came towards the end of his career
and was of the so-called Chicago thrill-killers, Richard
Loeb and Nathan Leopold Junior. These middle-class
youths were charged with the murder of 14-year-old
Robert Franks on 22 May 1924. Loeb's father was the
multi-millionaire vice-president of Sears Roebuck, and
Leopold's father, slightly less wealthy, was a retired
millionaire box manufacturer.

They collected a boy at random from outside his
school on the pretext they would take him back to his
parents' flat. On the way they smashed his skull with a
chisel. The body was then taken to a culvert alongside
the Pennsylvania Railroad where hydrochloric acid was
poured over the face to delay identification. The body
was then stuffed into a drainpipe. Shortly after midnight
they telephoned the boy's father and demanded a ransom

of $10,000 but by this time the body had been found by workmen.

Despite the abnormally high intelligence of the pair they were singularly inept at covering their tracks. The ransom note was traced to Leopold's typewriter and he had also dropped his glasses at the culvert. Loeb confessed first, implicating Leopold.

Darrow took over the defence from other lawyers at a fee of $100,000. The only question was whether he would be able to save them from the death penalty. In this he was not helped by his clients. Throughout the trial both boys behaved appallingly, sniggering and laughing and making gestures to each other. The public, never on their side, became even more hostile. Darrow was, however, able to show that Leopold was a paranoic with a severe manic drive and that Loeb was a dangerous schizophrenic. He displayed their emotional level to be that of a seven-year-old.

Darrow's was a bravura performance during which he wept for the victim and the defendants alike, recited to the jury in detail how the executions would take place, and invited the prosecutors to perform the execution. It was wholly as a result of his efforts that the defendants received life for the Franks murder plus 99 years for the kidnapping.

Over the years the boys received what was seen to be favourable treatment in Joliet prison with separate cells and a garden to tend. During the years Loeb became an aggressive homosexual and was stabbed to death in a fight in 1936. It was said wittily in the *Chicago Daily News*: 'Richard Loeb, a brilliant college student and master of the English language, today ended a sentence with a proposition.' Leopold's behaviour improved noticeably. He was paroled in March 1958 saying, 'I am a broken old man. I want a chance to find redemption for myself and to help others.' He wrote a book of his memoirs *Life Plus 99 Years* and then went to Puerto Rico to work as a hospital technician earning $10 a month. In 1961 he married a widow. He died in 1971. Darrow, after a good deal of effort, received $40,000 of his $100,000 fee.

Nathan Leopold, *Life Plus 99 Years*; Irving Stone, *Clarence Darrow for the Defence*.

23 May, 1936

On 23 May 1936 Norman 'Red' (because of his hair) Ryan was shot to death in a bungled liquor store hold-up in Sarnia. Also shot dead were Chuck McMullen, the brother of Edward, with whom Ryan had made a prison break in 1923 from Kingston, and PC John Lewis. Had the raid been successful Ryan and McMullen would have netted C$394.26. Hundreds queued to see the body of the man known as 'Ontario's Pet Boy'.

According to a highly colourful description of the shoot-out in the *Globe and Mail* the following day, Ryan threw his gun to the floor and 'as his lifeblood was spilling on the dirty floor and as it welled to choke him in the throat he gasped, "You've got me, boys. I've had enough."' Chuck McMullen was reported to have died in stoic silence.

There were various accounts of Ryan's colourful life. He was either born one of eight children on 18 July 1897, a boy who at an early age stole a bike, a chicken and then at the age of 15 shot a man, or (in a retrospective tribute) was from a middle-class family and had once saved a soldier's life when a punt capsized.

He had been in the Canadian Army from which he had deserted, as well as serving in the French Foreign Legion. He may have been held as a deserter in the Tower of London from which he claimed to have escaped. Almost certainly he went, after the First World War, to Australia and Nova Scotia where he robbed a series of banks.

In 29 years he was sentenced to a total of 116 years' imprisonment but such was his charm he only served a total of 16 and a half. In 1921, said to be earning a living as a tinsmith, he was convicted of robbing banks in Hamilton and Montreal. In 1923 he escaped from prison and lingered to stab a guard, Matthew Walsh, with a pitchfork. The papers gleefully reported that the following week Ryan wrote to his victim congratulating him on his efforts to stop the prison break.

He was recaptured in 1929 when he was shot in Minneapolis by a police officer. At the time Ryan was described as 'tall, lean, hard, handsome with rather fine blue eyes'. During his period on the run he had, it was said, used some of his cache of $120,000 to pay for the treatment of his sister who was suffering from tuberculosis.

By 1930 he was serving as an altar boy in the prison chapel after working in the hospital. On 24 June 1934 he met the Prime Minister when the latter visited the prison and from then on the clamour began for his release. It came, just over a year later on 23 July 1935, when he left the Kingston penitentiary on ticket of leave.

'For me to go back to a life of crime would be the biggest blow the ticket of leave system could ever receive,' he told adoring reporters. Jack Corcoran, a local wrestling promoter, obtained him a job at C$500 a week as a greeter at the Nealon Hotel in King Street, downtown Toronto and he also worked as a used-car salesman. He lectured at boys' clubs and had a box for the hockey at Maple Leaf Gardens.

A priest who had championed his release suffered a stroke and died within the year from, it was said, a broken heart. Ryan was correct about the effect his bad behaviour would have on ticket of leave men. After his death the number of those paroled dropped sharply.

24 May, 1992

On 24 May 1992 Graeme Woodhatch, 38, was shot twice in the head and twice in the chest as he was using the telephone at the Royal Free Hospital, Hampstead where he was recovering from an operation for piles. It was a contract killing and although his business partners Paul Tubbs and Deith Bridges were charged with his murder, initially the stipendiary magistrate, Mr David Fingleton, found there was no case to answer and they were discharged.

The prosecution's case was that Woodhatch had swindled Tubbs and Bridges out of £50,000 in their roofing business. Despite a lifestyle that included a Porsche and a Japanese-style house in Hertfordshire he was in serious financial trouble, owing £400,000 in tax and substantial business debts. Woodhatch was also becoming increasingly irrational and at the time of his death was on bail for threatening to kill his secretary.

A 27-year-old Maori woman, Te Rangimaria Ngarimu, was hired by Tubbs and Bridges for a fee of £7,000. She had met Bridges, another New Zealander, when she had been working as a barmaid in London in the late 1980s. At first when Bridges put the proposition to her she thought he was joking but almost immediately agreed. The money she earned was to be spent to fulfil her dream of buying a mobile home.

The plan was that she would shoot Woodhatch whilst he was in hospital and then immediately fly out to New Zealand. On her first visit she could not find the ward and, wearing a baseball cap, tracksuit and gloves, returned the next day. This time she shot him from a distance of three feet. Bridges, she said, had told her, 'Shoot him twice in the head and twice in the body to be sure of death.' She then caught the 4.30 pm flight from Gatwick, leaving the clothes and

gun at Bridges's flat in Camden Town to be disposed
of.

It seems that, at first, it was thought that Woodhatch
had died from a brain haemorrhage and it was not until
five hours later, in the mortuary, that the bullet wounds
were discovered. After the killing Tubbs telephoned a
friend and asked him to meet Bridges to help in getting
rid of the holdall. The friend looked inside and threw the
holdall in a pond, later helping the police retrieve it.

In early 1994 Ngarimu returned to England. She had
been contacted by the police but at first had told them,
'I couldn't kill a chicken. I am a vegetarian.' Over the
years, however, she had embraced religion and, after
at first fighting extradition procedures, she voluntarily
returned to England as she wished to clear her conscience.
Bridges and Tubbs were rearrested and were convicted
largely on her evidence. They had already pleaded guilty
to conspiracy to pervert the course of justice by disposing
of the gun and clothes she had worn. Bridges and Tubbs
were sent to prison for life with a recommendation
they serve 15 and 16 years' imprisonment respectively.
The trial judge, Sir Lawrence Verney, the Recorder of
London, added that he thought the Home Secretary
should consider making each man serve a further third
of the sentence. 'In my view it is necessary to protect the
public from serious harm from each of you.'

Five days later Ngarimu was sentenced to life imprisonment with no set recommendation as to how much she
should serve. 'I am satisfied that you are not a professional
killer,' said Sir Lawrence. 'You have expressed deep
remorse and I accept that, but it is not a thing which
it seems to me in a case of this nature can have very
much influence on my recommendation to the Home
Secretary.'

In a throw-back to the old Marshall Hall style of rheto-
ric, Oliver Blunt QC had told the judge that Ngarimu now
attended Bible classes three times a week and that her con-
version to Christianity was total. 'She knows that beyond
my Lord's sentence, she faces the judgment of her Lord.'

The case has two particularly interesting features. The first is that this appears to be the first use of a female hit man in this country. The second is that during the trial, which began in May 1994, Bridges was shot in the chest and leg whilst walking one evening in Ruislip, North Middlesex. The trial was adjourned until his recovery. No arrest was made over that attack.

James Morton, *Supergrasses and Informers*.

25 May, 1968

On 25 May 1968, the day before Mary Bell turned 11, the body of four-year-old Martin George Brown was found by some boys playing in an abandoned house in Newcastle. At first it was thought that he had swallowed pills he had found in a bottle. That day the father of Norma Bell found her being choked by her namesake who was no relation.

The next day a local nursery school was broken into and vandalised. A note left behind read 'Fuch of, we murder, watch out, Fanny and Faggot'. A second note read 'WE did murder Martain brown, fuckof you Bastard' (sic). Four days later Mary Bell arrived at the doorstep of the Brown home asking to see Martin. When told he was dead she replied that she knew that but wished to see him in his coffin.

On 31 May the police found both Mary and Norma in the nursery. They said they had never been in the school before and were sent home. It was not the first time the girls had been spoken to by the police. On 11 May that year a three-year-old had been playing with them and had fallen from the top of an air-raid shelter, suffering severe injuries. Later other children complained that Mary had been putting her hands around their throats and squeezing. Mary then appears to have begun telling her friends how Norma had killed Martin.

On 31 July three-year-old Brian Howe disappeared in the Scottswood area of Newcastle. Mary told the boy's sister that she had seen him playing on concrete blocks and his body was found there. He had been strangled and there were cuts on his stomach and legs. When she was interviewed, Mary Bell told the police she had seen a boy, whom she named, with Brian and carrying scissors. The boy was found to be in no way connected and as the police had not released the information that they had found scissors they turned again to Mary Bell. Norma now told the police that she had been with Mary when the boy had been killed and that when Mary began cutting the boy, she ran away.

Mary Bell had been suspected of the Brown killing for some time and an officer in the case had seen her rubbing her hands and laughing as the boy's coffin was taken from his home.

Both girls were charged and appeared at the Newcastle Crown Court on 5 December 1968. Norma was acquitted and Mary Bell was found guilty of manslaughter on the grounds of diminished responsibility. She was sent to an open prison. In September 1977 she escaped with another girl and remained at large for three days, boasting on her recapture that she had now lost her virginity.

Gita Sereny, *The Case of Mary Bell*.

26 May, 1901

At about 7.30 am on 26 May 1901 28-year-old Annie Austin was heard moaning in a cubicle in a lodging house at 35 Dorset Street, Spitalfields, London. She had been separated from her husband for about 10 days. When

she was examined by a doctor it was found that she had
been stabbed in both the anus and the vagina. When he
asked her if she knew who had done it, she said it was
by the man who had come in with her the previous night
but whose name she did not know.

She died in the London Hospital on 30 May. The police
had been called but did not arrive in time to interview her
and instead she had told the doctor her story. She said she
had slept with the man and then as he was getting up to
leave in the early hours she felt a sharp pain as if a knife
had been run inside her. She described her attacker as
short with dark hair and moustache and having a Jewish
appearance.

The hostel was managed by a Henry Moore and
his wife. His brother-in-law, Daniel Sullivan, sometimes
acted as his deputy. It was he who took the woman
to hospital. The lodging house rules, observed in their
breach, were that only married couples should share a
cubicle. The manager said that customers were insulted
if they were asked if they were married.

At the inquest the pathologist reported no signs of a
struggle and that Austin was healthy but for long-standing
syphilis. Moore said that he had allowed the man and
woman into the premises and that it was he who, the
next morning, had sent for Dr Dale and had called a cab
to take Austin to the hospital. His wife, Maria Moore, said
she had been up and about all that night but had heard
no screams. One of the unanswered questions was when
had the man slipped away or if indeed he was a member
of the hostel staff. Both Sullivan and Moore came under
suspicion because for some reason they gave the wrong
cubicle number to the police. At first they said Austin had
been in cubicle 44 rather than the correct number, 15. Was
the street door unlocked before her screams were heard?
If so it would indicate that the man had left. If it was
still bolted it would almost certainly be that the killer had
remained on the premises.

Maria Moore seems to have made some effort to divert
attention. She made a positive identification of Austin's

estranged husband but he was able to give a cast-iron alibi. There was also some suggestion that Daniel Sullivan had been the man with Austin that night but he gave an alibi that he had shared a bed with a man named Timothy Batty at 10 Paternoster Row. The coroner took the view that was not conclusive but in the absence of any contradictory evidence the jury should give weight to it.

The police, who felt the man was known to the lodging house habitués and was being protected by them, clearly had a hard time as the final report reads:

> From the first to the last we have to deal with a class of witnesses that are as low as they can well possibly be and it is difficult to know when they are speaking the truth. In some instances they lie without any apparent motive.
>
> Although we never despair I fear that nothing further can be done to elucidate this mystery and the perpetrator of this crime unfortunately goes unpunished as a result of the scandalous conduct of nearly the whole of the witnesses in this case.
>
> Thomas Divall (Inspector)

Apart from anything else the police were not happy that they had had to pay out the then not inconsiderable sum of £5 to sober people to round up the witnesses and make them keep their appointments.

After his career in the police ended Divall went into racecourse security, becoming closely involved with both the Sabini brothers and the Brummagen Boys who ran racecourse gangs. He wrote a number of books about his experiences but not the Austin case.

27 May, 1968

The small but flamboyant Essex villain, Tony Maffia, disappeared on 27 May 1968 soon after he returned from Belgium, where he had shown an interest in forged notes. Together with his longtime friend, prison escaper Alfie Hinds, Maffia had acquired a copper mine in Portugal and they worked together in various enterprises. They also both knew Manchester coal merchant Stephen Jewell.

For outside purposes Maffia was a car trader with a small firm, Justice Motors. Described as having bundles of personality and a man who couldn't keep his hands off a quick deal, he was one of the largest receivers of stolen goods to be found in England at the time.

The day Maffia disappeared he met Jewell who hoped to sell him forged £10 notes and on whom Maffia hoped to unload his cruiser, the *Calamara*, then in a marina at Wallasey Island. The price for the notes was £8,000 in real money against £32,000 paper value.

According to Jewell, when he saw Maffia's house in Buckhurst Hill he liked it so much he suggested buying it. The price, £12,000 was, even then, a bargain. Maffia was separated from his wife and a sale was needed. The pair drove in Maffia's green Jaguar, registration number MCC 932, to the marina to see the boat. Jewell carried a gun which, he said, Maffia had instructed him to bring. The gun, with its magazine housing bullets with a hole in every nose, was put on the front seat covered with a cloth. Jewell's car was then left in a pub car park. They certainly went to the marina where Maffia reversed a call to London to say he would be back in about an hour. After they left the marina he was never seen alive again. Maffia had been planning to fly to Jersey, where apparently he had important papers to sign, later that day.

His body was found on 1 June, Whit Saturday. One of the staff at the Midway Restaurant, so-called because it was between Southend and London, saw a dog sniffing at a green Jaguar which had been in the car park for the past few days. In the front passenger seat, covered by a tarpaulin, was Maffia. It had been a hot few days and his body was so bloated it was recognisable only by fingerprints and a gold ring he wore. He had been shot twice, by the right eye and behind the right ear.

Two days later Jewell, of his own volition, arranged to see Detective Chief Inspector Kenneth Drury.[1] His story was that, shortly after he and Maffia left the marina, they were stopped by three men in a Ford Zodiac, who told Jewell to go away whilst they talked to Maffia about a deal. When he returned both Maffia and the Zodiac were gone, as were the pistol and ammunition from the Jaguar. The car itself was still there. Jewell's overcoat, which he had left in the car, was bloodstained. He described the men, saying that one had a scar on his cheek.

He said he drove off in the Jaguar for London and after a time stopped to throw the overcoat into a field. It was just as well he admitted that, for the coat was found containing a live bullet and sale particulars of Maffia's house. A witness would later say he saw Jewell wipe the passenger door with the coat before it was thrown away. Jewell agreed he left the Jaguar in the car park of the Midway Restaurant.

Quite apart from the forensic evidence against him how did Maffia's body get into the Jaguar if it was not in it when Jewell drove to the Midway? It is impossible to believe that when Jewell dumped the Jaguar at the Midway, the killers then happened upon it quite by chance and in full view put Maffia's body in the passenger seat. Or had they followed him all the time, watching what he was going to do? Jewell was convicted by a 10 to 2 majority. Throughout the trial he had sought repeatedly to implicate Hinds, countering questions by saying that Hinds should be asked about the subject. After the trial

---

[1]Drury was later implicated in the great Porn Squad enquiry, convicted and sentenced to eight years' imprisonment, reduced to five on appeal.

Hinds was allowed to have a statement made in court denying any knowledge of the murder.

Why did Jewell go to the police in the first place? There were probably enough local candidates to keep the police happy in their enquiries for months. Presumably he wanted to get his story in first in the hope it would be believed. Unfortunately he changed the details on a number of occasions, although he stuck to the basic story throughout his trial and sentence. Whilst he was in Wandsworth he wrote to Arthur Maffia, Tony's brother, denying, yet again, that he had been his brother's killer and giving descriptions of the men whom he said had stopped the car. Arthur Maffia and other friends made what are quaintly described as 'their own investigations' and were satisfied the killer was Jewell. But Jewell still could find supporters for his story and in 1991 a television programme was made advancing his version of events.

There seems no really good reason why Jewell should have killed Maffia. It certainly wasn't a robbery. When the body was stripped, cash and cheques totalling over £700 were found, together with some rare gold coins. As always a number of theories were advanced. It was a contract hit – in which case it was extremely clumsily executed; Maffia was shot because he would not join in a forgery racket, which seems unlikely as offers such as this are made and declined on a daily basis without such major reprisals; Jewell had swindled Maffia and Hinds, which doesn't account for why he then shot Maffia; he was swindled by Maffia and Hinds, which would. There is no suggestion that Maffia was a police informer. Another theory is that on the way back to London Maffia, said to have had a spiteful tongue, simply taunted Jewell over a little con trick he had worked with the forged currency and had been shot in temper.

James Morton, *Gangland*; David Thurlow, *The Essex Triangle*.

28 May, 1982

The first of a series of killings which shocked both the Toronto public and police was on 28 May 1982. The partly clad body of Jennifer Isford, the 19-year-old cheerleader of the Canadian football club the Toronto Argonauts, was found on the lawn of a house five doors away from her parents' North York home. She had been raped and strangled shortly after she alighted from a Bayview Avenue bus after attending a cheerleading rehearsal. A $25,000 reward, later raised to $100,000, was offered for information leading to the arrest of her killer.

On 21 June, 25-year-old Christine Price was attacked whilst walking home after spending the evening with a friend. Her naked body was found in the West Rouge River near the Metro Zoo. She had been working as a nanny.

Just under a month later, on 10 July, the body of 38-year-old Judy Anne Delisle, a mother of four, was found in a lane near Woodcrest Avenue. Two days later, Claudia Geburt was stabbed to death in her Leslie Street home on her 21st birthday.

The spate of killings, together with a sex attack on a woman sunbathing in High Park, led to a review of safety on public transport and the establishment of a task force to combat violence against women.

Some of the killings were solved. Daniel William Wood was convicted of killing Judy Anne Delisle. He was also found to have murdered a woman in Calgary. Ms Geburt's killing was a domestic matter. Her fiancé and a girlfriend were found shot dead in a suicide-murder within the month.

In May 1995 a convicted sex offender was charged with the murder of Jennifer Isford.

29 May, 1979

Judge John Wood was shot in the back with a single dum-dum bullet as he went to get into his car in the parking lot of his apartment block in El Paso, Texas, about 8.30 am on 29 May 1979. He died an hour later. The 63-year-old judge, known as Maximum John and renowned for his tough sentencing in narcotics cases, had earlier been the recipient of death threats. Almost immediately the police announced they were seeking a curly-haired man aged about 20 who had been seen driving a small red car.

The killer of Judge Wood was not, however, a 20-year-old. He was Charles V. Harrelson, the son of a prison guard, who was convicted on 14 December 1982 of being the hit man in a $250,000 contract. He was sentenced to life imprisonment. Wood was the third man he had killed. In 1968 he had been charged and, despite eyewitness testimony, acquitted of the killing of a carpet salesman and then in 1973 he had been convicted of the killing of a grain dealer in Texas. For this he received 15 years' imprisonment and was paroled about eight months before shooting Judge Wood.

The prosecution alleged that Harrelson had killed Wood in a contract bought by El Paso drugs emperor and gambler Jimmy Chagra, who had been found guilty on drug smuggling charges and was due to appear before Wood for sentencing. Chagra's wife Elizabeth was also found guilty in the drugs conspiracy and Harrelson's third wife, Jo Ann, was found guilty of obstructing the course of justice. Elizabeth Chagra's conviction was overturned and a retrial set. By the time of his conviction on the Wood killing, Harrelson was serving a 40-year sentence for cocaine and weapons offences. He was a man possessed of considerable charm for women. Tape recordings made secretly whilst he was in prison have him promising three women he loved and wished to marry them. Jo Ann Harrelson's daughter gave evidence that she had had an affair of several months' duration with her stepfather.

Jimmy Chagra, then in his late thirties, was acquitted on the murder charge and received a total of 47 years for drug smuggling and impeding the course of justice over the Wood killing. His lawyer brother Joseph pleaded guilty to conspiracy to kill the judge and received a 10-year sentence.

The prosecution was keen to link the killing of the judge with the attempted murder of federal prosecutor James Kerr on 21 November 1978, and Joseph Chagra appeared in front of a grand jury to give evidence. The jury returned a two-count indictment with charges of conspiracy and assault against James Chagra.

By February 1986 the former lawyer, Joseph Chagra, was giving evidence in the case of his sister-in-law, Elizabeth, who was now charged with conspiracy over Wood's death. She was prosecuted by a husband-and-wife team, Ray and LeRoy Jahn. 'She was not an innocent bystander. She was a total conspirator,' said Mrs Jahn.

'The mere knowledge of a defendant that others have conspired to violate the law, even with her full sympathy, will not make her a conspirator,' defence lawyer Warren Burnet told the jury. 'You've got to find that Elizabeth formed an agreement with her husband, Jimmy Chagra, and that her intent at the time was to accomplish the murder of Judge Wood.' The prosecution's case was that she had delivered the $250,000 to Harrelson.

She was convicted after a retrial and was sentenced to 30 years in prison. She was eligible for parole in 1992 but was never released before her death from cancer in 1997. Over the years Harrelson has campaigned vigorously, protesting his innocence and alleging a governmental conspiracy. In 2000 the case was reopened with hearings in Denver and Florida.

30 May, 1992

Nineteen-year-old Amanda Duffy, who had just passed her audition for entry to the Royal Scottish Academy of Music and Drama, went celebrating with her friends. Within hours her half naked and battered body was found in a car park in Hamilton, Lanarkshire. Her body had been mutilated with twigs and branches in her mouth and nose – one had pierced her brain and penetrated her skull. She had also suffered a severe bite to her right nipple. At first it was thought this was a ritual killing.

It was possible to retrace Amanda's movements to early on the morning of 30 May 1992 when she had been walking home with friends through the pedestrian precinct in the town and had joined a queue for a taxi. Also in the queue, or at any rate passing, was 20-year-old bodybuilder and mechanic Francis Auld whom Amanda had known at school. She left her friends and walked away with him. She was not seen by her friends again.

Auld's account of the time spent with her was that they began kissing in shop doorways and later on a bench when another man who seemed to know Amanda had approached and she had left Auld for him.

Her body seems to have been discovered a little less than an hour after she died, for the pathologist estimated the time of death at 7.30 am, several hours after the ferocious attack on her.

When questioned Auld admitted biting her breast but said it was merely a love bite. The medical evidence was that it would have been bleeding and that if she had put her bra back on, as would have been expected before she left him with the other man, then it would have been covered with blood. It was found with no stains near her body. There was also a matching of Auld's hair snagged in a tree near the body. His jacket was never recovered. He said he had taken it off during the evening when, on his way home, he had decided to climb a tree and it had never been found. He had, he said, been drinking heavily and this was one reason why when the man went off with Amanda he had not protested.

Shortly after Amanda's body was found her parents received a telephone call from someone who appeared to be a young man who spluttered an apology for what he had done.

Auld was arrested and at his trial Dr Dallas Brodie, a psychiatrist, gave evidence that Auld apparently had no sign of mental or personality disorder. Defended by the leading Scottish counsel, Donald Findlay QC, Auld was released after the jury had returned a verdict of Not Proven. Later he appeared and was sentenced to 240 hours of community service for making threatening and malicious telephone calls to people whom he thought had boycotted him after the killing. In one he had said, 'You thought Amanda was the last. You are next after Caroline.' Caroline was the girlfriend of the recipient of the call.

In April 1995 Amanda Duffy's family took out civil proceedings against Auld. 'It is not really the money,' said her father. 'This is the only legal avenue open to prove once and for all who killed our daughter.' In October they were awarded £50,000 and costs. 'This is the end of a long fight. Someone killed Amanda brutally and horribly and we felt justice was not done. We have always thought Auld's actions were responsible for the death of our daughter,' said Mr Duffy. It is doubtful if the family will receive much of the award. When Auld had last worked it was as a motor mechanic.

31 May, 1994

On Sunday 31 May 1994 Shane Mills, the son of 47-year-old May Murrells, reported her and her 50-year-old former police officer husband, Ken, missing. On 29 May he had spoken to his mother at her Weymouth Avenue, Hillingdon, home when she told him they were planning to go to a horse show in Watford. When he did not hear from her the next day he rang relatives to try to locate them.

On 31 May he went with his aunt, Gay Cadden, to the Weymouth Avenue house, could not see the family car and then tried to trace the couple through friends and relatives. When he failed he contacted the police. In the evening he and his aunt broke into the Murrells' house and found May Murrells dead with multiple stab wounds. At 1.30 am the next day Ken Murrells's body was found next to his Nissan Prairie at Victoria Lane in Harlington, west London where he kept horses. He too had been stabbed. He had retired from the Metropolitan Police 14 years earlier after working in the Ealing and Hayes area and at the time of his death delivered leaflets for a mail-order company.

The Murrells kept themselves very much to themselves and a neighbour told the local paper, the *Hayes & Hillingdon Gazette*, that the windows of their house were never opened and, at one time, they had kept a pair of Alsatians indoors.

Their funeral took place at the end of January 1995 when Gay Cadden said she knew the person who killed the couple could well be at the funeral. 'May and Ken would have known this person really well,' she said. 'There is no way it would have been a stranger.'

A man was arrested in connection with the killing but no charge was ever brought. By the anniversary of the death the police enquiry had effectively been run down.

JUNE

1 June, 1993

On 1 June 1993 James Moody was shot dead in a contract killing in The Royal Hotel, Hackney. Moody had always been a shadowy figure in the London Underworld. Known as a hard man, in 1966 he had helped carry the wounded Frankie Fraser to comparative safety after the shooting of Dickie Hart at Mr Smith's Club in Catford (see 7 March). Moody was tried for his part in the affray that night and was acquitted.

He became an invaluable member of the Thursday Gang of the late 1970s, which specialised in hijacking, often with considerable violence, security vans in the London area. Wanted for a series of armed robberies he hid out in a lock-up garage which he furnished with books, food, bodybuilding equipment and a chemical toilet. He was caught when he visited his son's flat in Brixton. Charged with raids totalling £930,000 he was sent to Brixton prison to await trial.

In the 1980s it was still possible for remand prisoners to have food and drink brought in by friends and relatives. Moody's brother Richard brought, with the Sunday lunches, hacksaw blades, drill bits and other tools.[1]

---

[1]There is a full account of Moody's life and death in Cal McCrystal's 'The hit at the Royal Hotel' in the *Independent on Sunday*, 8 August 1993.

Together with his cell mates, Gerard Tuite, a Provisional IRA bombmaker, and Stanley Thompson, Moody cut through the cell's brickwork. Every morning the rubble was removed in their chamber pots at slopping out time. On 16 December 1980 they pushed out the loosened brickwork of their cell, stepped on to a flat roof where a ladder had been left by roofers and were away.

Thompson need not have bothered. The escape took place whilst the jury was out in his trial at St Albans and, in his absence, they found him not guilty. Tuite was later arrested in Dublin, becoming the first person to be charged in Ireland with criminal offences committed in England. He received 10 years. Richard Moody received two years for the help he had given his brother.

James Moody simply vanished. Apart from an unsuccessful raid on a flat in west London where his fingerprints and nothing else were found there was no sign at all of him for the next 13 years.

Then on the night of 1 June 1993, whilst drinking at the bar of the Royal Hotel, Hackney, where he was known as Mick, he was shot dead by a man described as being in his early forties and wearing a leather jacket. The man had ordered a pint of Foster's lager and put two coins down on the bar to pay for it. He then moved towards Moody and fired three shots. As Moody slumped to the floor, a fourth was fired into his back before the man was driven away in a stolen white Ford Fiesta XR2.

Where had Moody been and why was he shot? As to the first question there were suggestions he had been hidden out by the Provisionals but clearly he had been back in England some years, if indeed he ever left. At the time of his death he had been living in Wadeson Street, a back alley off Mare Street in Hackney. As to the second question, why was he shot, one theory was that it was a killing done on behalf of a cuckolded husband, for Moody was very much a ladies' man. A second version is that it was a part of the long-drawn-out struggle for power between the Arif family and other south London interests and that it was in revenge for the killing of

David Brindle in the Bell public house in Walworth in
August 1991.

There is, however, another theory over David Brindle's
death which fits the facts but has nothing to do with
the overall game plan of the south London warlords.
It was simply a personal matter. It has been suggested
that Jimmy Moody was working in a pub at the back of
Walworth under the name Tom and had been in the area
for 10 years. The suggestion is that since Moody was not
a man about town he could have worked the area and no
police officer would have recognised him. Some claim that
David Brindle had had a row with the publican and Jimmy
had crept behind him and beaten him with a baseball bat,
badly knocking him about. In turn Brindle told Moody
it wouldn't be forgotten. Moody and another man went
into the Bell in East Street and shot David Brindle and a
bystander. Immediately afterwards he went over to the
East End.

Once Moody had been traced to Hackney it became
common knowledge in south-east London that reprisals
were about to be taken.

Frankie Fraser, *Mad Frank*; James Morton, *Gangland 2*.

2 June, 1994

At 7.15 pm on 2 June 1994 a man wearing a balaclava
and gloves walked into the Mumutaz Tandoori restaurant
on the island of Orkney and shot the waiter, 26-year-old
Shaymol Mahmood, in the head. The bullet passed straight
through and lodged in the wall near where a family was
eating. The gunman then walked out of the restaurant, ran
down an alleyway, and was last seen near Kirkwall pier.

It was the first murder in Orkney for 25 years and
that time the killer had been arrested within 24 hours.

In this case, however, the police were unable to make an arrest. Some four thousand people, including tourists from Japan and Australia, were interviewed but without success. Theories for the killing included a feud in the Bangladeshi community, mistaken identity and a jealous husband but there was no evidence that Shaymol Mahmood had offended one of the latter or been involved in a dispute in the former.

After the murder the ports and Orkney airport were sealed and there was no evidence that a small boat had left any of the secluded bays on the island. Detective Superintendent George Gough, in charge of the investigation said, 'My experience tells me the murderer is more likely to be a local than an outsider, still there in the community.' By the summer of 1995 the investigation was scaled down.

3 June, 1991

At about 6 pm on Monday, 3 June 1991 Alison Shaughnessy was stabbed to death in her flat in Battersea. She had been struck 54 times. Police enquiries focused on 22-year-old Michelle Taylor, a former girlfriend of Alison's husband John Shaughnessy who had continued his relationship with her after his marriage. Their affair had ended in the autumn of 1990, some three months after Shaughnessy's marriage to Alison. Although Michelle Taylor remained good friends with both the Shaughnessys the motive, the police believed, was jealousy and the elimination of a rival.

Michelle Taylor was able to produce an alibi. She had been working in her job as an accounts clerk at a private health clinic in Lambeth Road, south London with John, who worked there as a gardener. On the evening of Alison's death she had been with him at about 6 pm, arranging flowers in patients' rooms. She had then spoken to a porter and at 8 pm she had given John a lift to his flat to collect two large flower pots. At half past eight that evening they discovered Alison's body. Michelle ran into the street screaming and called the police. When she was asked later that evening whether John had any girlfriends she said no. It was when, some weeks later, the police discovered the old relationship between Michelle and John that a theory was then constructed that Michelle could have stabbed Alison to death in her flat and returned to the clinic before 6 pm. Alison's movements could be traced back to the time she left work in the Strand very shortly after 5 pm.

There were problems with the theory. The first was a witness, a girl in the clinic called Jeanette Tapp, who said that Michelle and her younger sister, 19-year-old Lisa, had been at the clinic talking to her at 5.15 on the afternoon of Alison's death. The second problem was one of timing. How could Michelle and Lisa, who also became a suspect, have killed Alison after 5.40 pm, the earliest time she could have arrived home, cleaned themselves of all the blood from what was a truly savage attack and been back at the clinic at 6 o'clock? Jeanette Tapp adhered to her story on three occasions but, on 7 August, the police came to her home at 5.40 am and told her she was being arrested for conspiracy to murder. By the time she arrived at Tooting police station nearly three hours later she had changed her mind. She was now certain that she had not been with Lisa and Michelle at 5.15 pm. In fact she had not seen them until 7 pm. She was released without charge and the following day Michelle and Lisa were charged with murder.

There was no scientific evidence to link either of the sisters to the killing. Most surprisingly, no spot of blood could be found on the clothing of either of the girls. A doctor said he had seen two girls running from the flat at the time of the murder but he failed to pick out either of the sisters at an identification parade. There were five sets of unidentified fingerprints in the flat and there was some evidence that jewellery had been stolen. The defence was able to show that it was possible Alison had not arrived home until after 6 pm that day. What assisted in the conviction of both sisters was the alarming press coverage of the affair John had had with Michelle. There were stories that she was a jealous mistress and when it came out that she had slept with John on the way to Ireland for his wedding a further volley of abuse was fired at her. Much was made of an entry in her diary in October 1990 in which she had described Alison as an unwashed bitch and said, 'My dream solution would be for Alison to disappear as if she never existed.' She had also wrongly told the police that Lisa had never been to the Shaughnessy flat. The girls were convicted and sentenced to life imprisonment.

On 11 June 1993 the Court of Appeal released the girls, quashing their convictions which were ruled to be unsafe and unsatisfactory. The press coverage of the trial described as 'unremitting, extensive, sensational, inaccurate and misleading' had, said Lord Justice McCowan, 'created a real risk of prejudice'. There was also an evidential problem. The Crown's eyewitness, Dr Michael Unsworth, had also made another statement, not disclosed to the defence, in which he had said that one of the girls he had seen fleeing from the flat was black.

A possible alternative theory for the killing comes from a social worker who, on 5 June 1991, had telephoned the police to say that a man, whom he named, had told him he had 'done a girl'. The man had been in a squat in Battersea, had also been sleeping rough in the Strand and had carried a knife. The social worker and a colleague telephoned the police on a number of other occasions but when detectives finally went to interview the named man he had disappeared.

In July 1995 the sisters went to the Court to try to overturn a decision by the Attorney General not to prosecute various newspapers for contempt of court in their reporting of the case. They failed.

4 June, 1904

In what was one of the most sensational cases of the decade, the beautiful 22-year-old Nan Patterson was acquitted of the shooting murder on 4 June 1904 of Caesar Young in a hansom cab in Manhattan. She was a Floradora girl, replacing one of the original sextette who had married a millionaire and had left the troupe. Unfortunately she did not choose a millionaire for herself but, instead, fell in love with a married gambler, Francis Thomas Young, known to all as Caesar.

Although the couple were constantly seen together in public, Thomas seems to have rejected the idea of leaving his wife. He maintained her in one apartment and, conveniently, Nan Patterson in another in the same block.

By early 1904 he had paid for Nan's divorce – she had contracted a youthful marriage – and was about to leave his wife but, once more, he vacillated. Mrs Young persuaded him to sail for Europe with her where she felt that, in Nan Patterson's absence, she could finally win him back.

Young spent the day of 3 June with Nan Patterson. They drank heavily and quarrelled loudly. On the morning of Young's departure, on 4 June, they appeared to have made things up and took a hansom cab to drive down Broadway. En route the driver heard Nan call out, 'Look at me, Frank. Why did you do it?'

What the gambler was meant to have done was, tormented by the thought of separation, to have shot himself in the chest. There were, however, some serious difficulties with that scenario. The angles were all wrong and the dying man had put his gun back in his pocket.

Nan stood up well to cross-examination in three trials during which the prosecution's case was that it was she who had pulled out the gun and shot Young as he tried to take it from her. After three juries had disagreed, a motion was granted to discharge her.

Two thousand people cheered as she was released and children sang a quickly improvised little ditty:

> Nan is free, Nan is free,
> She escaped the electric chair,
> Now that she's out in the open air.

She went back on the stage but her career was short-lived. She remarried her first husband and that second marriage was also short-lived.

5 June, 1931

On 5 June 1931 the police forced open a window of the Lewis villa in Erith Road, Belvedere, Kent, only to find the furniture piled in the centre of the living room and the dining room walls stripped for repapering. The three beds were unmade and a sheet was missing from each. The police had been called because on 2 June Mr Lewis had telephoned the principal of the Stockwell college attended by his daughter Freda to say she would not be returning for the summer term. He had also written to various relatives saying that both Maude, his wife, and Freda had met with accidents and he would be forwarding details. When nothing further was heard and the telephone rang unanswered a relative called to find the house locked up.

When questioned, neighbours reported that they had seen the family, 60-year-old education officer Charles Lewis, Maude and the 20-year-old daughter Freda whom they had adopted after her father had died on the *Titanic*, digging a fish pond in the garden. The bodies of Freda and Maude were buried in the concrete surround to the pond. Sir Bernard Spilsbury found cyanide in their bodies. Lewis had blithely signed the poisons book when he purchased insecticide from a chemist in Eltham.

By the time the police found the remains of his wife and daughter he was on the high seas. In the name of Davidson he had booked a passage to Leith on the *Royal Scot* which left Wapping on 5 June. The boat was near Whitby when one of the passengers asked him about his limp – he had a withered leg. He limped out of the room and shortly afterwards threw himself overboard. His body was never recovered.

An audit at the education department showed that, over the years, he had embezzled some £600 (in those days enough to buy a decent detached house).

6 June, 1983

The Billionaire Boys' Club was founded in March 1983 with the concept that a group of wealthy young Californians would play the commodity and stock markets. The brains behind the scheme was Joe Hunt who had been on the Chicago Mercantile Exchange. There is little doubt that the 24-year-old possessed both charisma and leadership qualities. He had not had a successful time in Chicago and was almost broke but he persuaded two investors to put up $80,000 each and a third person to invest $20,000. More was needed and the name Ron Levin came up as a potential punter.

The 40-year-old bisexual con man agreed to put up $5 million with profits to be split in half. Within three months the investment was down to $1 million and then Joe Hunt managed to turn things around and made it all back. Unfortunately he had been the victim of a Levin scam. There had been no investment of $4 million by him. It had been done through a dummy account and Hunt had only made a paper as opposed to a real profit.

On 6 June 1983 Hunt and Jim Graham, the so-called head of security for the Club, visited Levin. There Graham, in a prearranged stunt, threatened both Levin and Hunt who now said that he was in debt to the Mafia and that Graham was one of their enforcers. Levin, convinced by the charade, wrote a cheque for $1.5 million on a Swiss bank account and was promptly shot. His body was taken to Soledad Canyon and dumped.

The killing unravelled fairly quickly. Hunt had written out his plan on seven sheets of yellow paper and carelessly left these in Levin's flat. They were found two months later. On 6 July 1987 Hunt was sentenced to life imprisonment without parole and after two mistrials Graham was allowed to plead guilty to being an accessory after the fact.

Since his killing a number of witnesses have come forward to say they have seen Ron Levin alive and well. One places him in a restaurant in Mykonos at Christmas in 1987. Hunt has continually maintained his innocence, alleging that Levin faked his death first to entrap Hunt; secondly to avoid his own prosecution on charges of theft; and thirdly because he was heavily in debt.

Murder Casebook, No 135, *Billionaire Boys' Club Murders*.

7 June, 1992

On 7 June 1992, the semi-naked body of 18-year-old Katie Rackliff was found by four schoolboys out on an early-morning walk after a night's camping. She had suffered a series of 27 stab wounds to her chest and neck. She had been with a friend to Ragamuffins, a nightclub in Camberley, Surrey, and they had become separated. It was alleged that Katie had been hoping to meet a previous boyfriend with whom she had broken up. A witness claimed that she had last been seen walking in a nearby car park calling out the name of her boyfriend.

Despite appeals from Katie's parents and the interviewing of nearly five hundred people who had been at the nightclub, the police made no progress with their inquiries until, in May 1996, 17-year-old Sharon Carr was arrested. She had been 12 at the time of Katie's murder.

At Winchester Crown Court on 26 March 1997, Carr was ordered to be detained during Her Majesty's Pleasure. The court heard that she had made a number of confessions, whilst detained at Bullwood Hall, for causing grievous bodily harm by stabbing a thirteen-year-old girl. She had also kept a diary in which she gave details of the killing and her feelings over the death. 'Killing did me good. Now I know what I am capable of and I will do it again.' Sentencing her, Mr Justice Scott Barr said, 'What is clear is that you had a sexual motive for this killing and it is apparent, both from the brutal manner in which you mutilated her body and chilling entries in your diary, recording what you had done, that killing, as you put it, turns you on.' Earlier, whilst on remand, she had tried to strangle two women staff at Middlesex Lodge Assessment Centre.

8 June, 1990

On 8 June 1990 millionaire Nicholas Whiting, former British saloon car champion driver, went missing after a raid on his showroom, All Car Equipe, in Wrotham, Kent. Along with him went five cars including a Ford Escort Turbo, and an Audi Quattro worth over £10,000. The cars were all recovered within a matter of days but of Whiting there was no sign.

Two weeks later it was suggested that he had staged his own kidnap and had gone on the run with John 'Little Lew'

Lloyd who was wanted in connection with the Brink's Mat gold robbery on 26 November 1983. In the robbery at a warehouse on the trading estate at Heathrow, guards had petrol poured over them and one was threatened with castration. The robbers had escaped with £26 million in gold. The reasoning behind the theory would seem to have been that Lloyd had been a long-standing friend of Kenneth Noye who, in turn, had been acquitted of killing an undercover policeman in the grounds of his home and then convicted of dishonestly handling part of the gold bullion. Noye had been sentenced to the maximum of 14 years' imprisonment.

The suggestion was proved totally wrong when on 1 July, following a tip-off, the police dug Whiting's body from Rainham Marshes in Essex. They believed he had been beaten, bound and gagged, and placed in the boot of a car. Later he had been frogmarched for some two miles before being shot in the head.

One suggestion was that his killing had been ordered by a major criminal then serving time on the Isle of Wight. Whiting was believed to have borrowed stolen money from the man to build houses on a plot of land he had bought and had been unable to repay it.

Two men were charged with his murder but on 16 August 1990 the Crown Prosecution Service offered no evidence against one of them who said that he had never met Whiting and that his arrest had been as a result of a malicious telephone call made to the police. On 13 December that year magistrates found the second man had no case to answer and refused to commit him for trial.

Jeffrey Robinson, *The Laundrymen*.

9 June, 1930

On 9 June 1930 Rose Elizabeth Tame, aged 10 years, went with her father and younger brother to Hampstead Heath on their way to Kenwood, north London. At South Hill park they saw a street entertainer performing a fire-eating act watched by a crowd of about two hundred. Rose left her father and, with her six-year-old brother, went into the crowd nearer the man. The act was a slight variation of the usual one in that 41-year-old William Richard Woodward saturated a cotton wool ball wired on the end of a rod, lighted it, and blew paraffin oil from his mouth which caused a large flame to develop, resembling a bursting shell. On this occasion there was a burst of flame which went into the crowd. Rose's clothes were set alight. Burned on her legs, buttocks and abdomen she ran away and her father chased after her. He took off his coat and extinguished the flames. She was taken to hospital but died from her burns on 13 June. Two other children were injured.

Two men who saw the act said that the performer gave no warning to the crowd and they believed the man was drunk. However, a police officer later gave evidence that he believed Woodward to have been sober.

Woodward, who had been performing the act for some five years without incident, was arrested and charged with manslaughter. He came before the magistrates at Hampstead on 18 June when the Chairman, who was also a lawyer, announced that no jury would convict and refused to commit the case for trial.

Wontners, the London solicitors instructed by the police, wrote in their report:

> We rather expected that the bench would have committed the accused for trial, although we think that it was almost certain he would have been acquitted by a jury. The circumstances were certainly of a most

extraordinary character and although the question was not altogether free from doubt our own view was that it was misadventure; for which the accused might be civilly but not criminally responsible.

10 June, 1967

Frances Barker disappeared on 10 June 1967. A year later her decomposed body was discovered at Glenboig, Scotland.

Earlier in 1967 Pat McAdam had also disappeared. The 17-year-old girl vanished on 19 February 1967 after accepting a lift, along with her friend, Hazel Campbell, from a lorry driver, back to Dumfries after a night out in Glasgow. Her friend was dropped off but Pat McAdam was never seen again. Three years after her disappearance a journalist from the Scottish *Daily Record* approached a Dutch psychic, Gerald Croiset, about the case. Croiset became convinced that Pat had been murdered and unsuccessfully endeavoured to identify the place of her death although he was able to describe a bridge.

A lorry driver, Thomas Young, was traced through a teenage girl who said she had been raped repeatedly by him after calling at his house looking for a friend. A search of his house at 71 Ashley Street, Glasgow turned up Frances Barker's powder compact and he was convicted of her murder. During police inquiries he admitted he had given a lift to Pat McAdam but said he had dropped her off at a layby near the bridge described by the psychic Croiset after he had had sex with her. He admitted to the police that he had had sex with over two hundred women in his lorry, some of whom he had raped when they would not consent. Pat McAdam's body has never been found.

Andrew Boot, *Psychic Murder Hunters*.

11 June, 1981

Issei Sagawa, a Japanese from a wealthy family, studying at the Sorbonne in Paris, invited a Dutch girl, Renee Hartevelt, out to dine on 11 June 1981. They had previously been to concerts and the theatre together. Sagawa was, apparently, particularly taken with the whiteness of her arms. After dancing they returned to his apartment in the fashionable 16th arrondissement, the Bois de Boulogne area, where he shot her in the back of the neck.

After this he chopped her into pieces and ate her. He recorded the sensations he underwent with meticulous care. First he noted that she had 'white breasts, a slender build, a long white neck and transparent white skin and a beautiful gorgeous face'.

At first he seems to have been in two minds which part of her he should eat first, settling on the right hip which he described as having the same texture as raw tuna. He moved to the thigh. He more or less ate the body in two days before putting the remains in suitcases which he threw into a pond in the Bois. Unfortunately he had not packed the suitcases properly and a severed arm attracted attention. He was arrested two days later on 15 June.

He was found insane and detained in a Paris asylum from where he was repatriated after a year to be sent to a mental hospital. His parents consented to his stay there but, since he had not been convicted in France nor had he been committed in the legal sense to the hospital, it was possible for his wealthy parents to obtain his release after little more than a year. On his release he became a celebrity, writing a novel, *Letters from Sagawa*, which won a literary prize, as well as his memoirs. He later became a television personality on a German station and a restaurant critic for a Japanese magazine.

His explanation for his cannibalism is that at the age of

five he dreamed of being boiled inside a pot. Over the years his fear became a desire.

12 June, 1993

On 12 June 1993 Emanuel Spiteri, a chef, died in what appeared to be a homosexual sado-masochistic killing. He was the last of the victims of Colin Ireland and a closed-circuit photograph taken of the pair as they left a cash point led to his killer's arrest. The killings had begun three months earlier when, on 8 March 1993, Peter Walker, a 44-year-old theatre director, had the day off from rehearsals for the musical *City of Angels* and went at about 5 pm to the Coleherne public house in Earl's Court, west London, a noted gay pub. The next day, when he did not appear at the theatre, friends contacted the police. Walker was found at his flat. He had been suffocated with a plastic bag. Two days later a man telephoned the *Sun* newspaper saying he had killed a man and that it was his New Year resolution to kill more.

Walker was probably the first of the victims of the twice-married Colin Ireland. Ireland's first marriage, in 1982, was to Virginia Zammit, a disabled sportswoman, who had obtained an injunction against him and who divorced him in 1987. He married again in 1990.

Ireland's *modus operandi* was to pick up men by pretending he was into sado-masochism, and torture them before killing them and getting their PIN numbers for their bank accounts. Apart from Walker his known victims were Christopher Dunn, killed on 28 May after he had been burned with a lighter; the son of an American Congressman, Perry Bradley III, whose body was found on 4 June having been whipped and strangled; Andrew Collier, found 7 June, beaten and strangled. Ireland had also strangled Collier's cat and placed it over his body. His final victim was Spiteri.

After the circulation of the photograph, showing him with Spiteri, Ireland gave himself up, denying his involvement in the murders. He confessed after hearing he had left a fingerprint at the home of Andrew Collier.

In his statement he said he was sober and not on drugs when he committed the offences. He had been a bouncer in a homosexual club but he himself was neither bisexual nor homosexual. Whilst he admitted he had experienced sado-masochistic sex with women he said he had only pretended with the men. He had not undressed during the encounters. Asked his motive for the murders, he said, 'I was a thin lanky little runt – always getting the worst of it. It was building up in me – a general dislike of people.'

13 June, 1919

Fleetwood Willats, a 72-year-old widower, was killed, seemingly for the fun of it, on 13 June 1919. He lived in Tottenham, north London and after he had been to his usual public house for a glass of beer he met two men who offered him a whisky. He drank two tablespoons of what he was able to say tasted like sweet wine and which burned his mouth. He declined any more.

The next day he was taken ill and died in hospital that evening. He had been given hydrochloric acid. He was unable to describe the men who gave him the poison and the joke never seems to have been repeated by them.

14 June, 1955

Judge Curtis Chillingworth and his wife Marjorie were not seen alive after they went to their beach house at Manalapan, Florida, around 9 pm on 14 June 1955. Two workmen, Frank Ebersold and Robert Force, who came the next morning to replace a window, found the house empty with the table laid for breakfast and the judge's car in the drive. With no one to direct them which window needed repair they decided to go for a swim. All the way down the steps to the beach they found what appeared to be a trail of dried blood and on the beach itself footprints leading to and from the house and out to sea. Ebersold telephoned the judge's secretary who in turn alerted the police. A search of the house showed the bed had rumpled sheets and there were two unwashed glasses. Of the judge and his wife there were no signs. The police confirmed the trail was blood. The judge and his wife were put on the missing persons list where their names remained for two years. The judge was not known to have had serious enemies and had not reported receiving threats from relatives of prisoners who had appeared before him.

Within a month of the disappearance of the Chillingworths, an attorney, Phillip O'Connell, began to receive anonymous telephone calls saying, 'You are next.' O'Connell, who had a substantial law practice, was also involved in the politics of Palm Beach County and stood in the way of another judge, Joseph Alexander Peel.

Whereas Chillingworth had a good reputation, Peel did not. In 1954 Peel had accomplished the difficult trick of representing both sides in a contested divorce suit, something for which he had been rebuked by Chillingworth. He also combined his judicial activities with an unhealthy interest in the Underworld. He was in association with Floyd Holzapfel, who worked as a private inquiry agent, and George David 'Bobby' Lincoln, offering protection to illegal distilleries and the operators of the Spanish betting game *bolita*. A grand jury refused to indict Holzapfel when he explained the reason he was associating with figures from the world of organised crime was that he was working undercover for a philanthropist who wanted the rackets exposed.

In 1955 Peel again mishandled a divorce and Chillingworth, as his senior, was this time preparing to do more than rebuke him. Disbarment would have been the end not only of his career but also – financially more importantly – of his ability to provide judicial protection.

Peel asked Holzapfel to organise a contract killing. On the night of 14 June he and Lincoln left the Rivera Dock and sailed for Palm Beach. According to Holzapfel, Peel had told him only the judge would be at home but when they arrived, posing as yachtsmen whose boat had broken down, both the judge and his wife were there. Holzapfel hit Mrs Chillingworth as she began to scream. This accounted for the trail of blood down the steps to the beach. The pair were tied and put on board the boat. Two miles out to sea they were pushed overboard with the judge fighting to the last.

Rewards, including one of $100,000 from the Florida legislation, brought no results and it was not until 1960 that the story began to unravel. By then Holzapfel and Lincoln had adroitly managed to sidestep a prosecution for the insurance fraud murder of Harold Gray, an attorney who worked for Peel. Holzapfel was also beginning to complain that he had not even had his expenses let alone a fee for the murder of Chillingworth and his wife. Reimbursement apart, he was leading a charmed life: a conviction for conspiracy to steal an arms cache, which had resulted in a 15-year sentence, had been overturned.

Unfortunately for Peel, Holzapfel committed another murder, disposing of a bootlegger, Lew Harvey, in similar manner to the way he had murdered the Chillingworths. Now Peel, fearing Holzapfel would talk, persuaded him to go to South Africa where, in turn, he took out a contract on the life of his protégé. Holzapfel was persuaded by the Florida police that it would be financially sensible for him to return and in what could be argued as a clear case of entrapment also persuaded him to confess all in a taped conversation during a three-day binge in a motel. He was arrested on 3 October 1960.

Holzapfel survived both an attempt to cut his own wrists and one by Peel to have him poisoned. He and Lincoln gave evidence against the judge who, to the anguish of the prosecution, who had sought the death penalty, received two life sentences. Holzapfel was sentenced to death but reprieved.

15 June, 1991

On 15 June 1991 Leslie Mahaffy disappeared from near her home in Toronto, Ontario. On 29 June 1991 Paul Bernardo and his fiancée, Karla Homolka, were married in a fairy-tale ceremony at the tourist trap resort of Niagara-on-the-Lake, a few miles from the falls. At the same time parts of the concrete-encased body of 14-year-old Leslie Mahaffy were being pulled from another lake. She had been strangled, sexually assaulted, and her body cut into pieces with a circular saw.

In 1993 Homolka received a 12-year sentence after she pleaded guilty to manslaughter in a deal with the police in which she agreed to testify against her husband. Hers was a story of perversion and murder which, she said, had begun when she met Bernardo at a Pet Shop convention in the Scarborough suburb of Toronto in 1987. She was then 17.

According to her story she had been subjected to a series of beatings and rapes. On Christmas Eve 1990 she had participated in the rape and assault of her sister, Tammy, after Bernardo had drugged the 15-year-old with an animal tranquilliser. The proceedings had been videoed. The girl was murdered and, said Homolka, she lived under the threat from Bernardo that he would tell her parents of her participation.

In 1991 whilst the pair were in Cape Cod another girl was lured to a rented home where she was drugged and subjected to sexual assaults. On 16 April 1992 Bernardo told Homolka he wanted a sex slave and with her help he lured a schoolgirl, 15-year-old Kristen French, into his car by pretending to seek directions. As Homolka spread a map on the roof of the car Bernardo came behind the girl, caught her hair and pushed her into the car at knifepoint. Once captured she was forced into oral sex with Homolka and sex with Bernardo. On 19 April, Easter Sunday, the girl was strangled after Homolka demanded they go to her parents for dinner. Bernardo had wanted to keep the girl hostage a little while longer. Her body was found on No 1 Sidewalk on 30 April.

On 17 February 1993 Bernardo was arrested at his home on Bayview Drive. DNA samples had matched him to sexual attacks in Scarborough. He was charged with rape and the killings of Mahaffy and Kristen French. Karla Homolka was arrested 13 weeks later and first appeared in court on 18 May. She waived her right to a preliminary hearing and a date for trial was fixed for 28 June. In fact she pleaded guilty on 6 July to the manslaughter of Kristen French and Leslie Mahaffy. In a plea bargain the court was told that the prosecution and defence agreed upon a 12-year sentence. In return she would testify against Bernardo. But for her evidence, the Crown said they would not be able to prove the circumstances of the death of her sister.

There were psychiatric reports on Homolka to the effect that her self-esteem had been completely destroyed and that in effect she had been brainwashed by Bernardo. According to another report she 'had intense need to be in a romantic relationship with a male who could project and maintain an image of dominance over others and financial/personal/family success in life'. From about

six months after they had first met, she said, Bernardo
had beaten and abused her, raping her, throwing knives
at her, punching her and pushing her downstairs. He
had also lessened contact between her and her family.
In January 1993 he had beaten her to an extent that
the emergency-room doctor had said the injuries were
the worst case of wife-assault he had seen.

Bernardo's trial began in May 1995 before an eight-
man, four-woman jury. Part of the evidence against him
were the video tapes made of the killings. Homolka began
her evidence against him on 19 June. Bernardo's only
defence was to discredit her and shift the blame for the
killings on to her, and much of the cross-examination was
designed to show that, far from being a beaten and abused
wife, she had been an equal sex partner and that she had
consistently lied over the death of her sister, Tammy.

Rather against expectations Bernardo gave evidence
claiming that Leslie Mahaffy's death had been an accident
and that Kristen French had been strangled accidentally by
Homolka.

The Bernardo jury retired on 31 August 1995, returning
the next day with verdicts of guilty on nine counts.
Bernardo was sentenced to life imprisonment with no
parole for 25 years. To the fury of the public Homolka
will be eligible for parole in 1997 and in the summer
of 1995 was entitled to have unescorted leave from the
prison.

Scott Burnside and Alan Cairns, *Deadly Innocence*.

16 June, 1919

Mabel Greenwood, the wife of a Kidwelly, Herefordshire
solicitor, died about 3 am on Monday, 16 June 1919. She
had been taken ill during the evening of the previous day.

On the face of it the Sunday had been a perfectly normal one. She had written letters and read in the garden. Harold Greenwood had toyed with his motor car. Luncheon had been a joint of meat, vegetables, gooseberry tart and custard and part of a bottle of Burgundy of which she had a glass.

She began to feel ill in the early evening, complaining of heart pain, and Harold Greenwood gave her a glass of brandy. Dr Griffiths was called and she said the gooseberry tart had upset her. He prescribed brandy and soda and bismuth. An hour later Greenwood told her friend Florence Phillips that she was very ill. Miss Phillips went for the district nurse. Griffiths returned regularly throughout the evening, saying that he believed it was gastroenteritis. Mrs Greenwood did not survive the night.

Greenwood was not a popular man locally. For a start he was a Yorkshireman and therefore was seen as an outsider. His practice was at subsistence level and it was said that the money for the smart Rumsey House, where the Greenwoods lived, came from his wife, a member of the Bowater paper family. He was thought to be a ladies' man and it was whispered that he had been seen with Dr Griffiths's sister sitting on his knee in a railway carriage. Four months after his wife's death he married Gladys Jones, 18 years younger than himself. Gossip reached fever pitch and it was only a matter of time before his wife's body was exhumed and found to contain a quarter of a grain of arsenic. From there it was a short step to the Assizes at Carmarthen where he was defended with great style by Marshall Hall. The prosecution's case that the arsenic, in the form of weedkiller, was placed in the bottle of Burgundy was destroyed when the Greenwoods' daughter Irene said she had had a glass from the bottle at lunchtime and two during the evening. Greenwood was acquitted.

He was, however, a ruined man. He changed his name to Pilkington and sold the house. In March 1922 he obtained £150 damages from a waxwork museum in Cardiff which had exhibited an effigy of him in the Chamber of Horrors.

In April of that year he reported the trial of Major Herbert Armstrong – another local solicitor, also charged with, and this time convicted of, poisoning his wife – for a magazine. He applied to become Clerk to the Ross Urban Council and was rejected. He died on 17 January 1929.

It is probable that had Greenwood not been acquitted, Armstrong would never have murdered his wife. His thinking appears to have been that the Director of Public Prosecutions, rebuffed by the acquittal of one solicitor, would never dare to prosecute a second in the same locality and in very similar circumstances. Major Armstrong was wrong.

17 June, 1935

On 17 June 1935 the body of 19-year-old Mildred Hallmark was found in a ditch in the cemetery of Peoria, Illinois. Her neck had been broken and her underwear cut from her body. Within a matter of days a number of women came forward to say they had been raped by a young, good-looking man and that he had then taken pictures of them.

Five days after the murder another young woman complained to the police. She had, she said, been waiting for a bus when a young man, giving his name as Lee Bridges, had approached her and offered her a lift. Somewhat foolishly she had accepted and had been lucky to escape with her life. Holding her neck with one hand he had hit her repeatedly with the other. He had cut off her clothes, raped her and then photographed her, saying that if she reported the incident he would send the pictures to her friends. He then drove her to within a block of her home.

This particular assault had occurred six months before the murder and she had indeed not reported her assault. The story was even stranger. She had, she said, some two months after the attack, met a man at a dance who closely resembled her attacker. She had challenged him but he denied the assault, saying his name was Jerry Thompson and that he lived with his grandparents.

Mildred Hallmark's father knew Jerry Thompson and so, he said, did his daughter. In fact they had lived only two blocks from each other. Gerald Thompson, a good-looking, curly-haired man of 25, was arrested. He was identified by the girl who had gone to the police but, given a lie-detector test, he passed with flying colours. There was, however, considerable forensic evidence against him. A search of his room revealed photographs of the naked girls who had been raped. The police also found a car cushion and trousers with bloodstains which proved to match the blood type of Mildred Hallmark. Thompson confessed to the rapes and the murder, saying that when Mildred had fought back he had strangled her, breaking her neck. When a collection was organised for her funeral he had contributed handsomely.

Found guilty he was electrocuted on 15 October 1935 after being moved to another town to prevent his being lynched. One worrying feature of the case was the way in which he had passed the lie-detector test, thought at the time to be an infallible, although not always legally admissible, test of guilt. Before he died Thompson explained that he had deceived the machine by thinking of another girl when he was asked if he had killed Mildred Hallmark. He had, so far as could be traced, raped some 16 women but had bragged to a friend that he had averaged over one a week for a year.

Carl Sifakis, *The Encyclopedia of American Crime*; Colin Wilson, *Written in Blood*.

18 June, 1988

On 18 June 1988, 22-year-old Marie Wilks, who was seven months pregnant, was driving on the M50 near Bristol when her car overheated. She had left her home, together with her one-year-old son and her 10-year-old sister, to visit her husband, a Territorial Army instructor, who was at a cadet training camp in Ross-on-Wye. She left her sister and her baby in the car and walked 600 yards to the nearest emergency telephone. Whilst she talked to the police operator she was attacked, stabbed in the neck and abducted. The killer drove her for two miles before throwing her over the motorway embankment where she bled to death. Her body was found three days later.

The police arrested Eddie Browning, 36, a former Welsh guardsman and nightclub bouncer from Cwm-Parc, Rhondda, who had a conviction for robbery. The evidence against him was slender and circumstantial. Witnesses to the abduction said the man had spiky blond hair which Browning had. They also said the car in which Mrs Wilks was driven away was a silver Renault. Browning had a silver Renault. When questioned he denied his involvement and said that on the evening of the murder he had driven to Scotland. The quickest route, and one advised by his father, was by way of the M50 but Browning said he had taken the M4 across the Severn Bridge. There were no traces of blood in his car although Mrs Wilks must have been bleeding badly after the stabbing. No witnesses identified him. The prosecution based its case on the premise that he was a violent man who had lied about the route he had taken. On 8 November 1989 he was convicted at Shrewbury Crown Court and sentenced to life imprisonment with an order that he serve at least 25 years.

His first appeal, on the grounds that the trial judge did not point out the inconsistencies in the prosecution's case, failed in May 1991. It later emerged that one of the key witnesses, an off-duty police officer, had been hypnotised and had given a description of a different make of Renault and a different numberplate from the one owned by Mr Browning.[1] This was not disclosed to the defence, nor were the contents of two telephone calls to the police which were at variance with the way the prosecution put its case. The Court of Appeal judges ruled that had this information been available to the jury they were not sure the same decision would have been reached. Browning was released. 'Justice has been done today,' he said outside the court. 'The past six years have been a living nightmare but I never, ever doubted I would be cleared.' Whilst in prison he had been the subject of razor attacks.

19 June, 1928

After their wedding at a fashionable New York, West Side address on 12 May 1928 Chung Yi Miao, a Doctor of Law from Loyola University, Chicago, and his bride Siu Wai Sheung, travelled to Europe, visiting Scotland and, on 18 June, arriving at the Borrowdale Gates Guest House at Keswick in the Lake District.

The next afternoon, 19 June, they went out for a walk. Chung returned alone about 4.30 pm. He had apparently had a headache and left his wife to walk into Keswick

---

[1]Evidence obtained under hypnosis has never been accepted as completely reliable by the English and American courts. In some States of America, once a witness has been hypnotised his evidence is inadmissible and, in England in 1987, the Home Office produced draft guidelines on the conduct to be observed by a police force when a witness is hypnotised. These draft guidelines were never made mandatory. After the Browning case Dr H. B. Gibson, President of the British Society of Experimental and Clinical Hypnosis, wrote to *The Times* (May 24), calling on the Home Office to make it 'mandatory for police forces totally to eschew the use of hypnosis'.

to buy some warm underwear. Around 10 pm when his wife had not returned he asked a maid whether he should inform the police but did nothing and went to bed. In fact, about 8.30 pm her strangled body had been found in Cumma-catta wood about 400 yards from Grange Bridge.

Chung was awakened later and told of the death of his wife. According to police reports he seemed to know that she had been attacked although they only told him she was dead.

There was some evidence to put him at the gate into the woods although there appears to have been a Japanese singer in the area at the time which confused identifying witnesses. More significant, however, was Siu Wai's wedding ring contained in a roll of camera film in their bedroom. There was also the fact that she had been strangled with a white cord of the same texture as that on their hotel blinds.

Opinion about Chung varied. A Charles Cyphers, close friend of Siu Wai who had known her since childhood, wrote to the Chinese Consul General saying the pair had stayed with him the previous Christmas and he had not been impressed with the prospective bridegroom whom he thought had a bad temper. He preferred to think that the killing had been done in a fit of insanity but mentioned the question of money which Chung had said he had lost in mysterious circumstances. There was no doubt that Siu Wai was personally wealthy – she had met Chung in New York where she had gone to sell a collection of jade left to her by her father – and the killing might have been done for her estate. Chung's New York landlady also wrote saying that Chung had remarked to her, 'I don't know why I'm marrying this girl. I don't love her.' On the other hand there is another letter on the police files expressing surprise and dismay that Chung should have done such a thing.

Chung's defence was that he was being followed by other Chinese, possibly seamen, and they had killed his wife who was known to go about with her jewellery in her bag. Curiously, none of the missing jewellery apart from the wedding ring seems to have been traced. Some enigmatic notes were found in the room written by Chung which read, 'Don't do it in the ship' and 'Be sure to do it in the ship'. A third read, 'Again consider on arrival in England'.

Tried before Mr Justice Humphreys, Chung was convicted on evidence which was almost wholly circumstantial but which was regarded as overwhelming. His appeal, which he conducted himself, was dismissed and he was hanged by Thomas Pierrepoint on 6 December 1928.

The killing was almost certainly for financial gain but there are alternative theories. The first is that after the marriage – which had at one time been intended to take place in China – Chung discovered his wife could not have children and he killed her so he could find another, more fertile wife. The other, and less plausible, is that the killing was, in some form or another, involved with Triad organisations and that Chung had been under an obligation to kill his wife.

Douglas G. Browne, *Sir Travers Humphreys*; Christmas Humphreys, *Seven Murders*; Travers Humphreys, *A Book of Trials*.

20 June, 1983

On 20 June 1983 66-year-old Zita Blum and Honora Lehman, three years older, were found shot and stabbed in their burned out home near Joliet, Ohio. Theirs were the first deaths in a series of killings that summer, most of which were finally laid at the door of Milton Johnson.

On 17 July, 18-year-old Anthony Hackett was shot as he slept in his car, parked by Interstate Highway 55 near Wilmington. He and his girlfriend were returning from the Great America Amusement Park in Gurnee. The girl was sexually attacked, bound, gagged and stabbed before being dumped on a road near Joliet. Amazingly, she survived to give evidence against Johnson.

He was also considered to be a prime suspect in the shooting of five people in Homer Township on 16 July. There was, said the police, ballistic evidence and a *modus operandi* to link him to those and other killings but that had not been sufficient to bring charges in respect of those deaths.

A receipt for the repair of a fishing reel which carried the name Sam Myers, Johnson's stepfather with whom he was living at the time, was found under the body of one of the victims. Myers was able to show that he was in Mississippi at the time of the killings and said that perhaps the receipt might have blown out of the pick-up truck when he was in the vicinity.

On 20 August four women were killed in a Joliet ceramics shop.

In February 1984 Charles Malinowski, a lieutenant in the Will County sheriff's department, came across a report of harassment of two women in July 1983 by a man driving a black pick-up truck. When he investigated the matter further he was able to link the truck to Sam Myers and through him to Johnson. A receipt for a Tasman devil doll bought by Hackett was found in the pick-up.

Johnson was convicted first of the Hackett murder and sentenced to death before being indicted in the murders at the ceramics shop. The prosecution alleged that his bloody fingerprints were found on the car belonging to one of the victims. He was convicted after a trial in which he defended himself. In early 1995 it was announced that lawyers for Johnson were asking for permission to examine the evidence used to convict him.

Those who had had dealings with the man, once questioned over the notorious I-55 serial killings, were in no doubt of his guilt and that this was simply post-trial strategy. 'He was completely amoral,' said Ed Burmile Junior, a former State attorney. 'He was a stone-cold killing machine.'

21 June, 1921

One of the more bizarre killings occurred on 21 June 1921 when shooting broke out in the lobby of a block of flats in Chicago.

Carl Otto Wanderer, who owned a butcher's shop with his father, had served with Black Jack Pershing and the First Illinois Cavalry. He was promoted to lieutenant and fought in France. Highly decorated, he returned to Chicago a hero. There he married 20-year-old Ruth Johnson and went to live with her parents at 4731 North Campbell Avenue. She became pregnant.

Wanderer now changed. He became moody and depressed, leaving the flat and, if the pregnancy was mentioned, hitting the walls with his fists. He seemed in better spirits when, on 21 June, he invited his wife to go to the cinema with him.

According to Wanderer, on their return, when they entered the lobby of the block of flats, the light was off. His wife was groping for the switch when he heard a man's voice say, 'Don't turn the light on.' Wanderer carried a gun, something by no means unusual in Chicago in the days of Prohibition, and drew it. He said the man then shouted obscenities and fired a series of shots. He returned the fire and within a matter of seconds 14 shots had been fired from the two guns.

Ruth's mother came out of her flat and saw her daughter dying on the floor. Also dying was a man dressed in rags. Wanderer, on his knees beside him, hit him with his empty revolver, saying, 'You've killed my wife, you bastard. You've killed my wife.'

The man was taken to Ravenswood Hospital where he died. There was no clue to his identity and he was dubbed The Ragged Stranger by the press. He had just under $4 on him.

Wanderer was again a hero. Interviewed in the press

he told of what he assumed was an attempted robbery. The two guns, both .45 automatics, were displayed side by side. Ben Hecht, the crime reporter for the Chicago *Daily News*, did not accept Wanderer's version of the killing. He could not understand why the stranger had not pawned an expensive gun rather than risk a random hold-up. He also thought it unusual that the guns were the same make. Could the stranger also have been a war veteran?

Hecht and his friend and later co-playwright, fellow newsman Charles MacArthur, checked out the second gun, tracing it through its first sale in 1913 to a telephone repairman who had some years previously sold it to Wanderer's cousin, Fred.

Tackled on the subject Fred Wanderer said he had lent the gun to his cousin on the day of the shooting and presumed that this was the gun which had been used by him. Hecht went to interview Wanderer and found him less than grief-stricken. Searching his apartment under the pretext of going to the lavatory, Hecht found love letters Wanderer had written to a man. It was also discovered that Ruth Wanderer had drawn out all the money from her bank account on the day she was shot.

The theory was now that, rather than go through the charade of having a child, the homosexual Wanderer had killed his wife. Hecht and the police again visited Wanderer and told him that his lover, James, was coming to the flat. He confessed all, saying that he had spent some time on skid row looking for a suitable man to help carry out his plan. There he had found Al Watson, a Canadian ex-soldier. He had told him that his wife did not accept him as a war hero and Watson was to stage a fake hold-up. He, Wanderer, would knock him down, and re-establish himself in his wife's eyes. Instead he had shot both his wife and Watson.

He was tried for the murder of his wife and sentenced to 20 years in prison. A newspaper campaign was launched by Walter Howey of the *Herald and Examiner* for him to be retried, this time for Watson's murder. Now he was sentenced to death.

Both Hecht and MacArthur visited Wanderer, who showed no resentment towards them, in the condemned cell. For a final joke they arranged that on the gallows he should read out a speech making complaints against the editors of their newspapers. However, when he was taken from the condemned cell Wanderer was tied hand and foot and so could not read the script written by MacArthur. Instead he sang 'Dear Old Pal of Mine'.

Later Hecht and MacArthur wrote the very successful play, *The Front Page*.

In an alternative version of the story the investigating journalists are Harry Romanoff and Walter Howey. In this version Wanderer is a womaniser who could not bear the confines of marriage. The other essentials are the same.

George Murray, *The Ragged Stranger* in *The Chicago Crime Book;* Jay Robert Nash, *World Encyclopedia of 20th Century Murder*.

22 June, 1954

Pauline Parker, plump and plainish, then 16, and her lesbian lover, the taller and more attractive Juliet Hulme, a year younger, murdered Pauline's mother by repeatedly hitting her with a brick in a stocking. They had been afraid they would be separated when Juliet's father, one-time Rector of Canterbury University College, Christchurch, New Zealand, took her to South Africa for a visit to relatives. Pauline was determined to go there with her and it seems the plan was to beat Mrs Parker into submitting to this idea.

The girls were pupils at Christchurch Girls' High School and had formed what, in those days, was seen as an

unhealthy relationship. Neither played games; Juliet had
contracted tuberculosis and as a child Pauline had a bone
disease which had left her with a slight limp. Between
them they had enacted a whole melodrama of pageantry,
assuming the identities of saints, Charles the Second, and
the Cornishman Trelawny of '. . . shall Trelawny die . . .'
The girls also planned to go to America together to have
their writings published. It was decided by their parents
that they should be separated for their own good.

On 22 June 1954 the girls ran into a teashop near a park
in Christchurch and told the staff that they had found Mrs
Parker's badly battered body. They said she had accidentally slipped and banged her head. However, detectives
found 45 separate injuries which the girls attributed to the
fact that they had carried the body and it had bumped on
the ground.

It was a totally unsophisticated crime. A brick wrapped
up in a stocking was found more or less next to the body.
The injuries to Mrs Parker included a fractured skull. It
is possible that the story that they intended to frighten
her into letting Pauline go to South Africa may have been
right because, when Juliet Hulme was questioned, she said
that '. . . after the first blow was struck I knew it would
be necessary for us to kill her'. But in her diary in April
of that year Pauline Parker wrote, 'It is she who is one
of the main obstacles in my path. Suddenly the means of
ridding myself of this obstacle occurred to me. If she were
to die . . .'

Efforts were made to show that the girls were insane.
Dr R. W. Medlicott told the court that he thought the girls
might be suffering from 'paranoia, a form of delusion, of
an exalted type of *folie à deux*, a term used to describe
communicated insanity'. The jury, however, preferred the
prosecution version that they were 'dirty-minded little
girls' and returned a verdict of guilty. Because of their
youth they were detained until Her Majesty's pleasure be
made known. That was in 1958 when they were released
shortly after Pauline had her twenty-first birthday. They
had both received psychiatric treatment whilst in prison.

Juliet Hulme had studied languages and Pauline Parker obtained a school certificate.

In late 1994 it was discovered that for some years Juliet Hulme had been living in seclusion in Scotland writing detective novels.

23 June, 1919

On 23 June 1919 the body of Zee Ming Wu, a Chinese factory worker, was found in a wood at Warley on the Warwickshire–Worcestershire borders. He had been battered to death, his head crushed and ribs and breastbone broken, and his post office savings book taken.

Djang Djing Sung was arrested when he tried to use the post office book. At his trial he tried to put the blame onto two other Chinese who were working in the same factory, saying that one of them had told him that Zee Ming Wu had cheated him of money and that he was planning revenge. All went out for a day in the country and, when Wu was distracted, another hit him on the head with a hammer. He had, he said, been an innocent bystander. Both men were able to produce alibis and, in any event, Sung, if innocent, had still to explain how he came to be cashing the post office book. He was unable to do so and was hanged on 3 December by John Ellis.

24 June, 1991

At 8 pm on 24 June 1991 the body of Ghislaine Marchal, owner of *La Chamade*, a villa on a street the locals called

Paradise Row at Mougins near Cannes, was discovered at her home by gendarmes who had been alerted by a neighbour. She had been stabbed 13 times and had been struck on the head. She had clearly struggled with her killer.

A widow in her mid-sixties, who drove a white Rolls-Royce, she died in her cellar, apparently after trying to write the name of her killer in her own blood on the wall. She had written 'Omar m'a tuer', a reference, the police said, to her Moroccan-born gardener, 31-year-old Omar Raddad.

Robbery was suggested as a motive and possibly a video recorder was taken. If so it was never traced to Raddad. Mme Marchal was said to have 3,000 francs in her handbag but again this was never found. Raddad's movements on the day of the killing could be traced, except for an unfortunate gap of around 30 minutes. He had been working in the garden during the day, observed by the 80-year-old next-door neighbour, Mme Pascal. At noon he had left on his moped and bought a baguette 20 minutes later. He had then returned to his apartment. At ten minutes to one he had set off for work again and had stopped to make a telephone call to his wife who was staying with her sister in Toulon, awaiting the birth of a second child. The owner of the next-door villa gave him an ice-cream at about 1.30 pm and did not notice any injuries on him or anything strange in his behaviour. The first two medical reports failed to state a definite time of death for Mme Marchal. After what was intended as the definitive autopsy, the time of death was stated to be a day later than originally indicated. This was then passed off as a clerical error.

Raddad always protested his innocence and at one stage of his detention embarked on a 40-day hunger strike. At his trial in Nice the prosecution did its best to destroy Raddad's character. They had trawled the prostitutes in the Côte d'Azur without finding one whom Raddad had patronised. So far as gambling was concerned, with its consequent need for quick money, the best they could do was to show he played the five-franc slot machines in the casino in Cannes. He was behind with his rent and he had been asking his employers for loans.

On the other hand his residence papers were in order and he lived quietly in a two-room flat in Cannes with his wife and child. He was described as polite and timid. He spoke little French and was barely literate. There was evidence that he had worked honestly and well for Mme Marchal and others in the neighbourhood who trusted him.

Nice was not a good venue for his trial. The townspeople there were not generally favourably disposed towards North Africans, who were looked on as a generally predatory race. He faced a hostile judge. When evidence was given that Raddad 'wouldn't hurt a fly', the judge remarked, 'No, but he would cut a sheep's throat.'

On 2 February 1994 Omar Raddad was convicted of the murder and sentenced to 18 years' imprisonment. There were many who thought the conviction to be wrong. Raddad's supporters point to the faulty grammar displayed by the dying woman when she wrote on the wall. The sentence should read 'Omar m'a tuée', something which should be known even to schoolchildren. They ask whether Ghislaine Marchal, by making such an elementary error, was trying to alert the police to the fact that she was writing under duress or whether the murderer, himself with no command of French grammar, was trying to implicate Raddad. Unfortunately no fingerprints of Marchal were taken and the body was cremated at an early stage in the investigation. Those who seek to uphold the conviction suggest that the grammatical error was a pardonable error by a dying woman.

Mme Pascal the next-door neighbour, who obtained some fame in the press as a sort of French Miss Marple, suggested that Mme Marchal had been very secretive about her bank accounts in Switzerland and that the police would do well to check out that end of matters. On the day of her death a car with Swiss plates had been seen near *La Chamade*. Nothing seems to have happened following her suggestions. Raddad remains in prison.

25 June, 1956

Tommy Smithson, an ex-fairground boxer with a penchant
for silk shirts and underwear, known as Mr Loser, died on
25 June 1956. Born in Liverpool in 1920 and brought to
London's East End two years later, he had served in the
Merchant Navy until his discharge in the 1950s. Back in
Shoreditch he found things to be different. The Maltese,
coming to England on subsidised passages, had moved in
and had themselves established a network of their own
gambling and drinking clubs and stables of prostitutes.
Smithson decided to set up his own protection racket
devoted to these Maltese businessmen.

Initially he worked for George Caruana as a croupier. At
the time Caruana and the other Maltese were keen to avoid
trouble and Smithson soon extended his interest to a share
of the takings in the clubs. Smithson took one shilling in the
pound from the dice games, earning up to £100 an evening.
He also obtained backing and opened up a one-room club
in Maidenhead Passage near Wardour Street.

But police raids followed and Smithson moved from club
to club and in so doing came into competition with the
powerful interests of Billy Hill and Jack Spot who, at the
time, controlled London's West End. He was involved in a
fight with Frederick 'Slip' Sullivan and, throwing him out
of French Henry's, cut his throat in the process. Sullivan,
who was later stabbed to death by a girl with whom he
was living, was the brother of a member of the Hill-Spot
partnership and reprisals were swift.

A week later Smithson was betrayed by the Maltese he
had been protecting. Told there was a peace offer on the
table, he was asked to attend a meeting and was collected
in a shooting-brake. On the dramatic signal of a cigar butt
tossed on to the pavement, Smithson was dragged from the
car and slashed over his face, arms, legs and chest. He was
then thrown over a wall in Regent's Park and left to die.

Smithson had not been wholly naive: two loaded revolvers had been taken from him before his slashing. Somehow he survived and 47 stitches were put in his face. His reward for honouring the code of silence was a party, the soubriquet 'Scarface' and £500 with which he bought a share in a club in Old Compton Street. This too was closed down by the police and Smithson took up receiving stolen goods as an occupation. For a time he was successful but then word began to spread that he was a police informer. This time he received a further 27 stitches.

It signalled Smithson's retreat from what he had seen as the big-time and he went back to the East End to provide further protection for the Maltese, but yet again he miscalculated. The new generation of Maltese had become more powerful. They may not have wished to have trouble but they were themselves preparing for a move into the West End and were not prepared to tolerate the likes of Smithson.

He had other pressing problems. At the time he was involved with a former prostitute, Fay Sadler, then on remand in Holloway Prison on forged cheque allegations. Money had to be raised for Fay's defence. Smithson collected £50 from his former employer George Caruana and complained bitterly it was not £100. On 13 June 1956 Smithson, together with Walter Downs and Christopher Thomas, went to a café in Berner Street, Stepney and confronted Caruana and Philip Ellul, a Maltese who ran a second- or third-division string of prostitutes. Smithson said he wanted more than £50 from Caruana and in the ensuing fight Caruana's fingers were slashed as he protected his face from a flick knife. Other Maltese in the café were held off at gunpoint by Thomas. Thirty more pounds were produced.

On 25 June 1956 Smithson was found dying in the gutter outside Caruana's house in Carlton Vale. He had been shot in the arm and neck. His last words were said to be, 'Good morning, I'm dying.'

In the 1970s Commander Bert Wickstead had been called in to investigate the Soho vice syndicates. One of the first men he wished to interview was George Caruana, who over the years had had three separate attempts made on his life. One plan had been for his car to be blown up and he had left the country to work a double act with his wife in a strip club in Hamburg. It was in Caruana's house that Smithson had been murdered in 1956. Now, in 1973, Caruana was located and made a statement but then, when it came to it, he declined to give evidence. In the ensuing enquiries club owner Bernie Silver was arrested.

One of the charges against Silver was conspiracy to murder Tommy Smithson. By now Wickstead had most of the story concerning the small-time hoodlum's death. Smithson's attempts to blackmail Silver to put up money for Fay Sadler's defence had come at a most unfortunate time. Silver was preparing his moves from Brick Lane into Soho and could not afford any hindrance. Nor could he allow himself to be seen as a weak man. Two contract killers, Philip Ellul and Victor Spampinato, had been given the contract and executed their one-time friend Smithson but they were never paid.

After the murder they had gone into hiding in Manchester where they received a message from the Syndicate telling them to give themselves up. A deal had been arranged that they would be charged only with manslaughter and once their sentences had been served need never work again. They were betrayed, and both were put on trial for murder. Spampinato was acquitted and Ellul sentenced to death before being reprieved on the eve of his execution. He served 11 years and on his release came to London to collect his money. Sixpence was thrown on the floor and he was told to pick it up. Later he was taken to obtain a passport and then to Heathrow.

Spampinato was found by Wickstead's officers working as a wine bar tout in Malta. Ellul was traced by the American police and telephoned Wickstead. Yes, he would come and give evidence against Silver. Spampinato gave evidence at the committal proceedings at Old Street Magistrates' Court but did not reappear for the trial. When next traced in Malta he owned a villa on the seafront at

Sliema, a new car and was said to be in possession of £30,000. His contract had been honoured at last.

Ellul was given police protection in a flat in Limehouse. He was kept under close observation but complained, saying that his time in the death cell had left its mark on him and he did not like company. The watch was relaxed and later Ellul said he wanted to return to the States, promising to return for the trial. He did not do so. It is said he was paid £60,000 which would roughly equal the payment made to Spampinato.

Silver was found not guilty on the charge of conspiring to murder Tommy Smithson but guilty of living off immoral earnings. He received six years' imprisonment. Others in the case received up to five years.

James Morton, *Gangland*; Bert Wickstead, *Gangbuster*.

26 June, 1989

Both Elmer 'Stormy' Woodall and his 81-year-old mother, Clemer, were shot at her home in Tallahassee, Alabama on 26 June 1989. Clemer died but Elmer, although mentally disabled from the head wounds, lived and managed to give evidence against his older brother, J. C. Woodall, who at the age of 65 was put on trial for the murder and attempted murder of his mother and brother in what the prosecution alleged was a murder-for-hire.

The gunman, Freddie Gleen Pope, pleaded guilty in a plea bargain and was sentenced to life imprisonment without parole. In return he gave evidence against Woodall. He said he had been paid $3,500 in two instalments for the contract. 'I guess I'm classed as a lowdown because I've done a lot of lowdown things but I could never be lowdown enough in my life to order my mother to be killed,' said Pope.

The murder, said the prosecution, had been about a dispute over family land in Tallahassee.

Elmer Woodall, speaking in a slurred voice and not looking at his brother, gave evidence that after he was shot he heard his mother call, 'Oh, no, not my baby.' Pope had then turned the gun on Elmer's mother. When the man had left Woodall said he crawled over to his mother and said, 'I love you.' He managed to dial 'O' for the operator because although he could not move his hand he had stuck his finger in the rotary dial and moved his body.

The defence claimed that J. C. Woodall had nothing to do with the killing and that it was a robbery organised by Pope and another man which had gone wrong. Pope had gone to the house under the pretext that he wanted to buy some land to mine gravel.

Woodall gave evidence that he was innocent but he cannot have helped his case by describing the judge as a 'zealot who is not qualified to settle a milk bill in a Kansas court'.

In January 1996 J. C. Woodall was sentenced to death. 'I want everybody to know the system does work and I am happy with the outcome,' said Elmer Woodall. In the arraignment hearing in June both J. C. Woodall and his lawyer had refused to speak and Judge Drinkard had entered pleas of not guilty and not guilty by reason of mental defect.

The lawyer had to be sent for and brought to the sentence hearing by a sheriff's deputy. He had had repeated clashes with the judge throughout the trial.

27 June, 1982

On 27 June 1982, when leaving his daughter's 11th birthday party, Nicky Gerard (see also 4 September) was ambushed by gunmen wearing boiler suits and balaclava helmets at the lock-up garage to which he had driven his Oldsmobile. Shots were fired through the windscreen and Gerard was hit in the stomach. He managed to get out of the car and to stagger 100 yards but his attackers followed him, smashing him so hard on the head with a gun that the stock shattered. He was beaten unconscious before one of the gunmen reloaded and shot him.

Gerard had not been sufficiently careful. Over the previous few days he had known he was being followed but he had thought his followers were undercover police.

'Gerard was one of the most feared men in the London Underworld. Although he was acquitted of being a hit man in the Knight case, he was the man who did the heavy business,' said former Commander Bert Wickstead. 'He would lean on anybody who took liberties. But he wasn't only a "muscle for hire" man. He was known and feared throughout the East End. His death could easily spark off a gangland war.'[1] In the event it did not.

On 22 November his cousin and 'best friend', Thomas Hole, was arrested and charged with his murder. He was tried at the Old Bailey in April 1983. He had been picked out on an identification parade by a 'Mr Fisher', the pseudonym given to a protected witness, who said he had seen a man with one rubber washing-up glove acting suspiciously. 'But,' he added, 'I am not sure it was the man I had seen that day in June in the car park.' Despite protests that the Crown had more evidence it had not been allowed to produce, on 27 April 1983 the judge stopped the case at the end of the prosecution evidence.

Thomas Hole was acquitted by direction of the trial judge, Mr Justice French.

'This, of course, was an appalling gangland murder, and any right-thinking citizen must be dismayed at the thought that no one has been brought to justice for that murder,' said Mr Justice French.

Hole, who left court with his friends, said, 'My head is reeling.' He later served a long sentence for drug-dealing.

[1] *News of the World*, 27 June 1982.

28 June, 1994

About 3.15am on 28 June 1994 petrol was poured on to the only staircase to the second-floor apartments above a garage at Seay Memorial Chapel at 711 Harrison Street, Riverhead, New York, and set alight. In the ensuing fire, five children died and three adults escaped with injuries after jumping from windows. It was the second-largest murder case in local history.[1]

Nearly a month later 32-year-old Raymond Dennis Smith was charged with the murders. According to the police he had made a five-page confession in which he admitted to starting the fire. He had thought that his estranged wife Victoria was staying with her friend Tina Fay who was badly burned in the fire and whose three children, Raheem Gregory, T'Keyah Gregory and Roger Gregory Junior, aged between six months and three years, died in the fire. Another three-year-old who was in the flat also died, as did 11-year-old Letitia Booker who was staying overnight.

'I want him dead,' said Tina Fay when she was released from the burns unit of the local hospital. 'I don't have my children no more, and he still has his. I want him to suffer.'

The police theory was that Smith had not intended anyone should be injured in the fire. Rather, he knew his wife was intending to move in with the Fay family and he wanted to ensure there was no place for her to go. According to newspaper reports Victoria Smith said she had been hiding in fear until her husband was

[1]The first was the so-called Amityville Horror case when, in 1974, Ronald 'Butch' DeFeo, aged 23, murdered six members of his family – his parents, two sisters and two brothers. After a day of drinking he shot them all with a .35-calibre rifle. He was sentenced to concurrent terms of 25 years to life. The house where the shooting occurred was said by subsequent owners to be the subject of 'evil forces'. Several films were made about the place and the killings.

Joy Adamson at the time of
filming her book *Born Free*
(3 January 1980)
(*Hulton Deutsch*)

Donald Urquhart with his girlfriend
(2 January 1993)
(Mirror Syndication International)

Kenneth Erskine,
the Stockwell Strangler,
is taken to court
(12 January 1988)
*(Mirror Syndication
International)*

Ted Bundy sits stone-faced as, after six and a half hours of deliberation, the jury returns guilty verdicts of murdering Lisa Levy and Margaret Bowman (1 February 1974) *(Popperfoto)*

Some of the crowd outside the Dewsbury Courthouse demonstrate that they feel current penalties are inadequate in the case of Peter Sutcliffe (10 February) *(Camera Press Ltd)*

A trio of young mourners kneel outside the home of the enormously popular Selena Quintanilla Perez after she was shot by Yolanda Saldivar, the president of her fan club (31 March 1995)
(Associated Press)

Yolanda Saldivar
(Popperfoto/Reuter)

Emanuel Spiteri, fifth and last victim
of Colin Ireland
(12 June 1993)
(Press Association/Topham)

Te Rangimaria Ngarimu, the contract
killer of Graeme Woodhatch
(24 May 1992)
(Rex Features)

Colin Ireland
(Press Association/Topham)

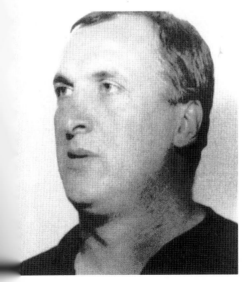

Diana Maw, killed by a
cross-bow bolt outside her
flat in West London
(20 July 1988)
(Mirror Syndication International)

Robert Black, found guilty of
murdering Caroline Hogg,
Susan Maxwell and Sarah Harper,
is led away from
Newcastle Crown Court
(30 July 1982)
(Press Association/Topham)

£1,000 REWARD
MURDER

A reward or rewards up to a total of £1,000 will be paid for information leading to the arrest of **HARRY MAURICE ROBERTS** b Wanstead, Essex, on 21-7-36, 5ft 10in, photo above, wanted for questioning in connection with the murder of three police officers on the 12th August, 1966, at Braybrook Street, Shepherd's Bush.

Information to be given to New Scotland Yard, S.W.1 or at any police station.

The amount of any payment will be at the discretion of the Commissioner of Police for the Metropolis

J. SIMPSON
Commissioner of Police

The wanted poster for Harry Roberts,
later convicted of killing three police
officers in Shepherd's Bush
12 August 1966)
Associated Press/Topham)

Margaret Allen, killer of
Nancy Ellen Chadwick
(28 August 1945)
(Mirror Syndication International)

Gordon Waddell
follows the coffin
of his murdered wife
Carol. He would later
be arrested and
convicted of her killing
(11 September 1994)
*(Press Association
/Topham)*

A reconstruction of the
face of the Pyjama Girl
(1 September 1934)

Was Linda Agostini really the
Pyjama Girl?

Philomena Morgan (second left) compared against photographs
of the charred face of the Pyjama Girl.

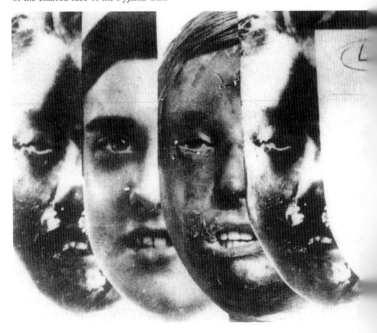

arrested. Meanwhile Smith had been beaten up by men who believed he had started the fire.

In February 1996 Smith's trial began with something of a sensation when it was announced that his wife would be providing him with an alibi. She had been with him on the night of the fire, said Smith's lawyer, Steve Wilutis, who said the defence would be presenting a story of sex, violence, drugs, prostitution and police coercion. Wilutis told the jury that the defence was that another man, who had an occasional relationship with Victoria Smith and whom she had accused of beating her two months after the fire, had equal opportunity and motive to set the building alight. The confession had, he alleged, been obtained whilst Smith was still suffering from the mental and physical effects of the beating.

At the trial it emerged that one of the men who had beaten and stabbed Smith was Roger Gregory, Tina Fay's boyfriend. He had not been prosecuted for the assault and, it was alleged, had cut a deal with the prosecution.

Smith was convicted and received a sentence of 125 years' imprisonment.

29 June, 1993

At about 9.30 pm on 29 June 1993, as her husband Peter worked in the garden of their home in Chester-le-Street, County Durham, Maxine Robinson, aged 26, told him she would go and check on the children, 19-month-old Christine and five-month-old Anthony. At 7 pm she had bathed them and put them to bed. She came downstairs saying they had both suffocated in their beds in separate rooms. 'I think the bairns are dead,' she told her husband.

It was not merely a double tragedy. Mrs Robinson's elder daughter Victoria from a previous marriage had suffered a cot death at the age of nine months in 1989.

In April 1995 the Sheffield Crown Court was told that
Mrs Robinson had killed her children and then watched
television for two and a half hours before thinking up a way
of pretending to discover the children were dead. After the
deaths of the children the windows of the couple's house
were smashed and the words 'murderers' and 'killers' were
daubed on the walls.

Mr Robinson, who was arrested three times for questioning with his wife before becoming a witness, told the
court that because he knew he had not harmed the children
it must have been his wife who had killed them.

After a ten-hour retirement the jury convicted Mrs
Robinson by an eleven to one majority. After she was
sentenced to life imprisonment the senior officer in the
case, Detective Chief Inspector Fred Taylor, said that the
police were no nearer finding a motive for the killings
than they had been at the start. There were no plans to
reopen the investigation into the death of Victoria who
had been put to bed after playing in the paddling pool.
Mrs Robinson's former husband had found Vicki all right
at 8 pm but about 10 pm Maxine had gone to check on
her and had come down the stairs holding her daughter
limp in her arms.

30 June, 1994

After Tony Armstrong pleaded guilty at Leeds Crown
Court to the murder of three-year-old Rosie Palmer on 30
June 1994 and was jailed for life, the police investigating
the case rejected criticism that they had failed to act on
suggestions that he had been responsible.

About 3.30 pm the red-haired little girl, dressed in red
and white checked shorts and a white T-shirt, had gone to
buy ice-cream from a van which pulled up near her home
in Henrietta Street on the Headland Estate, Hartlepool,

County Durham. She had not enough money with her but the vendor, who knew her as a regular, gave her a lolly.

When she did not return neighbours started a search and at 8.45 pm the police were called. The first time the police called at Armstrong's flat was the next day when the enquiries were part of a routine questioning of neighbours, trying to establish Rosie's last movements. They returned the next day, again as part of a routine search when all local homes were inspected. On the third day of the enquiry the police again spoke to Armstrong. The detectives noticed a change in his attitude. He now appeared dishevelled and on edge. He had, he said, been drinking heavily. Armstrong was arrested and a thorough search of his flat led to the discovery of the child's body in the hall cupboard. It had, apparently, been there from the time he had killed her. There had also been a violent sexual assault on the child.

Armstrong had been moved by the authorities to the Headland Estate, regarded by locals as a dumping ground for single men. He was a loner, disliked and distrusted by the other residents, with a number of convictions for dishonesty but none for sex offences. He also had a history of violence. As a child he had been adopted by a plasterer who had married his mother and whom he had subsequently robbed and beaten. In his teens he had discovered that he was the result of an incestuous relationship between his mother and her father. After that he said he had regularly had sex with his mother. Armstrong lived something of a fantasy life. Whilst on remand he told other prisoners he had the same sort of cancer which had killed his mother four years previously. He had told his workmates that he had been a commando in the Falklands War and that he had inherited a family farm. He liked to be called Rocky. He had, said his counsel at the trial, tried to commit suicide no less than 17 times.

His former wife, who had left him after six months and had since remarried, said of him that he had beaten her on her wedding night. 'He used to hit me all the time. I couldn't stand it. He was like an animal.'

Detective Superintendent Douglas Smith said of the enquiry:

> There was a lot of misinformation moving around. On the first night Rosie went missing, certain members of the public did come forward and suggest that a certain man was responsible for her disappearance. That man was eliminated from the inquiry on the very first evening and that man was not Shaun Anthony Armstrong.

JULY

1 July, 1928

On 1 July 1928, whilst New York crime boss Frankie Yale (born Uale) was trying out his new Lincoln coupé before sending it back to have bulletproof glass put in the windows, he was killed in a drive-by shooting. He had been in a bar when he had received a message that something was wrong at home and he was shot when a black Buick came alongside him and the occupants opened fire with a sub-machine-gun. His funeral was to set the standard by which other gangster funerals would be measured. His silver casket cost $15,000 and it was borne from St Rosalie's Church to Holy Cross Cemetery on an open hearse. One wreath said, 'We'll see them, kid.' Two hundred and fifty cars followed, passing through an estimated ten thousand people who lined the roadside.

The reason for Yale's death was twofold. First, he would not support Al Capone's nominee for the powerful position of head of the Chicago branch of the Unione Siciliane. Secondly, and worse, Capone's shipments of bootleg liquor bound for Chicago were not even getting out of the New York suburbs before Yale's men hijacked them. Capone, conspicuously holidaying in Florida, sent orders for the death of his one-time employer and mentor. In 1909 Yale had owned the Harvard Inn in Brooklyn where Capone had been barman-cum-bouncer.

It is recorded that Capone, watching the funeral, said

to Machine Gun Jack McGurn, 'I feel so sorry for this poor fellow . . . my heart is all broke up. Come, we go. I can't stand no more . . . this too much for me.'[1]

Yale's death also set something of a precedent. His death was the first by sub-machine-gun in New York. Before that they had been used exclusively in Chicago.

Laurence Bergreen, *Capone*; J. Kobler, *Capone*; F.D. Pasley, *Al Capone*; Robert Schoenberg, *Mr Capone*.

2 July, 1937

The body of Phennie Perry was found on 2 July 1937 on a path near the Long Island railway in the borough of Queens. She had been killed with a piece of concrete but her baby daughter was lying unharmed nearby. When the police arrived they found a bloodstained shoe with a hole in the sole, a strip of shirt, an electric iron and papers belonging to Ulysses Palm of 153rd Street, Jamaica. A witness had heard the sounds of a quarrel at about 10.30 pm the previous evening and had called the police. The officers had formed the opinion that the man, a nightwatchman, was drunk and had not carried out any further investigation.

In Palm's flat was found the other shoe, papers which showed he was a Deacon of the Amity Baptist Church and, significantly, the remainder of the torn shirt.

Both Palm and 22-year-old Arthur Perry, Phennie's husband, were taken in for questioning. Perry's version of events was that his wife had intended to go to spend a weekend with her sister but she had changed her mind and had told him that Palm had tried to break into her

[1]William Balsamo and George Carpozi Junior, *Crime Incorporated*, p 215.

bedroom that morning. A letter, in indecent terms, was produced which was apparently written by Palm to Mrs Perry and which carried the warning that if it was shown to her husband he, Palm, would kill her.

Forensic evidence showed that it was not written by Palm but the scientist could not take the next step and actually say it was written by Perry. However, Palm had a perfectly good alibi from his workmates for the time of the quarrel. The shoe belonged to him but he said he had lent it to Perry. In turn Perry said he had returned it. The piece from the shirt turned out to have been cut rather than torn. There was writing paper in Perry's flat which matched that on which the letter was written. Perry was arrested.

He was placed in a cell with a man he was led to believe was a wanted murderer, in reality an undercover police officer. Perry admitted he had killed his wife but was unable to offer a reason, saying he loved her. He was found guilty but his conviction was quashed and a retrial ordered. It did Perry little good. He was convicted a second time and on 3 August 1939 he was electrocuted.

3 July, 1942

Seventy-eight-year-old Samuel William Elbra, described as a jobbing gardener, was charged with murdering his landlady, the 82-year-old almost blind Elizabeth Buckenham, between 2 and 3 July 1942 by striking her with a long-handled broom.

He had been discharged from Chartham Mental Hospital near Canterbury the previous July and was in receipt of the old-age pension. He often came in late at night and after drinking he sang and caused a disturbance to the other lodgers. He was told to find fresh lodgings and this he resented.

After he killed his landlady he cut off her head and then dismembered and mutilated the body, amputating the fingers to remove her rings. Charged with murder, he replied, 'That's right. So would you. She's always been after me.'

In a statement to the police he elaborated on the shortcomings of his former landlady, describing her as 'a nasty bitch and as strong as a lion'.

> She had been after my body all the time, and she has struck me. She is a heavy woman and she has tried to poison me. She has poisoned me. She drinks like a fish night and day and you could see the murder in her . . .
> . . . She got blind drunk and she could hardly stand. She came after me again and I smacked her in the face with an open hand, and she fell down. I took her into the kitchen three times, but she kept coming for me, so I got a broom and jabbed her with that. She went down and I thought, now, you dirty cow, your time's come.
> I got my small table knife, went back to the kitchen and cut her head off. I then cut her up in great lumps. I didn't take her feet off, it wasn't necessary. I put the body in my room, there I sliced lumps off and flung them in the bushes. I intended to put the pieces in sacks and get rid of them outside, but then I thought the police might stop me, then I hadn't enough sacks. I had to do it so quick, it smelt so rotten and there was heaps of shit. I had to wash it all up twice, I had the kitchen already washed out when they came yesterday.

He had been born on 28 March 1863 and in 1900 was an inmate of Cane Hill Mental Hospital. He was back there in 1923 after having served in the army. There were notes on his record of a bout of insanity in New Zealand. He was in Barming Heath Mental Hospital in 1929 and in 1936 he was certified insane. He had, however, never been classed as dangerous. He was found unfit to plead on 9 September 1942 and committed to a mental institution.

MEPO/3/2224.

4 July, 1992

On the night of 4 July 1992 Kevin Fox, wearing a hood, was shot with his own gun after he had blasted landlord's son Mark 'Chalkie' Smith three times in the stomach at the Memory Lane public house, Plaistow, east London. Smith senior had announced that he planned to keep drug dealers out of the premises. Fox fired two more shots as the crowd surged towards him and he was hit over the head with a fire extinguisher, punched, kicked and then shot. Eleven people were questioned over the killing but no one was charged.

The case is similar to the killing on 10 July 1981, of Ken Rex McElroy in Skidmore, Missouri. It is another example of how members of the public can believe that summary justice was being done and they were not prepared to intervene.

McElroy, the local bully, had terrorised Skidmore's inhabitants for years, raping, beating up and stealing from the townspeople. His final act of terrorism came when he shot and wounded Ernest Bowenkamp, a local shopkeeper who had told one of McElroy's 11 children to return a sweet if she was not paying for it. McElroy had followed the much older Bowenkamp, challenged him to a fight and, when he refused, shot him in the shoulder and neck. Charged with wounding, McElroy was convicted and released on bail for sentencing hearings.

On 10 July, after he had been drinking at the D&G Inn, he was shot dead as he got into his pick-up truck. The shooting was watched by a crowd of up to 70 people, not one of whom was prepared to give evidence. T-shirts appeared in the town with the legend, 'Who killed K.R.?' on the front and 'Who gives a damn?' on the back.

5 July, 1930

The British Vice Consul, then acting Consul General in Marseilles, bachelor Reginald Arthur Lee, disappeared on 5 July 1930. To an extent his movements can be traced. That Saturday afternoon at around 5.30 pm he cleared his desk in his office in the Rue Arcole, leaving £12 in francs behind him, collected his car, drove it about 100 yards to the lock-up garage where he garaged it, spoke with the owner, went back to his flat in Rue de Valence, hung his coat on the peg in the hall and was never seen again.

Although he did not appear for work on the following Monday the Consulate committee did not report his absence to the police until the next day and a search only began on the Wednesday. From the start it was clear he had not slept in his bed on the Saturday night. His passport and the only key to the Consulate safe disappeared with him. According to his mother he was perfectly happy and was expecting her and his brother to come to stay with him during July. She offered a reward of £40 for the discovery of her son, alive.

A postcard in an envelope arrived for Lee after he had disappeared. It was signed Ida Bucher and was in a woman's handwriting. She was traced and turned out to be a Swiss girl with whom Lee had had an affair some years earlier. She made conflicting statements as to his relationship with her but she seems to have had nothing to do with his disappearance. Then a portmanteau was found on the shore near Marseilles. It contained a revolver, a whisky bottle now half filled with brandy, a pair of trousers which would not have fitted Lee and a photograph of an elderly woman. On the back was what appeared to be a farewell note: 'I am committing suicide; nobody is to blame.' Lee's concierge at first said she recognised the clothes but then changed her mind. Mrs Lee said that the handwriting was not that of her son.

It is possible that Lee, who had been in Havana on a previous appointment, was killed because of his involvement in breaking up one or more of the drug smuggling rings which were active at that time both in Cuba and in and around Marseilles. It was reported that he had been instrumental in the seizure of over a ton of morphine, cocaine and heroin shortly before his disappearance, and also in the arrest of two Turkish smugglers. One explanation was that he had been killed as a reprisal by the rest of the gang. Another version was that he had been decoyed by the beautiful 'La Rose Jaune', a girl working for a Japanese drug syndicate, and had been pushed into the sewers of Marseilles.

When in July 1936 Mrs Lee asked the High Court in London to declare that her son was dead, a representative of the Foreign Office gave evidence to say that Lee had never been involved, other than perhaps in the most routine way, in the fight against drugs. But then, as Miss Mandy Rice-Davies said on another occasion, 'Well, he would, wouldn't he?'

Harry J. Greenwall, *They were murdered in France*.

6 July, 1922

Clara Phillips, the so-called Tiger Woman, a 23-year-old former vaudeville dancer with a dazzling smile, killed her husband's mistress, Alberta Meadows, with a claw hammer on 6 July 1922. Armour Phillips, an oil stock salesman, had fallen in love with the widow during the spring of that year, masking his absences and late-night telephone calls with his business enterprises.

On 5 July Clara Phillips bought a claw hammer and the next day, with her friend Peggy Caffee, another former dancer, went to find Mrs Meadows at the bank where she worked in Los Angeles. They had both been drinking illicit liquor and it was an easy matter to persuade Mrs Meadows to give them a lift. In theory she was to drive them to Clara Phillips's sister in Montecito Heights. On the way she was asked to stop the car and Clara Phillips began to question her about the new tyres on the vehicle and the gold wristwatch she was wearing. When Mrs Meadows denied that Armour had bought them she was knocked from her car and chased down a hill. When the heel of her shoe broke Clara Phillips caught up with her and beat her to death with the hammer, more or less disembowelling her in the process. Meanwhile the unfortunate Peggy Caffee was being sick in the grass.

Clara Phillips returned to her husband in Alberta Meadows's car, told him what she had done and said she was going to bed. She would surrender herself to the police the next morning. Armour Phillips thought otherwise. She should escape and, in separate cars, they drove to Pomona to dump Alberta's car. On their return to Los Angeles he borrowed money to send her to El Paso from where she could cross into Mexico. There was little chance of the Mexican authorities sending her back. Relations between the United States and Mexico were still at a low ebb following Pancho Villa's successful raid into Arizona and the damaging reprisals led by 'Black Jack' Pershing in Mexico in 1917.

Alberta Meadows's body was discovered looking, said one of the police at the scene, as if she had been attacked by a tiger. Unfortunately, after his initial burst of solidarity Phillips could not keep it up. He went to see his lawyer who in turn went to see the police. Phillips could be a witness rather than an accessory. Clara Phillips was arrested in Tucson.

Her return to Los Angeles was something of a triumph.

She was feted at the train stops and willingly gave interviews. In her cell she received dozens of bouquets and boxes of chocolates. Her version of the incident was different from that offered by the prosecution. It had been Alberta Meadows who had started the fight after she had been accused of adultery. Alberta had broken Clara Phillips's finger – it had been broken in the fight – and the actual killing had been done by Peggy Caffee who had panicked. The jury returned a verdict of murder in the first degree. Clara received a sentence of 10 years to life and appealed.

Her story does not end there. During the trial she had made the acquaintance of one of the spectators, Jesse Carson, who promised that in the event of a conviction he would rescue her. On 5 December he did just that. He had smuggled in a hacksaw and Clara had cut the bars of her third-floor cell. They fled together to Pomona until early January, when they moved on to St Louis and then New Orleans. From there Clara sailed to Mexico, travelling on to Guatemala and then to Honduras, where she was traced by an enterprising Hearst newspaperman, Morris Levine. Extradition proceedings followed and failed. Still protesting her innocence she was persuaded to return to Los Angeles to continue with her appeal. Sadly, her lawyer, who had now died, had been late in filing the papers and she was out of time. She served until 1935. After her parole she practised as a dentist in California until the early 1960s, after which she retired to Texas.

Marvin J. Wolf and Katherine Mader, *L.A. Crime*.

7 July, 1960

Just as the English police did not know too much about
dealing with kidnapping when they investigated the disappearance of Mrs McKay, neither did the Sydney police
in 1960 when they were hunting for the kidnapper of
eight-year-old Graeme Thorne. It was probably the first
kidnapping case in Australia.

Basil Thorne, variously described as a country traveller
and typically middle-class, and his wife had won the
first prize in the $A100,000 Opera House Lottery on
1 July. They had two children, Belinda aged three and
Graeme aged eight. Despite their newly acquired fortune
the Thornes had no intention of changing their lifestyle.
He went back to travelling in the country and Graeme
continued going every day to school, waiting on the corner
of O'Brien Street where a Mrs Smith would collect him
and take him to school with her two sons.

On 7 July he disappeared. Mrs Smith had gone to collect
him as usual and, not seeing him there, dropped off her
sons, found he had not reached the school and drove
straight back to the Thornes' home. Graeme was not
there either and so the police were called. The first officer
to arrive was there when a telephone call came through.
A foreign voice said, 'I have your son.' Then followed a
demand for $A25,000 by 5 o'clock that afternoon.

The police officer, who had taken over the call, tried to
stall but the line went dead after the caller had said that
the boy would be fed to the sharks. Mrs Thorne said the
call must have been genuine because the family had only
recently had a phone installed and the number was not
in the local directory.

The only clue was that the night after the lottery win a
man had called on the Thornes saying that he was a private enquiry agent looking for a man named Bognor. He
was able to quote the Thornes' new telephone number.

The body of Graeme was officially found on 16 August under an overhanging ledge of rock on waste ground and wrapped in a carpet. Apparently two young boys had discovered the body some weeks earlier but had incorporated it into a fantasy adventure before a third child, who had become involved in the game, had told his father. The police were able to establish the approximate date of death by a botanical examination of spores on the body and could say it had been there for at least five weeks. Because plant particles were present from two species of cypress which rarely grow together, they were able reasonably quickly to find a house where both trees grew. It was only about a mile from where the body was found.

A member of the class of people euphemistically called 'new' Australians – in other words an immigrant Hungarian – had been living at the house. Stephen Bradley had moved out the morning of the kidnapping. He was traced to his place of work and interviewed. For the time being the police were satisfied with his explanation. Later the carpet in which Graeme's body was wrapped was identified as being one known to belong to Bradley. By this time he had left Australia for England and was taken off the ship at Colombo. He admitted the kidnapping but said the boy had died of suffocation in the boot of the car. Later at the trial he endeavoured to disclaim the statement but, found guilty, he was sentenced to life imprisonment.

Alan Sharpe, *Crimes that Shocked Australia*.

8 July, 1969

On 8 July 1969, 72-year-old Rachel Ross died at the County Hospital, Ayrshire. She had been the victim of a tie-up robbery off Racecourse Road, Ayr when one of the two robbers had knelt on her chest. Her 67-year-old husband, Abraham, had been hit with an iron bar and stabbed in the neck. Glasgow hard men Patrick Meehan and James Griffiths were prime suspects. One reason they were suspected was that Ross said that the men had called themselves Pat and Jim. It was also accepted by Meehan that he and Griffiths had been in the area. At a voice identification parade in which Meehan was the only one who spoke, Mr Ross identified him. Two girls to whom Griffiths and Meehan had given a lift also identified Meehan in another parade.

Shortly after Meehan's arrest at 10.30 am the police went to 14 Holyrood Crescent, Griffiths's home. Meehan had given them Griffiths's name and address as an alibi witness. When there was no reply to their knockings they kicked the door down and were faced with Griffiths wearing bandoliers of ammunition about his body and firing at them. He made off and later was himself shot dead after firing further shots at the officers as they burst through the door of his home to which he had returned. That day one civilian was killed and 11 were injured along with five police officers.

Meanwhile there were rumours in the Underworld that despite Griffiths's suicidal behaviour and his record of unpleasant robberies he and Meehan had not been responsible for the Ross murder. The name to come up regularly was that of Ian Waddell.

Under Scottish procedure if a defendant alleges that another has committed the crime then he must impeach or name him in pretrial procedures and Waddell and another man were duly impeached on Meehan's behalf. At the trial Waddell was invited to repeat the words, 'Shut up, shut up . . .' and Mr Ross, hearing him, said that although he was not sure, it did sound like the voice.

A majority verdict of the jury found Meehan guilty and he was sentenced to life imprisonment. Joe Beltrami, his lawyer, never gave up and used his Underworld contacts to discover the real killers in an endeavour to have the conviction set aside.

He had been half correct in having Waddell and the other man impeached. The correct half was Waddell. His actual partner turned out to be the noted hard man William 'Tank' McGuinness who had been a client of Beltrami's for some 15 years and was known for his partiality for tie-ups, along with his penchant for violence. Although not at present on a charge McGuinness began to pay visits to Beltrami's office on an informal basis, leaking more and more clues about the robbery. By the time of his last visit he had admitted that it had been Waddell's responsibility to telephone the police to get the Rosses released. Beltrami's problem was that these were confidential statements by a client. Without his express permission to use them he was bound by the lawyer's equivalent of the seal of the confessional.

On 12 March 1976 McGuinness was found in a coma in Janefield Street close to the Celtic football ground. He had been beaten unconscious and died 13 days later in the Royal Infirmary. He had never recovered consciousness. Although the allegation was never proved it was put about that McGuinness had been killed over his involvement in the Ross murder.

The death of McGuinness did at least release Beltrami from the confidentiality of the statements made to him by the man. It was established that Waddell's alibi was false and that, although he was unemployed at the time, shortly after the Ayr robbery he had been in possession of substantial funds. Meehan was pardoned in May 1976. Now Ian Waddell was charged with the murder of Mrs Ross and put forward the defence of impeachment against Meehan and Griffiths. He was acquitted by a majority verdict of the jury who retired for just over an hour.

His acquittal brought him little fortune. In 1982 he was murdered in Blackthorn Street, Glasgow by his friend, Andy Gentle, who received a sentence of life imprisonment.

An inquiry into the Meehan case undertaken by Lord Hunter offered a new and curious theory that all four men, Griffiths, Meehan, Waddell and McGuinness, had been

involved. Meehan finally received a pardon and the sum
of £50,500 in compensation. Beltrami had been hoping
for £100,000 and had to work quite hard to persuade
Meehan this was a reasonable sum.

   Meehan was singularly ungrateful for Beltrami's efforts
over the years on his behalf. He died from throat cancer
in a Swansea hospital in August 1994 at the age of 67.
He was described by one of his former solicitors as
'a thoroughly unpleasant, ungrateful creature – there
was not one single redeeming feature as far as I was
concerned'.

J. Beltrami, *A Deadly Innocence*; P. Meehan, *Innocent
Villain*.

9 July, 1983

On 9 July 1983, a 63-year-old antique dealer, Henry
Botton, who had led a chequered life, was shot to
death on the doorstep of his home in Shooters Hill,
Greenwich, south-east London. He had been watching
a Frank Bruno bout on television when he answered a
knock on the door.

   A leading light in the south-east London fraternity, in
1966 he had received five years for his part in the affray
at Mr Smith's club in Catford which had resulted in the
death of Dickie Hart. For that death Botton had pointed
the finger at the notorious 'Mad' Frank Fraser who was
acquitted of Hart's murder. Botton's previous sentences
had been up to eight years, including one for armed
robbery. Now, according to his sister, 'Henry was a sick
man, suffering from kidney trouble and an ulcer. All that
gangland stuff was in the past.'

   At first the police thought that the killing – a blast
from both barrels of a sawn-off shotgun – had been

a reprisal over money disputes but the truth was that Botton had not quite shaken off his past. In October 1984 Billy Clarkson, a member of a large family, was sentenced to life imprisonment for the murder with a recommendation that he serve at least 25 years. He had given out the contract for the killing to 19-year-old Colin Burke. The court was told that Burke, who was said to be under the complete domination of Clarkson, had dressed in a policeman's uniform to trick Botton into opening the door. Burke, who was sentenced to life youth custody, had told the police, 'I wanted to refuse the favour, but it was like being under hypnosis.' The killing had been to stop Botton giving evidence against Clarkson on conspiracy charges.

10 July, 1900

Charles Benjamin Backhouse was hanged on 16 August 1900 for the murder in Swinton, Yorkshire of PC Kew a bare five weeks earlier on 10 July. There had been bad blood between Backhouse, his brother Frederick and the officer. Charles Backhouse resented the fact that in a domestic quarrel with his wife, Kew had arrested Frederick whom he regarded as being an innocent bystander.

When another incident broke out near his home and Kew came to investigate, Backhouse saw the officer and shot him. He was convicted along with his brother Frederick, who was reprieved by virtue of his age two days before the execution.

11 July, 1906

Chester Gillette, also known as Carl Graham, took his pregnant, working-class girlfriend out in a rowing boat on Big Moose Lake in the Adirondacks on the morning of 11 July 1906. That night he registered alone at the Arrowhead Inn, Eagle Bay.

The 22-year-old son of Salvation Army workers, he was either orphaned or deserted by them at the age of 14. He then travelled the country working at various jobs before writing to his wealthy uncle in Courtland, New York, asking for a job in his skirt factory. He was employed on the understanding that he start at the bottom and work his way up. He created a favourable impression and was soon promoted to shop foreman. His social life improved and he courted a girl in local society. Unfortunately, he had also been taking out Grace 'Billie' Brown, a farmer's daughter from Utica, who worked as a secretary for his uncle. Grace Brown was by now pregnant and he arranged for her return to her father's farm, saying he would make things all right. He failed to follow her and in a series of letters she threatened to tell his uncle. In early July he took time off and travelled to Utica. They holidayed in a rented cottage and the next night took separate rooms at the Glenmore Hotel at Big Moose Lake.

The following day Gillette hired the boat, packed a picnic lunch in his suitcase and the couple rowed off. When Gillette arrived at the Arrowhead Inn about 9 pm that evening he sat on the beach, singing with other holidaymakers. Once the autopsy revealed that Grace Brown's drowning had been no accident it was only a matter of time before Gillette was arrested. He claimed she had attempted suicide by throwing herself in the lake but was unable to explain why he, as a swimmer, had not dived in to rescue her. He had, in fact, knocked her out with a tennis racquet.

His trial lasted 22 days and over a hundred witnesses were called. As is quite often the case, a number of women became infatuated with Gillette and he sold his autographed picture at $5 a time. He was executed in the electric chair at Auburn prison on 30 March 1908. His story became the basis of the novel *An American Tragedy* by Theodore Dreiser who attended the trial.

12 July, 1979

On 12 July 1979 as he sat on an outside patio at Joe and Mary's restaurant in Brooklyn, 69-year-old Carmine 'Cigar' Galante, the Godfather of New York, was shot dead along with his cousin, Giuseppe Turano, and his bodyguard Leonardo 'Nina' Coppolla. Galante, who had become the Godfather following the death of Carlo Gambino, had gone to the restaurant to say goodbye to his cousin who was going to Italy.

As a young man Galante had run a street gang and was said to have killed his first victim at the age of 11. He was sent to prison in 1930 when a young girl and a police officer were shot and wounded in a failed robbery. After he was paroled he became a hit man for Vito Genovese and later for Joseph Bonanno. He was part of the New York end of the notorious French Connection, a heroin smuggling operation which ran in the 1950s. He received 20 years in prison and, paroled on 23 November 1974, quickly re-established his authority.

In 1978 a drug war broke out between the New York families during which eight Genovese men were killed. At a meeting in Boca Raton it was decided that Galante was too dangerous to be allowed to continue and would have to go. He died with his cigar in his lips. The decision was said to have been a 'spur of the moment' one but during the meal one diner had 'felt

unwell' and left the restaurant and others had been to
the telephone.

'I used to say the rest of them were copper but he
was pure steel,' said Lieutenant Remo Francheschini of
the New York police. 'When he spoke, he made others
shudder.' Galante's death was almost certainly part of
the sequence which saw the death of Angelo Bruno of
the Philadelphia family.

Carl Sifakis, *The Mafia File*; Jay Robert Nash, *World
Encyclopedia of Organised Crime*.

13 July, 1953

On 13 July 1953, in his lodgings in Little Horton Lane,
Bradford, 42-year-old, well-built Father Henrik Borynski,
an exiled Pole, took a call, said 'All right I go', collected his
hat and coat and, watched by his housekeeper, walked up
the road, turned right past a hospital, and vanished. He
took only 10 shillings with him and left £300 in his bank
account.

He had left behind his wallet, money and personal possessions. He never returned to his lodgings. His landlady,
Irena Beck, telephoned the local police and both the CID
and MI5 were called in. The local community believed he
had been kidnapped and murdered by Communist agents
who were supposed to be prevalent in Bradford at the
time. The priest opposed them and their doctrines. There
was no evidence to support this theory.

A curious feature of the case was an apparent attack
on another priest, Father Boleslaw Martynellis who led
the Lithuanian community in Bradford. There was some
rivalry amongst the congregations, if not between the
priests. Shortly after Borynski's disappearance Martynellis
claimed he had been attacked and a message, 'Be silent,

priest', was spelled out in matchsticks and left on his table. Later he thought the attack might have been imagined because of his nervous state and he might himself have laid out the matches.

14 July, 1912

The Bennett case (see 22 September) had a curious sequel. On 14 July 1912 Dora May Grey told a Miss Eastick, with whom she lived in Yarmouth, Norfolk, that she had met a gentleman friend the previous Sunday at Lowestoft and had been on his boat, and was going to meet him again that evening.

Born in Norwich, Dora Grey, aged 18, was an illegitimate child who had been brought up by Miss Eastick and Mrs Brooks. She worked in a boarding house in Manby Road.

The last person to see her that night, apart from her killer, was a girlfriend, Emily Blythe. Dora Grey was wearing a big straw hat trimmed with roses. The next morning her body was found on South Beach near where Mrs Bennett's had been found. It appeared that she had been killed elsewhere and brought to the spot. She had however been strangled with a bootlace taken from one of her shoes, as had Mrs Bennett, which, together with her stockings, had been removed before her death. For a time it was suggested that she was killed by the same person as Mrs Bennett and therefore that Herbert Bennett was indeed innocent.

A more likely explanation is that it was a copycat killing. Indeed a local man was strongly suspected but no charges were brought.

Ivan Butler, *Murderers' England*.

15 July, 1992

In the summer of 1991, following the death of her
husband Harry, from cancer, Carolyn Taylor met a French
pilot, Gaeton Beissy, whilst on holiday in Corsica. He
moved into her £750,000 house near Dorking, Surrey
in the October, following a whirlwind romance. On 15
July 1992 Mrs Taylor was found stabbed to death at her
home. Her son, Mark, called the police. Beissy was found
in a drunken stupor in a wood on the estate. Two almost
empty bottles of whisky and port were found next to
him, together with a bloodstained knife. The prosecution
alleged that Beissy was the murderer, claiming he was
jealous because he believed Mrs Taylor was sleeping with
her physiotherapist. Mark gave evidence that he had been
woken at 6.30 am by his mother's screams. He said he
had found her body naked in the kitchen and that Beissy
entered as he, Mark, was telephoning for a doctor. He
said that Beissy then stabbed Mrs Taylor twice.
  Beissy claimed that it was Mark who had killed his
mother as she tried to prevent him attacking her lover
who would deprive him of his birthright. Two juries at
the Old Bailey could not agree on a verdict and Beissy
was released when the prosecution offered no evidence
after the second disagreement on 8 May 1993.

16 July, 1910

In the evening of 16 July 1910 43-year-old Wendon
Atherstone, sometimes called Thomas Atherton, a small-
time actor whose last engagement had been at the
Battersea Empire in a melodrama, *The Grip of the Law*,

was found by his son in the basement of the house where his former mistress, Elizabeth Earl (or Earle), had a flat in number 17 Clifton Gardens, Prince of Wales Road, Battersea, south London. He was wearing carpet slippers and had been shot. The 21-year-old son Thomas who, to complicate matters, was known as Anderson, had been dining with Miss Earl.

About 9.30 pm a chauffeur, Edward Noice, was driving in Rosenau Road, Battersea when he heard two shots. He saw a man climbing through the garden of number 19, then on a wall and, after leaping down on to the pavement, running off towards the Thames. The police went to number 17 where the door was opened by Miss Earl. She told him she had heard shots fired and that she had seen a man climb a wall. Thomas Anderson confirmed her story.

On investigation of the property, heavy breathing was heard and in the doorway of the downstairs scullery the body of Atherstone was discovered. He had been shot on the right-hand side of his face near his mouth. Atherstone was carrying a rudimentary form of life preserver, a piece of insulated electric cable wrapped in paper and covered in wool with a loop to pass over the wrist. The police officer found a visiting card in the man's possession and asked Thomas Anderson if he knew anyone by the name of Atherton. He replied he knew someone by the name of Atherstone and said that was the name under which his father appeared on the stage. He was taken to the police station and asked if the dead man was his father. He said that he did not think so as his father did not wear a moustache. He was told the man was clean-shaven and then began to cry, saying, 'I saw my father die.'

The case was something of a *cause célèbre*. What was Thomas Anderson doing dining with his father's mistress whilst his father was downstairs in the basement in his carpet slippers with a life preserver in his pocket? Various theories have been advanced, including the suggestion that Thomas, together with his younger brother and Miss Earl, conspired to do away with Atherstone as he was becoming a financial burden to them. Another is that Atherstone was killed by Anderson as he discovered his son and Miss Earl together. A third solution is that there was another lover who killed Atherstone when surprised by him.

Inquiries showed that there had been a number of burglaries in the area. The man seen escaping was in his thirties, rather than a young man like Thomas or his even younger brother. Atherstone had suffered a head injury some two years previously and had become increasingly suspicious of Miss Earl, believing that she had another lover, something of which there was no evidence. So far as dining with Thomas on a Saturday evening was concerned, he said Miss Earl had been like a mother to him and he had visited her often. There were no signs of a struggle or blood in her rooms. The police indicated they were satisfied that Miss Earl and the Anderson boys had co-operated fully with them.

The explanation is probably that Atherstone had been hiding to see if Miss Earl did have a lover whom he would then attack. Unfortunately, whilst he was hiding downstairs he encountered the burglar and was shot by him in the ensuing struggle.

Jonathan Goodman, *Acts of Murder*; Bernard Taylor and Stephen Knight, *Perfect Murder*.

17 July, 1995

'June Bug' Quentin Carter, one of the smallest students in his sixth grade class at Intermediate School 109 in Queens Village, New York, was shot to death on 17 July 1995, two days before his 13th birthday.

Known as a clown, he began to needle an older

boy, 16-year-old Brian Wright, pretending to beg a
quarter from him outside a neighbourhood grocery store.
Wright, poorly regarded by his peers and nicknamed
Shorty, enraged by the taunting, shot Carter with his
.38 handgun, emptying the clip into his body as he lay
on the pavement.

There had been a previous row between the youths
on the Sunday when Carter had gone through what he
regarded as an amusing routine. On that occasion Wright
had taken out the gun and said, 'Are you ready to die?'
Carter had begun to cry but had refused to back down,
sobbing, 'Go ahead and shoot me.' On this occasion an
adult had intervened.

Now, on the Monday night Carter, in company with
friends, had pointed Wright out and had once again begun
to taunt him. Wright pulled out his gun and shot Carter
in the back as he ran away. One schoolmate of Wright's
commented, 'If you carry yourself like you're a nobody,
you're going to get treated like a nobody. I think he felt
he had to take a little kid's life to show how big he was.'
Wright, who had no criminal record, was charged with
murder. He allegedly told the police he had shot Carter
because the boy had shown him disrespect.

18 July, 1981

Jack Henry Abbott, also known as Jack Eastman, had
become a literary lion from the prison cell. Convicted of
a variety of crimes, from robbery to murder, he had spent
much of his adult life in prison. In 1966 he killed another
inmate in the Utah State Penitentiary, running the defence
that he was warding off a homosexual attack. He received
14 years. He escaped in 1971 and was recaptured after
robbing a bank in Denver. During this sentence he started
corresponding with the author Norman Mailer who was

impressed with his talent and arranged for the publication of Abbott's letters under the title *In the Belly of the Beast* for which he received a $12,000 advance. Described by the *New York Times* as 'a work touched with dark greatness' it became a bestseller and, with Mailer and other literary celebrities campaigning on his behalf, led to Abbott's release.

In the summer of 1981 Abbott was sent to a halfway house in New York with a view to his being given full parole on 25 August. He did a certain amount of research for Mailer and was received in awe by the literati of New York. Unfortunately, the excitement of being outside proved too much and he returned to the Lower East Side. About 5 am on 18 July he stabbed 22-year-old Richard Adan, an actor and playwright, who was earning extra money as a waiter at the BoniBon, a small all-night eatery, owned by his father-in-law on Second Avenue and Fifth Street. Abbott had asked Adan to step outside after an argument in the restaurant. According to witnesses Adan had told Abbott perfectly politely that because of insurance problems customers were not allowed to use the staff washroom. After the killing, Abbott went on the run, hiding out in Mexico near the Guatemalan border before moving to the oilfields of Louisiana where he was caught on 21 September.

At his trial he was able successfully to run a defence of manslaughter rather than murder. He claimed that since he had spent all but 10 months of his life since the age of 14 behind bars he was incapable of living outside prison. He was jailed for 15 years.

In 1990 Ricci Adan, the widow of the waiter, was awarded $7.6 million in compensation for her husband's death. On this occasion Abbott had defended himself, aggravating the matter by suggesting that Mrs Adan's tears in the witness box had prejudiced the jury and were sufficient for the judge to order a mistrial. The money, or at any rate part of it, would come from the royalties from books and scripts written by Abbott in prison. *In the Belly of the Beast* had sold 40,000 copies in hardback and the film rights had gone for $250,000.

Jack Abbott, *In the Belly of the Beast*; Jay Robert Nash, *World Encyclopedia of 20th Century Murder*.

19 July, 1901

Tom Horn was one of the early undercover agents who worked for the Pinkerton Detective Agency. He had been an Indian-fighter and army scout before he arrived in Denver in 1890 with what were described as impeccable references. For the next few years he was the Pinkerton's Rocky Mountain operative, making a number of arrests of train robbers and cattle rustlers, killing a number as well. He also took time off to commit a robbery for himself in Nevada and was protected by the agency. Charles Siringo, an early chronicler of the Agency, wrote, in *Two Evil Isms*:

> . . .on one of his trips to Denver, William A. Pinkerton [one of the sons] told me that Tom Horn was guilty of the crime but that his people could not afford to let him go to the penitentiary while in their employ.

Despite the protection, let alone the salary the agency offered, Horn felt tied down, and resigned in 1894, becoming a freelance detective and hired gun of the Wyoming Cattleman's Association in their long-running fight against small ranchers who, they said, rustled their cattle, and sheep farmers.

Horn, born in 1860 and who is said to have once slapped the face of William Bonny, Billy the Kid, was described as a tidy, patient and skilful murderer. He would wait hours in driving rain, chewing bacon fat, to ensure he had the one necessary clear shot of his target. After each shooting he would leave a stone under the head of his victim so that there was no doubt as to the killer. In 1901 he made what proved to be his fatal error. On 19 July that year he killed 14-year-old Willie Nickell, the son of a sheep farmer, mistaking him, in poor light, for his father.

For two years, partially because of Horn's powerful protectors, the murder remained unsolved. His eventual undoing was by another semi-undercover man, Joe Lefors, a deputy US marshal who became Horn's confidant and, when the latter was well in drink, obtained a bragging confession from him. Lefors took the precaution of having the confession noted by a hidden shorthand writer and another witness.

Despite his pleas for help from his former employers and a donation of $5,000 to his defence fund from an unknown admirer, Horn was convicted of murder in 1903. He had tried to impugn the confession, suggesting that what he said was just a tall tale and that the stenographer had added pieces of his own. Whilst awaiting execution he escaped from prison but was quickly recaptured. He was hanged on 20 November 1903. In recent years efforts have been made, as has often been the case with outlaws, to rehabilitate Horn. In his book (see below) Dean Krakel has said that the confession should have been ruled inadmissible and that, indeed, he was not the youth's killer.

F. Morn, *The Eye that never Sleeps*; T. Horn, ed. D. Krakel, *Life of Tom Horn: Government Scout and Interpreter*.

20 July, 1988

Thirty-six-year-old Diana Maw's body, a six-inch cross-bow bolt embedded in her head, was found on the landing outside her flat at Stanley Court, Woodfield Road, Ealing on 20 July 1988. At the time of her death Diana, the daughter of an eye surgeon, was a high-powered executive in an employment company. She had also been planning to move into a £325,000 house with her boyfriend Michael Stevens. At first it was thought she had been shot by a mugger but inquiries led to the belief that she had been stalked by her killer for the previous six weeks. She had been receiving anonymous telephone calls.

In August Scotland Yard released a photofit of the man who had been seen carrying the weapon two days before Diana Maw was killed. He was described as between 19 and 21 and five feet eight inches tall.

On 30 November interior designer Jane Frances Salveson, the former girlfriend of Michael Stevens, was charged with the killing of Diana Maw. She had been picked out on an identification parade by a single witness. The allegation was that she was obsessed with the girl who had taken her place, that she had followed the couple and visited their homes whilst they were out. Through her solicitor she denied any involvement and appealed for witnesses to come forward. In the event she did not need them. The Crown Prosecution Service offered no evidence on 20 April 1989.

The allegations against her did not, however, end there. On 29 June 1990 she was remanded in custody accused of setting fire to Stevens's home and in the November she was accused of breaking into his yacht and stealing a diary. In October 1990 the Crown Prosecution Service again dropped the charges against her on the arson case and on 1 March 1991 she was acquitted by a jury at

Knightsbridge Crown Court of the theft charge. She claimed the police had been victimising her.

21 July, 1992

The In Memoriam notice in the *Daily Telegraph* read:

> **Lowndes** On July 21, 1992, tragically in Spain, Carmel June, much-loved wife of Jeremy, loving mother of John, dear grandmother of Katherine and David . . .

In fact it was the 'loving husband' Jeremy who stood trial for the murder of his 68-year-old wife who was suffering from cancer.

Carmel Maguire was one of the so-called Lovely Maguires, daughters of the Australian welterweight champion Mickey Maguire. Each did well for herself. One married into the Beaverbrook family, another went to Hollywood, another married Godfrey Davis, the car hire magnate. It was thought however that Carmel had done best of all. Her third marriage was to Jeremy Lowndes – she had previously married Derek Dunnet and Lord Kimberley by whom she had a son, John, Lord Wodehouse.

Her life with Lowndes was something of an aimless one. He would walk the dogs, discuss shooting prospects with his gamekeeper; there would be luncheon and dinner parties and from February until August they would charter a yacht. Soon Lowndes began to drink a bottle of Scotch a day. He lost money in the City; the farm was not doing well. In 1980, in a fit of depression, he tried to commit suicide, after which he required brain surgery.

In the 1980s the Lowndes sold much of their Suffolk estate to Sheik Hamdan Al-Maktoum and moved to

Sotogrande and then to the Côte d'Azur before, in 1991, they rented a house, *Villa Crepusculo*, at Sotogrande.

On 20 July 1992 they had friends, the Walkers, for dinner. They left after midnight, and during the night Carmel Lowndes was battered to death, receiving at least five blows to the head.

Lowndes would later tell the court: 'I was awoken by a terrible scream from my wife. I rushed upstairs and found the poor darling lying with blood everywhere.'

He went on to say that he believed he knew the name of her killer. This sat oddly with confessions he was said to have made to his stepson, John, to whom he said, 'I think I have just killed your mother,' and John's brother-in-law, Robert St John.

In turn St John told the court that he had rushed over from his villa nearby and found Lowndes pacing the living room in an agitated state, muttering, 'that bloody woman' and, significantly, 'I don't know why I did it . . . life's not worth living any more.' He then jumped from the terrace onto one by the pool. In doing so he broke both his ankles as well as damaging his spine.

Lowndes's defence was a veiled attack on his stepson, who was staying at the villa on the night of his mother's death, to the effect that there was a missing Georgian candlestick which might have been the murder weapon which was never found. The candlesticks which had been used at the dinner party had subsequently been taken back to England but, he claimed, one was missing. Lord Wodehouse said they were all safe in England.

There were criticisms by the defence of the investigation of the murder. Lowndes had no blood on his shirt and it was suggested that he had taken it off before killing his wife. Dr Iain West, called for the defence, said that he could not believe Lowndes was the killer, because there was no blood on his clothing or arms: 'I can see no objective evidence to indicate that Mr

Lowndes could have been the person who struck the deceased.'

In early June 1994 the court sitting in Cadiz and comprising three judges, took seven days to find 65-year-old Lowndes guilty and impose a sentence of nine years – the prosecutor had asked for a term of twenty. Nevertheless his Spanish lawyer, Señor Jose Maria Stampa, said he would appeal its severity. Money cannot have been the motive because Lowndes inherited only a life interest in certain of the property. It was generally thought that he had killed his wife whilst under the influence of a combination of drink and the drugs he had been taking regularly since his head injury, but others thought the evidence was less than satisfactory and that Carmel Lowndes might have stumbled across a burglar.

22 July, 1994

On 22 July 1994 Steven Chaifetz, a 50-year-old account-ant, and his wife, Charon, were sitting in a restaurant in Commack, Suffolk County, New York, when 25-year-old Peter Sylvester, from Long Island, began firing seemingly at random. Chaifetz was killed in what turned out to be a convoluted plot by Sylvester to create a smokescreen for a planned murder.

His intention had been to kill a topless dancer as an unsolicited favour to another topless dancer whose boyfriend had been stolen from her by the intended victim. Sylvester's intention was that the sniping attacks would lead the police to think that the girl was just another victim of these random attacks on restaurants and petrol stations. At his trial Sylvester pleaded guilty to killing Mr Chaifetz, as well as shooting a waitress, Kathryn Spatafore, at a Burger King restaurant whilst she was wiping down a table near the front window, and shooting at Ali Gocmez, a petrol station attendant who was protected by security glass. He also pleaded guilty to burglary, theft and attacking a sleeping girl with a metal object. Other counts in the 24-count indictment were dropped.

Under the plea bargain Sylvester was sentenced to a term of 35 years to life. The Suffolk County District Attorney, James M. Catterson, said he had agreed to the bargain because of the sentence and also to spare the victims the trauma of testifying at the trial. 'Justice is served and there is an end to it,' he said, describing Sylvester as 'the type of person who knows what's wrong but doesn't care'. The defence suggested that Sylvester, who was a customer of one of the topless clubs at the Bull Creek Inn, may have been 'spurred on or egged on by his friend, who was not charged, to murder her rival'.

As a result of Sylvester's shootings Long Island restaurants installed blinds and drew curtains whilst they had customers.

23 July, 1943

On 23 July 1943 Eric James Brown, whilst serving in the army, obtained a Hawkins 75 grenade mine and put it on the seat of his father's bathchair at his home in London Hill, Rayleigh, Essex. The anti-tank device blew up, killing his father, the 47-year-old Archibald Brown, and seriously injuring his father's nurse, Elsie Mitchell.

Archibald Brown had been badly injured in a motor accident three years before his marriage and had, in consequence, been a tyrant towards his wife and son Eric throughout the 20-year marriage. His wife had effectively been cut off from relations and friends and was the subject of constant verbal abuse, something which spilled over onto Eric Brown. Worse, in 1938, Brown senior developed spinal paralysis and lost the use of both legs. His behaviour to his son and wife became even worse. In a statement to the police Mrs Brown detailed how, when she displeased him, her husband would deliberately spill tea over her or, if she was standing too near him, pull her to the ground.

On the afternoon of 23 July Nurse Mitchell went to fetch the bathchair from the air-raid shelter in the garden but found the door locked. She went for help to Mrs Brown and both women were surprised to find that Eric was in the shed. He was evasive, saying he was 'looking for something'. What he had done was to put the mine, suitably modified, beneath the seat cushion. It detonated a few moments after his father took his place.

At Brown's trial for murder at Essex Assizes on 4 November 1943 the court heard that whilst at work before the war he had been prone to brainstorms. A consultant psychiatrist diagnosed that he was suffering from the early stages of schizophrenia. During the period on remand he had made a genuine attempt at suicide. The prison doctor gave evidence that having spoken to Brown every day since he had been in custody his conclusion was that he was sane. The jury returned a verdict of 'guilty but insane' and Brown was detained during His Majesty's pleasure.

Robert Church, *Murder in East Anglia*.

24 July, 1984

When Ron Lafferty appeared in court in 1985 charged with the murder of his sister-in-law Brenda, and Erica, her 15-month-old daughter, near Salt Lake City, Utah, on 24 July 1984, his brother, Dan Lafferty, who believes himself to be the Old Testament prophet, Elijah, gave evidence that he himself had carried out the killing at God's request and direction.

The prosecution claimed that 54-year-old Ron Lafferty had cut his sister-in-law's throat before handing the knife to his brother. The killing had been because Brenda, the 24-year-old wife of a third brother, Allen, had helped Ron Lafferty's estranged wife. Brenda had tried to encourage the Lafferty wives to stand up to their husbands who viewed women as property. As a result Dan Lafferty branded Brenda and her child 'daughters of perdition'. Their murders were 'the Lord's work', he said.

In March 1984 Ron Lafferty claimed he had received a divine revelation, ordering that Brenda and Erica be removed, along with two others who had helped his estranged wife. The others were spared – one was on holiday and in the second case, the Lafferty brothers missed the turn-off to his house.

They went to Allen's house and drove away when there was no reply to their knocking. Then, according to Dan, he had a strong impression that he must turn the car round. This time Brenda opened the door. Dan Lafferty wrestled her to the ground and after a quick prayer told his brother to get a hunting knife from his boot. Ron had cut the cord of the vacuum cleaner and tried to tie it around Brenda's throat but 'an unseen force' knocked it away. The brothers then took this as a sign of Divine intention that it should be 'Dan who killed Brenda and the child'.

'I am not ashamed about what happened,' said Dan, who saw himself as a secular David, holding the head of Goliath. 'It was just a matter of business.'

The defence was that it was only Dan who had killed. Ron Lafferty had, said his lawyers, been involved only because of mental illness and extreme psychological fatigue brought about by virtue of his earlier expulsion from the Church of Jesus Christ of Latter-Day Saints, and his divorce.

Dan Lafferty was convicted in 1984. One juror had held out against the death penalty and he received a sentence of life imprisonment. The sentence of death passed on Ron Lafferty in 1985 was overturned by the appeal court in 1991 and a new trial was ordered.

On Friday 31 May 1996 Ron Lafferty, who was convicted on the retrial of the murders, elected death by firing squad. 'I prefer to live,' he told the judge when given the choice between the squad and a lethal injection. 'You're guilty of murder in the first degree if you carry it out.'

He was sentenced to die on 18 July 1996 but the execution was stayed as he began a second series of appeals.

25 July, 1995

On 25 July 1995, so the police allege, Robert Joseph Silveria, who rode boxcars as a hobo, killed James 'J. C.' McLean in a camp next to the Southern Pacific railroad near the Albany–Berkeley border in California.

McLean, who had 'ridden the rods' for over 25 years, had settled down and built himself a shack on land just to the west of the tracks. He lived on Social Security cheques and from cashing in recyclables. He was regarded in the hobo community as a crusty but basically good guy who was quite prepared to share what little food or alcohol he had with other hobos. The theory is that Silveria, now named the 'Boxcar Killer', took advantage of McLean's friendship and then killed him.

After his arrest on 2 March 1996 for the killing of McLean, Silveria, who had once been a roofer in Redwood City but who had started travelling in the 1980s, told the police he had killed at least 20 people but he later reduced that number by four. He is alleged to have admitted killing William Pettit junior who was beaten to death in a boxcar on 1 December 1995 near Salem, Oregon, as well as a Bay area man, Michael Garfinkle, who was found beaten to death near railroad tracks in Emeryville on 2 August 1994. The police claimed that Silveria stayed at hobo camps throughout the Western States, working a month-long circuit. They claim he selected his victims carefully, causing confrontations and then waiting his time before murdering them. When arrested he had with him identification cards and papers for a number of people, including his alleged victims.

In June 1996 Silveria pleaded not guilty and it was suggested that his might be an insanity defence. By now Kansas and Florida were seeking his extradition.

26 July, 1966

On the evening of 26 July 1966 passers-by noticed a cardboard package in the quiet suburban street, Merton Rise, in Hampstead, north London. In it, naked, with all hair shaved from the torso, trussed like a chicken, was the body of a young black girl, 19-year-old machinist, Grace Fayodi. When Professor Francis Camps examined the body, which had multiple bruises, burns and stab wounds, he found the left thumb was crushed as if it had been shut in a railway carriage door. Although there was no single cause of death he thought that the crushing of her thumb had been the last straw.

Grace had been staying with a 36-year-old Nigerian law student, Kayode Orishagbemi, and his sister-in-law Evelyn Akolo. At the time Orishagbemi's wife was ill in hospital with tuberculosis. On 28 July when the police took him in for questioning Orishagbemi told them that Grace had said she was a witch and that he had tried to get her to disclose her secrets.

'When I tried to get her to tell me her witchcraft secrets she said she would die and another person too if she tells me,' he said in a statement to the police, adding, 'I just tied her up to the door. Very kindly I did it. She must have some kind of punishment, so I beat her . . . Witchcraft caused her death.' The statement went on to say that Grace worked witchcraft in her sleep and had killed two people by witchcraft in Nigeria. Orishagbemi added that she used a spider and would 'tie you up in the spider's web and you cannot move'. There was also a peanut which became invisible when someone was put in it and which could fly over rivers. Orishagbemi said he believed that Grace had practised witchcraft on both his wife and himself. On the day she died, he said he had given her a cup of coffee. 'She just gurgled and fell over, head down. It was too late to call the doctor. I could not call an ambulance. I could not call the police.'

The prosecution's viewpoint was a very different one. There was some correspondence found referring to Orishagbemi as the secretary of the 'London Girls' Modern College' in Plimsoll Road, Finsbury Park, London, and some letters saying he would be willing to pay the fares of Nigerian students to come to London. On enquiry it turned out there was no such college. When he was first questioned by Chief Inspector James Barnett Orishagbemi had said that Grace had run away a long time ago, and produced a diary with an entry for 17 December 1965 which read, 'Grace run away today about 4.30 pm.' When he was questioned further he said, 'She got to work to repay me the passage money. She is a bad girl. She come back. Then last July 16 she get two weeks' pay and run away again. I not see her since then.' That, said the prosecution, was what it was really all about.

Orishagbemi's defence was that he had not killed Grace but that she had ceased to wish to live. He said that he was not responsible for Grace's injuries and claimed that she had been pushed downstairs by a ghost.

On 5 December Mr Justice Glyn-Jones, sentencing Orishagbemi to life imprisonment after the jury had found him guilty of murder, said: 'You have been most justly convicted of a cruel murder. I think your treatment of the dead girl was so horrifying that I shall recommend that you be kept in custody for not less than 20 years.'

The judge, who later had enquiries made into the safety of others who might have 'attended' the London Girls' Modern College, ensured that help was available for Evelyn Akolo who had been found not guilty of assisting Orishagbemi in disposing of Grace's body. She returned to Nigeria shortly after the trial.

27 July, 1968

The likely day of death of 87-year-old Myles Daley was 27 July 1968. That at any rate was the medical evidence and it was the day the milkman brought the milk and saw him last. He called again on 30 July and, anxious that he had not seen the old man in the meantime, brought his employer with him. They forced the door and found that Myles Daley had been struck 27 blows to the head and chest with a slash-hook.

There were rumours in Mullaghoran, Finea, County Cavan, Ireland, where Daley lived, that a man had been seen locking the door of the cottage and throwing the key into a field. An extensive strip search of the field by the Gardai finally produced it and, in due course, a man was charged. After a five-day trial he was found not guilty on the direction of the trial judge, Justice Henchy, who said that too much of the evidence was 'neutral' for there to be a conviction.

28 July, 1950

The body of 40-year-old Catherine McCluskey was found
by a taxi driver on 28 July 1950 on the Prospecthill
Road in the Mount Florida district of Glasgow. From
the investigation it appeared that the woman had been
lying in the road when a car had been driven over her.
It had been stopped and then, possibly with the body still
trapped underneath, the driver had reversed.

The next morning the papers reported that a woman
had been knocked down and killed and within a matter of
hours a friend of Catherine McCluskey had come forward
to say that she had been looking after one of Catherine's
two illegitimate children for the evening and that she had
not returned.

McCluskey had claimed that the father of one of those
children was a 33-year-old police constable from the
Glasgow Southern Division, James Ronald Robertson. At
one time he had been regarded as a teetotal, nonsmoking
family man who was destined for promotion. More
recently he had, however, been found absent from his
beat in the Gorbals, then possibly the worst of many of
Glasgow's slum areas. He was also seen driving a large
black Austin car well beyond his means but which he said
he had been loaned long-term by a friend.

Police inquiries showed that once again he had been
absent from his beat on the night and at the time of
the murder. Robertson was arrested and placed on an
identification parade to be picked out by McCluskey's
friends and neighbours.

Robertson appeared for trial on 6 November 1950
before Lord Keith and the Scottish 15-member jury,
consisting this time of eight men and seven women.
The allegations against him were that he had struck
Catherine McCluskey with a rubber truncheon, battering
her senseless and then, driving a car with false plates, he

had run over her. He was also charged with breaking into a motor showroom and stealing a radio and registration books. A third allegation was that on another occasion he had stolen a motor car.

He gave evidence on the fifth day of the trial when he admitted knowing Catherine McCluskey. He had first met her the previous year when he had been called to a disturbance at her home. He had seen her many times after that. He denied stealing the car, saying that he had found it abandoned and had begun to use it. He denied breaking into the showroom. The court was, of course, primarily interested in his version of how his mistress had died.

He had met her by appointment at 11.10 pm when she had asked him to take her to see a friend some 14 miles away. This was, of course, impossible; he was still on duty. He refused and she began to cry. He told her to get out of the car in Prospecthill Road and drove away. He changed his mind and slowly reversed about 100 yards. He heard an increase in the exhaust and then a jarring. He braked, stopped and saw a face under the running-board. He used his torch to see that it was Catherine McCluskey and that she was, he said, quite dead. He tried to free her and failed and then panicked, reversing the car and then driving forward. After a few minutes he succeeded in freeing the body from the car. He denied that he was the policeman paying money to McCluskey for her child or that he had hit her with a truncheon. According to one report of the case his manner in the witness box was totally unconvincing and he 'literally talked himself to death'.

The jury brought in a majority verdict of murder within an hour of their retirement. Robertson lodged an appeal which was refused and, according to reports, it was only in the last few days before he was hanged at Barlinie on 16 December 1960 that he appreciated the reality of his situation.

Bill Knox, *Court of Murder*; Douglas Skelton, *A Time to Kill*.

29 July, 1954

The semi-literate Mrs Styllou Christofi was almost certainly a double murderess. On 29 July 1954 she killed Hella, the German-born wife of her son Stavros. She had been living for the previous year with the couple in South Hill Park, Hampstead and she did not get on at all well with her daughter-in-law of whom she was extremely jealous. It had been arranged that Mrs Christofi, who spoke little English, should return to Cyprus.

Shortly before midnight a neighbour out walking his dog saw Mrs Christofi trying to burn the body of her daughter-in-law by setting fire to newspaper in her back yard. At the time he assumed the naked body was a tailor's dummy. An hour later Mrs Christofi approached a couple in a car near Hampstead police station, saying, 'Please come. Fire burning. Children sleeping.'

The police were called and found that the 34-year-old Hella Christofi had suffered a fractured skull – she had been hit on the head with a metal ashtray – and had then been strangled. Her body was charred and smelled of paraffin. Her wedding ring was found in Mrs Christofi's bedroom. Although for once the prison doctors thought that she was insane, Mrs Christofi refused to allow that plea to be put forward. After her conviction, when the jury recommended mercy, she was again examined and this time three doctors found her to be sane. She was hanged at Holloway prison on 13 December 1954.

In 1925 she had been charged with murder in Cyprus. It was alleged she had pushed a burning torch down her mother-in-law's throat whilst the woman had been held down by neighbours. That had been part of a village vendetta and she had been acquitted. However, it is probably this killing which prevented her reprieve. There was at the time a tendency to reprieve women if at all possible. In 1952 Mary Wilson, the so-called Widow of

Windy Nook, had been spared despite the fact that she
had poisoned her second and third husbands. It may have
been her age – she was 66 – which earned Mrs Wilson the
reprieve or the fact, as is suggested by Fenton Bresler in
Reprieve, that Lord Butler, then Home Secretary, could
not bring himself to order her execution 'complete with
the ritual donning of rubber knickers'.

There was no public outcry for clemency but it is
thought that the execution of Mrs Christofi also told
against the reprieve of Ruth Ellis who shot her lover,
David Blakely, outside the Magdala public house, also
in Hampstead, on 10 April 1955. Then, William Connor,
writing in the *Daily Mirror* as Cassandra on 30 June 1955,
put the case for the abolitionists:

> Ruth Ellis does not matter any more than her two
> most recent female predecessors to the hangman's
> noose – Mrs Merrifield and Mrs Christofi. But what
> we do to her – you and I – matters very much, and
> if we continue to do it to her sad successors then we
> all bear the guilt of savagery untinged with mercy.

30 July, 1982

Susan Maxwell an 11-year-old girl, was kidnapped near
her home at Coldstream, near Kelso on the Scottish borders, on 30 July 1982. Her body was found in a layby near
Uttoxeter in the Midlands on 12 August. She was the first
known victim of Robert Black, an obese lorry driver who
had a noticeably offensive smell. He had agreed to stand
in for a workmate and undertake a weekend drive.

Black, who was born in 1947, had had a number of
previous brushes with the law. He had been admonished
in 1963 by the Sherrif's court at Greenock, Glasgow,
after he had choked a girl unconscious and indecently

assaulted her. A psychiatric report at the time seems to have suggested the offence was a one-off and he did not need counselling. In March 1963 he pleaded guilty to three cases of indecent assault and was sent to Borstal. In between there had been an indecent assault on a six-year-old girl in his lodgings but the family had decided not to prosecute. He came to London and was dismissed from his position as a swimming bath attendant after an allegation of assault on another young girl.

Black continued his work as a driver and over the next years killed and sexually assaulted Caroline Hogg and left her body at Twycross, Leicester where it was discovered on 18 July 1983, and Sarah Harper, whom he kidnapped at Morley near Leeds on 26 March 1986. Her body was found in the River Trent on 19 April.

Black was finally caught when he abducted a young girl in the Border town of Stow on 14 July 1990. He was seen by a neighbour of the girl who took down the registration number of his lorry and the police were alerted. Inexplicably, having driven away, he drove back into Stow where he was stopped and the girl was found, bound and gagged, but alive, in the back of his lorry.

On 10 August 1990 he pleaded guilty to plagium, the Scottish equivalent of abduction. His mitigation was that the offence was of an isolated character but he was given a sentence of life imprisonment. In 1994 he appeared at Newcastle Crown Court charged with the murders of Susan Maxwell, Sarah Harper and Caroline Hogg. He was found guilty and again sentenced to life imprisonment with Mr Justice Macpherson telling him:

> Neither you nor the public will expect me to say more than a few words in sentence. You are an extremely dangerous man . . . I expect you to be detained for the whole of your life, but on the murder counts I propose to make a public rec- ommendation that the minimum time for which you are detained is thirty-five years on each of the murder convictions. Take him down.

Black's application for leave to appeal was refused on
20 February 1995. During interviews with the police
he displayed some knowledge of the case of a young
girl, Genette Tate, who disappeared on 19 August 1978
near Exeter. Various continental police forces wish to
interview him in regard to the disappearances of young
girls in France, Holland and Germany, at times when he
was working as an overseas long-distance lorry driver.

R. Church, *Well Done, Boys.*

31 July, 1993

In February 1995 Jonathon Jones, then aged 35, stood
trial at Newport Crown Court accused of the murder of
his fiancée's parents, Harry and Megan Tooze, on 31 July
1993. The motive was said to be money, and the murder
committed so that their daughter, Cheryl Tooze, with
whom he had lived for eight years, would inherit an estate
worth some £150,000, for her parents owned a successful
six-acre fruit farm at Llanharry, Mid Glamorgan. Jones,
on the other hand, had only £99 in his current account.

The prosecution's case was that Jones had travelled the
200 miles from Orpington where he lived with Ms Tooze
to Ty-ar-y-waun farm and after having tea with them –
his left thumbprint was found on a cup and saucer – shot
the elderly couple through the head at pointblank range.
Their bodies were found in the cowshed. It was said that
he and Miss Tooze were often behind with payment of
their rent. He was arrested two months after her parents'
funeral.

The murder weapon was never found. Nor was there
any other forensic or identification evidence against Jones
who ran an alibi defence to the effect that, at the time
of the murder, he was in Orpington looking for office

space to launch a market research business. He could not, however, call any witnesses in support of his alibi. Cheryl Tooze gave evidence on his behalf, saying, 'If I thought he was guilty I would say so. He has been on remand in prison for a year for nothing. I don't really know what the future holds for us when this is over. I really don't know if we can rebuild our relationship, though I always think we will be the best of friends.'

She was not in court on 6 April 1995 when Jones was given two life sentences after being convicted by a 10 to 2 majority. Ms Tooze had become estranged from the rest of her family over the case and was living with Jones's parents. Jones lodged an appeal. Ms Tooze launched a £25,000 appeal for anyone who could give evidence which would lead to Jones's acquittal. In May 1995 the case took a dramatic twist when the trial judge, Mr Justice Rougier, wrote to the Home Secretary saying that he had doubts about the validity of the jury's verdict.

In May 1996 the campaigning of Cheryl Tooze paid off: the Court of Appeal quashed the conviction. Much to the fury of Mr Jones and the surprise of many, the police indicated that they were not pursuing other lines of inquiry.

AUGUST

1 August, 1957

Amateur photographer Harvey Glatman hired model Judy Ann Dull to pose for bondage pictures in his Los Angeles apartment on 1 August 1957. Once she was tied he raped and strangled her. Later he buried her body in a shallow grave some 125 miles from Los Angeles where it remained until 29 December of that year.

In 1958 Shirley Bridgeford disappeared after her first date with Glatman who, calling himself George Williams, had met her through a lonely hearts club. He took her to the desert, bound her and then began taking photographs. He also killed Ruth Mercado. He had broken into her home and raped and photographed her. He was caught when trying to kill another young woman, Lorraine Vigil. He drove her to the desert where he shot her in the leg. She managed to take the gun from him and hold him captive until she was rescued by a highway patrol officer.

At first Glatman claimed that the attack on Ms Vigil had been been a one-off but a search of his home revealed photographs of the bodies of his victims. In contrast to many cases, in which lengthy stays of execution have been granted, he was sent to the gas chamber on 18 August 1959. He had refused to appeal, commenting, 'It's better this way.'

Brian Lane and Wilfred Gregg, *The Encyclopedia of*

Serial Killers; Marvin J. Wolf and Katherine Mader, *Fallen Angels*.

2 August, 1921

During the evening of 2 August 1921 60-year-old Father Patrick E. Heslin was kidnapped from the Holy Angels Church in Colma near San Francisco. A man wearing a long overcoat with motoring goggles covering much of his face knocked on the door and when Father Heslin's housekeeper, Marie Wendel, opened it he said, in a foreign accent, that he would like to see the priest. The reason he gave was that his friend was dying, following a motor accident. Later she described the man as small, dark and rather foreign-looking.

Heslin put on his coat and left with the man, taking with him equipment to administer the last rites. He never returned. The housekeeper did not raise any alarm until the next day. It was not, after all, unusual for the priest to stay overnight with a dying person. When he did not call the next day she telephoned the Archbishop of San Francisco, Edward J. Hanna. He decided to wait a little more time before he contacted the police and, meanwhile, a ransom note demanding a modest $6,500 for the release of Father Heslin was delivered. The police were contacted and the press alerted. Massive hunts went on around the city but nothing was heard of the priest until eight days after his disappearance when a second ransom note was delivered. The same sum was asked for and the note seemed full of self-righteous pity: 'Fate has made me do this. Sickness and misery has compelled my action. I must have money. Please forgive this act if you can. The father is not dead YET.'

On 10 August a reporter for the *San Francisco Examiner* was due to interview the Archbishop when he heard a man explain that he was a William A. Hightower and could say where the missing priest could be found – on the beach near a billboard advertising flapjacks.

He told a complicated story of two girlfriends having cached some illegal liquor and that when he had gone to dig it up he had unearthed a black scarf. Eventually he led a police squad to the beach where Heslin's body was dug from the sand. The priest had been knocked unconscious, his skull crushed and two shots fired into his body. For some time Hightower stuck by the story of the buried liquor. One girl was found not to exist and the second denied anything to do with buried drink. The gun which had been used to shoot the priest had been pawned and was traced back to Hightower. Two tent pegs found near Heslin's body matched those found in Hightower's room.

Despite considerable public opinion in favour of an execution Hightower was sentenced to life imprisonment. In San Quentin he became a master chef specialising in pâtisseries.

Nick Harris, *Famous Crimes*.

3 August, 1990

The body of 44-year-old Ann Heron was found on 3 August 1990, the hottest day of that year. She had been sunbathing in the garden of her £300,000 home in the village of Middleton St George near Darlington. Her throat had been cut with a weapon similar to a Stanley knife and part of her bikini had been removed.

Her body was found on his return from work by Peter Heron, who owned a haulage business, and who offered £5,000 reward for the conviction of his wife's killer. Mr Heron appeared on television to make his plea.

The case was Durham's biggest murder hunt with the police conducting over seven thousand interviews and a total of over 100,000 police hours being used. The police said they were looking for a suntanned man in his thirties who was seen driving away from the Herons' home. No charges were brought.

Over an eight-day period in 1994 a series of anonymous letters were written to the police and the editor of the *Northern Echo* which began, 'Hello, editor . . . it's me, Ann Heron's killer!' It was signed The Killer.

Mr Heron, who had remarried in 1993, repeated his appeal for people to help catch his wife's murderer. The case remains Durham's only unsolved murder in 40 years.

4 August, 1952

On 4 August 1952 Sir Jack Drummond, a 61-year-old British biochemist who had a distinguished career with the Resistance in France, his wife Ann and their 10-year-old daughter Elizabeth, stopped to camp at the roadside outside Lurs in Provence. As they undressed for bed it is thought Drummond discovered a Peeping Tom in the bushes. He went to remonstrate with him and was shot in the chest. Ann Drummond was also shot and their terrified daughter beaten to death as she ran away.

Their bodies were found the next morning by railway workers and the police also heard from 33-year-old Gustave Dominici that he had discovered the bodies on the farm, La Grande Terre, which belonged to his father, Gaston.

An extensive police investigation by Edmond Sebeille, the superintendent of police in Marseilles, fixed on a member or members of the Dominici family. One of the railway workers told him that Gustave Dominici had said that Elizabeth was still alive, but dying, when he found her.

In November 1952 Gustave Dominici was charged with failing to come to the aid of a dying person and sentenced to two months' imprisonment, quashed on appeal. Throughout the next year Sebeille continued to put pressure on the Dominici family and accused Gustave of killing the Drummonds. In reply he said it was his father and, according to the police, this was confirmed by Clovis, another brother. Gustave later withdrew the allegation.

What had happened, according to Gustave, was that he had heard shots and run to the field where he had seen his father with a carbine rifle. He was afraid his father would kill him as well and when he returned at 5.30 am and found Elizabeth still alive he did nothing, for fear his father would find out he had seen the murders.

At first Gaston Dominici admitted the murders, rather claiming a *droit de seigneur* that he could do what he wanted on his land. Later he withdrew his confession and when, in accordance with the French police method, they re-enacted the crime in the presence of the suspect, he tried to commit suicide by jumping off a railway bridge.

He was sentenced to death after an 11-day trial in 1954 but the sentence was commuted to one of life imprisonment and he was pardoned in 1960. He returned to the farm and later to an old people's home where he died in 1965.

There have been considerable misgivings over the case and it has been suggested that he killed the adult Drummonds whilst someone else killed Elizabeth. Another theory is that he was not responsible for any of the killings but that he had confessed out of ignorance and confusion. A third belief, held by many French people, is that Drummond was killed because of his wartime involvement in the Resistance. A German, Wilhelm Bartowski, is alleged to have told British Intelligence that he and three colleagues murdered the Drummonds during a robbery.

Harry J. Greenwall, *They Were Murdered in France.*

5 August, 1927

Mary Josephine Waits, a 34-year-old American citizen who was employed as a stewardess on the *SS American Trader*, was charged with wilfully murdering Louis Fisher, a refrigerator engineer, on 5 August 1927 by throwing carbolic acid over him.

She had met Fisher in November 1926 and they had become friendly, with a suggestion they should marry once he obtained his engineer's ticket. She became pregnant and had an abortion in New York. The affair fizzled out in the summer of 1927 and Fisher spent his July leave with a Mrs Doris Ross, the wife of a seaman on the *American Merchant*, another ship in the line.

He had apparently been drinking heavily, to the point of delirium tremens. Much of his time was spent in the Queen's Hotel, Leicester Square and Waits went there on one occasion to try to persuade him to stop squandering his money. When they went aboard for the passage to New York Fisher said, 'Molly, are you very mad with me?' She replied, 'Yes, Louis, I am very grieved.' 'I am very grieved too, I am suffering the pangs of the damned, don't make it any worse for me,' he replied. She asked him if he would come home with her at the end of the voyage and he replied that he wanted to straighten himself out and would then join her. She advised him then to go and stay with his aunt and this he did.

There was talk about his not rejoining the ship and instead trying for his ticket but on 28 July she saw him again and he said, 'No, I am just going to hang round and you can do your damnedest and shoot.' He sailed with the ship. During the passage she sent him a note complaining that Mrs Ross was simply using him and that apart from her husband and Fisher she had yet another boyfriend.

On 5 August Waits sent Fisher a note saying she would lend him money if he needed it and when she went to speak to him he slammed the door in her face. She had a bottle of carbolic acid which she had been using to bathe her feet and she went to his cabin again about 3 pm. In a quarrel he struck her and told her to get out of his life. She threw the acid over him, thinking that she would mark him and he would not therefore be able to consort with Mrs Ross when the boat landed. He then beat her, saying, 'You're going to get yours.' She left him saying, 'Wash it off with soap and water and apply Vaseline. The longer you leave it the deeper it burns.' Fisher knocked the bottle out of her hand and ran to the doctor saying, 'Doctor, get up quick, this son of a bitch has thrown something on me.'

Fisher died in the ship's hospital that afternoon. The medical evidence was that death had been caused by shock set up by intense nervous irritability to which the acid was possibly a contributory factor. When questioned Waits said she had thrown the acid but had made sure none of it went into his eyes.

She was arrested when the boat docked and charged with wilful murder on the high seas. She replied, 'There is nothing like that in my heart. I loved the man. I love him now he is dead. I wouldn't intentionally hurt a fly or a cockroach.'

Her case was transferred to Bow Street. Because at the time of the attack the vessel was off the Scilly Isles and out of British waters and both victim and attacker were American citizens the court had no jurisdiction. On 9 August the charge was dropped and she was deported to the United States. The next day a coroner's jury at Rotherhithe Town Hall returned the verdict, 'syncope following a fright. Natural causes.' They added a rider, 'We do not think the prisoner intended to do him serious harm.'

On 19 September 1927 Waits, back in New York, and whose age was given as 24, pleaded guilty to a charge of manslaughter and assault. She was sentenced to a year and a day in the Federal reformatory.

6 August, 1986

It was 1995 before it became apparent that Monika Bottcher had been wrongly convicted for killing her two daughters, Melanie aged seven and her sister Karola, five, on 6 August 1986. Their bodies were found in a disused car park in Philippsthal, 90 miles from Frankfurt. One had been strangled, the other suffocated. The only people on whom suspicion fell were Monika, then aged 28 and a nurse, and her husband Reinhard Weimar, six years older and a locksmith. Their marriage had been happy until the birth of Karola after which, according to an interview Bottcher gave to a German newspaper, her husband began drinking and the marriage became hell.

She commenced an affair with an American soldier, Kevin Pratt, two years her junior. He omitted to tell her that he had a wife back in America.

The prosecution case was that the children were an encumbrance to her and that she killed them after driving them five miles from their home to the car park. Crucially, fibres from a yellow blouse found on a T-shirt were said to prove she had carried the bodies. Bottcher's relationship with the American led to a singular amount of prejudice against her. She was regarded in the ultra conservative village as a woman of loose morals and it was felt that she should be punished for adultery even if she was innocent of the murders.

At the end of the trial, which lasted 44 days and in which over a hundred witnesses were called, she was sentenced to life imprisonment. Over the years in which she was in prison her lawyer, Gerhardt Strate, was able to cast doubt on the fibre evidence. Experts said that they could have stuck on the blouse when the child was picked up as part of a normal family relationship. If they had been passed when the dead child was being carried there should have been many more.

On 4 December 1995 Bottcher was freed. She would receive, as compensation, £10 for each day spent in prison.

As for her husband, who was regarded as the only other possible candidate for the murder, his motive was that he was afraid she would go to America with the girls. He is alleged to have said to his wife, 'Now neither of us will have the children.'

It is unlikely that Weimar will ever stand trial. He developed signs of paranoia and in the periods when he is not in a clinic he lives with his mother.

7 August, 1994

On 7 August 1994 Ted Martin, aged 67, stabbed 80-year-old Warwick Batchelor more than 20 times. They had both been in love with the much younger June Cuxson. The fifty-one-year-old divorcee had met Martin, a former Army corporal, at a tea dance in Sussex and later took up with Batchelor, a former major and retired executive with Unilever, when they met at a bridge club. On the evening before Mrs Cuxson and Mr Batchelor were due to go to France on a coach tour with The University of the Third Age, a self-help group for retired people, Martin found his rival in the block of flats where Batchelor lived in Hassocks, West Sussex.

At the trial of Martin it was said that Mrs Cuxson played off both men but afterwards she told newspapers of Mr Batchelor: 'I felt so much for him and I could not help the way I felt.' Of Mr Martin, her ballroom dance partner, she said. 'He was clearly deeply attached to me but I didn't feel the same way about him.'

Sentencing Martin, who had maintained the killing had been in self-defence, to life imprisonment, the trial judge Mr Justice Wright said on 22 November 1995, 'You have been convicted on overwhelming evidence. The explanation for your offence at the end of a long and respectable life is only too clear. You were overcome by overwhelming jealousy.'

Afterwards Mr Batchelor's son commented, 'So far as we are concerned my father's relationship with Mrs Cuxson was platonic – he was 80 years old.'

8 August, 1963

John Berridge, a 23-year-old Broadmoor patient, was found just after 11 pm on 8 August 1963. He was unconscious on his bed in Block 4 and his fellow inmate, Gordon Gylby, was hovering over him. 'I thought he was having a fit,' he told the medical staff. 'He came over sort of queer. When I turned him on to his side to ease him a bit, he took a few deep breaths and then went all quiet. I think he's dead.'

Gylby was absolutely correct and, more bafflingly, the pathologist's report showed that Berridge had died from cyanide poisoning. This was especially puzzling because cyanide was not kept in the Broadmoor pharmacy. The official explanation was that the death was one of suicide, particularly as Berridge was a known suicide risk. But according to one former patient, Sidney Henry, he had been poisoned by the Russian Secret Service. Apparently he had received a suspicious parcel of what he thought was sugar some days before his death.

The reasoning behind this was that whilst Berridge was serving in West Germany in the RAF he had been approached by a man who had told him he was a Communist agent and would buy information about such things as squadron strengths and bombing tests on smaller atomic weapons.

Berridge had, he told Henry, supplied the information,

saying, 'It was easy money.' Then, back in Wales, he told his father who threatened to expose him. It was for this reason that on 25 April 1959 Berridge took a 12-bore shotgun and killed both his parents. He was found guilty but insane at Pembrokeshire Assizes and was sent to Broadmoor.

Henry was discharged in February 1964. He maintained that he had faked his insanity for his own purposes to rather too good effect.

9 August, 1982

On 9 August 1982, a former McLean, Illinois, county prosecutor, Jeffrey Gurga, blackened his face, scaled a gutter on to the balcony and climbed into the second-storey apartment of Kathleen Pearson in Chicago. There he stabbed her to death and attacked and wounded her 19-year-old daughter, Jeannine. He had never met either woman before. Mrs Pearson struggled and a neighbour going to her help found Gurga who said, 'My God, I've gone bananas . . . When are the paramedics coming? I don't know these women.' Mrs Pearson's throat had been cut almost from ear to ear and she had also been stabbed in the back. Her daughter had been stabbed in the kidney. She recovered.

Gurga was charged with murder and ran an insanity defence on the basis that he had been influenced by violence in films such as *Dressed to Kill* and *Bullitt*. Defence psychiatrists labelled him as a schizophrenic. There was, however, a note in his possession which indicated he thought that if he were to be convicted he would only have a 20 per cent chance of being sent to prison. In 1966 he had stabbed a student with a knife and told his lawyers that he prowled the streets looking for potential victims. At university he had told his friends that he was 'the world's greatest Jack the Ripper'. In the Pearson case the prosecution asked for the death penalty and the defence for 20 years. He was sentenced to 40 years' imprisonment.

The appeal court ordered the case to be remitted for re-sentencing on the grounds that Gurga had been mentally ill. In October 1987 Judge Maloney added the words 'mentally ill' to his judgment and re-sentenced Gurga to 40 years. Julius Lucius Echeles, who had acted for Gurga throughout the case, argued:

> Echeles: Your Honour, respectfully, has disregarded the mandate from the appellate court.
> Maloney: What mandate?
> Echeles: To reconsider the sentence.
> Maloney: I have reconsidered it and found it should stay the same.

10 August, 1948

In recent legal history there have been few attempted private prosecutions for murder. The most famous was probably that arising from the death of 27-year-old librarian, Joan Woodhouse. On 10 August 1948 the body was found – apparently strangled and raped – in the grounds of Arundel Park by 24-year-old labourer Thomas Stilwell. She was about five feet tall, of slim build with blue eyes, and Professor Keith Simpson estimated the date of her death as between eight and ten days previously, so putting it over the August Bank Holiday which in the 1940s was taken during the first weekend in the month.

She lay on her back stretched out on the slope of a hill, wearing pink camiknickers, a brassiere, elastic suspender belt and stockings. Her camiknickers had fastened at the crotch with two buttons but one was missing. The rest of her clothes lay in a neatly folded pile about 12 yards away. Simpson thought that she had either taken off her clothes to sunbathe and had been surprised or had agreed to some form of sexual foreplay short of intercourse. On the pile of clothes was a necklace and her handbag was nearby. Simpson found fingertip bruises in the muscles on both sides of the voice box and the hyoid bone had been fractured. The body was too infested with maggots to tell whether she had been a virgin before the attack.

Immediately after Stilwell had found the body he had been taken to the police station where he had been questioned for a number of hours. During the questioning he made a statement which he later retracted that he had taken a short cut through the park.

A major problem was what exactly Joan Woodhouse was doing in Arundel Park in the first place. Some time previously she had broken with a boyfriend over religious difficulties and had had something of a breakdown. After returning north she had come back to London and was living at the YWCA in Blackheath. She had arranged to spend the Bank Holiday with her widowed father in Barnsley, Yorkshire. She had told her roommate that she was going north when she left at 8.30 am on the Saturday morning, planning, she said, to catch the 10.10 am train. Instead she went to Worthing and checked her case into the left luggage office at the station.

The detective in the case was DCI Fred Narborough. A weekend case was recovered from the left luggage office and in it was a diary which contained the names of over a hundred men. Far from the promiscuity this suggested there was a simple explanation. She was the Honorary Secretary of the Old Students' Association which linked librarians throughout Britain. She had also drawn up a code for living which was in strict terms. The first of her resolutions was: 'I will offer the day's work to God on waking, pray for at least five minutes in the morning and at least ten minutes at night.'

Despite three months of sifting through Joan Wood-house's life, and the variety of 'sightings' of her alone and with a man over the Bank Holiday weekend, Narborough was never in a position to make an arrest. The inquest was reopened on 22 November 1948 and this time there were solicitors representing her family, the police and Thomas Stilwell who gave evidence. The jury returned a verdict of murder by a person or persons unknown. In those days it would have been open to them to name any person as the murderer.

Her family now offered a reward of £500 for infor-mation and then instructed a former CID officer, who interviewed over two hundred witnesses, at the end of which he presented a report to Scotland Yard saying there was enough evidence on which to launch a prosecution.

In turn Scotland Yard appointed Reginald Spooner – Narborough had retired – to conduct an inquiry. Six weeks later he reported there was no evidence to prosecute Stilwell. This did not satisfy the Woodhouse family and at the end of August 1949 her father applied for, and was granted, a warrant for the arrest of Stilwell on a charge of murder. It was the first time such a warrant had been granted for 85 years. As is the custom the Crown took over the prosecution.

The case against Stilwell, heard at Arundel Magistrates' Court, was based on what were said to be conflicting statements about his movements on the day Joan died and the fact that on the day he discovered the body he had walked almost straight to the spot. One of the witnesses, Nellie Petley, a young woman with three children and who suffered from lung trouble, gave evidence that on the Saturday she had seen a young couple, of whom Stilwell was one, and had spoken to them. Later, under cross-examination she admitted she was wrong and had not spoken to them. 'It was only in my mind,' she said. Earlier she had written 'I thought long ago each time I lay in hospital I could claim the reward and go away and get well.' The prosecution, whose heart was by no means in its case, called a witness to contradict Mrs Petley.

The evidence of another witness, who said she had seen Joan Woodhouse and recalled the girl because she was wearing a dress she admired and subsequently bought, was discredited when it was shown that the dress had been bought four days before Joan had disappeared. After a two-hour retirement the magistrates, to great cheers, announced there was insufficient evidence to commit Stilwell for trial.

The family complained and a letter was written to the then Attorney General saying that the opening for the prosecution had been an invitation to acquit. The matter was raised in the House of Commons and Sir Hartley Shawcross uttered the famous words, 'It is the duty of the prosecution to prosecute, not to persecute.' Three months later the relatives sought a Bill of Indictment from Mr Justice Humphreys at Lewes Assizes against a named person. He refused to grant it.

Spooner's theory was that Joan Woodhouse was not murdered. He believed that because of the decomposition of the body Simpson was wrong and that she had not been raped. He thought that she was a young woman who, because of the break-up of her relationship and hearing how other girls in the hostel were off for the weekend with their boyfriends, had decided to commit suicide. Given her religious beliefs it is difficult to accept this. Certainly Narborough did not agree and in his memoirs wrote: 'Down the years I had waited for a man to make his mistake. To take a drink too many perhaps and talk too loudly ... All the time there is that murder on my mind.'

Iain Adamson, *The Great Detective*; Fred Narborough, *Murder on my Mind*; Keith Simpson, *Forty Years of Murder*.

11 August, 1945

Shortly after 6 pm on 11 August 1945 Alfred Groves was
entering the block of flats where he lived in Shoreditch
when he was approached by a man who mumbled
something about coppers. Groves thought he was asked
for change for the telephone but the man said, 'I don't
want coppers, I want a policeman. I've done my old
woman in.' Groves thought he was joking but, even so,
pointed him in the direction of a police telephone box.
He started to wonder if there was anything in the man's
story and walked after him. He then saw him speaking
to a neighbour, Albert Webb, whom he knew. The man
asked Webb to telephone for the police.

Whilst waiting for the police he told Webb, 'I have
killed my wife. I have stabbed her. If I hadn't killed her
she would have killed me.'

The police went to Teale Buildings off Nile Street
where in flat number 1 the body was lying face down
with the head in a large pool of blood. There were no
signs of a struggle. According to the police report the
doctor who was first called out and 'who is a German
Jew [and] appears to have let the occasion override his
commonsense' had unfortunately allowed the body to be
moved. The victim had been attacked from behind and
stabbed.

When the man, Frederick James Hooker, was questioned he said, 'It's too late now. I don't want to blacken
her, but she drove me to it. I begged her to tell me about
the other man. She wouldn't.'

Hooker had been in the Pioneer Corps for the previous
five years and had left the Corps about three weeks
before. The couple had 11 children before the incident
and apparently had been happy together. In his absence
Hooker's wife had taken up with a man from an Irish
regiment. He was interviewed and, clearly assisted by the

police, wrote a statement ending: 'I am definitely sorry I formed the association and for the unhappiness which has been brought upon innocent people.'

Poor Mrs Hooker, she had tried to persuade the man to set up house with her but he had refused and had said he was returning to Ireland. Hooker appears to have previously attacked her during his first two weeks out of the army and she had been thinking of taking out a summons against him.

Hooker was found not guilty of murder and sentenced to five years' penal servitude for manslaughter.

MEPO/3/2305.

12 August, 1966

Harry Roberts, aged 59 at the time of writing, has served 30 years in prison. At about 3 pm on 12 August 1966 Detective Sergeant Christopher Head, PC Geoffrey Fox and DC David Wombwell stopped him, together with John Duddy and Jack Witney, in Braybrooks Street, Shepherds Bush near Wormwood Scrubs prison, west London, in what should have been a routine check. The men had been on their way to rob a rent collector when the police approached Witney about an out-of-date tax disc on his van.

In the *Evening Standard*, 17 May 1995, Roberts described what happened:

> DC Wombwell was talking to Jack through the window of our van. He was shouting and trying to get the door open. Jack said, 'Let the slag have it, Harry.' I shot him point-blank with the Luger, one shot at the bottom of his eye.
>
> As Wombwell fell I turned towards DS Head on

the other side of the van. He started running back towards their car. I aimed quickly and got him right in the middle of the back. He fell but he wasn't dead. I ran up and aimed at his head. I pulled the trigger. It misfired. I pulled the trigger again. It misfired again. He got up and staggered to the car but fell down in front of it. PC Fox tried to drive off but he jammed DS Head under the wheels. Then Duddy shot PC Fox in the head.

In November 1958 Roberts had attacked and robbed a 79-year-old man who died a year and three days after the attack. Had he died two days earlier a murder charge could have been preferred. Instead Roberts had received a seven-year sentence.

Duddy was caught shortly after the shootings in Glasgow. The blue Vauxhall van the men had been using when the killings occurred was traced to a garage in Lambeth rented to Witney. Roberts, who had learned survival techniques in Malaysia, was on the run for three months before he was found in woods in Hertfordshire. All were sentenced to life imprisonment with a recommendation that they serve not less than 30 years. Duddy died in prison. Witney was released in the early 1990s.

It is unlikely that Roberts will be released in the foreseeable future. Even though the crime was committed 30 years ago he still retains something of a cult status amongst certain football crowds who, in an attempt to annoy the police patrolling the ground, chant:

> Harry Roberts, he's our man,
> He shoots coppers, bang, bang bang.

In the spring of 1996, when it was mooted that the key to his cell had been thrown away, relatives of the police officers expressed their hopes that the Home Secretary would not parole Roberts.

Tom Tullett, *No Answer from Foxtrot Eleven*; Peter

Deeley, *The Manhunters*; Ernie Millen, *Specialist in Crime*.

13 August, 1930

Bessie Tobin, the common-law wife of Rocco Perri, the nearest that Toronto had to a major gang leader in the 1920s, was shot to death in her garage at 166 Bay Street South on 13 August 1930. On the evening of her killing she telephoned her maid shortly before 11 pm to ask her to make up her room and drove with Rocco Perri to their luxurious home. Their practice was for Bessie to take the garage key, turn on the lights and then go indoors leaving Perri to put their car away and lock up.

According to Rocco Perri this is precisely what happened at about 11.35 pm except that when Bessie went into the garage she was shot twice by men with shotguns. He panicked and ran for help. A third shot was fired. The police were called immediately and when the area was searched they found creased or chiselled shells, designed to cause the maximum possible damage to a victim.

Bessie had lived with Rocco Perri for some 17 years as he built up his business of racketeering and liquor smuggling to the United States during Prohibition. When her husband, Harry Tobin, whom she had left, along with two daughters, in 1913, was told of her death he was less than sympathetic. 'I can say thank God,' he told the *Toronto Star*. 'She dies as she deserved to die.' That, at any rate, was how the story was headlined.

Rocco Perri announced that the motive for the killing was robbery. This was not an explanation accepted by everyone, for none of Bessie's expensive jewellery had been touched. There were a number of more attractive

theories. First was that the killing had been carried out
by underlings in the Perri gang. Bessie was not simply
Rocco's mistress; she was the power and most probably
brains behind the organisation and took an active and
autocratic interest in day-to-day events. More probably
the killing was over a bundle of drugs for which Bessie was
refusing payment, telling New York State gangsters that
they could sue her. Her killers could have been members
of the Rochester organisation. It is possible that Rocco
Perri, although there is no suggestion that he took an
active part in her killing, knew it was likely to take place
but was powerless to prevent it.

Perri's fortunes sank, rose and sank after Bessie's death.
He was fortunate enough to meet and work with another
Jewish woman, Annie Newman, who also became his
constant companion and guide. He was less fortunate
to be interned during the Second World War. On his
release in 1943 he began to plan a campaign to regain his
territory, lost to the Magaddino family from Buffalo. On
23 April 1944, whilst staying with a friend in Hamilton,
Ontario, he complained of a headache and said he was
going out for a walk. He was never seen again. His body
was never discovered.

James Dubro and Robin F. Rowland, *King of the Mob*.

14 August, 1980

In 1980 Dorothy Stratten, born Dorothy Ruth Hoogstraten,
was named Playmate of the Year. Tall and blonde,
described in *People* as extravagantly sensual and 'so
beautiful she seemed luminescent, as if lit from within',
she was thought to be a potential new Marilyn Monroe.
She was the mistress of 40-year-old Peter Bogdanovich,
whizzkid film director of *Targets, The Last Picture Show*

and *What's Up, Doc*, whose career at the time was somewhat in limbo. Unfortunately she was also married to Paul Snider whom she had met two years earlier when, at the age of 18, she was working part-time in an East Vancouver snack bar. He is reputed to have told his friends, 'That girl could make me a lot of money.'

He wined and dined her, bought her clothes and persuaded her to be photographed nude. The pictures were sent to *Playboy* magazine and, on the strength of them, she was invited for a film test which she passed with flying colours.

Until her photograph was published as the centrefold in *Playboy* Dorothy worked as a Bunny cocktail waitress at a Los Angeles Playboy Club and lived with Snider near the Santa Monica Boulevard. He promoted wet T-shirt contests and male striptease; she appeared in television shows and had the lead in a small-budget Canadian film. It appears he had a Svengali influence over her life – he watched what she drank at parties, would not let her smoke and made sure she was able to reject the advances which are made to Bunnies. On 1 June 1979, against the wishes of *Playboy* and a few weeks before she was the centrefold, they were married.

Being Playmate of the Year brought substantial financial rewards – $200,000 cash, a gold Jaguar XJS, a sable coat and a brass hot tub. On the film front she now had the juvenile female lead in Bogdanovich's new comedy *They All Laughed* which was to star Audrey Hepburn and Ben Gazzara. Within a matter of weeks she was living with Bogdanovich in his New York Plaza Hotel suite.

She next saw Snider in Vancouver in May 1980 and returned to New York. At the time she seems to have been ambivalent about both relationships, saying that Snider would always have her heart, but a month later he received papers from her lawyers giving notice of separation. Now he arranged for a private detective to watch the pair.

They went to London and then moved into Bogdanovich's Bel Air home. Dorothy telephoned Snider and
arranged to meet him for lunch on 8 August. He believed
she was now going to return to him and was devastated
when she told him she loved Bogdanovich. She told him
to give most of her clothes to a 17-year-old whom he was
trying to promote as a second Stratten. Snider bought a
12-gauge Mossberg shotgun, saying he was wanting home
protection.

They agreed to meet on 14 August to discuss a financial settlement. It had been arranged that the inquiry
agency hired by Snider would keep in touch with him
by telephone throughout the afternoon but the private
detective's calls went unanswered.

About 5 pm the 17-year-old Stratten lookalike called
at the house, found the bedroom door closed and left.
The agent still received no reply to his calls and informed
the police. Dorothy Stratten was found in a crouched
position on the bed, her face blown away. The police
established she had been buggered after her death. Snider
was also dead, face down over the Mossberg. It was
an apparent murder followed by suicide but there have
been suggestions that they were both murdered by an
out-of-work actor over a drug deal in which Snider was
involved.

Bogdanovich did not work for some years after Stratten's
death. In 1989 he married her younger sister Louise in
Las Vegas.

Peter Bogdanovich, *Killing the Unicorn*.

15 August, 1949

Daisy Wallis, who liked to be called 'Dorothy', was the
36-year-old proprietress of a small business, The Adelphi

Secretarial Agency, with offices on the top floor at 157 High Holborn, London. On the evening of 15 August 1949 she was stabbed to death there. She lived with her parents in London and had saved from her earnings to set up her business with two second-hand typewriters, chairs and a filing cabinet. Two sisters who lived in the building heard her screams but did nothing about it. 'We often hear screaming and shouting,' said one, 'and take no notice of it.' The other commented, 'It was more than one scream. It seemed so close to us.' When asked if she could distinguish any words she said, 'Murder, I think.' It was a fairly rough area and much of the noise could be attributed to the postmen in the Drury Lane sorting office nearby.

Dorothy Wallis's body was found by her assistant, Sheila Bennett. When the police arrived they found that she had been stabbed repeatedly with a stiletto-like knife. She was wearing a pink dress which was covered in blood. She had bled so much that, when a sample was required for the autopsy, Professor Francis Camps had difficulty in taking one. The only clue the police had was that a man seen running away was dark-haired and of an Italian appearance. One witness described him as clean-shaven, fairly thick-set with dark hair brushed straight back from his forehead. Two witnesses said they had seen her on other occasions with a similar looking man, once in a restaurant in Piccadilly and the other in a public house in New Cavendish Street.

From her diary it was clear she had made an appointment to go out the night before but had cancelled it. The police found that every day she locked her office for a 90-minute lunch break but were unable to find any local restaurant in which she took it. She was also a member of a number of clubs but inquiries showed she rarely went to them. She did, however, keep a detailed account of her daily doings in one of 11 diaries, much of it concerning her sex life, which she wrote up in an old-fashioned and indecipherable shorthand. Fingerprints were taken in the office and all but one set of prints were eliminated from the inquiry. The owner of that remaining set did not have a criminal record.

One of Dorothy Wallis's clients volunteered the information that she had telephoned about 6 pm on the night of the attack and had spoken to a well-spoken man who said Miss Wallis had gone home. Earlier in the day a man described by Miss Bennett as a well-educated Pole had called twice saying he was desperate for work and also, curiously, offering Miss Wallis office space in a rather better building. He was never traced.

A month before her death her office had been burgled. Curiously, only the older and bulkier of the typewriters was taken, with the thief disregarding a new radio worth £20 and a cash box. At one time the police believed this to have some significance but the officer in charge of the investigation, Commander Harold Hawkyard, said it was eventually recovered and its theft was of no significance.

When the office block was demolished in May 1957 workmen found a sword hidden behind packing cases filled with rubbish on the second floor. The case was reopened but no arrests were made. The Metropolitan Police files are due to be opened in 1997.

Robert Jackson, *Francis Camps*.

16 August, 1969

Thirty-two-year-old Jemima 'Mima' McDonald was last seen alive on the night of 16 August 1969 when she left the Barrowland Ballroom in a poor area of Glasgow. Her partly clothed body was found on a derelict tenement at 23 Mackeith Street, Bridgeton. She was the second of three victims of an unknown serial killer known as 'Bible John'.

His other victims were 25-year-old Patricia Docker

whose body was found naked in the door recess of a lock-up garage on the night of 22 February 1968 and 29-year-old Helen Puttock. Her body was found fully clothed lying against a wall and with a sanitary towel in her armpit on the night of 30–31 October 1969. There was no evidence of sexual assault but the women, who were all strangled with a belt or tights, were all menstruating at the time of death. Helen Puttock's sister, Jeannie, had at one time spoken to Bible John and recalled him as a handsome man aged between 25 and 30, six feet tall, with beautifully barbered red hair. He smoked and quoted sexual and other passages from the Bible, hence his soubriquet. He said he was a teetotaller. Later she attended an identification parade, having said she was sure she would recognise the man. She did not make an identification.

The killing of Puttock was the last in the series. In 1983 a man who had been in Australia recognised an artist's impression of Bible John, circulated by the Crown Office, as a friend with whom he used to visit Barrowland. The friend was traced to Amsterdam but apart from being a lookalike there was nothing to link him with the killings.

There the matter ended until January 1996 when the police said they believed that they were now able to identify the killer through DNA sampling. The suspect, John Irvine McInnes, was formerly a guardsman, then furniture salesman, who committed suicide at the age of 41 in 1980. It was he who had been on the identification parade attended by Jeannie Puttock. He came from a devout Christian family. His father Robert and mother Elizabeth were regular attenders at the gospel hall in Stonehouse, a village near Glasgow.

On 1 February 1996, at first light, as is required by Scots law, his body was exhumed, as was that of his mother which had been placed on top of his in the family grave. It had been hoped that it would be possible to take cast marks of his teeth. Teeth marks on the body of Helen Puttock showed a deformity.

In May 1996, it was announced that because of the state of the body it was impossible to obtain sufficient DNA samples. As for the teeth, McInnes apparently had false ones which were not buried with him. His family complained about the handling of the exhumation.

Charles N. Stoddart, *Bible John*; Richard and Molly Whittington-Egan, *The Murder Almanac*.

17 August, 1991

Arthur Thompson, known as Fat Boy and son of Glasgow's King of Crime Arthur senior, was sentenced in 1985 to 11 years in prison on heroin dealing charges. The case was a curious one and until his death the Fat Boy maintained his innocence, claiming he had been framed by a Jonah McKenzie. For a time Arthur junior was able to demand a cut from his team, the Barlanark Gang, but he was by no means a popular leader and a rival organisation was in place within the year. By 1991 it was estimated that up to £200,000 a week was being generated in gang money by the manufacture, supply and distribution of cheap drugs. But so far as the Fat Boy was concerned he was isolated when the gang fractured and his percentage dried up. Before he came out on home leave as part of a parole plan in 1991, he vowed to kill the five men he said had ripped off his earnings.

The circumstances of his death were curious. Released on weekend home leave after serving some seven years of his sentence, on 17 August he arranged to have a meal with his sister in an Italian restaurant. Almost at the last minute the venue was changed and he went to Café India, a smart Indian restaurant in the centre of the city, with his mother and common-law wife, Catherine. Shortly before he arrived at the restaurant a man, later said to be a Paul

Ferris, had approached the manager, asked if there was a Thompson there and insisted on searching the dining area with its two hundred plus customers before he was satisfied there was not. After his meal Thompson returned to the council home where his father lived which had been converted into what amounted to a fortress, had a word with his father, and then walked to the end house to check whether his brother, Billy, was recording a film on the video recorder. He rang the bell and a woman in the house, who went to the door, sensed something was wrong. She saw the Fat Boy staggering away, shot. One bullet had grazed his cheek, one fractured two ribs and the third hit his heart. His last words were: 'I've been shot, hen. I'm going to collapse.' The family did not wait for an ambulance but drove him to hospital where he was found to be dead on arrival.

Now, say Underworld acquaintances, it was the moment for Thompson senior to show who really was the master. As his son's cortège went to the graveyard, it passed a car in which the bodies of the two men, Joe 'Bananas' Hanlon and Robert Glover, suspected of Arthur junior's killing, had been left shot in the head with a .22 pistol. Glover had, in fact, been arrested and released. Overall Hanlon had not led a happy life. A car he owned had been blown up; his ice-cream van from which he also sold heroin had been torched; and he had been shot on two occasions, once in the penis.

In 1992, after a trial lasting 54 days, a third man, Paul Ferris, suspected of being one of Thompson junior's murderers, was acquitted. The thread of the case – in which the prosecution was not successful – was that all three men had been involved in the killing. It may be that the prosecution had followed, too closely, Arthur Thompson's thought processes, reconstructed the case and found the evidence which would fit the theory.

Much of that evidence was from a fellow prisoner and supergrass Dennis Woodman, a Geordie, who told the jury Ferris had confessed to him in prison. How had Ferris made the confession? Shouting through the bars of his cell to Woodman, whom he had never seen, but who was conveniently in the next cell? How had Woodman been placed in the next cell? When he had been in another prison he had been found with escaping tools in his cell, something he, Woodman, said had been planted by the authorities, and as a result he had been transferred. (Woodman, cross-examined by Donald Findlay, told of the tragic death of his children in a road accident, something for which everyone had sympathy for several days until it was revealed the children were alive and well and living in England and, indeed, Woodman had sent them a Christmas card from prison after their 'death'.) Most of his evidence about the case could be traced, almost word for word, to pages from the Scottish editions of the *Sun* newspaper. As the trial went on Findlay quietly demolished Woodman, who became more and more wild in his allegations, including a suggestion that Ferris's solicitor had endeavoured to bribe him.

Much of the other evidence against Ferris came from a former girlfriend of Robert Glover who said that Glover had called her in the middle of the night saying he had to see her. At the time she was living with another man but Glover came round and they sat in a parked car for some hours during which time he told her of his and Ferris's involvement.

This presented something of a problem. Glover was dead and could not be cross-examined on the veracity of his statement. It was admitted into evidence but with considerable warnings from the trial judge, Lord McCluskey, as was the identification evidence that it had been Ferris in the restaurant combing the tables to find the Fat Boy.

There is little doubt that at the very least Ferris had been in the wrong city at the wrong time. He had flown to Glasgow from London on the day of the killing to buy clothes for his child by a woman in the city, heard of the shooting and had absented himself smartly, hiring a car and driving south throughout the night.

Ferris's defence was, in part, that the killer of young Arthur was in fact 'Blind' Jonah McKenzie, a man who

at the age of 37 had acquired 36 stab wounds and who
had been blinded by Bananas Hanlon in an attack in May
1991. This, it was said, was as a reprisal for the attack on
the ice-cream/heroin van. McKenzie, a staunch Thompson
man who had received seven years when young Arthur
had picked up his 11, vehemently denied the allegation.
The jury accepted Ferris's alibi for the murder. He had
sensibly written 63 pages of a notebook before his arrest.
The reason for doing this was that he had, so he said,
been fitted up by the police on a previous occasion and
as a result kept a detailed account of his movements. He
had, he said, been assisting another man in Glasgow who
had been slashed. 'There was blood spattered all over
his face – that's when I noticed his right hand. You
could actually see the white muscle tissue and the blood
streaming from it.'

Curiously, part of the defence was also to prove that the
dead men, Glover and Hanlon, were also innocent and a
substantial number of witnesses were found who, if they
could not completely alibi the men, could go a long way
towards doing so.

Ferris was also cleared of charges of supplying drugs,
kneecapping a former member of the Barlanark team,
Willie Gillen, and attempting to murder Arthur Thompson
himself.

So far as the attempt on Arthur senior's life was concerned, this could not possibly have been done by Ferris,
for Arthur himself, a great performer, went into the witness box to say he regarded Ferris almost as a son.

After Ferris's acquittal the *Daily Record* reported there
was a £30,000 contract on his life. Indeed in the ensuing
troubles Ferris's family had not escaped unscathed. Willie
Ferris, his father, received over a hundred stitches following an attack. He was beaten with a hammer and baseball
bat and his car, bought with a disability pension, had its
tyres slashed and was later set on fire.

In 1996 it was claimed by Bobby Glover's widow Eileen
that her husband had in fact been present when the Fat
Boy died. She maintained she knew who pulled the trigger.

Senior detectives confirmed they were looking into certain aspects of the Glover–Hanlon deaths.

James Morton, *Gangland 2.*

18 August, 1994

Forty-four-year-old Martin Cahill who, although he never acknowledged the soubriquet, was known as The General, and led what was described as the number one crime family in Dublin, was shot dead in an ambush in the Ranelagh area of Dublin on 18 August 1994. The shooting took place about half a mile from his home. Two men had lain in wait for him. One sat on a black motorcycle posing as a council worker checking registration numbers. When Cahill stopped his Renault 5 the man ran to him and fired a single shot. The car went out of control and hit a pole. The gunman then fired four more shots and escaped on the motorcycle.

Martin Cahill grew up in the Holyfield slums, at that time some of the worst in the Dublin area. At the age of 11 he was convicted of housebreaking for which he was given probation and in 1965, at the age of 15, he was sent to St Conleths, again for housebreaking. Four years later he married Frances Lawless whom he had met whilst working in Goodbody's making sacks. That was his last known job. He was next convicted of receiving cigarettes and a watch and was sentenced to four years' imprisonment, being released in 1973.

It was believed that The General led the Beit art robbery on 21 May 1986. The alarm went off at 2 am and when Gardai officers arrived they were told by staff that everything was all right. The loss of the paintings was not discovered until 9 am when the gallery opened to the public. Seven of the less valuable paintings were found discarded during the day. It was suggested that the gang had deliberately triggered off the alarm to lure the Gardai into a false sense of security. The stolen paintings included Vermeer's *Woman Writing a Letter*, itself thought to be worth in excess of £5 million, and a Goya portrait.

The General had first come to prominence in the £90,000 armed robbery at Rathfarnham Shopping Centre and a decade later in July 1983 he was regarded as the prime figure in the £2 million robbery of the Thomas O'Connor and Sons' jewellery factory in Harold Cross. It was a robbery about which the Gardai had advance information. On a number of occasions the premises had been staked out by them but no one had appeared. Now, on the night of 26 July, with only 25 of the 100-strong staff at work, the gang hid in a boilerhouse at the premises. As each member of staff arrived they were locked in a lavatory and, when all had been accounted for, the manager Dan Fitzgibbon was made to open the strongroom. It took 30 minutes for the gang to load their vans before they left, setting off a smoke bomb as they did so, something which led the locked in staff to fear they would be burned alive. By the time the Gardai was notified the jewellery was in parcels all over Dublin.

A reward of £25,000 was offered for information but not a single call was made. A fraction of the stolen property was recovered, some buried in a back garden in Terenure, a suburb near the Cahill home, and some more, but not much, in Norway. There were rumours that there had been an attempted drugs-for-jewellery swop in England but Cahill maintained he had never been involved in drug dealing. The raid broke the company, which was insured for only £900,000 of its £2 million loss. It went into receivership four years later.

In June 1988, acting on a tip-off, detectives went to Cahill's house where after a search the Gardai say they found a loaded .45 Colt in a water tank. The subsequent decision of the DPP not to prosecute angered senior officers who believe this was a cast-iron opportunity to score even a minor triumph. The thinking may have been,

however, that someone with a grudge against Cahill may
have planted the gun himself and then given the tip-off.

Initially a statement was issued claiming responsibility
for Cahill's murder by the Irish National Liberation Army,
with whom Cahill was known to have links. Within a
matter of hours, however, the IRA telephoned a Dublin
radio station to say that one of its members had carried out
the execution. The INLA then issued a statement saying
the first claim was false. No arrests have been made and
within months a new leader of the Dublin Underworld,
known as Mr Clean or The Monk, emerged.

James Morton, *Gangland 2*; Paul Williams, *The General*.

19 August, 1951

Beatrice Rimmer, a middle-aged widow who was reputed
to have a cache of money in her house, was murdered on
19 August 1951.

Edward Devlin and Alfred Burns had known each other
for some years before August 1951 when Burns was
on the run and being harboured by his friend. In one
of the all-night cafés in Liverpool frequented by young
criminals, Devlin and Burns explained to Marie Milne the
opportunity there was for robbing Mrs Rimmer without
too much difficulty. Milne, a 16-year-old who had been
recruited by June Bury, Devlin's girlfriend, was not completely enthusiastic. She said she would think about it.
The next day the men explained the plan to the girls.
June Bury said she wanted nothing to do with it but
Milne, thoroughly frightened, hedged her bets. Burns and
Devlin then recruited George MacLoughlin, a youth who
had spent 11 of his 20 years inside and who at 14 had been
the youngest person admitted to Walton prison. Marie
Milne was to keep watch until she was sure Mrs Rimmer

was in, knock and then engage her in conversation whilst Burns, Devlin and MacLoughlin broke in at the rear.

Things went wrong almost from the start. MacLoughlin was fortunate enough to be arrested for burglary two days before the planned robbery of 19 August. Milne was still not happy with her role. She was thoroughly frightened of her part in the robbery and more so when Devlin pulled a knife from his pocket and threatened her. She was still more frightened about what might happen if she went to the police.

Burns and Devlin decided to go ahead without waiting for MacLoughlin's release and on the 19th went by taxi with Milne to Cranbourne Street where Mrs Rimmer lived. When they arrived she appeared to be out and Milne was sent to a local cinema and told to wait outside. The men broke the kitchen window and were searching the premises when Mrs Rimmer returned. They attacked her, beating her with a piece of wood, and left her to die on the floor. She had 15 wounds in her head. When they met Milne she refused to go to Manchester with them but she still did not inform on them. That was done by MacLoughlin who, whilst serving his sentence in Walton, discussed the crime with other prisoners. Word was passed to the Governor in the weeks following the murder and then to Herbert Balmer, the officer in the case. In court MacLoughlin justified his informing on the basis that he was a professional burglar and did not approve of violence.

First the girls were traced and then the taxi driver. Milne told the police that when she had met the men after the burglary Devlin had asked, 'Will the woman live?' and Burns had replied, 'To hell with the woman. We will be out of Liverpool before long.' Devlin was arrested inside 24 hours and Burns three days later.

The pair ran an interesting defence at the Assizes. They said they had been engaged in a robbery at a clothing warehouse in Manchester from which they had stolen raincoats, suits and trousers and had spent the night at the home of a Joan Downey. Another man gave evidence that he was on the warehouse breaking with them but Mrs Downey flatly denied their story. The factory had been broken into some time between midday Saturday and early Monday morning when the crime was discovered. The trial judge pointed out that there was no reason why the men could not have committed the burglary which they admitted and the murder which they did not.

It was after the jury had found them guilty and the Court of Criminal Appeal had rejected their appeals that Rose Heilbron, who had defended Devlin, produced a statement from a 15-year-old girl, Elizabeth Rooke, saying she had heard June Bury say the men were innocent and that the real killer was the father-to-be of Bury's baby. This caused considerable upset. Lord Goddard, sitting in the Court of Appeal, refused to admit new evidence so the matter went to the Home Secretary. He appointed Albert Garrard QC and Commander Harold Hawkyard of Scotland Yard to enquire whether a possible miscarriage of justice had taken place. They found that the man named had been away from Liverpool at the time of the Rimmer killing and that the story of Elizabeth Rooke could not stand up. Both Burns and Devlin were hanged on 25 April 1952, protesting their innocence.

There were reprisals in the Liverpool Underworld. It was decided that Marie Milne should have her throat cut. In the end she was merely beaten unconscious in a back alley and needed 30 stitches. June Bury was beaten up in an all-night café and later was the subject of a further six beatings. She went to London, underwent plastic surgery and returned to Liverpool, secure in the knowledge she could not be recognised. She could; and was beaten yet again. MacLoughlin, correctly regarded in Underworld terms as a grass, was continually beaten, both in and out of prison. Joan Downey, who had refused to corroborate the Burns–Devlin alibi, had her home set on fire.

Even the minor witnesses suffered. The taxi driver who had taken the trio to Cranbourne Street was beaten up; another prosecution witness was shot and dumped in Blackpool. It was, wrote Norman Lucas, five years before the witnesses felt safe from the wrath of the remaining members of the Burns–Devlin gang.

Norman Lucas, *Britain's Gangland*; James Morton, *Gangland 2*.

20 August, 1993

Yusuf Carr, once known as Gordon, always referred to by his family as Captain Fidget, and an heir to the Peek Frean biscuit firm, was killed on 20 August 1993 at a house he had built in Lucknow, North India. Erected with separate quarters for men and women the house had been intended by Carr to be used as a kind of Outward Bound college for young Muslims. Carr, educated at Bradfield College, had gone to India for the first time in 1987 at the age of 20 and, after being taken ill in the Himalayas, he was nursed by two Muslims. He decided to settle there, adopted the faith and entered into an arranged marriage with Zeenat whose family came from a devout strand of Islam which devoted itself to the care of the poor. They had two children. At the time of the attack on their father Maryam was aged 18 months and Osamah was only a few weeks old.

In the middle of the night a number of young men arrived demanding 'papers'. They threw a servant off the roof, slashed the face of Zeenat and stabbed Carr who bled to death seven hours later. Some four thousand people attended his funeral.

One explanation was that the killing was the result of a dispute over the title to the land. Carr had paid about £10,000 for 20 acres to a petty prince, the Raja of Jehangirabad. There he grew mangoes and rice. Because of complicated property ownership laws the land had been made over into the name of the Raja's farm manager and it is possible he had passed on title to yet another person; hence the demand for papers. It is also thought possible that Carr's death was the result of a dispute he had with a local but powerful religious leader.

Arrests were made of the Raja, the farm manager and a known local thug but all were released. The religious leader was not arrested.

21 August, 1984

When Vera Kidwell of Jefferstown, Ohio died on 21 August 1984 of a heart attack the doctors attributed her death to natural causes. The 61-year-old woman had suffered from heart problems. The following spring Leah Proctor, Vera Kidwell's 10-year-old granddaughter, went to hospital complaining of stomach pains and suffering from weight loss. Tests showed that she had arsenic levels nine hundred times that normally found in the human body. Her sister Kimberly, aged eight, was also tested and a high level of arsenic was found in her body as well. On 12 April 1985 Vera Kidwell's body was exhumed and as a result the cause of her death was changed to one of arsenic poisoning. The girls' mother, Denise Kidwell Proctor, was arrested.

The police found a bottle of ant poison, containing sugar water and arsenic, in her sewing basket. According to employees at a local drugstore near the Kidwell home, 1984 had been a big year for sales of the ant poison.

On 5 December 1992 Denise Kidwell Proctor pleaded guilty to poisoning her mother and daughters, both of whom had survived. She had regularly given her mother a 'special glass of iced tea' said the prosecutor, Joe Gutmann.

Proctor had been in mental hospitals both before and after the poisoning and had herself been treated for arsenic poisoning. She had been in the same mental hospital as Lucy Pauline Rogers who had been convicted two years earlier of killing one husband and seriously injuring another by poisoning them.

Forty-one-year-old Proctor entered an *Alford* plea by which she pleaded guilty, accepting there was evidence against her, but maintaining that she was either innocent or was otherwise incapable of admitting guilt. She told the court she was pleading guilty because she needed to get on with her life. The trial had been delayed for seven years because she had repeatedly been found mentally unfit to stand her trial. She had, it was said, been diagnosed as having a multiple personality disorder and had been either in prison or in hospital. She was sentenced to 25 years in prison which meant she was at once eligible for parole. Gutmann said that he and family members, who had watched the proceedings on closed-circuit TV, would lobby against immediate parole.

22 August, 1973

Laura Lyn Harberts' body was found on 22 August 1973. The 18-year-old from Orlando, Florida had last been seen on 5 August. Twenty-two years later the *Miami Herald* and the Orlando *Sentinel* offered diametrically opposing views on the guilt of Joseph 'Crazy Joe' Spaziano, a member of the Outlaw biker gang, who had been on death row for 20 years. After eight months of exhaustive investigative journalism the *Herald* thought that Spaziano was a pathetic victim of injustice. The *Sentinel*, after a similar period of research, found him to be a 'dead-eyed' killer-rapist.

Just as the *Miami Herald* found poor-quality evidence, unreliable witnesses and a story of a senior investigating officer who toured the countryside in a car with a psychic holding a skull, so the *Sentinel* found incriminating evidence, staunch witnesses and a former Outlaw biker who said Spaziano had confessed to him.

The 1976 jury at the Seminole County Court believed Tony DiLisio who told them that Spaziano had shown him two mutilated bodies, one of which was that of Laura Harberts, at a dump in Altamonte Springs. The youth, a wannabe Outlaw, said that Spaziano had bragged of mutilating Harberts' genitalia when she was still alive. It was this particular aspect of the case which probably ensured Spaziano received the death penalty.

The police had no eyewitnesses or forensic evidence which could tie Spaziano to the murder and Harberts' body was too decomposed to determine the cause of death. DiLisio had been hypnotised by Joe B. McCawley and it was then he told the story of the visit to the dump. McCawley's evidence in another case, that of Pitts and Lee, convicted of the murder of two garage attendants, had come under heavy criticism and the convictions had been quashed. Evidence obtained under hypnosis has since been discredited and made inadmissible in many States but in the 1970s it was highly fashionable.

The *Miami Herald* was contacted by law teacher Michael Merlo who specialised in death row cases. In turn their reporter Lori Rozsa went to see DiLisio in Pensacola where he had become a born-again Christian. Eventually he agreed to speak to her and told her Spaziano had never taken him to the dump. He had, he said, made up the story to try and win favour with his father and the police. Spaziano's execution, scheduled for 27 June 1995, was stayed and an investigation ordered.

Meanwhile the *Sentinel* began to investigate the case, predisposed to the belief that Spaziano was indeed innocent. A *Sentinel* reporter saw DiLisio and became convinced he was now lying. Although he said he had been 'Christian clean' for a decade he had two convictions for driving under the influence and assaults on a girlfriend. He had gone into hiding after the trial and married. The 10-year marriage had been difficult with DiLisio into drink and drugs. In the mid-1980s his wife had contacted a local church. 'They said he was demon-possessed and he was throwing around 300-pound men at a men's retreat. They came and blessed our house with holy oil and that's when he gave up the drugs. And we were led to Pensacola.' The *Sentinel* believed that DiLisio's motives for lying now were the possibility of TV money and fear of the Outlaws as well as the allegation that Spaziano had raped DiLisio's stepmother.

Now the police found witnesses who said DiLisio had spoken of seeing the body before he had been hypnotised. There was also a witness who said she had been with DiLisio and Spaziano when they had dumped something she thought might have been a body. The execution was reset, but in January 1996 Spaziano was granted a new trial with Judge O.H. Eaton Junior saying that he had neither received due process of the law nor a fair trial at the first hearing.

23 August, 1995

On 23 August 1995 the police were called to a flat in St Petersburg, Russia. The day before, the severed head of Edik Vassilevsky, a 43-year-old mental patient, had been found in a rubbish container outside. The previous month another head, that of a homeless man, Mischa Bockov, had been found on Ordzhonikidze Street by a woman walking her dog. The police obtained a list of mental patients in the area and the name of Ilshat Kuzikov was first on the list. Posing as plumbers the police went to his flat. They broke down the door and in the flat found severed legs and arms, along with a saw, an iron mallet and a screwdriver. In a casserole dish by the oven they found human bones which had been picked clean. Pepsi bottles under the bath were full of human blood and a plastic bag hanging from the window contained marinated human flesh and onions.

In the video-recorded interview with Kuzikov he is shown a bag hanging on the kitchen wall and the questioning officer asks him what it contains. The answer is dried human ears. Kuzikov told the police on tape how he committed his crimes. He killed Vassilevsky with a blow to the back of the head before cutting his throat. Asked what he did with the pieces of the body he answered that he cooked them.

Kuzikov, a 35-year-old schizophrenic, had been in and out of mental hospitals all his adult life. It was thought that he had killed a number of other homeless people. Over the months neighbours had noticed strange rubbish in bins in the block of flats. One said, 'There were some really big bones in the rubbish heap a while ago. Nobody knew where they came from. But, I mean, you wouldn't think that they were a person's, would you?'

24 August, 1922

Alice Hilda Middleton almost certainly died on 24 August 1922. Her former lover, Cecil Maltby, shot himself at the moment when police and health workers broke into his flat in Park Road, Regent's Park, London on 10 January 1923. He had lived with the body decomposing in the bath in his flat for nearly five months.

Alice Middleton, the wife of a merchant seaman, had moved in with Maltby in the summer of 1922 while her husband was in the Far East. She was last seen alive around the middle of August 1922 and when Middleton returned in December he reported his wife missing. Maltby refused to let a police officer into the flat, saying Mrs Middleton had left him on 15 August. The police, watched by interested crowds, then kept a day and night watch on the premises until they obtained entry on the basis of an order authorising the Medical Officer of Health for the Borough to enter on the grounds that the premises were insanitary.

Mrs Middleton was found wrapped in a sheet in the bath in the kitchen. On her body was a note:

> In memory of darling Pat [Maltby's name for her], who committed suicide on 24th August 1922, 8.30 am.

Around the flat were other notes and nailed to the bedroom door was one which read:

> In memory of Alice H. Middleton who committed suicide on Thursday, August 24th, 1922. Pat darling why did you do it? Everybody loved you. I cannot live without you. When I can brace up my courage shall soon be with you
> — Cecil Maltby.

Another explained that Mrs Middleton had tried to commit suicide and Maltby had not been strong enough to wrest the gun from her. It ended:

> I put Mrs Middleton in the bath, and have not liked to part with the dear soul.

She had in fact been shot three times from behind. The medical evidence was that the bullets had been fired when she was either sitting or lying down.

E. Spencer Shew, *A Companion to Murder.*

25 August, 1958

Joyce Green was strangled in Denham, Middlesex at her home at Dawn Warren, Old Mill Road, on 25 August 1958. Her terrified son Stephen, six, ran to the next-door neighbour at about 10.45 am crying, 'Mummy's dead.' The police found Mrs Green lying naked except for a brassiere on the bed. A green flannel had been tied around her mouth. The house had been ransacked.

From Stephen's description a picture was built up. The killer was described as tall and heavily built. He was wearing a blazer with a green badge. Her killer was thought to have arrived on a Greenline coach at about 9.35 am.

On 19 October it was announced that a man was helping police with their enquiries at Hayes police station and a month later that, subject to the Director of Public Prosecutions's approval, a man would be charged. In the event he was able to provide a cast-iron alibi and no proceedings were brought.

The police were convinced that people in the village knew about the incident and were concealing information. On the anniversary of Mrs Green's death the police said they were determined to trace a couple who had spoken to the suspect on his way to the house and on his return. It was thought that Mrs Green may have known her killer and the ransacking of the house was a diversion.

No prosecution was ever brought. At the time it was suggested that there was a connection between her murder and that of 34-year-old Muriel Maitland who was killed earlier in the year in a bluebell glade in Cranford Park, Middlesex. Her shoes were never found and she, also, had been assaulted.

26 August, 1951

Michael Gelfand, one of Paris's gigolos of the 1940s, died on 26 August 1951. Two years previously he had shot and killed his mistress, Edith Tarbouriech, alleging she had insulted his honour. He then turned the gun on himself but survived. He was remanded in custody for two years awaiting his trial and was then given a two-year sentence. He was released on 11 August and died 15 days later. The bullet which had lodged near his heart had never been removed and it finally and poetically killed the man who had lived off women all his life.

27 August, 1964

Edmund Kemper was brought up by his grandparents on their seven-acre farm in the foothills of California's Sierra Nevada. His was not a happy life. His father had remarried, and his mother, with whom he stayed occasionally, regarded him as a 'real weirdo'. By the age of 15 he was six feet four inches tall. He had, apparently, suffered at his mother's hands as a young child. She had locked him in the cellar every night, putting a table over the trapdoor so he could not escape. He began to kill animals, including his own Siamese cat and a schoolfriend's dog which he shot.

He was sent to North Fork to his grandparents. His father's mother, Maude Kemper, who was an illustrator and writer of children's books, continually complained both about the cost of keeping him and the way he looked at her. She was constantly threatening to report him to his father. On the other hand he got on well with his grandfather, Edward, who had worked for California's

Division of Highways and was a man who was subservient
to his wife.

It was he who had given Ed Kemper the .22 rifle with
which he killed both his grandparents on 27 August 1964.
He had picked up the gun, saying he was off to shoot
rabbits. His grandmother told him not to shoot birds
and in a fit of temper he wheeled around and shot her.
He then picked up a knife and stabbed her repeatedly,
wrapped a towel around her head, dragged her body into
the bedroom and undressed it.

His grandfather was out at the time but, on his return, as
he stopped to get a box of groceries out of the car Edmund
shot him as well. He then put the body in the garage and
tried to hose the blood off the porch. When he failed he
telephoned his mother, saying, 'Grandma's dead. And so
is Grandpa.' She told him to call the sheriff. Asked why
he had killed his grandparents, he replied, 'I just wondered
how it would feel to shoot Grandma.' He had, he said, only
killed his grandfather to spare him the shock of seeing his
wife dead.

Diagnosed by at least one psychiatrist as a paranoid
schizophrenic, on 6 December 1964 Ed Kemper was sent
to the California State Hospital at Atascadero which
catered for both sex offenders and the criminally insane.
In September 1969 he was released to a halfway house and
three months later he was returned into the custodial care
of his mother. He had grown to six feet nine inches and
now weighed over 20 stone.

The next year he was refused a job in the police force
and instead joined the California Division of Highways.
In 1971 he began his career as a serial killer, picking up
women hitchhikers on the freeways. For the first year
he appears to have been merely practising his technique
because it was not until 7 May 1972 that he killed Mary
Ann Pesce and Anita Luchessa, first-year students at
Fresno State College. After that he killed Aiko Koo, a
15-year-old Korean girl who was late for dance class
and accepted a lift on 19 September. He then killed and
dissected Cindy Schall on 8 January 1973. On 5 February

he killed Rosalind Thorpe and Alice Liu, dismembering his victims and later visiting their burial sites. On 21 April he killed his mother with a hammer before cutting her throat at her home in Aptos, California. Later that day he strangled Sally Hallet, a friend of his mother. He then drove to Pueblo, Colorado from where, on 24 April, he telephoned the police.

He made lengthy taped confessions and showed the police the sites where he had buried his victims. His trial began in October 1973 in Santa Cruz when he pleaded not guilty by reason of insanity. The jury found him guilty on 12 November 1973 on eight counts of first-degree murder. He was sentenced to life imprisonment with a recommendation that he never be released. He did not appeal and began his parole hearings in 1978. Ten years later the parole board rejected an evaluation that he was now suitable for release. In 1981 he had been given a public service award for his work recording books for the blind.

Murder Casebook 89.

28 August, 1948

One modern example of a woman criminal who, although she never admitted it, probably killed for money was the unbalanced 42-year-old lesbian Margaret Allen who liked to be known as Bill. She had worked as a bus conductress in Rawstensall, Lancashire for four years from 1942 before giving up her job for health reasons. Later, she falsely boasted she had had a sex-change operation.

On 28 August 1948 she battered to death a 68-year-old woman, Nancy Chadwick, who worked as a housekeeper for a local man. The elderly lady was known both for telling fortunes and for counting her money in parks.

Consequently she was believed to have been in the habit of carrying large sums of cash with her. Her new red purse was never recovered. Allen had thrown her bag in the river.

Since the body was found outside Allen's house at 137 Bacup Road it was not surprising that the police wished to speak to her. At first she denied any involvement but she soon admitted battering the old lady with a hammer, putting the body in the coal cellar and then, in the early hours of the morning, dumping it in the street in the hope that it would look as though the injuries were from a motor accident rather than from nine hammer blows. Allen never admitted stealing the purse:

> I was in a funny mood and she seemed just to get on my nerves. I saw the hammer and on the spur of the moment I hit her with the hammer, I looked in her bag but there was no money. I didn't actually kill her for that. I had one of my funny moods.

She had originally kept the body in her cellar intending to throw it in the River Irwell but found it too heavy to move that distance.

At the Assizes a defence of insanity was put forward by W.A. Gorman KC with no success. The Home Secretary ordered a special inquiry into her mental condition but this did not save her. The one real friend she had in the town, Annie Cook, endeavoured to put together a petition for clemency but could only raise 152 signatures. It too failed. She was hanged on 12 January 1949 at Strangeways, the first woman to suffer the death penalty for 12 years. (The previous one was Charlotte Bryant, a part-time prostitute who poisoned her husband in December 1935.)

Apparently Allen kicked over the tray on which her last breakfast was brought to her, remarking that no one else was going to enjoy it. She told one visitor in the condemned cell, 'It would help if I could cry, but my manhood holds back my tears.' In his book, Edward Robey, who appeared for the Crown in the magistrates'

court, wrote that of· the people he had prosecuted and
who had died on the scaffold she was one of three whose
sentence should have been commuted to penal servitude
on the grounds that she was mentally abnormal.

The elderly man for whom Mrs Chadwick had acted as
housekeeper committed suicide shortly afterwards.

Edward Robey, *The Jester and the Court*; E. Spencer Shew,
A Second Companion to Murder; Renée Hugget and Paul
Berry, *Daughters of Cain*.

29 August, 1988

Wilfred 'Willie Boy' Johnson was shot and killed in
Flatlands, Brooklyn on 29 August 1988. He was a small
part of the empire of New York Mafia leader John Gotti
of the Gambino crime family, and the former boxer had
spent much of a sentence imposed in the 1970s for armed
robbery acting as a gofer for his boss who was also serving
a sentence. An enormous and enormously likeable man
within the limits of his trade, for the last 15 years of his
career with the Gottis the supposedly dumb-witted Willie
Boy Johnson was an FBI informer. Known as The Indian,
from his native American father, Johnson had known
Gotti for 30 years.

He had apparently become an informer after his bosses
had reneged on an agreement to look after his wife whilst
he was in prison.

In his account of his life as a contract killer Donald
'Tony the Greek' Frankos maintains that Johnson knew
the hit on him was coming but stayed in the neighbourhood and did nothing to avoid it. He was shot dead
with 19 bullets as he left his home shortly before 7
am and was about to get into his car. Asked about the

death Gotti is alleged to have said, 'Well, we all gotta go sometime.'

John Cummings and Ernest Volkman, *Mobster*; Donald Frankos, *Contract Killer*.

30 August, 1995

In early 1996 residents in the normally crime-free neighbourhood of Golden Valley, a suburb of Minneapolis, were advised by the police not to venture out at night. The warning came after the seemingly random execution of two men.

On 30 August 1995 Loren Busse was shot several times in the back with a large-calibre semi-automatic handgun as he was riding his bicycle home from work. From a reconstruction by the police it seemed he had tried to outride his killer.

On 15 December the police received a letter postmarked St Paul and typed on an old machine which said that the writer had been the driver in the Busse shooting. The letter named two men, both of whom had convictions and both of whom were released after questioning. The full text of the letter was not released by the police but the writer said that he had been told to turn the car round and follow Busse after he had been seen riding his bike on Mendelssohn Avenue. He did that and the passengers confronted the man, demanding money from a drug deal. One passenger had said, 'I can kill someone.' The second passenger had handed a gun over and Busse had been shot. The police interviewed 10 people whom they considered might have written the letter but no one admitted doing so.

The second killing came in February 1996 when Dan Neus was shot as he walked his dog on the 3300 block of Major Avenue North. A 1987 Ford station wagon, painted yellow and with wood side panels was seen driving away.

Neus had also been shot with a semi-automatic and he too had tried to outrun his killer. The police said they had 'pretty conclusive evidence' which linked the cases. Neither Neus nor Busse were regarded as being in 'high-risk' categories – police-speak for being involved in drugs or gangs. They do not appear to have known each other.

31 August, 1986

East Londoner Peter Morris was shot on 31 August 1986, possibly as a revenge killing for Micky Collins, killed the previous week in West Ham.

Michael Collins, owner of the Moonlight public house in Stratford Broadway, east London, was killed on 24 August 1986 when four men burst into the public house, sprayed ammonia and stabbed him and his friend, Mark Nattrass, with whom he was drinking, in the legs and buttocks. This was a traditional East End striping, otherwise known as noughts and crosses, in which the aim is to ensure the victim is unable to sit down for a period of time. Unluckily, an artery in Collins's leg was severed and he died on his way to Newham General Hospital where his attackers were taking him. Collins, whose pub had once been owned by the former England football captain Bobby Moore, had been boasting that he was going to take over the East End. It was not thought that his attackers intended to kill him.

Morris, aged 47, who ran a club in Canning Town, was axed, stabbed and shot three times as gangs fought outside The Telegraph pub a few hundred yards from where Collins died. No one was charged with either murder.

SEPTEMBER

1 September, 1934

On 1 September 1934 a girl's body, wrapped in the eponymous pyjamas which were to give the case the name The Pyjama Girl, was found on waste land near Albury, New South Wales, by a farmer bringing a bull back home from market. The body was so disfigured that it appeared at first to have been scalped. In fact, it turned out the girl had been shot and the body set on fire. The first problem was identification. There were difficulties in establishing identity through dental records because a bullet was lodged in her jaw. She was thought to be English and had distinctive ears in that they had no lobes. A Jeanette Rutledge claimed the body as that of her illegitimate daughter, Philomena Morgan, but she had something of a mental history and her claims were not accepted. The body was placed in a formalin tank at Sydney University where, for almost the next 10 years, desultory identification parades were held.

Meanwhile Mrs Rutledge was stepping up her campaign to have the body identified as that of her daughter and a totally eccentric Doctor Palmer-Benbow more or less gave up his practice to try to establish her claim.

In 1944, following pressure from lawyers urged on by Palmer-Benbow, a further inquest was arranged and almost on its eve, Antonio Agostini, a cloakroom attendant in Romano's, a Sydney restaurant, was arrested. He had been interviewed following the disappearance of his wife Linda, a former cinema usherette, some 10 years earlier. Then he had been shown photographs and said the body was not that of his wife. Now, in 1944, he made a confession. The body was taken out of its tank, make-up and a hairdo applied, and this time seven people identified it as that of Linda Agostini.

The inquest was devoted to an attack on the identification, with Agostini's representatives trying to prove the body to be that of Philomena Morgan. The eyes of the body, which might have helped in the identification, had been removed and suddenly disappeared during the hearing. Agostini's confession really did not stand up. Why had he driven so far to dispose of the body when, many miles nearer, there was a lake said to be bottomless? There were also suggestions that he was in trouble with the Camora, an Australian branch of the Mafia, and was not displeased to be out of the way. The jury found that the body was that of Linda Agostini and her husband was committed for trial.

Now, once more, Agostini changed his story. Yes, the body was his wife's, killed accidentally in a quarrel, after which he panicked. Despite an intervention by Palmer-Benbow who tried to reopen the whole identification question, the jury returned what the judge, Mr Justice Lower, described as a merciful verdict of manslaughter. Agostini was given six years and when asked what he wished to have done with the body replied that he did not mind as it was not that of his wife.

The body was buried at the State's expense in July 1944 and Agostini was deported to Italy on the liner *Strathnaver* on 22 August 1948, on completion of his sentence of which he had served three years and nine months. He told the authorities he would probably live with relatives in Genoa. Right to the time of sailing he continued to deny his involvement with the Pyjama Girl.

There are grounds for thinking the body was indeed that of Philomena Morgan, killed by the son of a Sydney detective. This would account for the enthusiasm the police had for proving the corpse to be that of Linda Agostini. Neither she nor Philomena Morgan were ever again seen alive. The body of the Pyjama Girl is buried in grave 8341 of the Preston Cemetery, Sydney.

Jack 'Ace' Ayling, *Nothing but the Truth*; Eric Clegg, *Return your Verdict*; Vince Kelly, *The Charge is Murder*.

2 September, 1982

In August 1992 Kevin Jackson was finally convicted of the murder of 51-year-old schoolteacher Meredith Levithan in her Lakewood flat in Brick Township, Florida on 2 September 1982. She had been stabbed 53 times and the medical evidence was that she probably lived for 15 minutes following the attack. In a taped interview Jackson said that he had gone to the teacher's flat that night and they had smoked marijuana before having sex. It was a claim which was firmly denied by her friends, one of whom had dined with her earlier in the evening. 'There was no way she would have any connection with that man at all.'

Jackson pleaded guilty to murder in 1986 and then tried to withdraw the plea during the death penalty phase of the trial in February 1987. Peter J. Giovine of the State Superior Court denied the request and Jackson was sentenced to die by lethal injection. He spent three years on death row before the State Supreme Court overturned the death sentence and ordered a retrial. In October 1992 Judge Donald F. Campbell sentenced Jackson to life imprisonment with a minimum of 35 years to be served before he was eligible for parole. In sentencing him he said that if it were within his power Jackson 'would never walk the streets of our society as a free man'. Jackson appealed, claiming that the court should have refused to allow his taped and signed confession in interview. Other grounds of his appeal had related to the prosecutor's attitude towards the defence lawyers, both of whom were black.

On 29 February 1996 the appeal court said:

> Although the prosecutor's remarks were occasionally improperly directed against defence counsel, returning, in part, treatment received from defence counsel, they occurred out of the jury's presence and had no capacity to influence the jury.
>
> Defendant's contentions that the verdict was against the weight of the evidence and that the sentence was excessive, are clearly without merit and warrant no discussion.

3 September, 1907

One of the great *femmes fatales* of the century stood trial after the shooting on 3 September 1907 of her lover. The Countess Marie Nicholaievna Tarnowska, part Irish like Maria Montez, was charged with complicity in the murder of her lover Count Paul Kamarovski, a colonel who had fought in the Russo-Japanese war.

Even before she had met Kamarovski she had had a chequered emotional career. Her brother-in-law and a doctor committed suicide over her; her husband shot her lover Alexis Borzewski who had, claimed the Countess, been trying to rape her; her lawyer, Donat Prilukoff, whom she persuaded to leave his wife and three children, began to embezzle from his client account to pay for her whims. Together they inveigled 21-year-old Nicolas Naumoff to shoot Kamarovski whose life they had insured. Her plan with the young man was an age-old one: the Count required her to perform any number of degrading acts; surely he would save her from this horrible old man. Accounts have him completely in her power to the extent that he allowed her to cut him with a dagger and cauterise the wound with eau de cologne. In Venice he shot Kamarovski in the Count's bedroom in his palazzo. However, Tarnowska's plan was botched. The lawyer was meant to have the police standing by to arrest Naumoff but unfortunately he had gone for coffee and the boy escaped. Nor was Naumoff's shooting accurate. The Count only died because of poor medical treatment. All were arrested immediately.

The trial in 1910 was a sensation with the Countess taking three months to give her evidence. Both men blamed the Countess, with whom both were infatuated. Naumoff received 40 months' imprisonment. The jury had found him guilty but that he was suffering from a partial mental collapse. The jury refused to return a verdict that the Countess was mad. They compromised by finding that her mental faculties were partially destroyed. She received eight years and four months. Prilukoff, with no such mitigation, received 10 years' solitary confinement. Tarnowska served only two years because of ill-health, and died in the 1920s.

4 September, 1974

After serving his sentence for the killing of David Knight (see 7 May) Tony Zomparelli ran a bucket shop travel agency in Frith Street in London's Soho. Much of his leisure time was spent playing the pinball machines in the Golden Goose around the corner in Old Compton Street (and not far from the A & R Club). It was in the arcade he was shot by two men wearing dark glasses and moustaches on 4 September 1974, a few months after his release.

It is not surprising that the police fancied Ronnie Knight for the killing. He does not seem to have hidden either his loathing of Zomparelli or his intention of seeking revenge for the killing of his brother. His alibi was that he was in the A & R Club and he named a substantial number of witnesses.

As in all these cases there were a number of theories offered for what was clearly a professional hit. Suggestions were made that Zomparelli was trying to muscle into the highly profitable amusement arcade business; another that he was involved in a stolen car racket of Lancias and Ferraris in Italy and their resale in London with claims on Italian insurance companies, and a third that he was a drug courier. The police interviewed over a thousand people including Knight but the enquiry came to nothing.

In 1980 Maxie Piggot *aka* George Bradshaw became the supergrass with most to confess in his generation. On 17 January 1980 he received a life sentence for the murder of Zomparelli with a 10-year concurrent sentence for all the rest of his crimes which included over a hundred armed robberies. He named Nicky Gerard, son of Alfie, as his co-hit man, the one who pulled the trigger of a .38 revolver.

He also named Ronnie Knight as the financier of the reasonably priced £1,000 contract and the supplier of the .38. He said that night he and Gerard received £250 of the promised £1,000. He also claimed that it wasn't the money which had tempted him but the added prestige in the Underworld which such an execution would bring him. Knight was arrested and charged.

But by 1980 supergrasses did not always have the ear of the jury. Ten years of practice had taught defence barristers how to overcome the witnesses' all-consuming repentance and desire to bare their souls so that justice could at last be done and they could receive a vastly reduced sentence. So jurors had grown rightly sceptical. Knight also had the bonus of his wife Barbara Windsor on his side. The jury acquitted both him and Nicky Gerard.

Nicky Gerard did not last long. He was beaten and shot to death after he left his daughter's birthday party in east London. His cousin was acquitted of his murder. Ronnie Knight fled to Spain after the Security Express Robbery in

London in 1983. In 1994 he returned and was sentenced to
seven years for dishonestly handling part of the proceeds.

5 September, 1995

Forty-two-year-old John Edward Honesty died on the
morning of 5 September 1995. Some days previously he
had injured his shoulder in a fight with James Lorance
Gross in a bar in Capitol Heights, Washington. He had
been treated in Prince George's Hospital Center and discharged. On the morning of his death he made a telephone
call complaining of breathing problems but when the
police arrived at his home around 8 am he was dead.
His right arm and shoulder were badly swollen.

The autopsy found his shoulder injury had been complicated by a rare flesh-eating bacterium, causing necrotising
fasciitis. Gross was arrested and charged with second-
degree murder. The prosecuting authorities equated the
death with one caused by complications after a shooting.

The bacteria normally enter the body through a cut
or other wound and then spread rapidly just below the
surface of the skin. They divide every 45 minutes and can
destroy an arm in a day. The disease is fatal in about 30
per cent of cases, of which there are between a thousand
and fifteen hundred annually.

6 September, 1976

At about 5.30 am on 6 September 1976, 44-year-old
newsagent Geoffrey Small was shot seven times with a
7.65 9 mm semi-automatic pistol as he stepped into his
shop in Westmead Road, Sutton, Surrey. One possible

reason suggested for his killing was that Small, who had been married for 20 years, had a mistress. But this was quickly ruled out because that affair had dwindled and was effectively ended by the summer of 1976. He and his wife had then bought a house away from the shop and had spent the summer doing it up.

The gunman had entered the premises though a ground-floor window and had sat and waited for Small. The killer then walked past an early customer who had come to collect a paper, and said 'Good morning.' He was described as 45 years old, five feet six inches tall, slim with brown hair and wearing a checked sports jacket and brown trousers.

The man took away with him Small's wallet containing £150 but no one seriously thought that the motive was robbery. According to former Detective Superintendent Beavan Moss who was in charge of the case there was no doubt it was a contract killing. 'Anybody but an absolute professional would find it very difficult in hitting the target. This bloke adopted what we call the double-tap method of firing, in as much as he fired two shots, bang bang, and then changed position, bang bang again.' (Fenton Bresler in the *Sunday Express*, 8 December 1985.) The gun was never found and only two of the seven cartridges were retrieved by the police.

One interesting if unsupportable theory was that he was killed in mistake for Bertie Smalls, the first of the British supergrasses who had once lived in the area and on whom there was said to be a contract still outstanding. In exchange for his testimony against his former colleagues he had been given immunity from prosecution and had, apparently, been given a share of reward money from the banks he had robbed. When it came to it, however, Small and Smalls looked nothing like each other. In November 1976 a former mercenary in Angola was arrested and questioned about the killing before being released without charge.

The local newspaper, the Sutton *Herald*, offered £1,000 reward for information leading to the arrest of the killer but over the years it has gone unclaimed.

7 September, 1979

On 7 September 1979 at around 6 pm Georgi Markov, a refugee from Bulgaria who had been living in Britain for 10 years, was stabbed with a poisoned umbrella tip. Markov was on his way to broadcast a World Service news bulletin to Bulgaria and was walking in the Strand, London, when he was stabbed in the right thigh with the point of an umbrella. He had driven his car to work that morning but, because of heavy traffic, he had parked it near Waterloo Bridge and walked the rest of the way to the BBC at Bush House. He was due to work late and at 6 pm he moved his car nearer the studio.

The man with the umbrella, who had been waiting at a bus stop, seemingly merely touched him, apologised and then hailed a passing cab.

When his leg began to stiffen Markov showed the wound – a bright red mark – to a colleague. Later he felt ill and, by the end of the evening, Markov's leg was completely stiff and he was feverish. The next day he was running a high temperature. His wife took him to hospital but the doctors were unable to explain the mark on his leg. His white blood count soared and he died on 11 September. In the postmortem a minuscule hollowed-out pellet, less than the size of a pinhead, made from an alloy of platinum and iridium, was found in his thigh. He had been poisoned with ricin, a derivative of castor oil seeds.

Another Bulgarian defector had been attacked in a similar way. On 24 August 1978 Vladimir Kostov was shot in a Paris street but on this occasion the pellet did not contain sufficient poison. He had felt nothing more than a stinging sensation in his back. Although never proved, it is reasonable to assume that both attacks were the work of the Bulgarian secret police, the Dazjavna Sigurnost.

Daniel Cohen, *Great Unsolved Crimes.*

8 September, 1935

The 'Kingfish' of Louisiana political life, Senator Huey Long, was shot to death on 8 September 1935 as he was attending a special session of the Louisiana House of Representatives in Baton Rouge. He had long been a major player in national politics and, depending on the speaker's point of view, was regarded as either the most-loved or most-hated man in the State. One of his ideas was a tax on the wealthy and a redistribution so that each family received seed money of $5,000. A man of enormous sexual appetites, he also had long-standing contacts with the Underworld and was probably instrumental in the introduction by Frank Costello, the successor to Al Capone, of gaming machines into Louisiana. His programme of building superhighways and leisure spas almost bankrupted the State and there was considerable dissent to his policies in Louisiana where people were beginning to appreciate the Square Deal policy of Long's enemy, Franklin D. Roosevelt, aimed at getting the country out of the Depression.

Long had five bodyguards with him when Dr Carl Weiss stepped from behind a pillar in the Capitol building and shot him with a .32 automatic. Weiss was knocked to the ground and shot an astounding 61 times. He died immediately; Long lived for 30 hours. His last words were reputedly, 'Why would anyone want to shoot me?' The motive for the killing is not clear although it is known that Weiss and his family hated Long. Suggestions have ranged from family insults, the rape of a relative and death threats to Weiss's father-in-law, Judge Benjamin Pavey, to the suggestion that Long was about to spread a rumour that the Pavey family was tainted with black blood.

A second theory for the killing is that Long was accidentally shot by his own guards; that when Weiss stepped forward he only hit Long with a punch and the guards then indiscriminately opened fire, hitting the senator. This version then has the guards taking Weiss's gun and firing into Long to cover up their own mistake. Another version is that Weiss was shot before he could get off a round.

Long was buried in the Capitol grounds; Weiss in an unknown grave.

9 September, 1900

On 9 September 1900 the third robbery of the year took place at the Birkenhead, Liverpool post office. George Fell, shoemaker, auxiliary postman and caretaker, failed to answer the gate when other postmen arrived for the evening shift at about 4.50 pm. They forced the door and found a pool of blood inside the doorway. Fell was found in the postmaster's room, his face covered with a postbag. A broken poker lay on the floor and a coal shovel had several dents in it. It seemed as though Fell had used it as a shield against the blows from the poker. £19. 15s. 2d. had been taken from the safe, along with £50 in £10 notes and three postal orders. Although details of the notes were circulated and their numbers printed in the national newspapers no single one was ever tendered.

One theory is that the killer may have had the gate opened to him by Fell some time during the day and immediately attacked him, which would account for the blood in the doorway. Another is that he may even have hidden himself in the cellar amongst postal baskets whilst the office was open and was later surprised by Fell.

The robber was never caught despite inquiries nationwide and as far away as Australia. At one time the Birkenhead police fastened on a man in the Grimsby area but that line of inquiry came to nothing.

On the two previous occasions that year when the post office had been robbed the employees were made to make good the loss. Each had a small amount stopped from his weekly pay until the money had been repaid. This time they were not docked their wages.

10 September, 1994

Jeffrey Gould's plea of guilty to the manslaughter of police officer James Bourke was accepted at Birmingham Crown Court. The judge, Mr Justice Rix, had heard how Gould, a 52-year-old paranoid schizophrenic, had battered his neighbour to death because of Mr Bourke's love of classical music.

Gould believed that Bourke had been sent 'by the Divine Lord' to spy on him and cause trouble. He did not believe that Mr Bourke lived next door or that he was a real man. He had developed a hatred of listening to classical music and had complained several times to the police but neighbours said that the music was unobtrusive.

On 10 September 1994 he battered the 50-year-old policeman with a mallet. The killing was seen by Gould's brother, James, who also lived nearby and saw blows being struck and then someone being dragged indoors. He telephoned the police but they did not arrive for an hour, by which time all was quiet. Mr Bourke's body was found the next morning when two women noticed blood on the front door. When details of the death became known Mr Gould's daughter, Rachel, reported the matter to the police.

11 September, 1994

Gordon Wardell was found by the police tied up in his
house on 11 September 1994. He had been there 16
hours. On his release he told the police how an armed
and masked gang had broken into his home and abducted
his wife, Carol, to force her to open the Nuneaton branch
of the Woolwich Building Society from which £14,000
was stolen. He had returned home after going out for a
drink and to post a letter, and had been attacked when
he interrupted the abduction. Carol Wardell's body had
been found by a passer-by on the A444 near Nuneaton.
She had been suffocated. Wardell appeared on television
in an emotional appeal for help in capturing his wife's
murderers.

At his wife's funeral he helped his distraught mother-in-
law as she collapsed on her daughter's coffin and he sent a
floral tribute with a card reading 'In loving memory of my
dear wife'. It was signed with a G and a kiss.

Public opinion turned against Wardell when it was
revealed that at the age of 17 he had been sentenced to
a term of four years' imprisonment for wounding with
intent, after he had indecently assaulted the wife of his
science teacher and stabbed her in the neck after luring
her to a wood. 'I am shocked and saddened this has been
dragged up again after 25 years,' said Wardell's mother,
herself a retired schoolteacher.

His tears and emotional appeal were, however, all a
sham, decided a jury when, on 20 December 1995,
Wardell was unanimously convicted of murder and theft
and sentenced to life imprisonment.

Wardell's story simply had too many inconsistencies.
The thieves had chosen a small branch of the building
society; they had left the automatic machine cash and
credit cards in the safe; they had not taken expensive
cameras from the Wardell home. Mrs Wardell knew an

easy way of sending an alarm – to gain entry to the building she had to tap a code; one number higher and a silent alarm would be triggered. Wardell himself had not the bruises which would have been expected from a fight; nor, despite being supposedly tied up for 16 hours, had he wet himself. He had, after all, drunk two pints of beer the previous night, but he could not produce a urine sample at the hospital. The knots on his wrists and the mouth gag could have been self-tied. There was also undigested food in the stomach of Carol Wardell. Had she eaten at seven, as Wardell said, the food would have disintegrated. This led the police to believe she had been killed much earlier.

'You are an extremely dangerous, evil and devious man,' said Mr Justice Cresswell. 'You killed your wife in a brutal manner then cynically attempted to escape detection by going to elaborate lengths to make it appear that your crime was the work of a gang of robbers. This murder was an outrage to your wife, her family and to everybody who knew her. Take him down.'

After the hearing the police said that they were considering questioning Wardell over the disappearance of two women, one a prostitute, in the Midlands. Despite telling the police he had a happy and successful marriage it was discovered he had been heavily involved in sado-masochistic acts with prostitutes.

12 September, 1982

Rudolph Tyner, a black convict, was blown up by a home-made bomb at the Central Correctional Institute, Columbia, South Carolina on 12 September 1982. At the time of his death he was involved in a series of appeals and stays in relation to his own execution for the killing during a robbery of William and Myrtie Moon who ran a small store.

Tyner's killer was Donald Henry Gaskins, known as Pee Wee because he was only five feet six inches tall. Tyner was his 14th victim. He had previously been convicted and sentenced to death – subsequently commuted – for the killing of 13 people, many with the assistance of a former cellmate, Walter Neeley, by shooting, stabbing and drowning. Eight of the bodies had been found in shallow graves in Prospect, South Carolina.

Gaskins, who had an irrational hatred of black people, had been recruited to kill Tyner by Myrtie Moon's son, Richard Tony Cimo, who was incensed by the delays Tyner was using to avoid the electric chair. Gaskins made several unsuccessful attempts to poison Tyner before succeeding with the bomb, disguised as a two-way radio.

Although initially it was thought that Tyner had accidentally blown himself up whilst trying to make a device for a prison escape, Gaskins was convicted and sentenced to death.

He too tried to avoid the death penalty and several hours before he was to die in the electric chair he cut his wrists with a razor blade he had swallowed some weeks before and had regurgitated. On 6 September 1991 he became the first white person to be executed for killing a black person in America since 1944. Cimo received a sentence of eight years and was paroled after six months. After his conviction his neighbours held a barbecue and lottery to raise money for his family. He was later the subject of a television film, *Vengeance: The Tony Cimo Story*.

James Bland, *The Book of Executions*; Brian Lane and Wilfred Gregg, *The Encyclopedia of Serial Killers*.

13 September, 1912

Seventeen-year-old Eliza Carter had her throat cut by
her boyfriend on 13 September 1912. Her parents had
forbidden her to go on meeting the 20-year-old engineer,
William Beal. On the evening of her death they were seen
kissing under a lamppost in Stratford, east London when
suddenly Eliza screamed. By the time the police arrived
she was dead. She had been nearly decapitated. Beal had
a wound to his own throat. His defence was that it was
she who had cut both his and her own throat. The medical
evidence was, however, that it was highly improbable that
the three cuts to her throat were self-inflicted and highly
probable that the cut to his was.

The jury made a strong recommendation to mercy
on behalf of Beal, who was described as not of very
sound mind. It helped him not at all. He was hanged
at Chelmsford prison on 10 December by Thomas
Pierrepoint. The gash in his neck opened with the
hanging.

14 September, 1954

Jean Townsend, a manageress with M. Berman, the theatrical costumiers, and a single woman who lived with her
parents in Ruislip, Middlesex, was raped and strangled
with her own black and gold-flecked scarf on the night
of 14 September 1954. She had been to a Pyramid party
which was then the current London craze. It worked on
the chain letter principle and, if successful, the person
on top of the Pyramid could expect to receive the tidy
sum of £128. It was expected that those nearing the top

should give a party and that night Jean had given one at the Londoner Club in Irving Street, London.

She was killed at a spot near an American Air Force base whilst walking home from South Ruislip station. There had been a considerable number of accostings and attacks on women in the area. Jacqueline Cliff of Bideford Road, Ruislip, who was the model for Norman Hepple's Royal Academy painting *Portrait of a Young Woman*, came forward to say she knew Jean and had been accosted by an American serviceman driving along the road about 11 days before the attack.

Townsend was a woman of habit. She always sat in the same compartment on the train; always walked along the left-hand side of the road and never varied in this. Yet her body was found on the right-hand side of the road. Two men had been seen quarrelling near where her body was found and the Scotland Yard reconstruction was that she had been approached by them; one man was to have sex with her whilst the other kept watch; she had run off, losing her shoes as she did so, but he had caught up with her and strangled her; he then returned to the other man and this was when the argument occurred.

At one time it was suggested that her killer might be the same man who murdered 'Red' Helen Carline in Pimlico but this seems unlikely since Peter Manuel, the serial killer (see 28 December), confessed to that murder.

In 1982 Detective Superintendent Tony Lundy said there were new clues to Jean Townsend's killer but no arrests were made. It was now thought that her killer had, indeed, been an American serviceman who had returned to the States shortly after the killing. Her mother later had a breakdown and went to see a clairvoyant who told her the person who committed the murder was a long way away, over water.

15 September, 1962

On the night of 15 September 1962, Harvey Leo Holford, the half-Belgian gun expert and owner of the Blue Gardenia Club in Brighton, shot and killed his 21-year-old wife, Christine. She had five bullets in her body and one in her brain. Holford was found in his club, cradling her in his arms. The self-styled King of Brighton and the 'Errol Flynn of the South Coast', he had married Christine Hughes in defiance of her parents' wishes. They had met just before one Christmas at his club, which he described as 'the most luxurious on the South Coast'. In reality it was little more than a drinker for the numerous Underworld characters of the town. In June 1960 they ran away to Scotland. Thirteen hours before they obtained the necessary Scots residential qualification to enable them to marry, an order was obtained making Christine a ward of court. Under the terms of the order she returned to Saltdean to live with her parents but Holford was allowed to continue to see her. By the August they were living together in a Regency-style terrace house in Queen Square, Brighton. By November her parents' resistance had been broken and they were married. She was then 19.

Within six months the marriage was effectively over. The Errol Flynn of the South Coast was no good in bed, Christine told her friends.

In the summer of 1962 Christine went to Paris where she met up with Vilasar Cresteff, a Swiss boy who had also worked at the Gardenia. She went with him to Cannes and San Remo. She then travelled to Juan-les-Pins where she had an affair with a drummer from a rock band. From Juan it was back to Cannes where she met John Bloom, the then washing-machine tycoon and his long-time friend and Conservative MP, Richard Reader Harris. She stayed with Bloom at his villa, and it was with him and the money he then had that, said Holford, Christine became obsessed.

In a quarrel she told Holford that their daughter was not his. After beating her he cropped her hair.

On Friday 14 September 1962, Holford and Christine went to the Press Ball at the Town Hall in Hove, later looking in at the New Hove Albany Club. Back home they went into the Blue Gardenia. It was the last time she was seen alive. The nanny was sent out to a coffee bar as, said Holford, he wanted a serious talk with his wife. When the nanny returned about 2.30 am she found Christine's wig on the draining board, covered in blood. On the stairs there was a cardboard carton, also covered in blood.

When the police arrived Christine was dead. Holford was lying beside her, drugged. He did not recover full consciousness until the following Tuesday. When he did so he made a statement to the police saying that after she had met Bloom she had changed and she could talk of nothing but money:

> I had just had enough. It was that bastard Bloom and money. I just got my revolver from the top cupboard in the kitchen and shot her. It is like a dream. How many times I shot her I do not know. Christine dropped on the floor. I picked her up and took her to the bedroom. I just wanted to die.

Holford went on to say that he laid her on the bed, went down to the kitchen and took all the tablets he could find.

It was, said Malcolm Morris QC, prosecuting, a clear case of capital murder.

Holford had a number of problems with his defence. The first was his possession of the gun. He had already been fined £15 for keeping one in his car. What was he doing with another, handy and loaded? The answer was that it was to protect him against the London gangsters Billy Hill and Albert Dimes. Holford had had an argument with a man named Gillett over the installation of a gambling game 'Legalite', a form of roulette, in the Blue Gardenia. According to a letter Holford had written and deposited with a firm of Brighton solicitors, 'To be opened in the event of my death, disappearance, or meeting with any accident that would incapacitate me, or if these events should happen to my wife', Gillett had apparently hinted that he had connections with Hill and Dimes who would deal with Holford.

But Holford overcame all his problems. There was sympathy for him because whilst in Lewes prison, to which he had been transferred from Brixton the night before his trial was due to begin on 4 December 1962, he threw himself from a balcony, fracturing his skull. His fall was broken by a warder. The newspapers were full of baby Karen visiting him. It was reported his 73-year-old Belgian-born mother, Celeste Holford, had also visited him. 'Mama, hold my hand – tightly', reported the *Daily Mirror*. There was more sympathy for him when Victor Durand coaxed the admission from Mrs Holford that she might have encouraged him to take sexual liberties with her when he was a child. By the end Morris, in his address to the jury, offered them some help and Holford a lifeline:

> If you accept as the truth what Holford says was said [about the paternity of Karen] then you will think that was strong provocation.

His acquittal on Friday, 29 March 1963 on the murder charge was well received, with the traditional cheers from women in the public gallery. The all-male jury found him guilty only of manslaughter. He received four years' imprisonment.

He was paroled on 2 October 1964. 'I am changing my name and going off in search of anonymity,' he told the *Daily Mirror*. 'I am not a poor man. I have the money from the sale of the Blue Gardenia club.' Calling her his little princess, a title he had given to Christine in happier times, he would, he said, never leave his daughter Karen again.

In February 1974, under the name of Robert Keith Beaumont, but disclosing that he was indeed Holford, he stood as independent candidate in the General Election for the constituency of Brighton Pavilion. He received 428 votes.

16 September, 1918

On 16 September 1918, 60-year-old Charles Chapin, editor of the New York *Evening World*, shot and killed his wife, Nellie, to save her from poverty. Over the years he had been a heavy gambler on the commodity markets and in 1914 was reputed to have lost the enormous sum of $100,000 when Germany declared war. He had previously been fortunate to escape criminal proceedings over a series of options in the sugar market.

Originally he had intended that the killing of his wife should be followed by his own suicide but he lacked the conviction to follow it through. He refused to offer a defence at his trial but a court-appointed lawyer succesfully argued that he should be imprisoned rather than receive the death penalty.

He had not been all that popular an editor in his time. Whilst he was in prison one of his former employees wrote to the warder:

> He was the worst curse our reportorial craft ever enjoyed. I used to think of him as a sort of devil sitting on enthroned power in the *World* office and making Park Row gutters flow red with the blood of ambitious young men. If you enjoy him I hope you keep him long and carefully.

In Sing Sing prison he edited the prison's magazine and laid out a garden, so earning himself the soubriquet of the Rose Man of Sing Sing. It may be that this title led to the later dubbing of Robert Stroud, also initially imprisoned for the murder of his wife, as the Bird Man of Alcatraz.

Neither was ever released. Chapin died in 1930 when he was 72 and Stroud in 1973 when he was 76.

Jay Robert Nash, *Murder, America*.

17 September, 1934

Kalli Georgiou, then aged 31, killed Thomas James at Torrington Square, Holborn, London on 17 September 1934, at the same time stabbing Margaret McKinnon.

Around 6.30 pm he went into the bar of the Marlboro Arms in Francis Street and drank a glass of bitter and when he ordered a second told the barman he was depressed. He said he had been living with a woman for eight months and gave her seven pounds a week. Now she was living with another man who had more money than he did. He was going to kill her. The barman, Arthur Talbot, told him not to be silly but Kalli showed him a visiting card of T. James, Torrington Square, together with a snapshot of the girl. He said he had some money and was 'looking for a sportsman to give it to, because you won't see me tomorrow. Tomorrow you'll see my name in the paper.' He had two more glasses of stout and a sandwich and left.

Kalli carried out his threat and stabbed Thomas James twice in the middle of his back and Margaret McKinnon in her arm in the living room of James's home. James staggered out of the house and died on the doorstep of 39 Torrington Square. Kalli then went to Cannon Row police station and surrendered himself, telling the police: 'Me live here. My name Kalli. I live with girl Margaretta eight months. I go home tonight and she in bed with Mr James. I say Mr James, you got my girl; she say 'no'. I take knife and put it like that [touching the officer on the left shoulder], I go and have drink and come here.'

Thomas James had been married with a grown-up son. He had owned a correspondence school, the Theiran School of Life, in Old Bond Street, but the business had failed and he had gone to manage the boarding house in Torrington Square. Margaret McKinnon had been a housekeeper there.

Kalli and Margaret McKinnon had been living together in nearby Lambs Conduit Street but she had become bored with staying indoors and had gone out to look for a job, eventually finding a position at 39 Torrington Square. She and Kalli had regularly quarrelled and she had left him.

Two days before the killing Kalli had again quarrelled with Margaret. He had wanted her to come back to him and she had refused. He had complained: 'You and Mr James are happy downstairs while I am miserable upstairs and crying.' She gave him some money and said, 'You are not going to get any more.'

Margaret McKinnon's version was that there was nothing sexual between her and Thomas James. She explained that he slept on a divan in the dining room on the first floor and she had a bedroom in which James kept his clothes but which, she said, she kept locked when she was in it. She had been to Brighton with James and had given him a photograph inscribed 'With fondest love, Margaret'. This she said was a joke. Her version of the stabbing was that Kalli came at her with a knife when she was kneeling on the floor to pick up a tray. She had refused to go to Cyprus with him. She called Mr James for help and he caught hold of Kalli, saying, 'I've got him now, you run.'

Kalli appeared in front of Mr Justice Goddard on 22 October 1934. He ran a case of self-defence and told the jury he had bought the sheath knife with which James had been stabbed some six months earlier for three shillings, to use for peeling vegetables. They found him guilty of murder with a recommendation of mercy because of provocation. James had, according to Kalli, told him: 'Get out of my house, you fucking bastard.'

Kalli was visited in prison by Michael Constantinides,

Great Archimandrite of the Ecumenic Throne, who wrote to Prince Nicholas of Greece, asking that he intercede. Kalli had, he said, 'in a moment of madness through the passion (pathos) of jealousy committed murder quite involuntarily'. There had, he said, been tremendous sympathy shown in Cyprus for the man. Kalli was reprieved and his sentence commuted to life imprisonment.

There was some dissent over the payment of £3 for the translation of the letter by a barrister. It had been written in ancient Greek which had not initially been recognised. The translator at Scotland Yard had thought it to be in modern Greek.

There may have been something in Kalli's overall version of events. Certainly his story about finding them in bed does not appear to be correct unless this related to an earlier incident. James was fully clothed when he was stabbed. There is, however, reference in the police file to an agreement made between James and Margaret McKinnon. His family refused to take out letters of administration to his estate.

PRO/MEPO/3/1696.

18 September, 1987

When Bob Moieni's mother and sister came home to their flat on 49th Avenue, Vancouver on 18 September 1987 they found the 16-year-old martial-arts expert, bound hand and foot, on the family-room floor. He had been shot through the forehead with a pistol to which a turnip had been added as a silencer.

Moieni was 11 when he came to Canada. His father had been an officer in the Shah of Iran's army. He had been expelled from three Vancouver schools for fighting. From there he had tried to join one of the teenage gangs prevalent in the city but, because of his nationality, he was never really accepted. He had first tried to join the Lotus gang but they would not have him because he was not Chinese. He joined Los Diablos, a Filipino-Hispanic gang who were affiliated to the Lotus gang, then in outright competition with the Red Eagle gang, and Moieni made enemies amongst these older Asians.

By the middle 1980s he had made a reputation for himself as a tough guy on the streets and was suspected of being involved in the day-to-day diet of a City gang – robberies of pizza parlours, petrol stations and local shops. He also had the reputation of being a big-mouth and was always trying to show off his martial-arts ability. A former member of the Red Eagles told the police that was why he had been killed. It was, thought the police, part and parcel of what essentially had been a series of tit-for-tat, drive-by, inter-gang killings.

19 September, 1978

On 19 September 1978, newspaper delivery boy Carl Bridgewater was shot and killed when he interrupted a robbery at Yew Tree Farm near Kidderminster in the West Midlands. His body was found about 5.30 pm by Dr Angus Macdonald who called at the farm on a routine visit to the owners, Fred Jones and his sister Mary Poole who, as it happened, were out. Carl had been shot about an hour earlier.

Four regular, if relatively minor, criminals were arrested – James Robinson, his close friend Patrick Molloy, Vincent Hickey and his cousin Michael Hickey. In the first days of December newspaper stories began to link the Yew Tree Farm case with another local burglary. On 4 December Vincent Hickey went to the police to confess to Chapel Farm. On 8 December Robinson was arrested and the same day Vincent Hickey confessed to being at Yew Tree Farm. Two days later he withdrew his confession. On 11 December Patrick Molloy signed a four-page confession to being present at the Yew Tree Farm murder and on 20 December Michael Hickey was arrested. Molloy's confession named Robinson as the man who had killed Carl Bridgewater whilst he, Molloy, had been upstairs, and also involved the Hickey cousins in the robbery.

Almost from that moment the confessions were hotly challenged by the defence. Throughout, Robinson denied any involvement in the murder. When he was finally arrested Michael Hickey also denied any involvement.

At the trial which began on 8 October 1979 at Stafford Crown Court, the prosecution's case was that the Hickey cousins had been drinking together in the Dog and Partridge in Selly Oak, a Birmingham suburb, and arranged with Robinson and Molloy, who had been in another pub, to meet to burgle Yew Tree Farm. They went there in a van and a Ford Cortina and were surprised by Bridgewater whom they shot. Surprisingly, there was no forensic evidence to support this. Against the individuals there was the evidence of Vincent Hickey's statements which amounted to a confession to the police. There was also evidence that he had lied when he said he had never met Robinson and that he had never been near Yew Tree Farm. A prison officer gave evidence that Vincent Hickey had told him he had bad dreams. 'I keep seeing the kid's face.'

Against Robinson there was the identification evidence of three witnesses, none of which could be described as cast-iron. He did have a sawn-off shotgun which he disclosed to the police. It was not possible to say whether the gun had been used in the killing but a cartridge found at Yew Tree Farm did not match those Robinson had. There was also evidence from long-serving prisoners that Robinson had made remarks which might amount to an admission. The evidence against Michael Hickey was a confession, said to have been made by him to a small-time villain in a shower whilst on remand. A taxi driver said

Michael Hickey had tried to arrange an alibi. Against Molloy there was his confession to the police.

At the trial Vincent Hickey and Michael Molloy maintained they had spent some time at the flat of Linda Galvin, the girlfriend of Vincent Hickey. Robinson denied any involvement. Patrick Molloy did not call evidence and did not go into the witness box himself. His confession therefore remained unchallenged and, although in law not admissible as evidence against the others, was put before the jury. They effectively followed his story, convicting Robinson and the Hickeys of murder and Molloy of manslaughter. Molloy went to prison for 12 years, whilst Robinson and Vincent Hickey were given life imprisonment with a 25-year recommendation. Michael Hickey was ordered to be detained during Her Majesty's pleasure. The three continued to maintain their innocence.

There followed what supporters of the men have seen as a significant fact which could lead to their innocence. A month after the trial Hubert Spencer, an ambulanceman, shot and killed Hubert Wilkes, who owned the farm next to Yew Tree, during a row at a drinks party. It has been argued since Spencer's conviction that he was the real murderer at Yew Tree Farm. Supporters of the men argue that Spencer dealt in antiques and therefore would have a motive for burglary, that he owned a shotgun, that he knew Carl Bridgewater and so would have a motive for killing him, that he knew Yew Tree Farm well, and that he owned a blue Vauxhall Viva. A man in uniform had been seen going into Yew Tree Farm in a blue Viva an hour and a half before the killing. The police had found only one man in the area who had such a car and wore a uniform. That man was Spencer. He consistently denied any involvement in the killing.

Both Michael Hickey and his cousin took a truth drug test and passed. If they hoped it would help them they were to be disappointed. In another case Mr Justice Tucker ruled that as a matter of principle such evidence would be inadmissible in an English court of law. On 12 June 1981 Patrick Molloy died. He had retracted his confession. In 1988, after a series of campaigns and protests, the Home Secretary referred the case to the Court of Appeal. It was dismissed in January 1989, the court finding the convictions neither unsafe nor unsatisfactory. The House of Lords then refused leave to appeal against that decision. Since then witnesses have admitted lying and, it was reported, the foreman of the jury now believes the men to be innocent.

The Home Secretary again considered the case in December 1995 and announced it was not likely to be his intention to refer the case yet again to the Court of Appeal. The police had not been able to confirm that Spencer had a shotgun in the summer of 1978 and if he had been sold one it was only for ornamental purposes. He also found that Molloy did not dispute his confession statement at the trial although on subsequent occasions he sought to refute it. The Home Secretary had information that up to Molloy's death, including the day of it, he continued to make admissions about the part played by him and his co-accused. He had, he said, received confidential information that would implicate Vincent Hickey and Patrick Molloy in the murder.

In April 1996 a television programme again tried to prove the men's innocence. The prosecutor said that Carl Bridgewater's bicycle, which had clearly been moved by his killers, did not bear the men's prints. Again there were calls for their release.

On 25 July 1996 the Home Secretary announced that he was referring the case back to the Court of Appeal. He was particularly disturbed over the non-disclosure of fingerprints, which were not those of the men, on the boy's bicycle.

On 21 February 1997 the men were finally released on bail pending another hearing before the Court of Appeal, listed to take place in April of that year. There was now grave disquiet over the confession of Molloy. Earlier two of the jurors in the case had come forward to say they now believed that the two men had been wrongly convicted. Their convictions were quashed by the Court of Appeal in 1997.

Paul Foot, *Murder at the Farm; Murder Casebook No 23.*

20 September, 1930

Eighty-five-year-old Margery Wren was found at about 6 pm on 20 September 1930 in her shop in Church Road, Ramsgate, Kent. A young girl called to buy some blancmange mix and found the door locked. Miss Wren eventually came to the door, bleeding profusely from a head wound. She served the girl who ran home to her parents to tell them of Miss Wren's condition. When the police arrived Miss Wren told them she had been attacked about a quarter of an hour earlier. She died five days later in hospital, during which time she had made a number of conflicting statements to the police about her attacker. Although a small hand-made velvet purse was the only thing stolen, robbery was almost certainly the motive because, although in reality she only had an income of £13 a year from her sister's estate and the money from the small shop, she had often boasted that she owned a number of properties. She had been attacked in broad daylight.

After initially saying she had been attacked she changed her story to say she had tripped and fallen but it was clear from her injuries that she had been repeatedly beaten, probably with a pair of tongs. Sir Bernard Spilsbury, the pathologist, said that an attempt had also been made to strangle her. When questioned further she made contradictory statements, saying that a man had attacked her, two people had attacked her and yet again that she had simply fallen. She also told the police it was an accident. In all there were six suspects, said Superintendent Hambrook at the inquest. Three of them were found to have cast-iron alibis and the murderer must have been one of the remaining three. Miss Wren went on to describe a red-faced man with a moustache.

When Margery Wren was invited to make a dying declaration she refused to do so with some satisfaction.

Finally she said, 'I do not wish him to suffer. He must bear his sins. I do not wish to make a statement.' As she rambled in a delirium she once said, 'He tried to borrow ten pounds.' Both the police and the coroner believed she was deliberately shielding someone, and preferred to rely more on a remark she had made whilst drifting into unconsciousness: 'You can't take it. Oh, don't.'

No charges were ever brought, although a young man then on probation was questioned and found to have lied about his movements. In 1930 a man serving a sentence in Dorchester prison made a confession. It was thought, however, he had done this to cause even more hurt to his estranged wife by bringing publicity on her. It was not until 1948 that the police wrote to her cousin's son asking if he wanted the carpet they had taken for forensic examination which had been in their storage. He did not.

Douglas G. Browne and Tom Tullett, *Bernard Spilsbury, His Life and Cases*.

21 September, 1987

On 21 September 1987, when she had not been seen for a week, two friends of a 'bag woman' known as Sis who lived in a shack built of tin and packing cases near a mission at Bloomingdale, Indiana, reported the matter to the police. Her body, without its head or hands, cut off to prevent identification, was found on part of the plot of land where she lived. The slash and stab wounds indicated a ferocious attack with a number of different knives having been used. There had been no sexual assault. Robbery could not have been a motive.

In her shack there was nothing to assist in identification. She was not in fact an elderly woman, as had been thought, but aged about 30, and when she first started going to the mission three years previously had been well dressed and appeared to have some money. She was well spoken. She had also grown vegetables on the patch of land. She was not, said the head of the mission, an average bag lady but one who kept herself clean.

Amongst her possessions was a book bearing the logo of a bookshop on the Indiana State University campus. A pencil inscription had been erased but, under laboratory conditions, the name Ellen Sears Marks was visible.

She turned out to have come from Connecticut, where she had attended the University, obtaining a degree in English Literature and History. She had then gone to Indiana State to obtain a Master's. Although she was considered a brilliant student she had dropped out halfway through the year, saying she wished to study how the poor lived.

There were no leads to her killer until a local landlord went to the police to say that he had accidentally seen a notebook on the table in the room of one of his tenants which detailed a killing ending with the removal of hands and head. The tenant, a 31-year-old night clerk, Robert Lee, was brought in for questioning. He said that he had been writing the first draft of a mystery novel. Given the illiteracy in the writing it was not an explanation the police could easily accept. Lee, who was now living some two hundred yards from Ellen Marks's shack, had been acquitted of a rape charge in New York in 1974.

A search warrant was applied for and in Lee's room were a number of knives. Forensic examination showed bloodstains outside his room all the way to Marks's shack. A cigarette stub of the type that Lee smoked was found in the grave where Marks's body was discovered. Charged with the murder he did not give evidence and, after the jury found him guilty of murder in the first degree without extenuating circumstances, he was sentenced to 60 years' imprisonment.

Georgina Lloyd, *The Part and Parcel Murders*.

22 September, 1900

There is no suggestion that either Herbert Bennett or his wife Mary were attractive people; the question is whether he killed her. They made their living selling faked violins. In a variation of the old con game she would pose as the young widow forced to part with her late husband's most cherished possession. They also indulged in the badger game[1] and insurance fraud. Their partnership ended with a quarrel and Bennett was heard by his landlady to tell his wife, 'I wish you were dead, and if you aren't careful you will be.'

Without his wife, he seems to have worked honestly at the Woolwich Arsenal, south-east London. He also took up with a parlourmaid, Alice Meadows, whom he promised to marry and to whom he gave an engagement ring. He seems, however, to have baulked at bigamy. On 14 September 1900 he went to Bexleyheath to see his wife and suggested she should take a holiday. Yarmouth was agreed upon and she took a room there under the name of Hood. Quite what they were up to is not clear because she told the woman from whom she rented a room that she had been escorted by her dead husband's brother-in-law who was both madly in love with her and madly jealous. It is probable that they were again going to work the badger game with Bennett playing the brother-in-law part.

The next week Bennett told Miss Meadows that he had to go to Gravesend to see his grandfather who was ill. On the Saturday, 22 September, he left his lodgings in Woolwich, telling his landlady the same story.

That night a courting couple on the sands at Yarmouth

---

[1] The badger game involves a young woman, pretending to be under age, or a wife, who solicits a man to have intercourse with her. Whilst they are in a state of undress, but before any sexual relations have taken place, the father/uncle/husband bursts into the room and demands reparation. This can include long-term payments for the 'psychological damage' the child has suffered from the trauma.

saw another couple on the beach and heard the woman call, 'Mercy, mercy.' There was then a moan. The courting couple got up and walked away. Later that evening, a man, identified as Bennett, took a room in the Crown and Anchor hotel, saying he had missed the last tram to Gorleston. He left the next morning.

Mary Jane Bennett's body was found that day. She had been sexually assaulted and strangled with a mohair bootlace tied around her throat. In fact she was not identified for some six weeks and was eventually traced through a laundry mark on her clothing. Bennett was arrested and, when his room was searched, the police found a long, old-fashioned gold chain, together with men's and women's wigs and a false moustache. There was also evidence that he had given a number of his wife's possessions to Miss Meadows.

There was no doubt that Mrs Bennett had a gold chain but whether this was the one she was wearing when she had her photograph taken during her week's holiday was not clear. The photograph produced by the prosecution was too blurred and witnesses could not agree.

Because of local prejudice whipped up by the press, the case was transferred to the Old Bailey where, for the defence, Marshall Hall called a Douglas Sholto who said he was out in Eltham on the evening of 22 September when he had been accosted by a stranger who had walked down the road with him. As they passed a barber's shop the man had remarked on the name, 'F.K. Bennett', on the fascia saying, 'A namesake of mine lives there.' They had been together for about an hour and had a drink together in the Tiger public house and he was convinced the man was Herbert Bennett. Although there was then no requirement on the defence to give notice of an alibi, one problem was why Douglas had waited five weeks before coming forward. A second and graver one was that Bennett steadfastly refused to give evidence. The summing-up was against him and the jury took only 35 minutes to return a verdict of guilty.

Marshall Hall, who firmly believed in his client's innocence, did what he could to obtain a reprieve. He was unsuccessful. As a souvenir of the trial he was given the gold chain. He later wrote to the dramatist, Sir Arthur Pinero:

> I should not be surprised if it were proved against him that he had committed six murders hitherto undiscovered. But he never murdered his wife on Yarmouth beach on 22 September 1900, unless I am sadly deceived.

Bennett was hanged at Norwich prison on 21 March 1901. As the black flag to announce the death was raised, the flagstaff snapped – a sign, said some, of Bennett's innocence.

The case raises a number of interesting points. First is the sexual attack on Mrs Bennett. If Bennett had killed her, why the attack – they seem to have been friendly enough at the time of her death – unless this was a stunning double bluff? Was Hall right about the chain being a different one? Why was Bennett so adamant about not giving evidence? One speculative version is that he had confessed his guilt to Hall, who therefore could not call him to tell what he knew were lies. In which case he could not have called Douglas either.

There is no doubt that during her week in Yarmouth Mrs Bennett had been seeing a man. Had he attacked her and Bennett, lurking in the wings, came on her body too late? Afterwards it was quite within his character to expediently give away her possessions.

And the second murder. Was that a copycat, the same murderer or just coincidence?

A second murder? On 14 July 1912 Dora May Gray was found strangled with a bootlace on the beach at Yarmouth. Her killer was never found.

George Dilnott (ed), *The Trial of Herbert John Bennett*; S.T. Felstead, *Sir Richard Muir, The Memoirs of a Public Prosecutor*; Nina Warner Hooke and Gil Thomas, *Marshall Hall*; Edward Marjoribanks, *The Life of Sir*

Edward Marshall Hall; Julian Symons, *A Reasonable Doubt*.

23 September, 1920

Fifty-eight-year-old Marks Goodmacher was only the third orthodox Jew to be executed in London for murder. On 23 September 1920 he killed his married daughter, Fanny Zeitoun, who lived with him at his home in Grove Street, St George-in-the-East. Life had been difficult for Goodmacher, his daughter and his son-in-law and they were not on speaking terms. In the evening of that day the son-in-law found his wife lying dead with her throat cut. Goodmacher was lying beside her and all her personal belongings, jewellery, and money had been destroyed.

The killing seems to have been because his daughter and her husband had refused to speak to Goodmacher on the Day of Atonement when he tried to bring about a reconciliation. After he had murdered his daughter Goodmacher attempted to commit suicide. He appeared before Mr Justice Darling on 18 November and a plea of insanity failed. He was hanged on 30 December by William Willis, in charge of an execution for the first time.

S. T. Felstead, *Sir Richard Muir, The Memoirs of a Public Prosecutor*.

24 September, 1905

On Sunday, 24 September 1905 Sophie Money, who

worked for a local dairy, left her home at 245 Lavender Hill, Clapham, London saying she was going for a 'little walk'. She called in at a local confectionery shop at around 7 pm and remarked that she was going to Victoria. Some four hours later her badly damaged body was found in the Merstham Tunnel on the London to Brighton line. There was little evidence about her death. At the inquest a guard on the 9.33 pm train from London Bridge said that he had seen a young woman who corresponded to Miss Money's description in company with a man at East Croydon. A signalman at Purley Oaks said that he had seen a couple struggling in a carriage as the trains passed each other. His evidence was subject to some criticism by the coroner who said that the struggle cannot have impressed him at the time and it was possible in thinking over the evidence he had thought he had seen more than he did. Miss Money's former employer, Arthur Bridger, was closely questioned about his relationship with her. He was asked if he had given her presents, something he denied, but there was also evidence that he had been seen with Miss Money on a day trip to Bognor.

The police theory was that she had met a man who had lured her onto the train under the pretext either that they should go for a ride or that he would see her home. She was then pushed, or fell, from the train. Three years later the police were still receiving information they were following up. An Albert Cooper wrote to them saying that he thought a William Wakeman was their man. The basis for this theory was slender. On the day before the Money killing Cooper had tried to borrow Wakeman's walking stick. He had been turned down on the basis that Wakeman was going to meet a 'very special Tart'. After the death Wakeman had some minor injuries and had kept to the basement for some six weeks, coming out only after dark and, when he did so, then with his hat well pulled down. Cooper and he had quarrelled and Cooper had said, 'I know something which could hang you.' Wakeman had, according to Cooper, turned pale. Nothing came of this or any other information.

The case had a curious sequel. Sophie's brother, Robert Henry Money, a dairy farmer, had affairs with two sisters. He had two children by one and another child by the other whom he married. In 1912 he took the whole entourage to Eastbourne and shot them all. He then shot himself. One of the women survived. There have been suggestions that it was he who killed his sister but apart from coincidence there is nothing to support the theory. It has also been suggested that John Dickman, the killer of John Nisbet (see 18 March) and named in the killing of Mary Luard, was Sophie Money's killer. There is little in the way of evidence to support that theory either and indeed an effort, based on the circumstances in which an identification was made, has recently been launched to clear Dickman's name of Nisbet's murder.

William Beadle, *Wrongly Hanged?*

25 September, 1937

The millionaire Chicago greetings-card businessman Charles P. Ross was kidnapped on 25 September 1937 by John Henry Sealund, a 28-year-old burglar who was working his way up in the criminal hierarchy, and his partner James Atwood Gray.

Ross was selected quite by chance – the attraction being his smart car – and he was stopped when Sealund drove in front of him in Franklin Park and produced a gun. The 72-year-old man was ordered into Sealund's car and his secretary, Florence Freihage, who was with him, was left behind. The motive appears initially to have been robbery but Ross remarked, 'I've often thought of being kidnapped,' and, on the spur of the moment, Sealund took him up on the suggestion.

Ross was driven to Wisconsin and there made to write

to a friend, 'I am being held for ransom. Try and raise $50,000.' The note was passed to the FBI where its maverick leader, J. Edgar Hoover, took a personal interest. A second note was sent to Mrs Ross who, obeying instructions, put an advertisement in a Chicago newspaper.

The notes, which had been typed on a new typewriter, were checked for fingerprints. A check was also made on all new machines bought in the Chicago area. A match was made at the rooming house where a young man who fitted the description of the purchaser was staying but he was gone.

The $50,000 had been delivered in marked notes in another drop which went wrong. The motorcyclist George Kukovac, all in white and on a white cycle, dropped the notes on a lonely road near Rockhampton. He waited until he saw a car's lights blink three times, the prearranged signal. But Ross did not appear to collect the notes and they disappeared, beginning during the winter to turn up at race tracks going in a westerly direction. It was anticipated that they might eventually appear at Santa Anita outside Los Angeles where there was a winter meeting. On 14 January 1938 Sealund was arrested as he tried to place a $10 bet. Asked of the whereabouts of Ross he replied, 'Dead, of course. I shot him.' He had also killed his partner Gray and had buried them both in a pit at Spooner, Wisconsin.

Sealund was electrocuted on 14 July 1938 in Cook County, Illinois.

Ross seems to have been an unlucky name so far as the kidnapped go. The first American kidnap victim was little Charley Ross, who was kidnapped from his parents' home in Germantown, Pennsylvania, on 1 July 1874 by Joseph Douglass and William Mosher. He was drowned by the organiser of the enterprise, William Westervelt, a former police officer. He killed the boy simply for gratification. Douglass and Mosher were shot in a Brooklyn burglary in early 1875. They had, they said, done it for the money.

J. Robert Nash, *Bloodletters and Badmen*.

26 September, 1923

The dead body of James Frederick Ellis, a drummer in the Leicester Regiment at Aldershot, Hampshire was found under some gorse bushes in Long Valley, near the garrison town, on 26 September 1923. His corpse, which had been reduced to that of a skeleton, had been wrapped over his mouth in his army greatcoat and strapped up with a webbing belt. The hands and feet were tied behind the back, and the knees pulled together in a position which would have caused considerable pain. He had been gagged and had suffocated.

He had been reported missing from his regiment on 24 May that year and when the other soldiers had been questioned only Lance Corporal Albert Edward Dearnley was able to give any information. He said that Ellis had suggested they desert together and go back home to Hull or even emigrate to Australia.

When Dearnley was questioned again after the discovery of the body he changed his story. Now he said that he and Ellis had been playing a game of Cowboys and Indians and he had tied Ellis up. There was some evidence that the pair had quarrelled over a girl. Two days later Dearnley changed his story a third time. He had, he said, tied up Ellis and left him 'as a bit of a punishment for insulting my sweetheart'.

Named as the murderer by a coroner's jury, Dearnley was tried before Mr Justice Avory at Winchester Assizes. He was prosecuted by Rayner Goddard and defended by R.E. Dummett. Bernard Spilsbury gave evidence to the effect that when Ellis had tried to move he would have suffocated. There was no way he could have made a sound. Dearnley's evidence was that he had tied up Ellis and decided to leave him overnight. He went back the next morning and found he had gone. He presumed Ellis had freed himself and had then carried out his intention to desert. Unfortunately there was evidence that he had told the girl, 'You need not worry any more about Ellis, he is dead, and he is not a mile from here.'

Dearnley was reprieved the night before his execution. Spilsbury had made it clear that Ellis was a masochist and liked being tied. There was also some doubt about the girl's evidence. The death sentence was commuted to one of life imprisonment.

Douglas G. Browne and Tom Tullett, *Bernard Spilsbury, His Life and Cases*.

27 September, 1912

At lunchtime on 27 September 1912 Stephen Titus, aged 28, a native of Armenia, went into the Horseshoe Hotel, Tottenham Court Road, London and asked for a glass of bitter ale. He was served by Esther Towers, the barmaid, who said, 'Hello! You are quite a stranger.' Titus said, 'Yes.' She said, 'Why have you neglected us, have you been away?' He said, 'No.' He drank his beer and left, returning a few minutes later to buy cigarettes. He lit one, produced a revolver and shot Miss Towers dead. He then shot another barmaid in the shoulder and after that shot a customer, Thomas Johns, hitting him in the cheek, wrists and hands. Johns died on 22 October. On the way out he shot Charles Hook who had been at the hotel looking for a job.

John Starchfield, a newsvendor, saw Titus running away and firing. He saw Hook shot and then crossed Tottenham Court Road where he tackled Titus. He was shot through the intestines with the bullet penetrating the bowel five times.

Eventually Titus was brought down by a bath attendant, George Alfred Holding, who, when Titus was reloading, fought for the gun and eventually tripped him up. On 11 November 1912 Titus was found guilty but insane. He had refused to plead and was declared mute by malice. The judge hoped he would never be released. Holding and Starchfield received £50 each for brave conduct.

When Starchfield applied for further compensation the police report stated that it should not be given to his wife who might drink it away.

PRO/MEPO/3/227.

28 September, 1917

In 1912 Annie Birkett, a widow in her thirties with an 11-year-old son, Harry, was courted by Harry Crawford, the coachman to a doctor in Wahroonga, Sydney, Australia. It was not an ideal courtship so far as Mrs Birkett was concerned. Harry Crawford was uncouth and she was hoping for better things. There was, however, little opportunity for socialising and so she would go with him to local amateur dramatic performances and drive with him to town.

She was also a thrifty woman who wished to work her way out of the drudgery of being a cook-housekeeper. She saved her money and bought a sweet shop in the industrial suburb of Balmain. Crawford followed her and, three years later, began to live with her. Their relationship was not a success and although the business prospered, Crawford drank and did not work. He also produced a daughter from a previous marriage, the 16-year-old Josephine, who came to live with them. Annie Birkett decided to leave. She sold the shop and moved to Kogarah but Crawford followed. Later they moved together to a slightly smarter suburb, Drummoyne.

On 28 September 1917 Harry Birkett, Annie's son, went

to the beach for the day and, on his return, was surprised to find his mother had gone. Crawford reassured him. There had been a tiff and she had gone to stay with friends in North Sydney.

Soon afterwards Crawford sold the furniture, Josephine went to live in the city and he and Harry Birkett took lodgings in Woolloomooloo. Crawford's drinking habits continued and Harry was sent to live with his aunt who began to question him about his mother. Not satisfied with the boy's replies, she reported her sister missing. But, by now, Harry Crawford had disappeared. His landlady, in a device to get rid of him, had said detectives had called. Crawford had packed his bags.

Meanwhile, although so far unidentified, Annie Birkett's charred body had been found in Lane Cove. It would later be identified by a greenstone pendant still on the body and a dental plate. The search for Crawford continued, complicated enormously by the revelation by Josephine that Harry Crawford was not her father but her mother. The relationship with Mrs Birkett had been maintained by the use of a wooden phallus. Possibly the reason for the murder was the discovery by her of the truth. She had to be silenced to prevent disclosure. The police now feared that Crawford had switched sexes once more, making it almost impossible to trace him.

For two years Harry Crawford eluded them until he married again, this time at the register office in Canterbury. Some months afterwards Crawford was arrested – the 'marriage' had again been maintained by mechanical means – and at the trial the true story, or at any rate something approaching it, emerged.

Crawford had been born Eugénie Fellini (sometimes Falleni) in Florence, Italy on 25 July 1886. Her parents emigrated to New Zealand where, at the age of 16, she signed on as cabin boy of a trading barge in the Pacific Islands. On board was another Italian and by the end of the trip Fellini was pregnant. The daughter, Josephine, was boarded out and Fellini continued to find work as a man.

Crawford's defence at the trial at Darlinghurst Central Criminal Court in October 1920 was that there had been no quarrel with Annie Birkett and, so far as she knew, the woman was still alive. Crawford was found guilty, sentenced to death and reprieved. She served more than 10 years in prison until in 1931 she was released. Under the name of Mrs Ford she ran a boarding house in Paddington, an inner-city Sydney suburb. On 10 June 1938 she was knocked down by a car and fatally injured.

Tom Gurr and H. H. Cox, *Famous Australian Crimes*; Alan Sharpe, *Crimes that Shocked Australia*.

29 September, 1927

Dai Lewis, a former professional welterweight boxer, was stabbed to death on 29 September 1927 in St Mary Street, Cardiff, after falling foul of Edward and John Rowlands, brothers, who ran racecourse protection rackets. 'Tich' Lewis ran the 'chalk and water' concession, a smalltime protection racket at Monmouth races, and in doing so upset the brothers who regarded that unnecessary service as one which they and their followers alone would provide for the bookmakers.[1]

The day before he had been warned that the Rowlands brothers were not pleased with him and, despite a certain amount of bravado, he took the precaution of staying away from home that night and slept in an hotel in St Mary Street.

The next day was business as usual. He went back to

[1] Bookmakers at racecourses were obliged to buy chalk at an exorbitant price from their protectors. They were also obliged to allow a young boy to bring round a pail of water to wipe off the odds from the boards after a race. Refusal would undoubtedly result in a beating or possibly a slashing.

the races at Monmouth and in the evening back to St Mary Street and the Blue Anchor public house where he drank all evening, ignoring the Rowlands brothers and their friends, Daniel Driscoll, John Hughes and William Price.

He was set upon shortly after closing time outside the Blue Anchor. John Rowlands had previously warned Lewis about muscling in and he was the instigator of the attack, as he had been of many others. Lewis's throat was slashed in a wound seven and a quarter inches long and one and a quarter inches deep. As he lay dying on the pavement, 'prostitutes rushed to his aid, ripping off their petticoats in a desperate effort to staunch the flow of blood'. He was taken to the Royal Infirmary hospital where the police went to his bedside, waiting for him to name his attackers. It was whilst they were there that two calls came, inquiring after the state of Lewis. The second was traced to the Colonial Club in Custom House Street and there the police found the Rowlands brothers, Driscoll, Hughes and Price.

In the early hours of the morning a local magistrate and the clerk to the justices came to Lewis's bedside to take a dying declaration. Edward Rowlands and Daniel Driscoll were also brought to Lewis's bedside.

The boxer maintained the code of the Underworld. 'I do not know how I have been injured,' he said. 'I do not remember how it happened. There was no quarrel or fight. Nobody did any harm to me. I did not see anyone use a knife.'

Then he added to Eddie Rowlands, 'You had nothing to do with it. We've been the best of friends,' and to Daniel Driscoll, 'You had nothing to do with it either. We were talking and laughing together. My dear old pal.' To his wife he gave £3 5s 0d — what was left from his earnings at the races.

The funeral, on 5 October, was attended by up to 25,000 people who lined the streets as the cortège passed. A week later John Rowlands made the admission that he had stabbed the boxer. Lewis had, he said, attacked him with a knife, they had wrestled for it and Lewis was accidentally stabbed. Driscoll and Eddie Rowlands both said they had seen the fight but had made off, not anxious to be involved. At the magistrates' court John Hughes was discharged and the other men committed for trial at the Glamorgan Assizes.

At the trial the evidence was confused; witnesses were not able to agree on what had happened. Some said that John Rowlands had the knife as he approached Lewis but a police officer said Driscoll was holding Lewis whilst Edward struck him in the face.

Driscoll did not help himself. He called a patently false alibi which in turn cannot have helped his colleagues. Although Price was acquitted, the jury found Driscoll and the Rowlands brothers guilty after an hour's retirement.

The verdict was not well received. £600 was collected for an appeal and a petition mustered a quarter of a million signatures demanding that the Court of Appeal look at the verdict. The appeals were dismissed on 11 January 1928. On the way there, however, John Rowlands went berserk and, certified insane, was sent to Broadmoor where he died many years later.

A Harley Street doctor returned from a holiday in France to give his opinion that Lewis had died from a heart attack rather than from loss of blood. Three Cardiff doctors who attended the postmortem supported him.

The case had already been raised in the House of Commons and two members of the jury travelled to see T. P. O'Connor, the Father of the House, with a petition from eight members of the jury.

O'Connor managed to obtain an interview with the Home Secretary but this did not produce any result. 'No regard can be paid to expressions of opinion by individual members of a jury by which a prisoner has been convicted.'

The night before the execution Driscoll asked for a bottle of port and Eddie Rowlands told his family, 'I have told the truth all through. Don't forget me at eight o'clock tomorrow. They can break my neck but they can't break my heart.' Rowlands was apparently shaking and had to be helped when he went to the scaffold but, when confronted with the two nooses, Driscoll remarked, 'Which is mine?' Both maintained their innocence to the end and Driscoll's last words were said to be, 'Well, I'm going down for something I never done, but you don't have to pay twice.' Outside the prison a crowd of over five thousand gathered and sang hymns.

Ex-Detective Superintendent Power took the view that Driscoll had indeed tried to stop the fight and that if he had not given the false alibi he might well have been acquitted. As for Eddie Rowlands, the belief was that all he had intended was that Lewis should be marked rather than killed. The case became known in Cardiff as the Hoodoo murder. John Hughes died within 12 months and one of the prostitutes who had given evidence committed suicide by jumping from a second-floor window. One of the detective sergeants involved in the case committed suicide, two other officers died, one from tuberculosis and another from cancer, whilst a third died from a stomach complaint. All were relatively young men. In September 1928, Harold Lloyd, the solicitor who represented Price, was sentenced to five years' penal servitude for embezzling client monies.

James Morton, *Gangland 2*; D. Thomas with R. Grant, *Seek out the Guilty*.

30 September, 1994

The successful Newmarket racehorse trainer Alex Scott was shot dead by his stud groom, William 'Clem' O'Brien, on 30 September 1994. He was the youngest son of the Lord Lieutenant of Hampshire, married with three young children, and had charge of the 1995 Derby winner, Lammtarra as a two-year-old for the Maktoum family.

O'Brien was a groom on the Glebe Stud at Newmarket which Scott had bought two years previously. The prosecution alleged that O'Brien had been there for seven years and viewed the stud as his own. He was upset that he no longer had more or less absolute control over the day-to-day working and resented what he regarded as interference by Scott.

The pair frequently quarrelled and there had been a furious row when O'Brien had refused to allow blood-stock agents to see a yearling which was for sale. Scott complained that he had lost potential business and O'Brien replied with the taunt that Scott was 'fucking mad', a reference to the depression from which his employer had sometimes suffered. Scott sacked the groom who thought he would be allowed to work out his notice. When Scott arrived to help him clear out a barn next to his tied cottage, O'Brien shot him. He was seen by Robin Forster, one of the other workers. Forster's evidence was that O'Brien shot his employer, saying, 'This is for you, you bastard.'

O'Brien claimed that he had lost control when Scott called him 'a fucking Irish bastard' but he had not mentioned this in earlier interviews with the police. O'Brien, who said during the trial, 'I am deeply sorry for what occurred, but there is nothing I can do to put it right now,' was convicted of murder by a ten to two majority after a five-hour retirement by the jury. He was sentenced to life imprisonment.

Lammtarra won both the Derby and the King George VI and Queen Elizabeth Cup in 1995.

OCTOBER

1 October, 1993

The abduction of 12-year-old Polly Klass on 1 October 1993 from her own bedroom in Petaluma, a farming community some 45 miles north of San Francisco, whilst she was holding a pyjama party, brought a nationwide reaction. The news of her disappearance was spread worldwide and actress Winona Ryder, a native of Petaluma, offered a $20,000 reward. It led to the arrest of Richard Allen Davis whose palm print was allegedly found in Polly's room.

A man entered her bedroom at about 10.40 pm, asked which of three girls lived there and abducted Polly at knifepoint. The others were left bound and gagged. At 11.42 pm a woman called the sherriff's office to report a trespasser east of Santa Rosa, some 20 miles north of Petaluma. The police responded to the call and found Davis whose car was stuck in a ditch. His car was searched but nothing suspicious was found. At the time those searching it did not know of the kidnapping of Polly.

On 30 November Davis was arrested on a charge of driving under the influence and, it is alleged, confessed to the murder. It is said he led the police to Polly's body which was found on 4 December. She had been strangled.

Davis's trial was scheduled to begin in July 1994 but

the trial judge decided it would be impossible to select an impartial jury in Sonoma County. The case went to Santa Clara County where in February 1996 the judge began jury selection. The trial was scheduled to begin in April and was expected to last up to five months. During jury selection Polly's relatives were ordered to remove buttons, bearing Polly's smiling face, which they were wearing in memory of the girl outside the courtroom.

A Polly Klass Foundation was set up to assist in finding missing children and her death led in a substantial part to the 'three strikes and you're out' law under which repeat offenders face mandatory sentences.

On 5 August 1996, Davis was sentenced to death by the jury which took 21 hours to come to its decision.

2 October, 1973

At lunchtime on 2 October 1973 Albert Taylor called on his girlfriend Gillian Seston's home in Mountsteven Avenue, Peterborough, Northamptonshire to tell her about an interview he had attended for a job. He found her sister, 15-year-old Jackie, stabbed to death and with a dog lead around her throat. She had 17 stab wounds and had been sexually assaulted.

Instead of calling the police he panicked and ran, caught a bus and went back to his room at the Great Northern Hotel in Peterborough. He noticed he had blood on his trousers from the time he had knelt by the body to see if Jackie was alive and took them to the cleaners. He then met Gillian as she left the local technical college but did not tell her of the murder. She went to another class and Taylor went to her home. The police had already arrived.

His alibi at the trial was that he had been on Peterborough railway station buying a newspaper at 1.15 pm.

Then he went for his interview which lasted half an hour
and then he went to the Sestons' house. He said he knew
it was 1.15 pm when he was at the station because
of the peculiar ticking noise of the station clock. The
prosecution, however, called evidence to show that the
clock was electric and did not tick.

After his conviction, for which he was sentenced to
life imprisonment, Taylor complained about the police
handling of the case and Detective Chief Superintendent
Peter Crust of the Essex police was appointed to head
an investigation. He traced the clock which had been
removed when the station was modernised and found
that it did tick but only in cold weather and then at
certain times of the day. It would have ticked at 1.15
pm on the day of the murder.

Taylor explained the reasons why he had not told his
girlfriend of the death of her sister by saying that he
thought he had imagined it. As to the cleaning he said
if he had killed Jackie he would have burned his clothes
and anyway there was blood on his coat which he had
not had cleaned. So far as running away from the scene
of the crime was concerned, he said both that he had had
trouble with the police before and that as a child he had
seen a cyclist killed under a bus. As a result he could not
stand the sight of blood.

Giving judgment on 13 April 1979 Lord Justice Lawton
said:

> We have changed from side to side and we con-
> sidered it outside the court for a very longish
> period. But we have borne in mind that in a case
> where we have wavered from time to time there
> is some indication that there may well be some
> doubt. Certainly two of us are not all that clear
> about where the real truth is. The doubt in this
> case has been almost impossible to find but at the
> end of the day it is there.

Taylor had served five years and five months of his

sentence, hoping he would win back his girlfriend's
love after he was freed. Meanwhile Gillian Seston had
married someone else and told the newspapers she did
not wish to see Taylor again. He changed his appearance
and advertised in his local paper for a new girlfriend. He
received £12,000 compensation.

On 23 May 1980 Taylor tried to rescue Donna, the
four-year-old daughter of his common-law wife, when
a fire swept their home at Bancroft, Tamworth. Their
three-month-old baby was saved when Taylor caught the
child, thrown from a window. He was taken to hospital
with serious injuries received after he had returned to
the house.

3 October, 1995

In March 1996 14-year-old Lauren Stoetzer pleaded guilty
to assisting Michael Est, another 14-year-old, to kill his
father, Thomas, at their home in High Ridge, St Louis,
Kentucky.

The children had apparently known each other only for
a few weeks when they began practising shooting, with Est
senior's pistol, into books, with a stereo system turned on
high to drown out the noise. On the day of the shooting
Stoetzer had smoked marijuana and again the stereo had
been turned on high, this time to attract the attention
of Thomas Est and bring him inside the house. There,
according to the prosecution, on 3 October 1995 he was
shot once in the back of the head and three times in the
chest by Michael Est with a 9 mm handgun. The pair
then took some cash and a truck and drove to Oklahoma
where they were arrested.

Had Lauren Stoetzer been charged a few months earlier
she would have been released by the time she was sixteen.
As it was she was tried as an adult and on 22 July 1996

received 24 years in prison. Earlier in the day, in another case, Circuit Judge Gary P. Kramer had sentenced a girl who killed her mother when she was fourteen to thirty years. Kimberley Depew had pleaded no contest.

4 October, 1922

There is no doubt that Frederick Bywaters intended to kill Percy, the husband of his mistress, Edith Jessie Thompson. What is certainly not as clear-cut is the part she played when her husband was stabbed to death as he walked along Belgrave Road, Ilford in the early minutes of 4 October 1922.

The Thompson marriage had not been a happy one, with the attractive and vivacious Mrs Thompson smothered by her husband's behaviour. According to her, at best he was pernickety and at worst a wife-abuser. He was 32, she four years younger and Bywaters only 20.

She was a great romantic and fantasist. Bywaters, a steward on the P & O liner, *Morea*, had known Edith when he was at school with her brothers and in 1921 he took lodgings with the Thompsons. She fell passionately in love with the younger man, writing him a series of ardent letters which were to become her death sentence. Because of his job Bywaters was abroad for lengthy periods and the letters Edith Thompson wrote him whilst he was away were to become a pivot of the prosecution's case at her trial. She destroyed his letters and it is even possible that he kept hers with a view to blackmailing her at a later date.

On his last leave the pair met in a café in Aldersgate Street on 3 October 1922. That night she went with her husband to the Criterion Theatre. As they reached home Bywaters attacked and stabbed Percy Thompson. She was heard to cry, 'Oh, don't, oh don't', and ran to help her husband. When a doctor arrived she complained he had not come soon enough to save her husband. Both were arrested and taken to the police station where, when she saw Bywaters by chance, she called out, 'Oh, God, what can I do? Why did he do it? I did not want him to do it.' She continually denied that she had known Bywaters's intentions. Unfortunately, in the past she had written in one of the letters to him that she had tried to poison her husband on three occasions by giving him powdered glass. When Sir Bernard Spilsbury examined Thompson's body he found no trace of poison or of the powdered light bulbs of which she had written.

Mrs Thompson gave evidence, much against the advice of her counsel Sir Derek Curtis-Bennett. The judge, Mr Justice Shearman, was wholly against her – he ruled the letters to be admissible – and she made a terrible witness. Both she and Bywaters were condemned to death. Any reprieve for which she may have hoped was dismissed by the Home Secretary. Two things counted against her: first the outcry there had been over the recent reprieve of Robert True, from a wealthy family, for the murder of prostitute Olive Young, and also because of a newspaper campaign which suggested that she had led a younger and weak-willed man astray.

It is now generally accepted that Edith Thompson should not have been convicted on the evidence before the court but that she was tried and convicted for what was seen to be her lack of morals.

Both were hanged on 9 January 1932, he at Pentonville and she at Holloway. It is possible that she was pregnant but no examination of her by a jury of matrons took place.

Douglas G. Browne and Tom Tullett, *Bernard Spilsbury, His Life and Cases*; Frederick Porter Wensley, *Detective Days*.

5 October, 1949

On 5 October 1949 the body of Stanley Setty, brother of Max who ran the fashionable Blue Angel nightclub in Berkeley Street, Mayfair, was dumped from an aeroplane into the Essex marshes. Known as a banker for the black market and born Sulman Seti in Baghdad, he ran his business from the pavement around Warren Street, then home to the London secondhand car trade and all sorts of dishonest dealing.

On 4 October he had drawn £1,005 from his bank to pay for a car. On the next afternoon Brian Donald Hume, a 29-year-old pilot, hired an Auster from the United Flying Services Club at Elstree, flew over the Essex coast and dropped two parcels. He landed at Southend aerodrome and rented a car to bring him back to his flat in Golders Green. The next day he returned to Southend from where he flew the plane over Gravesend and dumped another parcel wrapped in felt and tied with twine. Unfortunately, his calculations were wrong. He thought the parcels had been dropped far enough out to sea; instead, on 22 October, at Tillingham on the Essex marshes, one of the parcels, brought in by the tide, was recovered by a wildfowler, Sidney Tiffen.

When he unwrapped it, there in pale blue silk underpants and with a cream silk shirt but without head or legs, was much of Stanley Setty. A postmortem showed the head had been cut off with a sharp instrument and the thigh bones sawed through. Setty had been killed with five stab wounds in the chest. He was identified though his fingerprints; he had a conviction for fraud.

It was not too difficult to trace Hume through the Flying Club and he was questioned on 26 October. The interview culminated in Hume saying, 'I'm several kinds of bastard, aren't I?'

He then told a story about how he had agreed with

two men, 'Mac' and Green, to pilot an aeroplane for them on a smuggling trip. On 5 October they had called at his home with parcels containing what they said were 'hot' plates used for forging clothing coupons. He agreed, for a fee of £50, to fly them out to sea and drop them. After the first flight, on his return to Golders Green, he found them, along with a third man called 'Boy', waiting outside his flat and he agreed to drop the third parcel for another £100.

He put this third parcel in the kitchen cupboard and on the way down heard a gurgling from the parcel. He thought it might be a body inside and, possibly, even that of Setty of whose disappearance he had heard. That was something he denied at the trial, saying it had been put in later. As for the men, Green wore a green suit and might have been Greek or Cypriot. Mac was tall and fair, in his thirties, and Boy, who wore steel-rimmed spectacles, had subsequently telephoned him to warn him to say nothing.

Hume was charged with murder. His first trial aborted when, after some 20 witnesses had been called, Mr Justice Lewis became ill and the trial was restarted before Mr Justice Sellers.

The evidence against Hume was formidable. Notes which Setty had drawn from the bank were traced to him. He had taken a carpet to be cleaned on the morning of 5 October and a garage hand identified a knife which Hume had asked him to sharpen on that morning. For the defence it was argued that there was not a single fingerprint of Setty's in Hume's flat, nor had any neighbour heard suspicious noises on the night of 4 October or the next morning. The prosecution maintained that Setty had been killed in Hume's flat and that was where the dismemberment had taken place. 'It is impossible to go on dictating to one's secretary if human bones are being sawn through in the vicinity,' said the pathologist Dr Francis Camps. There was therefore every reason for the jury to disagree, particularly in those days when there was neither the majority decision available to them nor was it the custom to leave jurors locked in a war of attrition for days on end.

Although a second jury was sworn the prosecution had some reluctance to have the man on a capital charge the second time. He pleaded to being an accessory after the fact. Hume confidently expected a short sentence and was not pleased with the 12 years handed to him.

He was released in 1958 and immediately sold his story, 'I killed Setty . . . and got away with murder', to the *Sunday Pictorial* for the sum of £2,000. He had, apparently, stabbed him with a knife in a quarrel. During his time in prison Hume's wife, who had given evidence for her husband, had married Duncan Webb, the maverick reporter for *The People*, who did so much to bring down the Messina vice gang.

Hume continued his winning ways. In the later part of 1958 the police wished to speak to Donald Brown, to which Hume had changed his name, in connection with the shooting of a bank cashier in August and another in November. Both victims had survived. In January 1959 he shot and killed a taxi driver who tried to prevent his escape from a bank raid in Zurich. He was sentenced to life imprisonment, after which the President of the Court declared: 'Life imprisonment for this kind of man means for life. He will never be let out of jail – not this one.'

But eventually he was returned to England and subsequently released.

Rupert Furneaux, *Famous Criminal Cases* 6.

6 October, 1985

On 6 October 1985, PC Keith Blakelock was hacked to death during a riot on the Broadwater Estate, Tottenham, London. His death arose from an incident the previous

day when officers had searched the premises of a Mrs
Cynthia Jarrett, looking for her son, Floyd. She had
suffered a heart attack and had died. There had been a
series of difficulties between the police and ethnic minority
communities both in and out of London in the preceding
weeks and at the least a demonstration that weekend, if
not more serious trouble, was expected.

There was a large police presence in the area and a
substantial presence of local youths. Fighting took place
between 7 and 10.30 pm. A number of shots were
fired and pavement slabs were torn up and thrown,
as were petrol bombs. A supermarket was set on fire.
One witness estimated that in less than five minutes
more than fifty petrol bombs were made on the streets.
Forty-seven wrecked cars were later towed away. Two
fire officers believed that the fire from the supermarket
might spread to nearby flats and tried to get near the
building to discover the extent of the danger. They were
beaten back by a crowd of youths throwing bottles and
were later escorted by police officers to the building where
they all came under a renewed and more violent attack.
They then made a run for safety, chased by the youths.
During the chase PC Blakelock tripped and sustained 40
wounds caused by knives or other weapons. His head was
nearly severed from his body and there was a knife driven
nearly six inches into his neck.

Reports of the fighting were necessarily confused and
at one time local councillor, Bernie Grant, even suggested
that PC Blakelock's death might have been caused by
another police officer.

Over three hundred people were arrested in the course
of the enquiries and three, Winston Emanuel Silcott, Mark
Braithwaite and Engin Raghip, were convicted of murder
and riot on 19 March 1987. Primarily, the evidence
against them consisted of their confessions which, said
the police, had been contemporaneously recorded. In
December 1991 Silcott's conviction was quashed when
the Court of Appeal heard evidence that the Crown
accepted the evidence of expert witnesses who showed his

confessions had not been contemporaneously recorded. Raghip and Braithwaite's convictions were also quashed when the court heard that, because of their low intellectual capacities, the lengthy questioning they underwent could have produced unreliable answers.

The police reopened enquiries into the killing of PC Blakelock but no further charges have yet been brought.

Lord Gifford, *The Broadwater Farm Inquiry*.

7 October, 1944

Although the criminal career of 18-year-old Elizabeth Maud Jones lasted less than a week, by the end of it she was fortunate to escape the hangman. She was convicted, along with Karl Gustav Hulten, of the murder of a taxi driver, George Edward Heath. Hulten, then aged 22, a Swedish-American deserter from the parachute regiment of the US forces in Britain, met her in a café in October 1944. He was posing as Lieutenant Ricky Hulten and she as an actress. In reality she was working as a striptease artiste under the name of Georgina Grayson and lived in a room in King Street, Hammersmith, near the Broadway. He fancied himself as a gangster and she as a moll. Together they set out on a nightly campaign of robbery, attacking pedestrians and cyclists. One woman, hit repeatedly with an iron bar, was then nearly strangled and thrown in the nearby Thames.

Their reign of terror in west London was shortlived. On 7 October 1944, four days after their meeting, they hailed a cab driven by Heath and during the journey Hulten shot him. The proceeds of the robbery – of which Jones said:

I knew the meaning . . . he wanted me to go with

>   him to rob a taxi driver . . . I saw a flash and heard
>   a bang. I was surprised that there was not a loud
>   bang because Ricky had told me it would make a
>   big noise.

– yielded nineteen shillings, a silver pencil and a cigarette case.

The pair drove on to Staines where they dumped the
body in a ditch. Despite the fact that the body was found
the next morning and a description of the missing Ford
V8 cab circulated, Hulten and Jones continued to drive
around for a further three days until on 10 October
Hulten was arrested in the Fulham Palace Road with the
gun and ammunition still in his pocket.

Jones did not last long on the outside. Speaking to a
policeman friend who had commented that she looked
pale, she said, 'If you had seen someone do what I
have seen done you wouldn't be able to sleep at night.'
They were both sentenced to death – with the jury
recommending mercy for Jones – on 6 January 1945
after a trial lasting six days at the Central Criminal Court.
Despite strong representations by the American Ambassa-
dor who visited the Home Secretary, Lord Morrison, and
spent an hour arguing for a reprieve, Hulten was hanged
by Albert Pierrepoint on 8 March. Jones was reprieved on
the grounds of her youth, a decision apparently regretted
by Sir Winston Churchill, and released from prison in
May 1954. In 1992 a film starring Kiefer Sutherland
and Emily Lloyd was made about the case which had
become known as the Cleft Chin Murder, a reference to
the taxi driver.

Fenton Bresler, *Reprieve*.

8 October, 1923

On 8 October 1923 Angus Murray and Richard Buckley robbed Thomas Berriman as he left the Commercial Bank at Glenferrie railway station, Hawthorn, Australia, carrying a briefcase containing A£1,851. Murray was a prison escapee whilst serving a sentence for armed robbery and both worked for the driver of the getaway car, Leslie (known as Squizzy) Taylor. Buckley had a long record of violence and was on parole at the time of the robbery.

Berriman refused to hand over his bag and was shot by Buckley. He died two weeks later from blood poisoning. On 10 October police, acting on a tip-off that men had been seen burning a briefcase in a yard in St Kilda's, one of the loucher suburbs of Melbourne, arrested Murray and Taylor. Murray was identified as being with Buckley and Squizzy Taylor as the driver. At the trial, completely against the odds, Taylor was acquitted. Although it was accepted that Murray did not fire the fatal shot, he was sentenced to death. Of Buckley there was no trace.

Taylor did at least have the courtesy to try to assist his former employee. He attempted to organise one more prison break which failed when the warder who was to be bribed told the police who, in turn, seized a car outside the prison, arrested the four men in it and confiscated a rope ladder. All four, together with Taylor, were subsequently acquitted of conspiracy.

Murray was hanged on 14 April 1924 in Melbourne jail. He is reported to have said from the scaffold, 'Never in my life have I done anything to justify the penalty passed on me. I have tried to forgive those who have acted against me and I hope those I have injured will forgive me.' Quite often Australian criminals of those days tended to be reported as making speeches of a similar nature at their execution. When the noose was put over his head he is said to have added, 'Pull it tight.'

two men, 'Mac' and Green, to pilot an aeroplane for them on a smuggling trip. On 5 October they had called at his home with parcels containing what they said were 'hot' plates used for forging clothing coupons. He agreed, for a fee of £50, to fly them out to sea and drop them. After the first flight, on his return to Golders Green, he found them, along with a third man called 'Boy', waiting outside his flat and he agreed to drop the third parcel for another £100.

He put this third parcel in the kitchen cupboard and on the way down heard a gurgling from the parcel. He thought it might be a body inside and, possibly, even that of Setty of whose disappearance he had heard. That was something he denied at the trial, saying it had been put in later. As for the men, Green wore a green suit and might have been Greek or Cypriot. Mac was tall and fair, in his thirties, and Boy, who wore steel-rimmed spectacles, had subsequently telephoned him to warn him to say nothing.

Hume was charged with murder. His first trial aborted when, after some 20 witnesses had been called, Mr Justice Lewis became ill and the trial was restarted before Mr Justice Sellers.

The evidence against Hume was formidable. Notes which Setty had drawn from the bank were traced to him. He had taken a carpet to be cleaned on the morning of 5 October and a garage hand identified a knife which Hume had asked him to sharpen on that morning. For the defence it was argued that there was not a single fingerprint of Setty's in Hume's flat, nor had any neighbour heard suspicious noises on the night of 4 October or the next morning. The prosecution maintained that Setty had been killed in Hume's flat and that was where the dismemberment had taken place. 'It is impossible to go on dictating to one's secretary if human bones are being sawn through in the vicinity,' said the pathologist Dr Francis Camps. There was therefore every reason for the jury to disagree, particularly in those days when there was neither the majority decision available to find the gun before the police did. She took Power to the beach and when they had dug the gun from the shingle the police arrested her and, so it seemed to her, Power. Power was then used to persuade her that the only way to save herself was to betray Williams and eventually she made a statement that he had confessed to her. She made a pitiable figure in the witness box when, realising how she had been tricked, she withdrew her statement. Of Power, Sir Patrick Hastings who defended Williams wrote, 'Never in my life have I met a more utterly contemptible human being.'

Before Williams was hanged Seymour was allowed to take her newly born child to see him. Williams is said to have pressed a piece of bread into the child's hand saying, 'Now nobody can ever say your father has never given you anything.'

Sir Patrick Hastings, *Cases in Court*.

10 October, 1949

About 9 pm on 10 October 1949 Leopold and Esther Goodman went to see their daughter in the Muswell Hill Maternity Home, north London. Married to a successful advertising agent, 23-year-old Daniel Raven who went with them, she had given birth four days earlier.

Leopold Goodman was a businessman with dubious connections who kept large amounts of cash and valuables in his house in Ashcombe Gardens, Edgware. He was involved in the black-market and had been burgled in the past. Now he feared another attack, possibly instigated by his rivals. Raven drove the middle-aged couple home and offered to stay the night. They said there was no need and he then drove to his home, bought for him and his wife by the Goodmans, about five hundred yards away.

At 10 pm another relative, Frederick Fraiman, called

and, failing to get a reply at the front door, climbed in through an open window. The bodies of the Goodmans were in the dining room. Both had been beaten to death with a television aerial base. Curiously, there was no sign of a break-in. A pile of banknotes was visible and untouched as well as another pile under the mattress in the bedroom.

Raven was told of the deaths by the police and in a smart suit and clean shirt went round to their house where he sat sobbing, 'Why did they tell me to go? Why didn't they let me stop?' It cannot have been a convincing performance. He was arrested immediately and taken to Edgware police station.

Once the police learned that Raven had been wearing a blue suit earlier in the evening they searched his house. In the boiler was part of a bloodstained blue suit. In the garage was a recently washed pair of shoes and although he had washed the upholstery of his car it was still damp. All contained traces of blood which could be matched with the Goodmans.

At first he could not explain the bloodstains but later said that he had in fact been back to the Goodman home and found his parents-in-law dead. It was when he knelt by the bodies, he said, that he got the bloodstains. He had fled in panic.

No motive was ever established for the murders and at the trial it was argued that the killing was done by Goodman's business enemies. The defence was not successful. Raven was hanged on 6 January 1950.

11 October, 1923

On 11 October 1923 the d'Autremont brothers, twins Roy and Ray, and Hugh, attempted to rob the Southern Pacific railroad mail train, killing four people in the process. Whilst the train was moving slowly through the Siskiyou mountains in Oregon two men climbed on the tender and ordered the driver to halt as soon as the mail car had cleared the tunnel. A third man then dynamited the mail car. The mail was destroyed and the mail clerk was burned alive. The robbers then shot to death the driver, a fireman and the guard. Although posses were set up to try to track down the robbers they failed.

The only evidence left by the trackside was a detonator with batteries, a revolver, a pair of denim overalls, apparently covered in grease, and some shoe covers soaked in creosote. This would thwart any tracker dogs.

A garage mechanic who worked near the tunnel was arrested. The police sent his clothing and the other exhibits to Edward O. Heinrich, a lecturer in criminology at the University of California. His previous work had included the Black Tom explosion in 1916 and he had given evidence in the rape case brought against Roscoe 'Fatty' Arbuckle. His first act was to say that the marks on the overalls were not car grease but pitch from fir trees and the mechanic should therefore be released. He then gave the detectives a profile of the wearer of the overalls. He described him as being a thin, light-brown-haired, left-handed lumberjack who had worked on the Pacific coast. The man was fussy about his appearence, five feet ten inches tall and rolled his own cigarettes. In true Sherlock Holmes fashion the explanation was easy. There were Douglas fir needles common to Pacific Northwest forests attached to the overalls; they had been regularly buttoned from the left, suggesting a left-hander; there were fingernail clippings which suggested a fastidious nature; a light brown hair was attached to a button. There was, however, one more crucial piece of evidence which Heinrich was able to extract. In the hem of a trouser pocket was a wad of paper. It had been washed repeatedly but Heinrich was able to identify it as a registered mail receipt and its number. It belonged to Roy d'Autremont of Eugene, Oregon. The investigators went to see his father.

Enquiries showed that he was unhappy about the disappearance of his sons who had vanished on the day of the
attempted robbery. Roy was known to be neat and tidy,
was indeed left-handed and rolled his own tobacco.

There followed one of the greatest manhunts in American
history and, over three years later, Hugh d'Autremont was
found in Manila. The twins were working, under the name
of Goodwin, in a steel mill in Steubenville. All were given
life imprisonment.

Heinrich, born in 1881, died at the age of 72.

Carl Sifakis, *The Encyclopedia of American Crime*.

12 October, 1962

In what was believed to be the first capital murder
case in which two juries disagreed – on 12 February
and again on 6 March – 19-year-old Robert Reed was
eventually acquitted on 9 March 1963 of the Holy Lady
of Clerkenwell murder when the prosecution offered no
evidence.

The allegation was that Reed had robbed and battered
to death 73-year-old Annie Mary O'Donnell in her rosary
shop in Victoria Dwellings, Clerkenwell Road, London
in the early evening of 12 October 1962. The murderer
had stolen probably less than £5 and had missed nearly
£600 kept in a body belt. Miss O'Donnell had been to
Mass earlier in the evening and had probably been killed
during the tolling of a church bell at about 7.50 pm.

At an identification parade Reed had been picked out by
one witness who had known him as a boy. His fingerprints
were found on a Catholic newspaper and on a piece of
glazed paper in the shop. The witness said he had seen
Reed outside the shop mopping his face shortly before
8 pm. When questioned Reed denied involvement and

told the police he had been off work with an injury to his thumb.

He told the jury that he had been to the shop a few days previously to buy a St Christopher medallion for the baby his 17-year-old wife was expecting. Asked if he was short of money he said, 'Not by a long shot', adding he had about £37 in savings. His defence was an alibi saying he had been with his wife, mother, father and grandmother at home before going out to a club.

13 October, 1987

In December 1989 Michael Lee Lockhart, 29, originally from Toledo, Ohio, was given his third death penalty sentence in as many States when he pleaded guilty to the murder of a 14-year-old girl in Land O'Lakes, Florida.

Lockhart had begun his killing spree when on 13 October 1987 16-year-old Windy Gallagher was found bound and gagged and stabbed 21 times at her home in Griffith, Indiana. Lockhart's fingerprints were found in the flat where she lived with her mother and younger sister.

Three months later, on 20 January 1988, 14-year-old Jennifer Colauer was also stabbed to death in her Land O'Lakes home. Her nine-year-old brother returned home to find his sister had been mutilated and sexually assaulted. Lockhart had been seen near the flat earlier in the afternoon.

On 20 March 1988 he was captured in a stolen red sports car after shooting and killing a Texas policeman. After his arrest he told the police that he had killed between 20 and 30 people in a 30,000-mile rampage during which he had stolen guns and cars in Ohio, attacked his former wife, committed robberies in Wyoming, Louisiana and Missouri, as well as killing Windy and Jennifer.

By the time he came to face the Florida jury he had already received the death sentence in Indiana and Texas. This third trial was, said Assistant State Attorney Allen Allweiss, an insurance policy in case he escaped the death penalty in the other States. Lockhart, acting on his own, said he did not want a trial so he could spare the Colauer family grief but the trial judge, Maynard F. Swanson, refused to sentence him to death without a jury's recommendation.

> 'I'm not going to stand before you and make excuses for myself,' he told the jury. 'I believe in God. The one last thing I can do in this world is accept responsibility for what I have done.'

After the sentence was imposed he was taken back to Texas. Lockhart was then also the only suspect for killing a 12-year-old girl in Las Vegas, Nevada.

14 October, 1995

Four days after the death of teenager Tanya Smith in Abbotsford, British Columbia, the raspberry capital of Canada, her killer began making a series of telephone calls to the police.

In the early hours of 14 October 1995, 16-year-old Tanya and her friend Misty Cockerill were dropped off a few blocks from Tanya's home after attending a party together. A neighbour later told the police that she had seen a man struggling with what she thought were two drunken teenagers but since she could hear little by way of protest she thought they all knew each other and it was a bit of horseplay.

Later that morning Tanya's naked body was found by

a fisherman in the Vedder River, some 10 miles away. She had been severely beaten and drowned. Misty Cockerill was more fortunate. She managed to get herself to hospital where it was found that she had a fist-sized hole in her skull. Their attacker was almost certainly a man with a receding hairline about six feet tall.

Shortly after three o'clock on the afternoon of 18 October Tanya Smith's killer made his first call to the police. 'I'm the killer,' he said. 'Are you having trouble finding the killer? .... I'm the one ... giving you the chance to try and find me. I'll be scurrying around looking for someone else.' The call was taped and traced but by the time the police arrived the caller had fled. Edited tapes of this and other calls were released in the hope that someone in the 105,000-strong community would be able to identify the voice.

Twenty minutes later the caller was back on the telephone asking if the police thought he would be foolish enough to leave fingerprints behind when he made a phone call. Three hours later he telephoned again, this time threatening to strike once more.

On 31 October he called from outside a bar. A waitress recalled seeing a man who had asked for a telephone. She had told him that there was a freephone but he declined to use it and made his call from the parking area.

On 1 December a man who fitted the identikit drawing of the attacker was arrested. He was not released until 26 January 1996 when DNA evidence cleared him.

On 6 February the police, possibly as a bait, issued a statement saying that they believed the man had left the area. On 17 February Tanya Smith's gravestone was stolen in the middle of the afternoon. The local radio station received a telephone call telling a producer to check what was in the parking lot. There was the gravestone. Over Tanya's picture someone had scraped threats. 'I'm still out there. I'm the one.'

Two days later another call was received from a payphone two blocks from the police station. Shortly after that a note wrapped around a wrench was thrown

through the window of a family unconnected to the case.
It led the police to believe the man would strike again.

15 October, 1934

> This is the queerest murder case I have seen and
> although it sounds ridiculous I doubt whether it
> was murder at all. I should have liked another,
> or indeed several other medical opinions so as to
> be quite convinced that this odd, odd man could
> not have done it himself. The extraordinary lack of
> noise is very striking . . .

So said the coroner investigating the death of Horace
Butcher who was found dead on 15 October 1934.

The 50-year-old eccentric marine store dealer – each
night he set the table for himself and his brother who
had died six years previously – was found at his home
at 151 Middlegate Street, Great Yarmouth, Norfolk. He
was lying in a reclining position on his right side on the
couch. His feet were touching the floor. There were a
number of wounds to the head, including a bruise to
the left eye. There had been considerable bleeding. His
arms were crossed and his hands bloodstained. He was
fully dressed and it appeared that he might have urinated
into his trousers which were wet. There was no evidence
of a struggle. A damaged weight, variously described as
between seven and 14 pounds, was found either in the
hallway near the living room or by the couch. The
police officers who went to the scene of the crime were
at variance with each other.

Suspicion fell on a local man who was reputed to
have said somewhat enigmatically, 'Yes, Mr Tuttle [the
officer] came down to where I am lodging and took a

lot of particulars and I expect they will soon say I did the murder. I have known Mr Butcher a long time and could go over his place in the dark.' At first the man said he had been drinking in a public house but then denied he had been out during the evening. 'If anyone says I left the house where I live after 10.30 pm on 15 October they are telling infernal lies.'

A Toni Siani, also known as Alfred Peachey, claimed he killed Butcher. He was interviewed in Durham prison where he was serving a sentence for store breaking and larceny but the officers were satisfied his confession was untrue.

Despite the view of Dr Aldington, the police surgeon, there were many local people and police officers who agreed with the coroner that the wounds were self-inflicted.

MEPO/792.

16 October, 1953

John Harries, a 63-year-old Welsh farmer, and his wife Phoebe were last seen on 16 October 1953 by one of their neighbours, William Morris, who had tea with them at Llanginning, Carmarthenshire. Whilst he was there the Harries's nephew, Ronald, called in and was still there when Morris left.

Another neighbour, Ronald James, called the next morning and found the place empty with the cows unmilked. Ronald Harries, who lived nearby, told neighbours his uncle and aunt had gone to London for a few days' holiday. Later he told the police he had driven them into Carmarthen on the previous Saturday to get the train to London. It was to be a secret kept from the neighbours. They had stopped to buy some things and then went to the station. They had given him the use of their car and paid him to look after the farm whilst they were away. It was not an unreasonable story. He was known to be a favourite nephew. Indeed he was a well-liked man in the community, always ready to help out. No one, however, could recall the trip, either at the station or in the shop. Harries had also told a friend that he had bought the A40 car.

Further enquiries showed that Harries had now moved his aunt and uncle's cattle to his father's farm at Cadno Pendine. It was discovered he was in debt to the tune of £300. A search of the farm proved negative and the local police called in Scotland Yard. Detective Superintendent John Capstick was sent to Wales. Harries's story remained constant. He said he had left before Morris, returned to collect his aunt and uncle the next day and then had driven back to milk the cows. Capstick questioned him about a cheque for £909 made out to Harries's father by his uncle and endorsed into his, Ronald's, own account. It had been dishonoured as there was ony £123 in John Harries's account at the time. Closer inspection showed the cheque to be a forgery. The original amount had been £9 0s 9d.

A check on Harries's movements showed a gap of an hour and a half on the evening of 16 October. Despite further searches no bodies were forthcoming. The local gossip was that they had been placed in sinking sands near Pendine but Capstick, known as Charlie Artful for his cunning, devised a scheme which he hoped would flush Harries into the open. He and his detective sergeant drove to Harries's parents' farm at Cadno and spent a profitable half hour tying thread on the gates. As they left they saw a light come on in Ronald Harries's bedroom. Next morning a check showed that the thread on one gate, that leading to a field of kale, had been broken. An examination of the field showed that one row of kale was yellower in colour than the remainder and not as well grown. It seemed it had been dug up and replanted. The bodies of John and Phoebe Harries were discovered and medical evidence showed they had been killed with blows to the head, probably with a hammer.

Charged with murder, Harries repeated his story. His clothing was sent for forensic examination and blood on the lapel and lining indicated he had been wearing it when he dug the field of kale. A hammer was later found hidden in a hedge. Harries claimed he had lost it. His defence at the trial was unconvincing and he made wild allegations about the witnesses, saying the real murderers had dumped the bodies to throw suspicion on him. It seems he genuinely thought he would be acquitted and asked his parents to arrange a celebration party for him. He was hanged at Swansea on 28 April 1954.

John Capstick, *Given in Evidence*.

17 October, 1977

The so-called Hillside Strangler was, in fact, two cousins, Kenneth Bianchi, then aged 25 and by far the more intelligent, and the almost subnormal and considerably older Angelo Buono Junior, then aged 42. In 1977 Bianchi, who had been raised by foster parents, went to Los Angeles to stay with his cousin who ran an upholstery business from his garage.

On 17 October 1977 they killed 19-year-old Yolanda Washington and left her naked body in the grounds of the Forest Lawn cemetery where it was found the next day. It had been throughly cleaned by the pair. They had begun their spree of killing women, who were often semi-professional prostitutes, with Elissa Teresa Kastin just under a fortnight earlier, on 6 October. After Yolanda Washington, their next victim was 15-year-old Judith Miller, found raped, sodomised and strangled on 31 October. There were three victims on 20 November and another on 23 November. Three more girls were murdered by them over the next three months. Then, as the police said they believed they were closing in on the Strangler, the killings stopped. The reason was that Bianchi, tired of the poor conditions in which his cousin lived, moved up to Washington. There he raped and killed two college girls and was caught because he had been seen with one of them shortly before she disappeared.

Bianchi was clever enough to strike a plea bargain. In return for giving evidence against his cousin who, he said, was the real Strangler, he would not only escape the death penalty but would be allowed to serve his sentence in a Californian prison where the regime would be less severe than in Washington. He then proceeded to fool a series of psychiatrists into believing that he had a multiple personality and so could not testify against his cousin.

Buono was tried two years later in November 1981 and convicted two years after that on 14 November 1983. Much of the time had been taken up with the disruptive behaviour of Bianchi. He gave evidence that he was completely innocent. Buono was sentenced to life imprisonment without the possibility of parole. Bianchi was regarded as having broken the terms of his plea bargain and consequently was sent to the harsh Walla Walla prison in Washington to serve a life sentence without the possibility of parole until 2005. The judge, Ronald George, sentencing them said, 'I'm sure, Mr Buono and Mr Bianchi, that you will only get your thrills by reliving over and over again the tortures and murders of your victims, being incapable, as I believe you to be, of ever feeling any remorse.'

Darcy O'Brien, *Two of a Kind*; Jay Robert Nash, *World Encyclopedia of 20th Century Murder*; T. Schwartz, *The Hillside Strangler*.

18 October, 1941

Irene Louise Valeska Coffee, aged 29, and her mother, Margarete Salamon Brann, aged 55, a German citizen, of 33 Castellain Road, west London, entered into a suicide pact between 11 and 18 October 1941. On that day the police entered the house and found the mother dead and Irene Coffee in a semi-conscious condition.

Coffee, a Jewish refugee, had arrived in the United Kingdom in 1937 and two months later had entered into a marriage of convenience with Aaron Coffee. In February 1938, travelling as a British citizen, she went to Germany and returned with her mother. She then obtained work as a secretary and was her mother's sole support.

They were both refugees and in October 1941, during the German advance on Russia, they both became extremely depressed and apprehensive about what would happen should there be a German invasion of Great Britain. They decided to commit suicide by poisoning themselves with veronal and phanodorm.

Irene Coffee was defended by Victor Durand in one of his earliest cases at the Bar and in an effort to save his client from the gallows he appears to have urged the jury to disregard the arcane law that the survivor of a suicide pact must be guilty of murder. She had written in a statement to the police, 'I did not murder my mother. We decided to die together. I was unfortunate. I did not know it was a serious thing to do.' In joint wills they left their property to German refugees.

Although he clearly had great personal sympathy, Mr Justice Humphreys would have nothing of the argument. He pointed out that in fact the law had been clear since 1821, and as long ago as 1823 there had been a case where a man and woman decided to die by drowning together, with the result that the survivor was tried.

The jury retired for 11 minutes, returning a verdict of

guilty, with the strongest recommendation to mercy. Mr
Justice Humphreys then said he believed their recommendation would receive sympathetic consideration.

At the Central Criminal Court on 6 December 1942
Irene Coffee was sentenced to death, a sentence commuted
nine days later to one of life imprisonment.

MEPO/3/2196.

19 October, 1994

Gerald McQuade, aged 41, and Paul Bootland, 15 years
his junior, were convicted of the murder of old-age pensioner David Dunn on 19 October 1994. Together they
had been convicted, along with Robert Smith, aged 34, of
killing Dunn in a car park in Bonnyrigg, Midlothian when
he had tried to prevent their getaway in a robbery.

Smith had shot the pensioner in the chest as he swung
a bag of groceries at him after a raid on a branch of the
Bank of Scotland which had netted £185,000.

All three had been sentenced to life imprisonment and
McQuade and Bootland appealed in February 1996 on a
complicated point of procedure. At the trial Smith, who
was the only one to give evidence, had said that both
the others knew he was carrying a loaded shotgun. The
defence claimed that under Scottish law they should have
been given prior notice of the allegation. In Scotland if a
defendant is seeking to exculpate himself at the expense
of a co-accused or anyone else he must give prior notice
of this.

The Court of Appeal ruled that the men had suffered
no prejudice. Notice, the judges said, was unnecessary.
Smith had not been trying to free himself of blame. His
claim was that he had committed culpable homicide (the
Scottish equivalent of manslaughter) and not murder.

Lord Hope, the Lord Justice General, said notice was needed only when an accused was trying to remove the blame from himself entirely and place it on his co-accused. This was not the position in the present case. The appeals were dismissed.

20 October, 1976

On 20 October 1976 Jimmie Wayne Jeffers lured his former girlfriend and fellow drug user, Penelope Cheney, to a Tucson, Arizona motel with the promise of more drugs. There he injected her with a fix of heroin which, said the prosecution at Jeffers's trial, was sufficient to kill a horse. He had suspected his victim had informed on him to the police. When Cheney did not die immediately Jeffers strangled and then beat her, finally forcing his companion, Doris van der Veer, to inject more heroin.

Cheney's body was left in the shower stall for three days before he wrapped it in a sleeping bag and buried it outside Sedona, not far from the Grand Canyon.

Jeffers was executed by lethal injection on 14 September 1995 after a final appeal, that his lawyers at his trial in 1978 had presented an inadequate defence, failed. According to reports his last words to Corrections Director Sam Lewis were a stream of obscenities. A small group of protesters held a vigil outside the prison gates. Jeffers was the fourth person to be legally executed in Arizona in 1995 and the 34th in the whole of the United States.

21 October, 1994

Michael McCormack, director of an indexing company with offices in the area and John Ogden, his works manager, were shot on 21 October 1994 in what had all the hallmarks of a contract killing in Cavendish Road, Balham, south London.

The lone gunman, who had been waiting in a sandwich bar, followed the men as they returned from a lunchtime drink at the Prince of Wales public house on Clapham Common. He shot them both in the back of the head with a .45 Colt and then ran to a D-registration Vauxhall Cavalier which was later found burned out in Streatham. It had been bought in a false name for £1,500 cash from a family in nearby Catford.

Neither man was known to be a major figure in the Underworld. The police could not discount the view that the killings were a case of mistaken identity and that the killer had confused one of them for a target in the long-running drug territory war which had raged in south London over the previous years.

22 October, 1995

In the early hours of 22 October 1995, 39-year-old Leo Yoelson, who was described by neighbours as a man who worked long hours in the pizzeria he and his mother owned in Greenwich Village, and who lived quietly with her and a golden retriever dog on 35th Avenue in Bayside, Queens, New York, began firing weapons no one knew he had possessed. He had previously said he intended to shoot a colony of mice which were breeding in his back yard, but tenants had said they thought he had meant this as a joke.

However, the shots appeared to be random ones until a neighbour, Santo Puleio, who had reported the gunfire and was directing the first police car that arrived, was shot in the back. Yoelson then wounded a police officer who was getting out of the car. After that, whilst pinning down the police over a 90-minute period, he killed his dog and his 55-year-old mother, Rosaurita Yoelson. Traffic was stopped on the Clearview Expressway near Yoelson's home whilst he continued to shoot at a seven-foot barricade on wheels brought by the police. Finally he emerged, firing at the police. Told to surrender he fired again and was killed in a hail of bullets.

There were conflicting reports over Yoelson's behaviour. Some said he had been drinking heavily since the break-up of a relationship with a girlfriend. A woman who rented an apartment said that he was macho, troublesome and argumentative. Others spoke of a peaceable man who liked to go fishing.

23 October, 1929

Although, over the years, both Sidney Fox and his elderly mother, Rosaline (known as Rose), had been confidence tricksters of some talent, their abilities were on the decline and by 23 October 1929 they were staying, without visible means of support, at the Hotel Metropole, Margate, Kent.

Old Mrs Fox had been ill and probably was suffering from Parkinson's disease. Sidney, with a lazy left eyelid, was a handsome man, if a bit down at the heel. They had, he said, been visiting the graves of his brothers in France. She let it be known that she was the widow of William Fox, founder of Fox's Flour Mills.

At 11.40 pm Sidney Fox, wearing only a shirt, ran down the stairs of the hotel shouting there was a fire. Samuel Hopkins came out from the billiard room and ran back with Fox to his bedroom. Smoke was everywhere and Fox said, rather touchingly, 'Mummy's in there' pointing to room 66. Hopkins crawled into the room, saw a pair of bare legs and pulled Mrs Fox from the smoke-filled room. Another man tried to put out the fire which seemed to be in an armchair near the gas fire. He dragged the chair from the room whilst yet another guest stamped out the fire on the carpet. Fox was so upset he was given an injection of morphine.

Later, he told the police that his mother had walked into his room at about 9.45 pm and asked for the *Evening Standard* which he had given her. He said goodnight and went downstairs for a drink, returning and going to sleep about an hour later. He woke, smelling burning, tried to get into her room, was beaten back by the smoke and went in search of help. He was concerned about his mother's handbag which, he said, held at least £24. The bag was found without the money.

The medical evidence at the inquest was that it was possible Mrs Fox had undressed before the fire and her underclothes or part of the newspaper had caught alight and smouldered. It was postulated that she had been asleep and, waking to find the room full of smoke, had been too shocked to raise the alarm. The verdict was death by misadventure and Fox set out to collect £3,010 in short-term life insurance policies which would have expired at the midnight following her death. The insurance companies were not happy. Fox had taken out the policies in August and September and had extended them saying, on the last occasion, that his mother would not travel abroad unless she was insured. They went to the police.

Sadly, Mrs Fox had not been the widow of the mill owner but of a railway signalman whom she had left for a porter, Fox's father. True, two of her sons had died in France but she and Sidney had not been to see their graves. When they had arrived at the hotel they explained their lack of luggage by their travels abroad. In fact Mrs Fox had only two dresses, both of which she wore simultaneously. Fox had a long record of dishonesty, starting early with fraud on charities and theft from his employers. As he grew up his alter egos included Captain Owen Smythe and the Honourable S. H. Fox.

His last venture had been to befriend a Mrs Morse, whose husband named Fox in a divorce petition. He persuaded her to make a will in his favour and then insured her life. She awoke one night to find the gas tap on. They parted and Fox took her jewellery with him. For that he had received a sentence of 18 months.

By the time they reached the Metropole the pair had left a trail of unpaid bills throughout Kent. Fox was arrested for obtaining credit by fraud. Scotland Yard was called in and an exhumation of Rose Fox by pathologist Sir Bernard Spilsbury found there was no soot in the air passages. Therefore she had died before there was any smoke in the bedroom. The case against Fox was that he had made his mother drowsy with port and then strangled her. A telling factor was that he had shut the doors to both his own and his mother's rooms when he went to raise the alarm. He maintained it was to prevent the fire spreading.

The medical evidence from Professor Sydney Smith for the defence was that it was impossible to strangle a person without breaking the hyoid bone. Spilsbury maintained he had seen bruising on the larynx, something which Smith claimed could have been a transient mark of putrefaction.

He was one of the few murderers not to appeal against his conviction and was hanged at Maidstone on 8 April 1930. His supporters claim that the murder of his mother was to save her from the further debilitating effects of Parkinson's disease rather than for the money. Sydney Smith went further, writing in his autobiography that he did not think that a jury would have convicted on the evidence of anyone but Spilsbury, adding, 'Perhaps Spilsbury

did not fully realise that fame brings responsibility as well
as honour.'

Jay Adams, *Double Indemnity*; Sir Sydney Smith, *Mostly
Murder*.

24 October, 1917

On 24 October 1917 James Petty called the police to his
home in North Kensington where his wife and son were
apparently dead on the floor of the back room at the top
of the house. She was in fact still alive and was taken
to Kensington infirmary. At an inquest on 22 November
1917 a verdict on the death of the boy, Arthur James
Petty, was that of wilful murder by his mother. It was
accepted she had been cruelly treated by her husband.

   On her discharge from the hospital on 13 November
1917 she was arrested. She was committed for trial and
discharged. The judge remarked he failed to see on what
grounds the coroner's jury returned the verdict.

25 October, 1957

Albert Anastasia, the so-called Lord High Executioner
of Murder, was killed in a classic barber's shop chair
shooting on 25 October 1957. At the time he was having
a haircut in the Park Sheraton Hotel in Manhattan. His
bodyguard, who had been informed of the likelihood of
local difficulties, had gone for a walk when two men
entered the shop, pushed Arthur Grasso, the barber, aside
and shot Anastasia.

After his arrival in the United States in the 1920s, Italian-born Anastasia had, along with his brother, 'Tough' Tony, gained a position in the longshoreman's union. He had been a close associate of Louis 'Lepke' Buchalter as the working arm of Murder Inc. In 1951 he moved several rungs up the ladder with the murder of Phil Mangano whose New York 'family' he took over.

His downfall may have come directly from the killing of the bystander, and therefore outsider, Albert Schuster, who had given the police information which led to the capture of bank robber Willie Sutton. Outsiders were, as a general proposition, not to be harmed. Anastasia's rage at Shuster's behaviour in informing the police about a man who was not even a family member was regarded by his colleagues as too dangerous to go unchecked.

In theory the killing of Anastasia remains unsolved but the contract was almost certainly given to the Gallo Family from Brooklyn. Anastasia's brother, 'Tough' Tony, died of natural causes three years later.

26 October, 1995

On 26 October 1995 four teenagers were kidnapped by Ace Crew gang members and put in the boot of a truck before being driven to a flat in Banner Road, Nepean, Ottawa. There, according to the unidentified 19-year-old witness who had driven the teenagers in her mother's truck, 17-year-old Sylvain Leduc was asphyxiated and beaten to death and another teenager was beaten whilst a girl was badly burned with a curling iron. The second girl was found unharmed just outside a storage room in the flat.

Three members of the gang, John Richardson, known as 'The Devil', Kurton Keith Edwards and Mark Williams were charged with first-degree murder. A female teenager who cannot be identified under the provisions of the Young Offenders' Act was given a separate trial.

The witness told the court that she had picked up six gang members and was told to drive downtown. On Marier Street in Vanier they picked up a teenager and told her to lie in the boot. 'I didn't know why we were going there, but the Devil told me where to turn,' the witness said in evidence. The Devil had told the girl to get in the back and she climbed over and did so. 'She wanted to know what was happening, but was told to shut up.'

On a second trip the gang had kidnapped the two male teenagers and another girl. Then they were beaten and tortured. The witness said she was outside the room in which this was happening, doing her French homework with another girl. 'I heard a female voice near the entrance say 'no', but she was not yelling and I didn't recognise the voice.'

On 3 April 1997 three of the Ace Crew were sentenced to three years in a detention centre, the maximum permissible. The adults were still awaiting trial.

27 October, 1927

On 27 October 1927 Leslie 'Squizzy' Taylor (see 8 October) and John 'Snowy' Cutmore, rival Australian gang leaders, were found shot dead in a suburban house in Melbourne.

Taylor, born in 1888, began his working life in a racing stables and progressed through gambling, running a sly-grog shop (or unlicensed premises), jury fixing, armed robbery, drug-trading and murder.

The power of Taylor, the one-time king of the Victorian Underworld, had, since the hanging of Murray, fallen into decline. It was thought Taylor was a police informer. There were also rivals for his empire and for control of the burgeoning and lucrative cocaine trade. In the previous June, Norman Bruhn, one of Taylor's men, was shot in Sydney. He had robbed a drug trader who had good connections in the New South Wales Underworld. Bruhn's killer was thought to be Cutmore.

There followed a series of shootings and knifings in what came to be known as the Cocaine War. The battles were indecisive and Cutmore, determined to put an end to the matter, travelled with a friend to Sydney. On 26 October Cutmore was drinking heavily at a bar in St Kilda's which was under the protection of Taylor. Cutmore smashed the premises and stripped a woman naked before turning her onto the street.

According to one version of the double killing on 27 October, Cutmore was in bed at his home in Fitzroy when Taylor walked in and shot him. Cutmore, who had a pistol under the sheets, returned the fire. He died on the bed and Taylor was taken to St Vincent's Hospital, Melbourne where he died. Although the police accepted that Cutmore and Taylor had shot each other, another version has emerged. It is that somehow Taylor shot Cutmore first and was then, himself, shot by a travelling companion.

If this is correct it was almost certainly set up by Henry Stokes who, as a result of Taylor's death, became for a time, the King of the Victorian Underworld. Stokes had at one time been Taylor's partner in a number of gambling schools in Melbourne.

28 October, 1992

The man who killed her thought that the name of the young girl found dead in a Bayswater hotel on 28 October 1992 was Becky and that she came from East Germany. Colin Findlay had found her begging on the streets, bought her a meal, taken her to the hotel and raped and strangled her. He was, however, by no means sure of her identity and the task for the police was not to find her killer but to discover who she was. They could not trace her through her fingerprints or details from the missing persons lists. Her dental characteristics were no help either. Details of the jewellery she was wearing – a ring shaped like a scorpion – and an artist's likeness of her face were circulated again without any success. Her details were also circulated abroad via Interpol. Eventually her ring was sold by the Westminster Council to help pay for her grave.

Her identity was eventually discovered. She was indeed German but her real name was Kirsten Hochstetter, born on 21 January 1965, who had come from Gladbach. Her mother and sister saw the Interpol pictures and made an identification of her from the postmortem photographs and her scorpion ring. They did not need to come to England to see the corpse. Findlay received a sentence of life imprisonment.

29 October, 1993

In May 1995 Shahid Walayat, aged 22, was sentenced to life imprisonment at Leeds Crown Court for the murder of 18-year-old Julia Baines on 29 October 1993. He had seen her as she was walking the four miles to her home in Crofton in West Yorkshire after she had been on a night out in Wakefield. It was never clear why she had chosen to walk home that night.

Walayat had seen her as he and a workmate shut down a takeaway pizza store. He attacked her with such force that her features were barely recognisable. She was raped and then strangled with her skirt.

Walayat was arrested seven weeks later. A collection of pornographic videos was found at his home.

Julia's father, Geoffrey Baines, is writing a book about his daughter and her death, provisionally entitled *Julia and My Faith*.

30 October, 1968

Twenty-two-year-old Paul Ferguson and his brother Tom, five years younger, were convicted of the murder of the former silent film star Ramon Novarro on 30 October 1968 because they made a telephone call whilst they were torturing and beating the elderly homosexual.

They had been picked up by him as the latest in a line of one-night stands and taken to his home in Hollywood. On the streets they had heard a rumour that he kept at least $5,000 in cash in the house and whilst one beat him the other brother made a long-distance telephone call to a girl they knew in Chicago. After ransacking the house without success they left with only the money Novarro had in his pockets. They had stuffed a dildo down his throat.

In a routine check the police traced back the calls made on Novarro's telephone line and the girl they had called, Brenda Lee Metcalf, confirmed that she and the boys had been old friends until the brothers had left for California.

With Tom still a juvenile Paul attempted to persuade him to take the blame for the killing – an almost token punishment would have resulted – but both were tried in the adult court and, with the one blaming the other for the killing, both were convicted and sentenced to life imprisonment without parole.

31 October, 1908

The most positive outcome of the death of Teddy Haskell was that a directive was issued to provincial police forces that, if the assistance of Scotland Yard was required in a case, steps should be taken to preserve rather than to destroy the evidence. The lack of a conviction in the case was almost certainly because the local police had allowed the bloodstained area to be washed before a proper investigation had been made.

On the night of Saturday 31 October 1908, between 10.20 and 10.30 pm, 12-year-old Teddy Haskell had his throat cut whilst in bed in his home at 40 Meadow Road, Fisherton, Salisbury, Hampshire where he lived in a two-storey cottage with his 34-year-old mother. The knife stroke was through the jugular vein and below the vocal cords. He was an enormously popular child in the neighbourhood. His father had died some four years previously of consumption at about the time that Teddy had his right leg amputated below the knee as a result of a bone disease. He made light of his disability, playing football and running with his crutches. By all accounts Flora Fanny Haskell was a devoted mother. 'She was all a mother could be,' said one witness at the trial.

Her movements at the time of the killing can be timed up to 10.20 pm and then after 10.30 pm. She worked as a laundress and that evening did her shopping in Salisbury, came home at about 8.30 pm, went and collected Teddy from his uncle's next door, took him to buy a comic and was back indoors by 8.45 pm. She said that she had then given Teddy his supper, given him a footbath for his good leg and put him to bed.

At 10.05 pm a delivery boy, John Wyatt, was sent with a package to number 42, could not get a reply and so knocked on Mrs Haskell's door and she took it in for her neighbour. He was to say that she appeared absolutely normal and the time was 10.20 pm. Ten minutes later Percy Haskell, Flora Haskell's nephew, called round at the back door and, when he found it fastened, knocked. Mrs Haskell called, 'All right' and he heard first what he described as the sound of a kitchen chair scraping. Then he heard what he later described as a jump, the sound someone would make if they leaped the last few stairs. There was a scream and Mrs Haskell came to the back door, shouting, 'Go and stop that man! He has killed my poor Teddy! Go for a doctor, quick.'

Haskell could see no one he did not know in the street. Another neighbour, a Mrs Chivers, went back to the house with Mrs Haskell and was asked by her to go to the bedroom. At the foot of the stairs was a bloodstained knife. Mrs Haskell then said, 'There is the knife. I fancied I heard footsteps upstairs. Someone came down the stairs and threw the knife at me. Look, there is blood on my sleeve.' There were some small bloodstains on her blouse.

Dr H. L. E. Wilks said that the call for his assistance had come at 10.30 pm and so the time of the murder can be fairly accurately pinned down to those 10 minutes between 10.20 and 10.30. Wilks found that the force of the knife thrust was such that a spurt of blood had sprayed a chest of drawers near the bed. It is difficult to see, therefore, how Mrs Haskell if, as was said, she was the killer, could have avoided being covered in blood. She had no time to clean up and change.

Search parties for the man who had jumped down the stairs were organised and a police description shows that a man of five feet six or seven inches tall, dressed in a dark suit but with no collar was being sought. Mrs Haskell seems to have been questioned throughout the night and somewhere around 3.30 am asked a police sergeant whether 'the money' was all right. This was a reference to money kept in Teddy's room. He had been saving to buy an artificial cork leg and had put together eight pounds in gold and two shillings. When the sergeant checked, only three sovereigns and a half sovereign remained.

There is no doubt whatsoever that the investigation was thoroughly mishandled. At about 6 am Mrs Haskell's mother, Mrs Carter, decided, and was allowed, to scrub the bloodstain from the bottom of the stairs where the knife had been found. The bedding had also been rearranged and Teddy Haskell's body was washed. The all-night search was fruitless and it was then the Chief Constable called in Scotland Yard.

Chief Inspector Walter Dew, who would become famous for his arrest of Harvey Hawley Crippen, arrived the next morning and, finding some newly washed men's clothing, questioned Mrs Haskell. She said that on the night of the murder a man had called asking for lodgings. She had turned him away. Asked about the clothing and the local rumour that she was planning a remarriage, she said that the clothing belonged to an Alfred Mold who was a steward on the liner, the *Adriatic*. He slept in the house whilst on shore and she did his laundry in his absence. Dew also found eight sovereigns in Mrs Haskell's purse. She said she was keeping them for her mother who confirmed the story.

On Tuesday 3 November 1909, Mrs Haskell was charged with her son's murder and she was remanded to Devizes prison. A defence fund was set up by neighbours to pay her legal costs. A coroner's jury returned a verdict of wilful murder against her and the magistrates committed her for trial. Mrs Haskell had the time and the opportunity to kill her son. The only motive which could be advanced by the prosecution was that she was contemplating marrying Alfred Mold and that Teddy was an impediment to the union. That, at least, had been the line which counsel for the police had taken during the inquest and committal proceedings. When it came to the Devizes Assizes things had changed:

The only theory which the Crown are able to present is that this woman committed this act in one of those abnormal conditions of mind which overtake human beings sometimes, and which it is impossible for medical men or legal experts to give any adequate explanation of. During her stay in prison, the accused has been under the observation of the prison doctor, and he is of the opinion that she is perfectly sane.

Flora Haskell was represented by Rayner Goddard, later the Lord Chief Justice, in his first and only major murder trial for the defence. Mr Justice Ridley summed up against her but the jury disagreed, after a three-hour retirement. The next hearing was before Mr Justice Darling, who was no more sympathetic to Mrs Haskell.

Goddard had not called Mrs Haskell to give evidence and Mr Justice Darling was not happy that the jury had not heard an explanation for the bloodstains on her clothing. But the jury retired for only 10 minutes before returning a verdict which sounded extremely like the Scottish 'Not Proven' verdict: 'We find her not guilty on the ground of insufficient evidence.' The public gallery erupted in applause.

Fenton Bresler, *Lord Goddard*; Walter Dew, *I Caught Crippen*.

NOVEMBER

1 November, 1957

The date of her death on her tombstone reads 1 November 1957 but the body of one of Germany's most celebrated prostitutes, Rosemarie Nitribitt, was not found until 4 November by her charlady who saw unopened milk bottles outside her flat at Stiftstrasse 36 in the centre of Frankfurt and called for help. She had been strangled on her Persian carpet. Born in 1933, the blonde, long-legged, most highly paid courtesan in post-war Germany was used in satirical cabarets to portray the symbol of the Economic Miracle *Wirtschafts-wunder*. Her symbols of wealth included 50 pairs of hand-made shoes, nine fur coats and two custom-built sports cars. After her death her Mercedes coupé H70-6425 became a collectors' item. All her rooms were fitted with mirrors, one of which had concealed cameras, and there were hidden microphones in all rooms. Robbery was clearly not a motive for her killing. The only things missing were films from the cameras, tapes from the microphones and her green dossier, the prostitute's 'black book'.

It appears she had been in some fear for the past months. Callers were only admitted if they used the word Rebecca. Some thought she may have been working for the communists. Numerous explanations appeared in the German papers, including one that she had been hypnotised over the telephone.

Her death sent tremors of panic through the business and political communities. Anyone questioned found his name in the headlines with disastrous consequences to his family and business life. Two financiers committed suicide, several others sold up and emigrated.

Six months after the murder her friend and confidant, Heinz Pohlmann, was arrested. When he was released after nine months in custody he wrote his memoirs. The film he was making was stopped when Heinz said he had sold the copyright to protect the brother of a German industrialist. The figures quoted for the sale varied from £4,500 to £18,000. The celebrated German actress Nadja Tiller appeared in a rival production, *Die Schöne Rosemarie*.

2 November, 1975

The homosexual Italian film director Pier Paolo Pasolini was found battered to death on wasteland at Ostia, the Rome bathing resort, on 2 November 1975. He had, apparently, picked up a young male prostitute, Pino Pelosi, outside the railway station in Rome and, after a meal, had driven to the resort with him. There, according to his confession, Pelosi, having refused to perform sado-masochistic acts, beat Pasolini with a wooden sign, kicked him repeatedly in the testicles and then drove Pasolini's car over his body as he escaped. To account for the fact that when he was arrested there were no bloodstains on Pelosi it was explained he had stopped to wash in a fountain.

The Italian Left Wing never accepted the version given by Pelosi and it was suggested the confession that he had acted alone had been made to please the authorities and so obtain a lighter sentence. In April 1976 he received a sentence of just under 10 years' imprisonment. The conspiracy theory goes that the Right Wing wished to be rid of this highly articulate critic of corrupt members of the dominant Christian Democrat Party. The theory has gained credibility with the release of the film *Pasolini, un Delitto Italiano* [*Pasolini, an Italian Crime*] at the Venice Film Festival. In the autumn of 1995 it was announced that a Rome magistrate, Italo Ormanni, was studying a request by Pasolini's family for a new investigation. The request was based on a statement by a former detective who was 'promoted' to other duties because of too close an investigation into the murder.

3 November, 1994

On 3 November 1994 John Penfold, a trainee manager with Woolworth's at their Teddington, Middlesex branch was stabbed to death by Ian Kay when he tried to prevent a robbery at the store. Kay escaped with £165 and the court was told 'had no problem with what he had done'. He spent the night with his girlfriend.

Two hours earlier he had tried to rob a Woolworth's store in Yiewsley in West Drayton. He took £200 from the till but the cashier snatched it back. Kay was annoyed at his failure and went looking for what he saw as another easy target.

At the Teddington store he came to the counter with a packet of Quavers and a 50 pence piece. Believing him to be a customer, John Penfold told the assistant to serve Kay. As the till was opened Kay tried to snatch the contents and when Penfold tried to stop him he was stabbed in the chest. He died later in hospital. When questioned Kay said that Penfold had been 'fair game and a necessary hazard in a robbery'.

At the time the 24-year-old Kay was on home leave from an eight-year sentence imposed in December 1991 for 16 shop raids. He had previously been allowed out on home leave in January 1994 and had stolen £2,000 from a Maidstone post office before returning to prison. On 25 August 1994 he had been given yet a further period of home leave and this time absconded. On 31 August he began his series of raids on shops until he killed John Penfold. Kay was also dealing in drugs. Two days before the killing he had produced a knife and run it over the neck and chest of a Woolworth's assistant, telling her, 'Open the till or I will use it.'

Awaiting his trial he gave psychiatrists a picture of a man plagued with violent fantasies and obsessed with the occult. This time he was sentenced to a term of life imprisonment with a recommendation that he serve at least 22 years.

4 November, 1928

Arnold Rothstein, one of the new breed of Jewish Underworld figures who now had a very thick finger in the New York crime pie, was shot and killed on 4 November 1928. He had been born in 1882 into a relatively wealthy Jewish family and was privately educated. His father had a fine reputation as being both pious and even handed. He was called 'Abe the Just' by New York Governor Al Smith. Unfortunately his son did not inherit these qualities. He was a gambler through and through, often pawning his father's valuables in the morning to get a stake and redeeming them with his winnings before nightfall and the return of his parent. He soon came to the attention of Big Tim Sullivan who asked him to manage the gaming at the Metropole on 43rd Street. From then on Rothstein scarcely took a backward glance as he moved ever upwards in demimonde society.

He was always open to approach to finance an illegal

operation for which his fee was 90 per cent, and for muscle he used first 'Little Augie' Orgen and then, after Orgen's death, Louis Lepke. When bootlegging was at its height he backed not only Jack 'Legs' Diamond but also Waxey Gordon, Owney 'The Killer' Madden, Frank Costello, Frank Erickson and Meyer Lansky.

Rothstein also backed Luciano and Diamond when in the 1920s they were involved in a drugs cartel and it was in the midst of these dealings that some of the stolen bonds reappeared in France and Cuba. A little earlier they also surfaced in England, Nassau and Bermuda where they were used to finance the purchase of liquor during prohibition.

Rothstein rarely involved himself in inter-gangland affairs as such, although he intervened in the Schultz–Diamond beer war, aligning himself with Diamond to such effect that Schulz called a meeting to discuss a truce. Just as his father was regarded as a great arbitrator so was Rothstein regarded in the Underworld. He would sit as judge in disputes, taking a fee from the party against whom he made his ruling. It is said he was paid $250,000 by Diamond and Gordon to arbitrate when they quarrelled over Manhattan territory.

Now a millionaire several times over, in 1928 Rothstein went to pieces, developing a hand palsy and eye twitch and slurring his words, but not through alcohol. He had had a poor year from investments and loans and the police suddenly began to make inroads into his empire, raiding his gambling establishments. His horses began to lose and he had lost over $130,000 in bets at Belmont Park, the racetrack in Queens. On 8 and 9 September he played in a two-day poker game in a room in the Park Central Hotel in New York with several West Coast gamblers including 'Nigger' Nate Raymond and Alvin Clarence Thomas, known as Titanic Thompson. Rothstein lost over $320,000 including side bets of $50,000 on high-card draw. He declined to pay, saying he would settle in a day or so because he did not have that amount of cash on him. Later that night he was heard in the popular Broadway restaurant Lindy's to claim that the game had been fixed, saying the other players had conspired to defeat him.

It appeared his gambling luck had turned again on the day of his death. He had been betting on the presidential election, favouring Herbert Hoover to beat Governor Al Smith, the man who thought so well of Rothstein's father. On 4 November about 10 pm he received a telephone call at Lindy's. One of the players in the game, George F. 'Hump' McManus, wished to see him, he said. He was found by a lift attendant three-quarters of an hour later, near the lift at the Park Central Hotel. Asked by the police who had shot him Rothstein replied, 'Never mind. Get me a taxi.'

According to the taxi driver who was called, the gun which had been used to shoot Rothstein was thrown from a window of the hotel and landed on the roof of his cab. Rothstein died in the Polyclinic Hospital two days later, without having named his killers. McManus, to whose room a trail of blood could be traced, was indicted for the murder but never brought to trial. Raymond produced a blonde woman who told the court she had been in bed with him at the time of the murder and he was released. His lawyers suggested that, in despair over his losses, Rothstein might have shot himself. Although his wife was left comfortably off, much of the gambler's reputed wealth had disappeared.

It is possible Rothstein was killed over the gambling debts but it is more likely that the powerful syndicates thought his financial acumen was failing and he could soon be an expensive liability. There have been suggestions that the contract was undertaken by killers from the feared Purple Gang of Detroit. His empire was divided between various interested parties including 'Lucky' Luciano who took over the bootlegging enterprise, Costello the political and police protection, Lepke the garment interests, and Frank Erickson the gambling.

Damon Runyon, *New York American*, *November–December 1929*. Partly reprinted in Jonathan Goodman (ed)

Masterpieces of Murder; Albert Fried, *The Rise and Fall of the Jewish Gangster*.

5 November, 1972

In the early hours of 5 November 1972, two gunmen forced their way into the Barn Restaurant, Braintree, Essex. When the owner Bob Patience refused to hand over the keys to the safe they shot him, his wife, and daughter Beverley, in quick succession. Muriel Patience died later in hospital. George Ince, already charged with a major silver bullion robbery, was identified as one of the gunmen and was charged with the murder.

The trial of Ince at Chelmsford Crown Court for the murder took place in May 1973. It was presided over by Mr Justice Melford Stevenson, the judge who had tried the Kray twins in their first trial for the murder of Cornell and McVitie and who was not noted for his sympathy towards defendants. Ince was defended by Victor Durand QC who frequently clashed with the judge. Ince continually protested his innocence and was sent down to the cells whilst Beverley Patience gave her evidence that she identified him as one of the attackers. It was after this that Ince, who had already made an abortive application to change the judge and who, during the trial, had had a telegram sent to the Lord Chancellor asking for Stevenson to be removed, sacked Durand and his junior, Robert Flach. Now he was on his own. Both his barristers remained in court, taking no further part whilst Ince stayed in the dock with his back to the judge, occasionally interrupting the prosecution witnesses. He offered no defence until he asked whether he could be allowed to take the truth drug. Stevenson said no but asked if Ince would like his defence counsel reinstated. Ince replied that he would not and said once more that the judge was both biased and rude. After a retirement of six hours at 9.30 pm before a tense court the jury returned to say they had failed to agree on a verdict.

Within the week Ince was on trial again. This time before a much more sympathetic judge, Mr Justice Eveleigh. Durand and Flach were reinstated and this time Durand called a crucial witness, a Dolly Gray. Ince had apparently been unwilling for her to appear. He had thought that when, as it must, her real name was given, it would act against him and also that she would suffer reprisals.

Mrs 'Gray' had bravely gone to see her husband, Charlie Kray, in Maidstone prison before she testified. It seems that he did not know she had been seeing Ince before she told him and this 'Dear John' was a shattering blow to a man serving a 10-year sentence. To his great credit, however, he did not attempt to prevent her giving evidence to the effect that on the night of the murder she had been in bed with Ince.

On 23 May the jury retired for over three hours before they acquitted Ince, to wild cheers from the public gallery. Three weeks later a northerner, John Brook, was found in possession of the murder weapon and was later convicted of the murder of Muriel Patience.

The Barn murder case was one of a number of similar cases of mistaken identity which led the Court of Appeal to formulate guidelines on the dangers of convicting on identification evidence.

6 November, 1946

On 6 November 1946 a police officer discovered the body of 57-year-old widow Olive Nixon, beaten to death some 50 yards from her home in a mews off the Marylebone Road, London not far from Madame Tussaud's. She had been returning from a church social. She had not been sexually attacked nor had a valuable pearl necklace and other jewellery been stolen.

It was not until 10 August 1956 that the puzzle of her death was solved. Adam Ogilvie walked into the local police station at Albany Street and confessed to the murder. He said he feared he might kill again and had been worried since the death of Mrs Nixon. Not all that worried because in 1948 he had served a three-year sentence for an assault on a woman in Torquay, hitting her over the head with a brick. In his confession he said:

Last Wednesday night I met a girl on Hampstead Heath. She said her name was Jean and she lived in Golders Green and had been locked out. We walked down a footpath and I had a terrible urge to kill her. I grabbed her by the arms and tried to pull her down. She screamed and I pulled myself together and told her I was sorry.

Going back to the night of the death of Mrs Nixon, he said he had had a quarrel with his wife and so had gone to a billiard hall in nearby Warren Street. Going back home:

In Park Village East I saw a woman walking towards me. When she was passing me I picked up a brick and hit her on the side of the head, near the back. I think I only hit her once. She fell down and was lying on her back. I threw the brick away and shook the woman, but she was lying quite still and I think she must have been dead.

He then pulled her to the back of a bomb-damaged building where he left her.

He appeared at the Old Bailey in the November of

that year when he recanted, saying he had only confessed to prove his innocence to his wife. This was strange because she had left him some years earlier. He said he had the necessary details of the killing (which in accordance with police practice had not been released) from a stranger, a Jamaican he had met at a coffee stall. He had had a row with his wife when he got home late and he said he had killed someone and would do the same to her if she nagged him. She left him in 1950 and had never been, he said, convinced he did not commit the crime. The police had, he claimed, suborned witnesses and themselves committed perjury.

> I pretended to her I did the killing and told her I would murder her, too, if she didn't stop quarrelling with me. I thought if I was acquitted she would come back.

On 20 November 1956, after a retirement of only forty minutes, the jury convicted him of murder. He was sentenced to death but was reprieved under the Homicide Act 1957.

7 November, 1949

On 7 November 1949 Jean Lee, together with Robert Clayton and Norman Andrews, tortured and then strangled and stabbed William 'Old Bill' Kent, a 73-year-old bookmaker, for his money. At the time Lee, known also as Smith, White, Brown, Duncan, Marjorie Brees, and Marie Williams, was an attractive red-headed 32-year-old woman, from a respectable working-class home in Dubbo, New South Wales. After leaving school she worked for a milliner, then as a waitress, then as a clerk and finally in a factory. At the age of 18 she married a man from Sydney and had a daughter. When, at the beginning of the war, her marriage broke up, she became a prostitute working in the King's Cross area of Sydney. She acquired a number of convictions and then realised she needed a minder. She took up with Robert David Clayton, described as a bludger or ponce. Soon they latched on to the badger game as being an easier and more profitable form of work.

She would go with men to hotel rooms or the backs of cars, only to be 'discovered' by Clayton who, as the aggrieved husband, demanded financial recompense. When Clayton discovered that some of the victims were prepared to fight it out with him it was necessary to recruit another member of the team. In 1949 Norman Andrews joined the team as 'husband's friend' and he supplied the strong-arm stuff when the victims showed any reluctance to pay.

Unfortunately one of their victims went to the police and reported the beating and robbery he had sustained. Doubly unfortunately, although the police were able to identify the trio from the descriptions, they did not arrest them immediately.

On 7 November 1949 they took to a bar in Lygon Street, Carlton, a Melbourne suburb, and latched on to the small and fat Kent. It was only a matter of drink and time before he was persuaded to go with Jean Lee to a rooming house in Dorritt Street. She got him drunker and tried to pick his pocket. When he would not let go of his wallet she hit him on the head with a bottle and then a piece of wood and, joined by the others, tortured him. Kent was placed on a chair with his thumbs tied together with a bootlace whilst he was repeatedly kicked and beaten.

With the money Clayton bought tickets for a flight to Sydney and in the meantime the trio went to a nightclub to celebrate. They returned to their hotel room to find the police waiting for them.

The case is interesting not only because it is a classic example of the badger game but because after all three were arrested the statement of one prisoner was used to extract confessions from the others. When the jury announced its verdict Lee threw her arms around Clayton, screaming, 'I didn't do it.' When the convictions were quashed by the State Court she had to be physically separated from Clayton and was led from the dock, laughing. The High Court reversed the State Court's ruling and restored the death penalty sentence. A reprieve was denied and they were hanged at Pentridge prison on 19 February 1951. Outside the jail a part of the crowd sang 'Nearer my God to Thee'. Lee was the last woman to be hanged in Australia.

V. Kelly, *The Charge is Murder*.

8 November, 1921

Annie Black had married an insurance salesman 18 years her junior. They were, according to friends, continually quarrelling over money.

On 8 November 1921 insurance agent Edward Black disappeared from his home in Tregonissey, near St Austell, Cornwall, owing money to clients. His wife Annie who had a small confectionery shop died three days later. A popular woman locally, her death was at first diagnosed as being from gastroenteritis, of which an epidemic was sweeping Cornwall. Neighbours were not satisfied, however, and brought pressure for a postmortem. However, no substantial amount of poison was found in her body.

Shortly after the postmortem a local butcher, who was a family friend, received a letter, posted in Liverpool, from Edward Black. In it he suggested that his wife's death would have been as a result of a weak heart which

Dr Andrews, one of the doctors who had carried out the postmortem, had himself diagnosed. He also wrote of the shame he felt about the accusations of theft from his clients and said that he might commit suicide.

He did not. He was arrested on 21 November in a Liverpool hotel. There was, however, a wound to his throat. When he was returned to Cornwall he stood trial at Bodmin Assizes where he was defended by the young and inexperienced John Pratt, the brother of the actor Boris Karloff. Quite apart from local prejudice the evidence against Black was that of the local pharmacist who said that Black had signed the poison book for two ounces of arsenic. It would seem that Pratt could have made more of the defence. He did not, by accounts, establish an alibi which Black claimed he had for when the poison had been purchased. Black's neighbours, however, were quite convinced of his guilt. The cause of death on his wife's death certificate had already been written as 'Arsenical poisoning by Edward Ernest Black'.

He was hanged by John Ellis at Exeter prison on 24 March 1922.

9 November, 1944

Winifred Mary Evans was strangled on 9 November 1944 at Ellough near Beccles, by LAC Arthur Heys, a married man with three children. Serving in the WRAF, Evans left her barracks at about 12.10 am. She was already late for duty and it is assumed it was then she encountered Heys. He had been drinking and wanted sex. He pulled off one of the buttons on her greatcoat. She fell in a ditch and whilst lying there Heys jumped on her back, causing her liver to burst and begin to haemorrhage. He pulled her shirt up, tearing the buttons. He then tore off her slacks, dislodged a sanitary pad and took her from the rear.

She was 18 years old and worked as a wireless operator. Described as a pleasant and reserved girl with no boyfriend she was not one who would associate with strangers. On the night of her death she had been to a charity dance at the nearby American base.

Her body was found the next morning by a special constable cycling along the Ellough Road, shortly after 8 am. Corporal Margaret Johns, who had also been to the American Red Cross dance at Horsham St Faiths had, shortly after midnight, seen a man on the site with a badge of LAC. The man was later identified as Heys who said he had been to a dance in Caxton Hall, Beccles.

When questioned he said he had returned to his barracks after being at the Beccles dance and had fallen asleep. His trousers seemed to have been recently washed around the crotch. There were cat hairs on Mary Evans's clothing which matched some found on Heys.

Heys had been born on 1 November 1907 at Colne, Lancashire and had convictions for dishonesty. On the file was the unsolved murder of a female in Colne who was stabbed in the back.

He had been suspected of an attack on a LACW at the RAF Station Leuchars but he could not be identified and his explanation that he was in the lavatory vomiting through excess alcohol had been noted. Heys had also been on site when another woman had been assaulted, this time at Thornaby.

He was not without cunning. Whilst awaiting trial, from the prison he wrote an anonymous letter purporting to come from the murderer saying Heys was innocent. In the supposed confession the man said how he had had an appointment to meet Winnie Evans shortly after midnight, that he had seen a drunken aircraftman (Heys) and that Winnie had arrived after that.

He referred to the woman as being 'unclean' (menstruating), a fact which had not been revealed at the inquest and which only the killer could know. Police enquiries showed that he had access to paper and crayon and that the letter had, in all probability, been smuggled out by a discharged prisoner. The fingerprint and handwriting expert, Superintendent Fred Cherrill from Scotland Yard, gave evidence that the letter had been written by Heys and it was this which largely led to his conviction.

Heys was executed on 13 March 1945.

PRO/MEPO/3/2282; Fred Cherrill, *Cherrill of the Yard*.

10 November, 1960

On 10 November 1960, shortly after hearing on the radio that his friends Francis 'Flossie' Forsyth and Norman James Harris had been hanged at Wandsworth and Pentonville respectively, Victor John Terry shot 61-year-old bank guard John Henry Pull at pointblank range in Lloyds Bank, Durrington near Worthing, Sussex. Along with Phillip Tucker and Alan Alfred Hosier he stole £1,372. Bravely, if perhaps foolishly, Pull had tried to seize the gun.

Terry and his girlfriend then travelled from Worthing to Portsmouth where he bought another shotgun. Terry was traced, with his girlfriend, to a hotel in Glasgow where he had registered under the name of Diamond. He had told a taxi driver to keep the change from a 10 shilling note when the fare only came to half a crown. Tried at Lewes Assizes in March 1961, Terry, in a defence of diminished responsibility, claimed he was controlled by the spirit of Jack 'Legs' Diamond, the New York gangster of the 1920s and he was supported in this by two defence doctors.

His defence was rejected by the jury. His appeal, on the grounds that the judge, the fairly eccentric Mr Justice Stable, had not properly reviewed the medical evidence for the jury, was dismissed by the Court of Criminal Appeal. What the judge had done was to hand the jury a copy of the transcript of the medical evidence which he had marked in red, and the really significant pages of which he had turned down. The Court said that this was objectionable but because the whole question was not an evaluation of the medical evidence but whether Terry was trying to fool the psychiatrists there was not much else the judge could have done. Hosier received life imprisonment for non-capital murder and Tucker was sentenced to detention under the Children and Young Persons Act 1933, s 53(2). Terry's girlfriend was given a year's probation for receiving part of the stolen money. Terry was hanged at Wandsworth prison on 26 May 1961.

Terence Morris and Louis Blom-Cooper, *A Calendar of Murder*.

11 November, 1994

In January 1996 three teenagers, Nicholas Pinero, Thomas Crook and Anthony Rienzi, were found guilty of the third-degree murder of 16-year-old Edward Polec in Philadelphia on 11 November 1994. He had simply been in the wrong place at the wrong time.

After what turned out to be untrue rumours that a local Abington girl had been raped, two gangs of youths from Abington and Fox Chase had driven into Philadelphia for a pre-arranged fight. Shortly after 10 pm five cars from Abington pulled up at McDonald's on Oxford Avenue and a number of youths came from

Fox Chase. Seeing that the Abington youths had baseball bats, the Fox Chase contingent ran. The Abington youths then drove to St Cecilia's Roman Catholic Church, where they found Edward Polec, who had once sung in the choir, and beat him to death. It was 45 minutes before the police arrived because, despite repeated calls from by-standers, 911 operators apparently failed to notify them or paramedics of the urgency. As a result, new equipment was installed and training given. Originally the operators were dismissed but were reinstated after suing the city.

Rienzi and Pinero, both 18, were sentenced to the maximum 15 to 30 years and Crook received 14½ to 30. The prosecution had asked for convictions for first-degree murder and in sentencing the youths Judge Greenspan said she had received thousands of personal letters from the community asking her to impose the maximum sentences. 'I needed no encouragement from the communities for the sentence I impose today,' she said. 'The jury in this case has shown all the sympathy and mercy that those defendants deserve.'

12 November, 1941

Although Abe 'Kid Twist' Reles, a high-ranking soldier in Murder Incorporated, whose leaders were Albert Anastasia and Louis Lepke, had been arrested some 42 times over the previous 16 years he had served only short prison sentences and his real position in society was unknown to the police. In 1940 he was charged with robbery, possession of narcotics and six charges linked to murder. He feared, probably correctly, that some of those arrested with him might endeavour to arrange a deal by informing on him and, so to speak, he had the first drop on them. The police were able to clear up some 49 killings in Brooklyn alone. He named Frank Abbandando and Charlie Workman in the killing of Dutch Schultz and his evidence was in a large part responsible for the conviction of his superiors, Louis Lepke and Mendy Weiss, for murder.

For a year Reles was, like so many subsequent informers, held in protective custody. His safe home was the sixth floor of the Half Moon Hotel on Coney Island, New York, where he was kept under constant surveillance by six uniformed police officers. It was from there he travelled to the New York courts to give his evidence. On 12 November 1941 he fell from the window of his room, landing on the pavement, and was killed. One of the more ingenious theories into his death is that he was playing a practical joke, climbing out of the window on knotted bedsheets and then running back upstairs to frighten the guards outside his room. Another is that he committed suicide. To do this he must have lowered himself to the third floor and then jumped. As his body was found 20 feet out into the street this seems unlikely.

The much more plausible account is that it was a gangland hit. At the time Reles was due to testify against Albert Anastasia who was on trial for the killing of waterfront labour leader, Peter Panto. After Reles's death the case against Anastasia was dropped and although it was reopened in 1951 no progress was made. He was also due to give evidence against 'Bugsy' Siegel but the charges were now dropped. Charles 'Lucky' Luciano was later to say that the killing had been done by police officers who had thrown Reles from his room and that the contract price had been $50,000. Later Meyer Lansky said the fee paid had been $100,000. There is also some evidence that Reles's confessions were being used not simply to obtain convictions against organised crime figures but to blackmail them.

13 November, 1993

On 13 November 1993 Roger Severs, the 36-year-old son of a middle-class Yorkshire family, travelled to their bungalow village of Hambledon and shot his parents, Eileen and Derek.

Severs had been well educated but, according to his mother, had wasted his life. A compulsive womaniser and fantasiser he was, at the time of his parents' death, trying to re-establish a relationship with Jain Galliford, whom he had met through a Lonely Hearts advertisement, telling her he was a gynaecologist. She ran a country hotel and they had had a son, Tom, born in October 1991 on whom his parents doted.

According to the evidence at the Nottingham Crown Court, when Roger Severs had gone to visit his parents on the afternoon of 13 November, his 69-year-old mother had challenged him about his mounting debts and his failed relationship with Jain, with whom they remained on the best of terms. She had a blazing row with him, telling him that on her death and that of her husband he would get nothing in the will and their estate would be left to Tom.

Severs followed her to the bathroom where he hit her eight blows with a steak tenderiser. She collapsed on the floor, taking some 30 minutes to die. His father Derek returned from the local pub and as he got out of his Land Rover Roger hit him with the mallet 10 times. He died almost immediately. Severs then wrapped his mother in a blanket and put her in the boot of the Land Rover. He bound up his father's body and strapped him in the back seat. Then he drove them to a wood and buried them in a shallow grave.

Back at the house he did what he could to conceal the murders. He burned stained clothes and carpets, dumping some at the local tip. He delivered raffle prizes his mother had been in charge of, telling the recipients that he was doing this for his mother who, with his father, had gone to the south of England to visit friends.

Jain had arranged to speak to Mrs Severs on the Tuesday but when she asked Roger if his mother was all right he was non-committal. Now he suddenly had money and invited her out to dinner, paying cash. The story about his parents changed. His father had had a stroke and was away convalescing. Neighbours who had heard the different versions called the police. Severs was arrested on 18 November at Stamford cattle market where he had taken Tom.

Jain Galliford had known Roger Severs to be violent. He had blackened her eyes and on another occasion dislocated her thumbs but, as she told the *Daily Mail*, on 16 February 1995 '. . . although I knew he was violent, it never occurred to me that he had killed his own parents and was now calmly spending their money.'

Roger Severs was sentenced to life imprisonment.

14 November, 1983

On 14 November 1983, 32-year-old Johnny Watkins Junior shot and killed Betty Jean Barker during a convenience store robbery in Danville, Virginia. On 22 November he killed Carl Douglas Buchanan in a second robbery. He was finally electrocuted on 3 March 1994 when, for what was likely to be the last time, the switch was thrown on the chair at the Greensville Correctional Centre, near Jarratt, Virginia. In its history 258 men and a woman had been electrocuted. Watkins was the 23rd man executed in Virginia after the Supreme Court restored the death penalty and the sixth in 1993–4. As from 1 July 1994 inmates had the option of electing death by lethal injection, an option almost always exercised in other States.

Watkins had appealed for clemency on the grounds that all-white juries were racially motivated. His lawyers had noted that no white person had ever been sentenced to death in Danville, a small town in which the Confederate flag is still flown, near the North Carolina border. The State's governor had rejected his appeal in a terse statement saying 'The facts of the case do not warrant exercise of the extraordinary remedy of executive clemency.'

Almost unheeded by the abolitionists Watkins was electrocuted after spending the day with his lawyers and having a visit from his girlfriend. None of his relatives came to the prison. It was reported that there were calls from spectators of 'God bless you' and 'Go with the flow' as he was taken into the chamber.

15 November, 1993

On 15 November 1993, so he told the court in Tucson, Arizona, space aliens forced Robert Joe Moody to shoot Michelle Malone, aged 33. Five days later they told him to beat 55-year-old Patricia Magda to death. He complied with their request.

The prosecution's version of events was more mundane. They alleged Moody had killed the women, both of whom he knew, for money to buy drugs. During his three-week trial, during which Moody represented himself, a defence psychiatrist had given evidence that, in his opinion, Moody suffered from a multiple personality disorder, a claim challenged by expert witnesses for the prosecution.

Moody, 37 on 29 March 1996, the day he was sentenced, appeared not displeased at the guilty verdicts and told Superior Court Judge, Howard Hantman, 'We have finally come to the point where I get my birthday wish. I hope you grant the appropriate sentence to allow me to complete my mission.' He went on to say that the aliens would resurrect him to prove their existence.

16 November, 1949

Abraham Levine, the owner of the Albion Watch Depot in Leeds, Yorkshire was killed on 16 November 1949 in a raid on his jeweller's shop. At 10 am that morning Walter Sharpe, then aged 20, and Gordon Lannen, three years younger, staged a robbery. They produced guns and demanded money but Mr Levine attempted to fight them off, grabbing hold of Lannen by the collar, before he was obliged to release him under a hail of blows from the butt of a revolver. Two shots were fired and the youths ran across the road, firing as they went. Witnesses could not agree whether they were firing to discourage pursuers or whether, by this time, the youths were in panic and firing randomly.

Levine staggered out of the doorway of his shop and onto the pavement where he collapsed. 'Two men came in,' he told helpers. 'They tried to hold me up. I struggled with them. One hit me on the head, the other shot me.' That evening he died. He had wandered in and out of consciousness and was able to give the police a description of his attackers. On 18 November the men were arrested in Southport, Lancashire.

At the trial Lannen pleaded guilty against the advice of his counsel and the trial judge, Mr Justice Streatfield, then ordered that a plea of not guilty be entered. In evidence Sharpe said that the pair had broken into a gunsmith's and stolen four revolvers. They had gone to rob Mr Levine and when he had seen Lannen held by the jeweller he also heard an explosion. He did not know then that it was his revolver which had been fired.

Mr Justice Streatfield described the case as nothing

short of gangsterism. It had, he said, shocked him as it must have shocked the jury 'when vast sums of money are spent on education to think that two young men have not had inculcated into them a better sense of right and wrong'.

Both were found guilty and Sharpe was sentenced to death. Lannen, because of his age, was detained during His Majesty's pleasure. The crime was blamed on the influence of the cinema. Sharpe had, it was said, been in the habit of visiting the cinema 'as many as three times a week' to see what the judge called 'these wretched gangster films'. He was hanged at Leeds prison on 30 March 1950.

17 November, 1961

The last men to be hanged in Canada were Ronald Turpin (see 11 February) and 54-year-old black Detroit numbers runner, drug dealer and pimp, Arthur Lucas. They were hanged back-to-back at Don prison, Toronto on 10 December 1962. So far as Turpin was concerned there was no doubt that he shot and killed a police officer.

Lucas's case was rather more difficult and for years afterwards many believed that he had been wrongly convicted. They included his lawyer on appeal, Walter Williston, who commented, 'I do not say he was innocent but I believe there are serious doubts about his guilt.'

The victims of the murder on 17 November 1961 at a rooming house, 116 Kendal Avenue, were police informer Therland Crater, also from Detroit, and his prostitute girlfriend, Carolyn (or Carol) Newman. Detroit mobsters had filed a Bill of Particulars to force the authorities to disclose the names of witnesses to a Crime Commission and so had discovered that Crater had turned against them. The FBI believed that another Detroit drug dealer,

Gus Saunders, had offered C\$1,000 and two ounces of heroin to anyone who could find Crater, who had been hidden by the authorities in Toronto.

In the days before the witness protection scheme was streamlined witnesses could often be left to fend more or less for themselves and there is no doubt that Newman, who traded as Rochelle, and Crater were hard up. Possibly old habits die hard and on 12 November they were arrested for keeping a bawdy house. They were held in custody for four days – something of which the Detroit police approved – but unfortunately for them were released on bail. A Toronto lawyer, Mannis Frankel, lent them C\$1,000 against their Ford car on the Thursday afternoon and within 13 hours they were both dead. Carolyn had her throat cut, Crater had been shot and his throat had also been slashed. Medical evidence was that the cutting was not the work of an amateur.

The motive for the killing was said by Henry Bull, for the Crown, to be that Saunders had wanted Crater silenced and that, as the only eyewitness to his killing, Newman had to die as well. The following day Lucas was arrested. He was regarded as having a subnormal IQ but lawyers said he was a skilled draughts player. He had, undoubtedly, been in the numbers racket and one of the witnesses for the Crown, Morris 'Red' Thomas, said that Lucas was a cutter and packager in the narcotics trade although he was, himself, not an addict. He was married to an Englishwoman, Dolores Chipps, also known as Jean, who worked for him as a prostitute and by whom he had a small son. Shortly before the killing he had been living with Lilian Boykin whom the newspapers of the time rather quaintly described as a 'coloured harlot'. Lucas owned an apartment on Burns Avenue in Detroit. He had convictions for a number of offences including armed robbery.

The case against him was that he knew both Saunders and Crater and more particularly where the latter was living. He drove a car belonging to Saunders to Toronto and back around the time of the killing. The car was found to contain bloodstains and bloody rags under the sun visor. There were other bloodstained items found at Lucas's home but none appears to have matched the blood group of the victims. Human blood was found under Lucas's fingernail but again it did not match. There was no identification of Lucas at the scene of the crime and, apart from his general bad character, probably what counted the most against him was that his zircon ring was found on the bloodsoaked sheets beside Newman's body.

He gave his story to the police almost immediately after his arrest. He had known Crater for some time. Lilian and Carolyn got on well together and the men had discussed the possibility of setting up a brothel in Toronto. After Crater had left Detroit he, Lucas, had heard no more and determined to visit his friend to finalise the business. He had left Detroit on the morning of 16 November and had crossed the border at Windsor, driving Saunders's Chevrolet Impala. He had met a man in a bar, Willie White, near Spadina Avenue and had offered to share a room with him costing $8. They checked into the Waverley Hotel at College and Spadina, with Lucas giving his correct name and address.

Lucas made two calls to the Crater-Newman home and then after the second at 3 am left the hotel. At 4.51 am he also made a long-distance call collect to his home on Burns Avenue. He returned to the hotel just after six. He had, he said, left his friends half an hour earlier and had had a coffee in a shop in the city and, indeed, during the trial he identified a police officer sitting in court as having been in the coffee shop at the time. He checked out of the hotel around 6.30 am and the desk clerk noticed nothing untoward about his clothing or his behaviour. He then drove to Cleveland to discuss prostitution with a Paul Brown and then returned home to his wife, arriving about 4.15 pm. As for the ring, he knew that Crater was hard up and wanted to redeem the Ford car. He lent him the ring, saying Crater could pawn it and repay him later. No witnesses were called for the alibi or his visit to Cleveland. He was convicted by the all-male jury after a retirement of five hours. His appeal was dismissed but one judge, J. R. Cartwright, delivered a 21-page dissenting judgment. After two stays of execution Lucas was hanged.

He appears to have behaved very well whilst awaiting his execution. Williston described him as 'rather a gentle individual'. The Salvation Army officer, Colonel Cyril Everitt, who acted as the padre for both Lucas and Turpin said, 'Lucas is the bravest man I ever knew in my life.' In an interview some years later Everitt recalled that Lucas had said to him the day before the execution, 'When a man thinks he has been tricked out of his life, it's hard.'

In the middle 1970s there was some talk that Lucas should receive a posthumous pardon. His supporters argue that his behaviour was inconsistent with his guilt. Why register in the rooming house under his own name? Why make a collect call which could be traced back to him? They argue that the defence was hampered by a lack of time and funds and that the judge should not have allowed the prosecution to introduce the damning evidence of Lucas's lifestyle.

He and Turpin were buried in numbered graves in Toronto's main cemetery. Until he had a heart attack in the 1990s Colonel Everitt visited the graves regularly.

18 November, 1995

Sixty-two-year-old Jacqueline Levitz, widow of furniture magnate Ralph Levitz, was last seen alive on Saturday, 18 November 1995 when at about 4.15 in the afternoon she called into a lumber store in Vicksburg, Alabama to collect some wallpaper samples.

Two days later, when relatives had not heard from her, they called at her modest redbrick house with views over the Mississippi River. The front door was open and there was a bloodstained mattress in her bedroom. There did not appear to have been a robbery. Her handbag was missing, as was a diary, but a safe with a quantity of jewellery had been left unforced.

Levitz had had a lifestyle worthy of an airport novel. A local beauty pageant queen she had been born into a poor sharecropping family and was said to be able to pick 300 pounds of cotton a day. She preferred to ignore a first marriage, only admitting to the second and third. The first marriage had been in 1956 and had ended when her husband's boatbuilding business failed.

She had met her second husband, Banks 'Smitty' Smith, a local restaurateur, when she was a waitress and had been hired by him to be his greeter. They had married in 1964. He already had a history of heart trouble and on 7 April 1969 suffered chest pains and had difficulty with breathing. Jacqueline took him to hospital but, claimed Smith's family, not fast enough and she had stopped at a bank on the way. Smith died shortly after his admission there. There had been problems in the marriage. Smith was a man with an uneven temper and a separation agreement had been drawn up 18 months before his death, if never executed.

During her time with Smith she had embarked on a role as a society hostess and had made a fortune for herself investing in blocks of flats and redeveloping property.

She met Ralph Levitz when he invited her to redecorate his mansion on South Ocean Boulevard, Palm Beach. They married in 1987 and six weeks after the wedding he suffered his first stroke. With her help he recovered sufficiently to play golf and host receptions. In 1989 they renewed their marriage vows and at a reception at Breakers Hotel she was accompanied by 42 bridesmaids all in white lace dresses and matching hats. She was then 55 and Levitz 76. From then on Levitz's health deteriorated and he died in the spring of 1995. Jacqueline moved to Vicksburg to be near her sisters. She was popular in the neighbourhood, free of the social airs and graces of a former Washington hostess or a woman who had just inherited $18 million, and devoted her time to renovating the house.

Two men were arrested for burglary of the Levitz house but were not thought to have been involved in the disappearance. A reward of $100,000 for information about the murder has gone unclaimed. Speculation has ranged from a kidnapping – but no demand has been made; robbery – but nothing was taken; and even that she staged her own death – but why?

In the spring of 1996 television companies were hovering over the houses of her sisters, hoping to obtain the rights for a mini-series or film of her life.

19 November, 1943

About 2.15 pm on 19 November 1943 what appeared to be a sack was discovered by two sewermen from the Luton Corporation, Bedfordshire as they checked on the water level at Osborne Bridge Road. In fact it was four sacks containing the battered and naked body of a young woman. The pathologist Keith Simpson was called in and he estimated that she had been killed within the 36 hours before her body was dumped. He thought she was aged between 30 and 35. She had been beaten about the head with a blunt object and her upper and lower jaw had been fractured. She was five and a half months pregnant and had already given birth to a child in the past. She was missing her false teeth. None of her clothing was in the sacks. A mark, M. F., on one of them showed it belonged to the Ministry of Food and had come from a potato merchant from a nearby village.

Photographs of the woman's restored face were circulated and lantern slides were displayed in cinemas asking for help. Enquiries were made in local cafés and dance halls but without success. Nearly 40 people came forward to try to identify the body as one of their missing relatives but no identification was made.

Finally, three months later, a dog nosed out a shoulder pad from a woman's dress, part of a bundle of rags on a rubbish tip. Quite by chance the officer in the case, Chief Inspector Chapman, was nearby and it was handed to him. It revealed a dyer's tag V1 2247. It was traced to the Sketchley dye works in Luton and from there to Caroline Manton who lived at 14 Regent Street, Luton. In a house-to-house inquiry the two teenage children living there had been shown the photograph but had failed to recognise their mother.

Bertie Manton, a former boxer then working for the National Fire Service, told the police he was a single parent looking after four children. He said that his marriage to Caroline had disintegrated following quarrels over her associations with soldiers and she had left to go and live with her brother in Grantham and had then moved on to London. Further inquiries showed that Mrs Manton's mother had received three letters from Hampstead. The police were not satisfied, however, and Fred Cherrill, the fingerprint expert, found a print on a pickle jar in the cellar. It was matched with the body. Blood splashes were found on a door jamb in the front room and on an envelope in the cellar. They were Group 'O' and also matched that of the body. When Manton was asked to write the word Hampstead he omitted the letter 'p'. This writing appeared to match the handwriting on the letters which also made the same spelling mistake.

At first Manton maintained his wife had left him but he changed his story, saying that he had killed her following a quarrel in which she complained that he did nothing but work. She had, he said, thrown a cup of scalding tea over him. 'I lost my temper, picked up a heavy wooden stool . . . and hit her about the head and face several times.' He then said he had a blackout and when he recovered he found his wife was dead. He had taken the body to the cellar and when the children were out that evening had put it on the handlebars of his bike and dumped his wife in the river. When the children asked where their mother was he told them they had quarrelled again and she had left once more. He had destroyed her teeth because his children knew their mother was never without them.

He was convicted of murder and his appeal refused. The death sentence was commuted after a petition which garnered over 30,000 signatures but, already a sick man, he died in Parkhurst prison in 1947. In his autobiography Keith Simpson points out that the coat from which the shoulder pad came was unstained with blood. Had Manton not tried to dispose of it he would almost certainly have got away with murder.

Fred Cherrill, *Cherrill of the Yard*; Keith Simpson, *Forty Years of Murder*.

20 November, 1991

A week after the killings of four members of a Korean family in Grenada Hills, Los Angeles, on 20 November 1991 the police had found no motive for their murder. Nor, as the years have passed, has further progress been made in the investigation.

Hee Yoo, aged 36, his wife Gyung, two years younger, their seven-year-old daughter Pauline, and five-year-old son Kenneth had been killed by what the police described as 'sharp force' wounds. The parents were found underneath a blanket in the living room, the children in bedrooms in their nightwear.

Hee and Gyung had failed to attend a dental appointment and their relatives went to their home where they found the bodies at about 10 am.

Neighbours had heard the sounds of arguments the previous evening and there had been reports of strange cars parked nearby. A murder-suicide was ruled out.

21 November, 1984

Colin Pitchfork, from the village of Littlethorpe near Leicester, was convicted of the murders of two young girls from the area. He was the first person in England convicted of murder by virtue of DNA evidence.

On 21 November 1984 15-year-old Lynda Mann left her home in The Coppice, Enderby to visit a friend. The next morning her body was discovered. There were traces of semen in her pubic hair. A second murder occurred on 31 July 1986 when another young girl from Enderby was murdered in the early part of the evening. She too had semen in her pubic hair which suggested that in both cases the attacker had ejaculated prematurely. It was clear that he was a local man.

One of those seen in the neighbourhood was a kitchen porter who worked at the local hospital. Questioned, Richard Buckland, then aged 17, gave a detailed confession saying he had probably gone mad. He was arrested and charged but the officer in charge of the case, DCS Baker, was unhappy. The man was regarded as unstable, and false confessions in high-profile cases are regular.

At the time Dr Alec Jeffreys had been carrying out pioneering work at the Department of Genetics at Leicester University. Using body fluid, blood, semen, saliva as well as hair roots he claimed to be able to match samples which would be the equivalent of genetic fingerprints. No two people in the world would have an identical pattern. Asked to test material from the youth and the semen sample found on the bodies of the girls he said unequivocally that they did not match. Buckland was released after three months in custody.

The police decided to obtain samples from all men in the neighbourhood aged between the ages of 17 and 34. This ambitious and expensive project was not a unique one. All men in Blackburn had been fingerprinted after the killing by Peter Griffiths of four-year-old June Anne Devaney in Queen's Park Hospital, Blackburn on 15 May 1948. Griffiths's fingerprints matched those on a bottle on the child's bedside table.

There could be no compulsion for a man to give a sample but those who refused would be subject to special scrutiny. The scheme was thwarted by Richard Kelly who gave a sample on behalf of his work superior at Hampton's Bakery, Colin Pitchfork. Later he discussed this quite openly in the Clarendon public house in Leicester. The manageress of the bakery reported the conversation to the police and inquiries showed that the signature on an early statement he had made as to his whereabouts and that on the consent form for the blood sample did not match. Pitchfork also had two convictions for indecent exposure prior to his marriage in 1981.

He was arrested on 19 September 1987 and confessed to the murder in front of his wife. Asked why he had killed the second girl he replied, 'Opportunity. She was there and I was there.' His more detailed explanation was that in both cases he had initially intended to expose himself to the girls but they had seen who he was and so could identify him if they saw him in the village. They had effectively backed him into a corner. It was, he explained, their fault. He claimed he had exposed himself to a thousand women. On the day he killed the first girl at 7 pm he had taken his wife to an evening class where she was studying sociology and had collected her at 9 pm. Their baby had been in a carrycot on the back seat of the car when he had stopped, raped and killed the girl.

He pleaded guilty at Leicester Crown Court and was sentenced to life imprisonment. Kelly, his stand-in at the blood test, was given a sentence of 18 months, suspended for two years.

Joseph Wambaugh, *The Blooding.*

22 November, 1987

The body of 15-year-old Diane Cho was discovered, partially clothed and bound, in the cupboard of the bedroom of her home near Richmond, Virginia on 22 November 1987. She was the third victim of Timothy Spencer who, in a short spree between September and December 1987, raped and killed four women in the area. He was the first person to be convicted of murder by DNA evidence in the United States.

The first victim was 35-year-old Debbie Davis who was found raped and strangled in her flat. The second was Dr Susan Hellams who was attacked in her flat and her body pushed into a bedroom cupboard on 3 October. The press gave the killer the name 'The Southside Slayer'.

In December the body of 44-year-old Susan Tucker was discovered in her flat in Arlington. She had been raped and strangled a week earlier. The officer in the case noticed the tidy way in which the murderer had left the flat and linked it to the behaviour of Timothy W. Spencer, from Washington DC, whose *modus operandi* was breaking into houses whilst the occupants were asleep. He had no convictions for sexual offences but he had been at liberty, living in a halfway house, when the killings occurred. He was questioned initially as a routine suspect but, when asked to give a blood sample, asked if it had anything to do with rape. At the time he had only been told he was being questioned in connection with burglaries.

The match came from a semen sample removed from Susan Tucker's body and the laboratory gave the chance of a match as 135 million to one. There were also matches with samples from Debbie Davis and Susan Hellams.

In July 1988 Spencer stood trial for the murder of Susan Tucker. The defence argument was to be that since Spencer shared the same genetic make-up as his relatives, they were just as capable of committing the murder as he. The trial judge ruled that if this line of defence continued he would allow evidence of the other murders to be introduced. On 17 July Spencer was convicted of first-degree murder and sentenced to life imprisonment. On 22 September 1988 he was convicted of the murders of Debbie Davis and Susan Hellams and was sentenced to death. In the case of Diane Cho there was not a sufficient sample to provide a match.

23 November, 1908

Around breakfast time on Monday, 23 November 1908, the body of 60-year-old semi-invalid Dorothy Oliver, also known as Dorothy Allen, was found lying on an Ilkley couch in the breakfast parlour of her home at 6 Alexandra Road, Southport, Lancashire. She had been shot twice in the back and once in the head whilst in what was described as a stooping position. From evidence given at the inquest it appears she would still have been able to walk after the shots in the back. The third shot was in front of the right ear. The gun must have been held within six inches of her head and this was the shot which killed her. Jewellery had been stolen.

Fifty-four-year-old Henry Jackson, a local man who had known Mrs Oliver some years previously and who dealt in jewellery, was interrogated by officers regarding the murder and later committed suicide. He had been traced when he sold some of the stolen jewellery. He had been behind with his rent but he had an alibi provided by Ann Rimmer, his landlady. He left a note protesting his innocence but a quantity of Mrs Oliver's jewellery was found at his house together with a bloodstained Webley revolver.

Chief Inspector Bower, sent by Scotland Yard, interviewed Jackson at length after searching his rooms where he could find nothing relating to the murder. He did, however, find a quantity of powder which Jackson said was harmless. In fact it was strychnine and, as the Chief Inspector wrote in a subsequent note, he must have taken enough to kill 50 people. In some self-justification Bower wrote, 'I took a statement of 36 sheets of foolscap from the man, and no doubt the fact of my taking the statement killed him.'

The police came in for some criticism in the locality for failing to arrest Jackson before he killed himself but, at the inquest, the jury dissociated themselves from the strictures. They considered the fact that the police had not arrested Jackson was completely justified and, as Bower wrote in another memorandum, thought Mrs Rimmer 'deserving of severe censure for frustrating the efforts of the police and for her unsatisfactory evidence today [19 December 1908].' She admitted she had lied, saying Jackson had not been in on the Sunday night and that she had found the remainder of the jewellery and the revolver Jackson used in her part of the house. Asked why she had lied she told the coroner's jury that she regarded it as her duty as a landlady to oblige her lodger.

24 November, 1961

William Wentworth, prison guard at Kingston Penitentiary, Ontario, was stabbed to death on 24 November 1961. In the early hours of the morning Wentworth, the only officer in charge of C dormitory containing 42 inmates, was attacked in the washroom and stabbed 11 times with two knives which were later found in a wastepaper basket.

It was not until October 1994 that charges were brought against Ralph Cochrane who was serving a sentence for armed robbery at the time and who, by

the time the charge was finally brought, was serving a
life sentence for another string of robberies. He denied
the offence. Explaining the gap between offence and
arrest, Gerald Rice, the Chief of Police of Kingston,
said that unsolved cases were reviewed periodically and
that people involved in the murder 'have matured' and
that new scientific methods had been developed. 'They
used any number of things to re-evaluate the evidence
and re-interview witnesses.'

Wentworth's family was critical of the way the investigation into his death was conducted. Although C dormitory was a pre-release facility, at the time of the attack
it was housing a high proportion of dangerous men,
including Edwin Alonzo Boyd, head of the notorious
Boyd gang, who were noted prison breakers. Boyd was
released 10 months after the stabbing. In March 1995 he
returned to Kingston to give evidence in the preliminary
hearings against Cochrane.

William Wentworth's son Michael believed 'the rest [of
those in the dormitory] were accessories after the fact.
None of these men should have received parole until it
was proved who did it.'

On 1 May 1995 Judge Thomas Lally stayed the murder
charge against Cochrane saying that the 34-year delay
in bringing the case violated Cochrane's constitutional
rights. Subject to any appeal this effectively meant the
charge had been dismissed.

25 November, 1929

On 25 November 1929 commercial traveller Kurt Erich
Tetzner gave a lift to a young man. Four days later,
on 29 November, his burned out car was found near
Ettershausen, Bavaria. A charred body was found at
the wheel and Tetzner's wife identified it as that of her

husband. The not inconsiderable sum for depression-hit Germany of £7,250 was payable on his death and the insurance company stalled. Earlier in 1929 they had already paid out £500 after insuring his mother. Now Tetzner's wife began to receive calls from a Herr Stranelli in Strasburg at a neighbour's flat and the French police were asked to investigate. They arrested Stranelli, who soon confessed to being Tetzner.

Tetzner made two conflicting confessions. The first was that he had killed a tramp to whom he had given a lift, and then burned his body to deceive the insurance companies. A second statement slightly modified this in his favour. He had accidentally knocked down a tramp who, whilst being driven to hospital, had died. He had only then devised the fraud. In court Tetzner offered the second as the correct explanation. On cross-examination he agreed that he had discussed a fraud with his wife who had suggested that he dig up a body rather than commit murder. He had replied that there must be blood about.

He went on to describe two attempts he had made to secure a victim. The first, a young man, had refused to get into the car; the second, a mechanic, Alois Ortner, he had met near Ingolstadt. He had bought him a collar and given him money to pay for a shave so that he would resemble his killer. He asked Ortner to crawl under the car to check an oil valve and when he emerged hit him with a hammer. Ortner had managed to escape into the forest and now gave evidence at the trial.

Tetzner was found guilty and made a full confession before his execution on 2 May 1931. He had given a lift to a youth. The man complained of the cold and this gave Tetzner the opportunity of wrapping him in a heavy rug and pinioning his arms. He then strangled him with a piece of rope. Near Ettershausen he had driven the car into a tree, opened the petrol tank and laid a trail over the mudguard into the back of the car which he had then set alight.

The case bears considerable similarity to the English

case of Alfred Arthur Rouse, who also set fire to a tramp and who was hanged on 10 March 1931.

26 November, 1995

On 26 November 1995 Harry P. Kaufmann, a 56-year-old clerk, was attacked and then set on fire in his booth at the Kingston-Throop Avenue subway station in Bedford-Stuyvesant, New York.

On 14 December an 18-year-old Brooklyn man, James Irons, described by his family as mentally slow, was arrested for the murder. According to police reports he had confessed on videotape and his account of the killing seemed credible. Mr Kaufmann had been killed because he refused to open his booth and hand over the money without a struggle. As a result one of his attackers had sprayed an incendiary liquid through the coin tray and another had started to drop lighted matches, telling Kaufmann to leave the booth. There was an explosion as the vapours were ignited by the flame.

The attackers had gone fully armed. They ran, leaving behind an M-1 carbine with a loaded clip and a charred glove which suggested a blow-back from the explosion.

Irons's family said that James had dropped out of school because of poor reading skills and his brother, Randall Clark, said he doubted James understood half the questions being put to him. Miriam Graham, Irons's mother, said she and her son had been together when the explosion occurred. He was warming up soup whilst she was watching television.

According to reports Irons had said that he had not wished to participate in the hold-up because he lived too near the subway station and might be identified. He had capitulated and had agreed to go on the raid a few days later.

The Brooklyn District Attorney was quick to deny suggestions that the attack was inspired by the recently released film *Money Train* which had featured token-booth fire scenes. The death of Mr Kaufmann was followed by another seven similar attacks within a matter of weeks. There were suggestions that the film, which starred Wesley Snipes and Woody Harrelson, should be withdrawn. Columbia executives said that the attacks on token booths in the film had been based on a series of 1988 attacks in New York subway stations.

On 17 December 1996 Irons, 19-year-old Thomas Malik and 18-year-old Vincent Ellerbe were all sentenced to 25 years to life. 'You have rights,' said Judge Francis Egitto, 'but who protects the rights of Mr Kaufmann?' Malik and Ellerbe continued to maintain their innocence.

27 November, 1978

The murder which obliquely did much to promote the struggle for gay rights occurred on 27 November 1978 when former police and fireman, Dan White, shot George Moscone, Mayor of San Francisco, and Harvey Milk at their offices. White had resigned his position as a city supervisor because he said the pay of $9,600 was not sufficient for him to support his wife and family. Later he asked to be reappointed. The mayor Moscone was at first predisposed to do so but the move was opposed by Milk, another supervisor. An hour before a replacement was to be announced White went to their offices and first shot the mayor four times and then Milk.

White's defence – which became known as the Twinky Bar defence – was an ingenious one. He was, it was said, suffering from the results of consumption of junk food and, consequently, his judgment was affected. On 22 May 1979 White was acquitted of premeditated murder and convicted only of manslaughter, receiving the maximum sentence of seven years and eight months.

Milk had been a prominent gay activist and the gay community felt that this was the reason White had been acquitted of murder. The community in San Francisco rioted, with some five thousand protestors causing over $1 million-worth of damage. White was released on 6 January 1984 and committed suicide the next year. He had attached a garden hose to the exhaust pipe of his car. He left a suicide note on the windscreen: 'I knew you were going to find me this way. Sorry you had to find me in this condition. Sorry for any inconvenience.'

28 November, 1911

The self-styled Lord George Sanger, owner of the circus bearing his name and actually of Hungarian origin, was beaten to death at his home in Finchley, north London, on 28 November 1911 by Herbert Cooper, the son of his farm manager. There had been trouble with Cooper who had been banned from sleeping in the main house because it was said he had been over-familiar with the wife of another employee, Harry Austin.

About 6 pm on that day Sanger had been sitting talking with Harry Austin, when Cooper rushed in with an axe and struck Austin. He then attacked Sanger, striking him on the head and behind the left ear, and rushed out. Cooper then went into the kitchen where he said he had come for his gramophone. He went into a scullery and returned, saying it was all dark. He then put his hand over the mouth of Arthur Jackson, another member of Sanger's staff, and cut him on the throat with a razor.

Although the police arranged for a magistrate to take a dying declaration from Sanger he never recovered consciousness. The wound had penetrated to the bone which was laid bare.

Telegrams were sent to all ports, and photographs of Cooper were sent to all newspapers. In the event they were not necessary. Cooper had not gone far. His body was found on the up railway line near Crouch End at around 7.30 am on 30 November. Thomas Potter, the ticket collector at Highgate station, told the coroner: 'His brain was lying in the centre of the fourfoot [track] about three yards from the body and a portion of the face and skull lay near the inner rail of the up road.'

Amongst his possessions was a letter:

Dear Dad

Something at the farm has happened I dont remember doing it I can only call to mind someone speaking I seemed to come to my sences no one knows what i have gone through the govener turned against me what for I dont know and blamed me for things I never knew anything about after spending six years with him and Jenny Beasley and George Austin with ther lies as turned my brain she is the worst woman I have ever heard of i cant send this by post as I havent got a stamp but all what belongs to me share out between you you must look behind the pictures over wash table you will find some money I drew from one of my old books and havent put it all away dont think of me any more I have been greatly wronged by that woman Good bye all my brains has turned hope you will forgive me for some great wrong Good bye Tom Dick Len and you Dad your broken hearted son Herb.

Another letter intended for Austin read:

Dear Harry

I am sorry things should have come to this know one

knows what I have gone through what I told you was the truth and Mr George turned like he did after all that time I have been with him I couldnt stand it I have blamed Jenny Beasley for all and let her think it over. Good bye

Thirteen pounds in gold was found and as the relatives of Lord George did not claim it the money was given to Cooper's father.

There was some insanity in Cooper's family. His grandmother's brother died in an asylum. The coroner's jury returned a verdict of suicide whilst of unsound mind.

Over the years into the 1930s the police received letters which suggested that Cooper had not died but had escaped to Australia or Canada, and two people said he was working in a circus in Ontario. There were also a number of letters from the continent suggesting that the writers should share in Sanger's estate. Apart from a number of small bequests, Sanger had left his money to his daughter.

PRO/MEPO/3/216B

29 November, 1930

Apart from her killer the last person to see 59-year-old Marie Louisa Bossano, a British subject of Spanish extraction, alive was a baker's boy who made a delivery around midday on Saturday 29 November 1930.

When she had not been seen at church on the Sunday the police went to her house in a residential part of Gibraltar and the front door was forced. Her body was found in her sitting room. She had been struck 16 or more times with a blunt instrument. Regarded as 'of a religious turn of mind, peculiar in temperament and very methodical', she lived alone and was a property investor. From the forensic evidence it seemed that she had first been attacked in her bedroom and then had been carried or walked into the sitting room where she had collapsed. There was no evidence of robbery; money and jewellery had been left undisturbed. She had probably been dead for some 30 hours, putting the time of death at no later than 4 pm on the Saturday.

In the flat at the time was another British subject of Spanish extraction, Ernesto Opisso, who was employed as a general handyman. At 1.45 pm a police constable had seen him leave the flat. The only front door key to the flat was found some 200 yards away.

When questioned Opisso said he had not been to the flat since 7.30 on the Friday night and put forward an alibi that he was working on another house. There was a fingerprint in a diary which could have been that of Opisso but insufficient ridge characteristics were found to make an identification. It was, however, on a page which related to work done by him.

The theory was that there had been a quarrel over work done and that in temper Opisso had struck his employer. Opisso was arrested and in the first execution in Gibraltar for 35 years was hanged on 3 July 1931. The previous day a petition for a reprieve had been refused and the police were called out to deal with demonstrators. The crowd demanded that the Roman Catholic bishop should intervene to prevent the execution and when he refused they attacked the police and stoned windows. Troops were then called out and, armed with hockey sticks, charged the crowd. There were no such incidents on the day of the execution but shops remained closed.

30 November, 1993

In March 1995 Sicilian Domenico Finocchio was convicted at the Old Bailey of the murder of his brother-in-law Domenico Ranno, on 30 November 1993. The prosecution had alleged that Ranno's wife Sebastiana had summoned her brother to her help after she found her husband had been sleeping with her sister.

The court was told that Sebastiana Ranno had married her husband at the age of 16 when they eloped to England. Ranno ran two south London restaurants, Donna Ina and Donna Ina Two – Ina was the nickname of Mrs Ranno – which he used as cover for drug dealing. Finocchio, who had 19 previous convictions in Italy, came to England to avenge his sister who alleged that her husband, apart from his infidelity, had been cruel to her. Finocchio shot Ranno twice in the head with his own gun at his home in Helix Road, Kennington whilst he was ordering tomatoes for the kitchens. A love-bird with a broken neck was found at the scene.

Finocchio was caught because a small-time Italian criminal saw the murder reported on television and went to the police. He allowed himself to be wired and discussed the killing with Finocchio. On one tape the court heard that Finocchio had said, 'With the first blow, I got him, bang. He fell to the ground. With the second I ran out. I told him farewell and I will see you in the next life. He got what he deserved.' Later he said, 'When you murder someone always shoot the final shot, for even if you shoot him in the head he can stay alive. The best thing to do is put the barrel in his mouth and shoot.'

The informer, who was given a new name and identity, gave evidence from behind screens, shielded from the public gallery.

Mrs Ranno, who had been accused of ordering the murder of her husband, was acquitted. His Honour Judge Capstick told them that her silent tacit acquiescence did not make her guilty. Before they convicted her the jurors had to be sure that she instigated the plan and encouraged her brother in it. Finocchio was sentenced to life imprisonment. Judge Capstick told him, 'It was an execution and you were proud of it.'

DECEMBER

1 December, 1902

Edgar Edwards attacked and killed John William Darby
and his wife, Beatrice, on 1 December 1902. They had
a small but profitable grocery shop at 22 Wyndham
Road, Camberwell when Edwards arrived carrying a
5lb sash-weight wrapped in newspaper. By the time he
had left the shop he had nailed up the premises and
attached a note saying the business had closed down
but would soon reopen under new management. Over
the next week, helped by local people to whom he paid a
few shillings for their time, he emptied the contents of the
shop and the living quarters, taking them to his new home
at 89 Church Road, Leyton. Amongst the contents were
black sacks containing the dismembered bodies of the
Darbys and their young daughter, Ethel, whom Edwards
had strangled.

The police were called, not to investigate any murder
but because it was thought that the Darbys had run off
with the Christmas Loan Club savings, amounting to
nearly £200.

For some weeks Edwards appears to have behaved
perfectly respectably until, with money running out, he
attacked another grocer who survived to give a description
of his assailant. At Edwards's home the police found bill
heads belonging to the Darbys and from then it was only a
question of digging in the garden to retrieve their remains.

In 1903 Edwards ran an unsuccessful defence of insanity at the Central Criminal Court. His mother and a great-aunt had died insane, his father was an alcoholic, two cousins were mental defectives and a third in an asylum. He does not appear to have minded greatly when the jury refused to return a verdict in his favour. As the black cap was being placed on the head of the judge, Edwards commented, 'This is quite like being on the stage.' On his way to the gallows at Wandsworth prison on 3 March 1906 he is said to have remarked to the prison chaplain, 'I've been looking forward to this a lot.'

E. Spencer Shew, *A Second Companion to Murder.*

2 December, 1919

On 2 December 1919 the 56-year-old Ambrose J. Small, a theatre owner in Toronto, Ontario, sold the shares in his companies for $1 million. His wife, Theresa, banked the money and went home to await her husband for dinner. Small told his lawyer that he would be keeping his bookkeeper John Doughty and went to pay off his other staff. He was never seen again.

Doughty disappeared shortly afterwards, together with some $100,000 of bearer bonds from Small's bank deposit boxes. Whilst there were a number of false sightings of Small, Doughty was traced to Oregon where in November 1920 he was found working in a lumber camp. In the meantime it had become apparent that Small was not the homeloving man he had been thought to be. He had kept a love-nest at the Grand Opera House, furnished with oriental decor. It was also apparent that Doughty and Small did not get on. Small had fought with his bookkeeper on at least one occasion.

When he was extradited to Canada, Doughty was

convicted of stealing the bonds and received five years' imprisonment. Curiously, suspicion now fell on Theresa Small. There were suggestions that she had murdered her husband to provide money for the Catholic church, and obscene pictures were printed of her. The family home was searched but nothing incriminating was found, let alone Small's body.

He was officially declared dead in 1924 and Theresa died 13 years later. When the Opera House was pulled down in May 1944 the police were on hand to see if a body had been hidden. Nothing was found.

Fred McClement, *The Strange Case of Ambrose Small*.

3 December, 1980

On 3 December 1980, then aged 50, Colin 'Duke' Osborne was found dead on Hackney Marshes, east London. A minor public schoolboy and gambler who had once owed money to the Kray twins and later became their armourer, he had served five years for possessing firearms. In prison he became something of a cigarette baron and in 1980 he put together a drugs importation scheme involving Lennie (also known as 'Teddy Bear' or 'Silly Eddie') Watkins. Deals were set up in Pakistan to smuggle a high-grade cannabis, 'Paki Black', and four successful runs were made. Container lorries were fitted with false floors exporting, at least theoretically, sanitary equipment and returning with sports shoes, netting some £10 million at street prices. Watkins, however, had a predilection for lighting cigars in public with £20 notes, something which drew him to the attention of the authorities and justified the 'Silly Eddie' nickname. The last operation, involving some £2.5 million worth of cannabis, was monitored by a joint police and customs exercise in the course of which Watkins shot and killed customs officer Peter Bennett, on 20 October of that year.

Both the Customs and Excise and other members of Watkins's team still at large wished to see Osborne. Certainly the former failed to do so but the latter may have managed it. An open verdict was recorded at the inquest. Suggestions of the cause of his death include suicide (a version favoured in his book *Villains We Have Known* by Reggie Kray), a drug overdose or that he died of a heart attack, possibly during questioning by his former colleagues as to the whereabouts of the proceeds. It was thought that his body had been put in a freezer immediately after his death whilst a decision was made about its disposal. Watkins was sentenced to life imprisonment for the murder of Peter Bennett and committed suicide in prison.

Duncan Campbell, *The Underworld*; Reggie Kray, *Villains We Have Known*; James Morton, *Gangland*.

4 December, 1982

In early February 1996 prosecuting attorneys in Orlando, Florida finally dropped a first-degree murder charge against Michael Marley. He had been accused of the murder of his wife, the spunky and jitterbug-loving Joyce at their home in Orlando on 4 December 1982. For good measure it was alleged he had sliced off her finger which carried the heart-shaped diamond engagement ring he had given her.

According to Marley the day began as usual when he woke around 4 am to go to his job at Disney World. His wife made the coffee and kissed him goodbye. He

left around 4.30 am and a neighbour found her in her
nightgown on the bedroom floor, covered in blood,
around midday. The house had been ransacked. Clock-in
records showed Marley had been at work all morning.
Although Marley was questioned the case was never even
brought before a grand jury.

There the matter rested for a decade until the case was
passed to Tom McCann of the Orange County Sheriff's
office. Now scientific investigation had progressed and
a detailed stomach analysis was obtained. According to
this Joyce Marley had probably died whilst her husband
was still at home. Over the years he was also alleged
to have made a remark to a neighbour that he would
slice off his wife's finger to get back the engagement
ring if she would not agree to a divorce. Marley, now
aged 51 and remarried, was indicted by a grand jury in
September 1993.

However, a Gainsborough doctor's analysis challenged
the prosecution's claim that Joyce Marley had died
between midnight and 2 am. There were, said Ed Kirkland,
Marley's lawyer, strange hairs on Joyce Marley's body as
well as on a door which appeared to have been forced
open. A neighbour said she had seen a shadowy figure in
the Marley yard.

Marley was understandably angry. 'It's just showed me
that life isn't what you think it is. You can be taken away
at any time. I'm not the person I used to be.' Of his wife,
whose picture he still carries, he said, 'Feisty as hell. She
was just fantastic.'

5 December, 1924

Elsie Cameron, an unattractive, neurotic, and poorly
educated girl who worked as a typist, was last seen
carrying a small dressing case on the afternoon of 5

December 1924. She was besotted by, and engaged to, a similarly unintelligent young man, Norman Thorne, who struggled to make a living running a poultry farm near Crowborough, Sussex. She had stayed the night at the Crowborough farm and that month told Thorne she was pregnant. She had consulted a fortune teller who had told her that the two-year engagement would end in December in a wedding. Thorne had also become involved with a rather more attractive local girl, Elizabeth Coldicott. He was trying to break off the engagement to Cameron but was vacillating. Elsie came to the farm one final time, determined to drive off her rival once and for all.

There followed a series of telegrams. On 10 December her father telegraphed Thorne asking for news of his daughter. Thorne replied saying he did not understand. He had been expecting her on the morning of 6 December but she had not arrived. The police were called and Thorne was co-operative, anxious to help both them and the press who were staking out the farm. He allowed himself to be photographed holding one of his hens in his arms.

The local police appear to have disregarded the stories of two local men which placed Elsie near the farm on the evening of 5 December and it was not until 10 January 1925, when a third witness reported she had seen Elsie going through the gates of the farm, that Scotland Yard was called in. Thorne made another statement which merely elaborated on his earlier story that he had been expecting his fiancée who had not arrived. On 14 January the police, who had been digging over the farm, found her dressing case. Now Thorne made another statement.

'I want to tell the truth about what happened,' he lied. In this new and improved version Elsie had indeed come to the farm and announced she intended to stay until their wedding. He had gone out that evening to see Elizabeth Coldicott and her mother. When he returned about midnight Elsie was hanging on a crossbeam in the chicken shed. There had, he said, been no quarrel before he left her.

He had sawn the body into uneven quarters. The head he put into a tin box where it was effectively stuck; the trunk and the legs were wrapped in sacking. The portions were buried in the chicken run, at the spot on which he had, the previous month, allowed himself to be photographed. On the afternoon of 6 December he had gone to the cinema with Miss Coldicott.

Bernard Spilsbury conducted the first postmortem and, two months later, Robert Bronte, who had been Crown Analyst to the Government of Ireland before coming to England in 1922, undertook a second. It would not be unfair to say that Spilsbury regarded him as an inferior.

Thorne's trial was effectively conducted as a medical battle with Spilsbury lined up against Bronte and six other doctors. His evidence was that the bruises on Elsie Cameron's body, including a massive one on the temple, were caused before her death. Bronte argued that if the blow had been of the force Spilsbury advocated it would have broken the skin and cheekbone, something which had not happened. The main problem was, however, whether she had been hanged. The final version of the defence was that she had tried to commit suicide, Thorne had cut her down but that she had died from shock. Spilsbury would have none of it. There was, he said, no medical evidence to suggest a hanging of any kind. Death had been caused by shock following the bad beating she had sustained.

Thorne was defended by James Cassels and, by and large, given the string of lies he had already told, made a reasonably credible witness. He really had no answer to the questions put by Curtis-Bennett for the Crown:

Q: If your story is correct, when you went out at half past nine she still believed from you that you were going to marry her if she was pregnant?

A: Yes.

Q: Then why should she commit suicide?

With some presence of mind he replied that since his
fiancée had left no note he could not say. This, coupled
with the medical evidence, was sufficient to secure a
conviction. The jury retired for less than half an hour.

At the appeal the Court rejected a suggestion that the
medical evidence should be referred to the arbitration of
a medical commissioner, something which the court had
power to do under the Criminal Appeal Act 1907. There
was then considerable pressure for a reprieve. The *Law
Journal*, in an early attack on the ability of juries to
understand complex matters, argued that 'The verdict of
a jury on a question of pathology is valueless. Thorne is
entitled to feel that he has been condemned by a tribunal
which was not capable of forming a first-hand judgment,
but followed the man with the biggest name.' The Home
Secretary was not impressed. Thorne was hanged on 22
April 1925.

Douglas G. Browne and Tom Tullett, *Bernard Spilsbury,
His Life and Cases*; Edward Grice, *Great Cases of
Sir Derek Curtis-Bennett KC*; Helena Normanton (ed),
Famous British Trials: The Trial of Norman Thorne.

6 December, 1953

On 6 December 1953, 17-year-old Marion McDowell
went for a drive with James Wilson, a 19-year-old scaffolding rigger. They had been out together a few times
in the preceding weeks. According to Wilson at about
7.40 pm they parked in a place for courting couples in
Scarborough, a suburb of Toronto, Ontario. Whilst they
were necking, something which lasted for two hours, the

passenger side door was opened and a flashlight was
pointed into the car. They were told, said Wilson, 'This
is a stick-up.' He identified the attacker as being about
five feet eight inches tall with a narrow face and, he said,
carrying a handgun, either a Walther .38 or a Luger.
Wilson was told to hand over his wallet, which he did.
He was then hit on the back of the head with two blows
and later required 17 stitches.

Wilson's recollections of the subsequent events were,
unsurprisingly, vague. He recalled being in the back
of his own car with Marion's body across him, then
being alone and of the bandit getting into a second car
and driving off. Of Marion there was no sign. He got
back into the driver's seat and went back to his father
who took him to the police. Wilson directed them to
the yard where he had woken and there the police
found broken locks and a chain. They also found a
bar of laundry soap. The back seat of his car was
covered in blood, some his and the rest was believed
to be that of Marion. His wallet was found back in
Scarborough.

There was considerable discussion as to the significance
of the soap. There were street suggestions of a botched
abortion rather than a robbery but there was anecdotal
evidence that McDowell had suffered menstrual pains the
previous month. As the last person seen with her, Wilson
was under considerable suspicion but, although regarded
as none too bright, he both held firm under lengthy
interrogation and came through a lie-detector test with
flying colours.

In the late summer of 1954 Robert Fabian of Scotland Yard was brought into the case by the Toronto
Telegram. He was on a lecture tour in America promoting his latest book and, apart from an effort to
solve the mystery, was roped in to boost circulation
in a slack period. He was unable to throw light on
the case and returned to America and continued his
signing tour. The body of Marion McDowell was never
found.

The case has interesting comparisons with the Brown–Watson case in Boulder, Colorado, in which Keith Brown was acquitted of killing his girlfriend, Kelly Watson, who was trying to break off their relationship. His defence was that on 13 October 1985, whilst they were at Chapaqua, a courting site near Boulder, two men had approached the car, forced him to drive to Table Mesa some 15 miles away, knocked him out, and strangled his girlfriend.

Derrick Murdoch, *Disappearances*.

7 December, 1928

Bookmaker William Holmyard, then aged 72, but still fit and muscular and weighing 13½ stone, was found with blood running down his face, holding on to the railings outside his home in Tachbrook Street, Pimlico, London on 7 December 1928. He was taken to the Westminster Hospital where he was diagnosed as having a fractured skull and where he died three days later.

His much slighter 24-year-old grandson William John Holmyard, a former Army bandsman, was tried for the murder and claimed self-defence. He told the court he had gone to see his grandfather about getting a job and had been abused by him as a spendthrift and a rat. His normally placid grandfather was in a foul temper and had picked up a chair and struck him. In turn he had picked up a pair of tongs to ward off the blow, 'but he still kept coming at me. As I was cornered I struck him again.'

He was spiritedly defended by Venetia Stephenson, the first time a woman barrister appeared in a murder case. She was complimented by the judge, Mr Justice Humphreys, on her ability: 'A serious responsibility lay on the shoulders of counsel for the defence but Miss Stephenson might feel that she had discharged her duty to her client in a manner which reflects the highest possible credit on her carefulness and on her own ability.' But it did not help Holmyard. She first tried to get a confession excluded on the grounds the police had set a trap for Holmyard but Mr Justice Humphreys refused. She then argued that youth had as much right to defend itself as old age, but the jury did not accept Holmyard's version of the fight. Unfortunately, according to the prosecution evidence, he had said to the arresting officer, 'I hit him on the floor.' In court he said, 'I left him on the floor.'

His appeal was conducted on the interesting point that whilst the question of the admissibility of the confession was being argued the jury had retired to their room where they were shown a newspaper report in which the confession was discussed. With Lord Justice Avory sitting with the Lord Chief Justice it was not likely the appeal would be successful and it was not. Holmyard was hanged at Pentonville by Robert Baxter, the hangman who was a part-time lay preacher and who officiated at almost every execution in London from 1924 until the late 1930s when he retired.

Douglas G. Browne, *Sir Travers Humphreys.*

8 December, 1944

On 8 December 1944 Harry, known as 'Harry Boy', and Thomas Jenkins, members of the Elephant and Castle Gang, took part in a raid on a jeweller's in Birchin Lane in the City. With them was Ronald Hedley, known as Silver because of his blond hair. He was the driver who knocked down Captain Ralph Binney who had run into the road, arms outstretched, to signal the getaway car to halt.

Hedley did not stop and passed right over the gallant retired naval captain. Hedley then put the car in reverse and, with Binney trapped under the car, drove off at high speed. Binney was dragged for over a mile before being dislodged. At the trial Hedley was found guilty of murder and Jenkins of manslaughter. Hedley was sentenced to death, reprieved and released after serving nine years. Thomas Jenkins received eight years.

Old-time villain Frank Fraser recalls:

> Harry Boy wasn't charged. When they took Harry Boy into the police he had this brilliant idea and he chinned the police sergeant, knowing full well he'd be mercilessly beaten up. As a result everyone on the ID parade had to be plastered up with tape and so he wasn't picked out. He eventually got Borstal for the assault on the copper.

Harry Jenkins was not so fortunate on the next occasion when someone was killed. He was hanged for his part in the death of Alec de Antiquis on 29 April 1947. De Antiquis received the Binney Medal posthumously for gallantry.

Robert Fabian, *Fabian of the Yard*; Frank Fraser, *Mad Frank*.

9 December, 1992

Described as a small-time gang leader, 25-year-old Jamie Ramos of the Maniac Latin Disciples was put on trial for the murder of 10-year-old Gabriel Martell who had been killed by a misplaced sniper's bullet whilst his father was parking his Buick on North Kedzie Avenue in Chicago about 10 pm on 9 December 1992.

The case against him was based on the eyewitness evidence of a 14-year-old girl who, through fear, had at first

refused to name the shooter, saying she could not identify
him. She had later named Ramos and the police had
rehoused her in another part of the city. She was traced
there by members of the Maniac Latinos and threatened
about the consequences of giving evidence. Finally she
was moved to California to live with relatives.

After two days of deliberation the jury acquitted Ramos.
His lawyer said that the police, feeling pressure over a
similar case two months earlier, had arrested the wrong
man. In the first case seven-year-old Dantrell Davis, out
walking with his mother in the Cabrini-Green public
housing development, had been killed by a stray bullet.
In the Ramos case the prosecutor paid tribute to the
courage of the witness, commenting on the lack of others
who would give evidence: 'The gangs count on that. They
do things when no one's around and intimidate the ones
who are out there. This was the only girl with the courage
to tell them what she saw.'

10 December, 1945

For Charles Templeman Brown, 10 December was a
significant day in his life. Shortly after 7.30 in the evening
of that day in 1945 he carried out a raid on the station
master's office at Pollockshields East station in Glasgow.
There were three staff on duty – William Wright, Anne
Withers and 15-year-old Robert Gough. It was Gough, a
porter, who first saw Brown at the window and then in
the doorway. He was shot in the stomach by Brown who
shouted, 'This is a hold up.' Wright was also shot, as was
Annie Withers. In her case the first bullet lodged in her
thigh after entering under her armpit. The second bullet
entered her stomach and exited through her back. Brown
then rifled the safe, stealing a wage packet containing £4,
and left the injured people on the floor of the office.

Wright, the least injured, tried to stop a train that was passing through the station. The guard did not believe him and the train went on through the night. Wright then managed to telephone the police. Before he died two days later Gough was able to give the police a description of the robber – white, between 30 and 35 years old, five feet seven inches tall, clean-shaven and with ginger hair. Annie Withers also failed to survive her injuries.

The Glasgow Corporation offered a reward of £1,000, which led to some undignified wrangling. The idea had been to take the money from the police fund but this was vetoed by the Lord Advocate, and the Secretary of State for Scotland then said that any money would have to be put up by the council, in other words from the ratepayers. It was left to the *Scottish Daily Express* to offer the reward but no information was immediately forthcoming.

It was not until 8 October the next year that the police, as a result of a tip-off, visited Brown's mother's home. He was away working as a fireman on an engine. The next day Brown went up to a policeman and asked him to telephone Glasgow Central police for him. When asked why, he replied: 'I did a murder – the Pollockshields job.' He was taken to a police box where he handed over a Luger and 13 rounds of ammunition. Whilst waiting for the police he wrote a note to a friend with whom he had been in the army, saying he had tried to commit suicide but had failed and hoped that he would not forfeit the man's friendship. He then told the detectives that he had only fired because Gough had dived at him. Sadly, Gough had not been diving at him. Seeing the gunman he had tried to cover Annie Withers.

On 10 December 1946 Brown's trial, in which he apparently took little interest, began at the High Court in Glasgow. His defence was that his psychological state was in doubt. He was addicted to swing music and as a tribute to Frank Sinatra sported bow ties and a white whipcord jacket of which he was so proud he wore it to collect his wages. Dr William Blyth, physician in charge of mental and nervous diseases, pointed up the difference between the law and medicine. He said he thought Brown was suffering from a form of schizophrenia. Asked if he was prepared to certify Brown as insane, he replied, 'Medically yes, legally no.' Brown was convicted by the jury after a retirement of less than an hour and sentenced to death. On 30 December he was reprieved. In 1957 he was released on parole and worked as a travelling salesman.

On 10 December 1960, following his release, he was killed when his car hit a wall on the A9 road to Dunblane.

Bill Knox, *Court of Murder*; Douglas Skelton, *A Time to Kill*.

11 December, 1978

Around 9 pm on 11 December 1978 15-year-old Robert Piest went to a pharmacy in his home town of Des Plaines, Illinois, to discuss a holiday job. His family did not think he would be long. He was due back for his mother's birthday party. When he had not returned by 11.30 pm his mother, Elizabeth Piest, and her husband called the police. Working on renovations at the pharmacy was John Wayne Gacy, a man with a string of convictions for sexual offences, which had finally earned him a 10-year sentence. There had also been a complaint made about him earlier in the year when 27-year-old Jeffrey Rignall claimed he had been lured into Gacy's car with the promise of marijuana. There he had been chloroformed, and taken to a house where he had been beaten and sodomised before being dumped in a park. Gacy was investigated over this assault and agreed to pay $3,000 medical expenses to Rignall.

Gacy was put under surveillance and on 19 December invited the officers in to have breakfast with him at his home at 8213 West Summerdale Avenue. They noticed an unpleasant smell. Gacy explained that he was having trouble with his sump pump. A warrant was obtained and under a trapdoor the police found seven complete bodies in various stages of decomposition, along with parts of others. There were eight more in lime pits in the garden and garage. Five more, including that of Robert Piest, had been thrown into the Des Plaines river. In all Gacy admitted to killing 32 boys and young men during, before and after sex, over a period from 1972 to 1978. He had forgotten one, the total count being 33.

Gacy was born on 17 March 1942. As a child he had been struck on the head by a swing and as a result had suffered from fainting fits throughout his life. He attended a business school and became a successful shoe salesman. His first marriage broke up when he was sent to prison for 10 years and his second marriage also failed. He then set up as a renovation contractor.

He was well known in the local Junior Chamber of Commerce where, as Pogo the Clown, he was a popular children's entertainer. He claimed that he was not homosexual and, indeed, disliked homosexuals. At his trial the prosecution displayed a 10-foot high placard with photographs of 22 of Gacy's identified victims. He did not give evidence at his trial and an insanity defence was rejected by the jury. On 13 March 1980 he was sentenced to death but a series of appeals kept him on Death Row at the Statesville Correctional Centre until 1991 when in April an application for a writ of *habeus corpus*, in which constitutional errors at the trial were alleged, was heard.

Gacy was finally executed with an injection in May 1994. Crowds who waited outside the prison were mainly supportive of the execution, calling out, strictly inaccurately, 'Turn that frown upside down, they have just fried the clown.'

Clifford L. Linedecker, *The Man Who Killed Boys*; Terry Sullivan with Peter T. Maiken, *Killer Clown*; Brian Lane and Wilfred Gregg, *The New Encyclopedia of Serial Killers*.

12 December, 1994

Jason Mitchell, then aged 23, began a rampage on 12 December 1994 when he attacked retired stationmaster Arthur Wilson and his wife, Shirley. He had been granted limited release six months earlier from a mental hospital after two mental health tribunals had ruled his condition had improved after treatment. He had been ordered to be detained indefinitely on 10 September 1990 after he had attacked 70-year-old church cleaner Jim Powell with a baseball bat. On that occasion he had told the police, 'I heard voices in my head and they told me to kill the vicar.' On 18 August 1994 he was transferred to a hostel in Lowestoft. There he did not get on with other residents and was returned to St Clements' Hospital in Ispwich, allowed to come and go as he pleased during the day. On 9 December he failed to return to the hospital.

Mitchell broke into the Wilsons' bungalow next to the Methodist Church where Shirley Wilson played the organ at Bramford, Suffolk. He waited for two hours and, when they returned, bound them hand and foot. He first strangled Shirley Wilson with her scarf and then Arthur with a pair of her tights.

He then went on along the street to where his father, Robert, lived, killed him and cut up the body with a hacksaw and knife. He was found by the police sitting in the dark at his father's house. He hid the arms and legs in the attic. Mitchell, who suffered from paranoid schizophrenia and who was described by one psychiatrist as 'a pleasant young man with no sign of malice' had intended to eat his victims but decided they were too old. He had wanted to kill his father since the age of six. He was using the Wilsons as practice to prove to himself he could kill people. He cut up his father as training for a future younger victim.

Mitchell, who had a tattoo of a cross in the middle

of his forehead, together with one of a snake slithering out of the eye sockets, was sentenced to three terms of life imprisonment with a recommendation that he serve at least 20 years.

13 December, 1991

The body of Ghebre Luul Kassa, an Ethiopian refugee, was found hanging from a tree in West Heath Road, Hampstead, London about 8 am 13 December 1991 by a woman walking her dog. It had been bound with white washing-line rope and Kassa's face blindfolded with a red silk tie. He had been killed close to where his body was found and he had then been hanged. His gold and black onyx ring with the letter 'K' was missing. His briefcase was found nearby, opened and with its contents scattered. The area was known at night-time as a meeting point for homosexuals, prostitutes and the criminal fraternity. The police received a telephone call about 2.45 am saying that a body was hanging on the Heath.

Kassa had spent the previous day at a café in Crickle-wood Broadway owned by his brother Yohannes. Kassa had told his brother he had obtained a job working as a chauffeur for a wealthy Arab family. Whilst with his brother he had made several calls to the garage off the Finchley Road where his employer's Mercedes was being repaired. After he left the café around 6 pm he was not seen again.

Kassa was thought only to have been on the fringe of a group of exiles although from a small wage he was able to contribute around £100 to help other refugees. One theory was that the killing was a mugging which had gone wrong but homosexual activity was ruled out. There was, however, a suggestion that Kassa had been on Hampstead Heath about 10 pm waiting for someone. The police did not succeed in tracing either the Arab family or the garage where the car was supposed to have been left for repair. Despite an appeal on BBC television's *Crimewatch*, when the tape of the call was played the voice was not recognised. The case was never solved.

14 December, 1953

Stanislaw Sykut was last seen alive on 14 December 1953 when he took a cob to be shod by the local blacksmith at Cefn Hendre near Llandilo, Wales. He was the partner of Michail Onufreczyk, a well-decorated former sergeant-major in the Polish Army, in the 120-acre farm they owned in the valley. Things had not gone well with Onufreczyk since he had bought the farm. Sykut, a former nurse, was his third partner in four years. Now, after suffering a good deal of bullying from the man known by locals as Mr Whiskers because of his white beard, Sykut had complained to the police and had a solicitor draw up a notice to dissolve the partnership. If Onufreczyk did not buy out Sykut then the farm would be put up for auction.

On 30 December when the local police officer paid a routine visit to the farm he was told Sykut had gone to London for a fortnight. When Sykut did not reappear in the small community further enquiries were made. This time Onufreczyk said that around 8 pm on 18 December three Polish men had come to the farm in a car and, after Sykut had sold his share for a down payment of £450 with the balance payable in May, he had driven off with them. Onufreczyk produced the receipt, apparently witnessed by a man called Jablonski. How had he, Onufreczyk, raised the money? He had, he said, borrowed it from a Polish lady in Holloway, north London, a Mrs Pokora. She denied this.

Sykut's mail was left uncollected in the Cwn Du post office and there were no drawings against his post office savings account. When questioned again Onufreczyk said his partner must have gone to rejoin his wife behind the Iron Curtain. When the police began a search of the farmhouse they discovered two thousand tiny blood specks on the walls and ceilings with, in one, a spicule of bone. There was also a large bloodstain on the Welsh dresser. There was, however, no body.

Despite this Onufreczyk was arrested on 19 August 1954 and charged with the murder of his partner. The trial began in Swansea in November and was the first conviction in modern times of murder on land in which there was no body: Modern cases at sea had included James Camb, convicted of murdering Gay Gibson in what became known as the Porthole murder, and a 1936 Irish case of Edward Ball who was convicted of killing his mother.

Quoting a New Zealand case the judge, Mr Justice Oliver, said that in the absence of the body:

> Before he can be convicted the fact of death must be proved by such circumstances as render the commission of the crime morally certain and leave no ground for reasonable doubt. The circumstantial evidence should be so cogent and compelling as to convince a jury that upon no rational hypothesis other than murder can the fact be accounted for.

The jury convicted and Onufreczyk, now sentenced to death, appealed. Lord Goddard, the Lord Chief Justice, now set out the requirements in a case where there was no body: 'The fact of death can be proved, by circumstantial evidence, that is to say by evidence of facts which lead to one conclusion, provided that the jury are satisfied and are warned that the evidence must lead to one conclusion only.'

Onufreczyk was reprieved. Despite the evidence which

seemingly led inexorably to his guilt the Home Secretary, Gwilym Lloyd George, was unhappy. He told Elwyn Jones QC who defended Onufreczyk that he was afraid that if the death penalty were carried out there might be someone from behind the Iron Curtain who would come forward and claim to be Sykut. Onufreczyk, who apparently spoke almost no English and spent his time in prison playing chess, was released in 1965. The next year he was killed in a car accident in Bradford where he was now living.

15 December, 1988

The prosecution alleged that an orgy of violence took place on the night of 15 December 1988. The first victim of what became known as the M25 gang was 57-year-old hairdresser Peter Hurburgh. He was participating in homosexual activities in his car, parked in a field in Blackman's Lane near Chelsham, Surrey, when the gang came upon him. He and the other man were dragged from the car at gunpoint and tied up. Hurburgh, who was badly beaten, had a heart attack and died. Both men were doused with petrol by the gang before they left with Hurburgh's Austin Princess. At about 3.40 am they then attacked the home of 66-year-old Richard Napier. His son Timothy tried to defend his father and as a result of the fight lost four pints of blood from two severed arteries. The men then took the Napiers' Toyota and broke into a house in Fetcham where the owners were tied up and gagged whilst the house was ransacked.

At the Old Bailey on 30 March 1990 Randolph Johnson, Michael Davis and Raphael Rowe were sentenced to life imprisonment for Hurburgh's murder. Their convictions have not been the end of the matter, however. There have been persistent claims that the men were innocent and that they were convicted on the word of informers and accomplices.

At a preliminary hearing of the Johnson, Davis and Rowe appeal, prosecuting counsel handed a document to the court which was not shown to defence counsel. Crown counsel invited the court to give a ruling on disclosure either in the absence of the defendants and their legal representives or on the undertaking of defence counsel not to disclose what took place to their clients. Defence counsel declined to give such an undertaking and withdrew from court at the direction of the court. The prosecution application went ahead *ex parte*. After the hearing the court endorsed the stance the Crown had taken and declined to order disclosure of the contents of the document.

The content of the document held by the Crown in the 'M25 Three' case has never been made public. There has, however, been speculation that it related to the identity of an informant or to reward money paid to a witness. The appeals of Johnson, Davis and Rowe were dismissed in 1994. Their case went to the European Commission on Human Rights and was later returned to the Court of Appeal when in 2000 they were released after their convictions were declared unsafe.

16 December, 1935

The body of 29-year-old actress and highly regarded comedienne Thelma Todd, whose best known films were the Marx Brothers's *Horse Feathers* and *Monkey Business*, was found in her open car in a garage overlooking her roadhouse restaurant near Malibu, Los Angeles, on the morning of Monday 16 December 1935. The doors were closed and the ignition was switched on. There was blood on her face, on her dress, her coat, on the car and spots on the garage floor. It was thought she had been dead for over 30 hours. If she had been murdered the motive cannot have been robbery because her jewellery had been left.

In 1932, at the height of her fame, she had married Pat di Cicco, a theatrical agent, with whom she had eloped to Arizona. The next year she had opened Thelma Todd's Sidewalk Café with Roland West who had originally cast her in his 1930 film *Corsair*. According to West she had a half-share in the business but no financial investment. Her name was the lure to the customers and sufficient to earn her a share of the profits. In March 1934 she had divorced di Cicco on the grounds of cruelty but they had remained friends.

The Saturday before she died she had been at a party with the British actor Stanley Lupino and his daughter, Ida, who went on to direct successfully in Hollywood. Di Cicco had been expected to dine with them but had been with another actress in the same restaurant. Ida Lupino said that Thelma Todd had been in good form at the party and had said she was having a relationship with a businessman in San Francisco. At 3.30 am she returned by chauffeur-driven limousine to the café, over which she had rooms. She probably was not seen alive again although a shopkeeper said she had called at his drugstore to use the telephone. She had been joined by a man and they had walked off together.

Earlier in the year West and Miss Todd had been approached by Los Angeles gamblers to allow them to turn a large room in the tower over the living quarters into a casino. They had turned down the proposition.

The inquest verdict was that she had died of carbon monoxide poisoning. It was a verdict which satisfied few. If she wished to kill herself then why should she attempt this in an open car when there was a sedan in the garage? The blood on her face and clothes was never explained. The popular version of events is that she was killed by gangsters on the orders of Lucky Luciano to whom di Cicco was linked, as a reprisal for not allowing her restaurant to be used for gambling.

However, the Hollywood reporters Marvin Wolf and Katherine Mader came up with a very plausible alternative theory. Her death was something of an accident. They interviewed the director Hal Roach who told them that Roland West had confessed to the police on 17 December but had not been charged. He had told Roach that he was piqued when Todd had not returned home by 2 am and in his power struggle with her he had shut her in the garage overnight as a punishment, intending to release her the next morning. West was never charged but never directed another film. Apparently he repeated his confession to Chester Morris with whom Todd had starred in *Corsair*.

John Austin, *Hollywood's Unsolved Mysteries*; Marvin J. Wolf and Katherine Mader, *L.A. Crime*.

17 December, 1992

At about 3.15 pm on the afternoon of 17 December 1992, Jonathan Zito, aged 27, was killed at Finsbury Park Underground Station, London by a paranoid schizophrenic, Christopher Clunis. In a totally unprovoked attack he stabbed Mr Zito in the eye. At the Old Bailey Clunis, who had been a saxophone player before his illness, was found guilty of manslaughter on the grounds of diminished responsibility. He was sent to Rampton, a secure mental hospital.

In December 1995, rather to the amazement of the general public, Clunis began an action against the Camden and Islington Health Authority, seeking in excess of £50,000 for 'failure to care', on the basis that its negligence in discharging him led to his being convicted of manslaughter which, in turn, led to him being sent to Rampton. Mrs Jayne Zito, Jonathan Zito's widow, who established the Zito Trust to assist victims of community care, in turn sued Clunis. She was not able to sue the Health Authority because, in law, they owed no duty of care to either her or her husband.

18 December, 1931

Jack 'Legs' Diamond – his nickname came either from his prowess on the dance floor or because of a childhood ability to outrun pursuing police officers – was shot dead in his room in Albany, New York on 18 December 1931 in what was a typical gangland execution.

Born in 1896 he had begun his career as a sneak thief in New York, working his way up to become an enforcer and bodyguard to Jacob 'Little Augie' Orgen, then a leading racketeer. Diamond, allegedly a bodyguard, was shot in the arm and leg when Orgen was killed in Norfolk Street on the Lower East Side in 1927. Once out of hospital Diamond divided Orgen's businesses with the killers, Louis Lepke and Gurrah Shapiro, retaining the bootleg liquor and drugs trade for himself. He opened a club, the Hotsy Totsy, on Broadway between 54th and 55th and it was from there a number of gangland killings were carried out. In 1929, he and his right-hand man, Charles Entratta, killed a rival, Red Cassidy, in full view of both employees and customers. Both men fled and then organised a series of contracts to eliminate the witnesses and so undermine the police case against them. They duly surrendered and were charged but released because of a lack of evidence. In his absence Diamond's business was taken over in a large part by Dutch Schultz. In the ensuing quarrel the Underworld sided with Schultz and over the years Diamond survived at least four assassination attempts in 1924, 1927, 1929 and early in 1931. He then traded on the reputation of being a man who could not be killed. In

August 1931 he was found guilty of operating an illegal still, fined $10,000 and given a four-year jail sentence. He was released on bail pending an appeal.

By this time he had fallen out with most of the other leading Underworld figures, first because he could no longer be trusted and, secondly, because he wanted a larger share of Joey Fay's nightclub rackets and the bootlegging operation of Waxey Gordon. It was never known which, if either, of these operators organised the contract on Diamond. It may have been on the orders of Meyer Lansky or even Lucky Luciano, who both saw themselves as potential targets for the over-ambitious Diamond. Whoever organised the killing this time it was a successful operation. He was asleep when three men entered his hotel room. One man held him by the ears and the others shot him in the head.

19 December, 1995

On 19 December 1995 five people were shot dead in Little Chester Shoes, a shop near the Zoo in the Bronx. The shooting had broken out when, so he said, 22-year-old Michael Vernon, a man with a history of drug-taking and psychiatric problems, quarrelled over whether the store had Nike sneakers in his size. He wanted a size 13½ and apparently could not understand that it was not a common size stocked by all shops. The clerk had apparently refused to order them and it was then the shooting started. In the ensuing dispute he killed five people including Kwong Bae whose husband owned the shop, Maria Carrasquillo and her two young sons Rafael and Richardo, and another customer, and seriously wounded three others. The gunfight ended when Vernon was shot in the groin and right wrist by the police as he tried to escape using a hostage as a shield. The police maintained that Vernon's story was incorrect and that his motive was one of robbery.

The police also maintained that Vernon had confessed to shooting a cab driver, Steven Fineman, on 3 November 1993 and to two armed robberies in August 1995. Vernon's court-appointed lawyer said that his client remembered nothing after the refusal of the store clerk to order the shoes and denied involvement in the other killing. According to the police Vernon had tried in July 1995 to confess to Fineman's murder and other offences when he had been arrested over a minor assault. Instead of being questioned he had been released on bail to appear in court on the assault charge.

Vernon was admitted to Bellevue Hospital for assessment and it was there, double-handcuffed to the bed, he was arraigned in a special hearing. A defence request for a psychiatric examination was granted. During pre-trial hearings in July 1996 his lawyer announced that, although he was competent to stand trial, he would be pleading insanity.

20 December, 1958

When nine-year-old Mary Olive Hattam did not return for tea on the afternoon of 20 December 1958 her parents did not mind. She had gone to play with her brother Peter and another boy on the beach near Ceduna, South Australia. During the afternoon her brother and his friend returned to the house to get a tin tub in which to float. They left Mary on the beach. It was then she was lured into a cave and there raped and killed. Her body was found shortly before midnight. Two elderly Aborigine trackers were invited to look at footprints by the cave and both agreed that they had been made by an Arandan man who had lived with white people.

Rupert Max Stuart, an Arandan, had been employed by a small carnival which had been in Ceduna on the day of the killing but he had been sacked for absenteeism and being drunk. He had stayed on in Ceduna working as a labourer for the Wheat Board. Two days later, when questioned by the police, he was evasive. Later he said that he had seen the killing, done by a white man who had forced him, Stuart, to carry the girl's body. Finally, he admitted that after a day's drinking he had lured the girl into the cave under the pretext of showing her some birds and had raped and killed her with a stone. After his confession had been taken – he could neither read nor write and he had no access to a lawyer – the trackers agreed that the footprints were Stuart's. Stuart had two previous convictions for assaults on women. At the time South Australia had no forensic science facilities which would have provided evidence for or against him.

At his trial no effort was made by his defence lawyers to exclude the confession on the grounds that it had been obtained by violence. Stuart did not give evidence but made a short statement from the dock saying, 'I cannot read or write. Never been to school. I did not see the little girl. I didn't kill her. Police hit me. Choke me. That's what I wanted to say.' His lawyer had wanted a much longer statement to be read out detailing the alleged police brutality and for Stuart to say that it was correct. The court declined to allow this to be done. Stuart was found guilty and sentenced to death.

There followed a series of legal battles to quash Stuart's conviction. Stuart endeavoured to call a partial alibi that he had been with another girl around the time of the killing. The execution was repeatedly postponed, once on the day he was due to be hanged. South Australia was evenly divided as to whether there had been police brutality. The rest of Australia was, by and large, on Stuart's side. There followed also a Royal Commission into the conduct of the police and an appeal to the Judicial Committee of the Privy Council, which was the English House of Lords sitting under another name.

Stuart's conviction was upheld but his sentence commuted to one of life imprisonment. The Royal Commission found that there had been no brutality and that the new evidence in the form of the alibi did not affect the case. In 1973 Stuart, who had learned to read and write whilst in prison and who was continually in difficulties with warders and other prisoners, was quoted as saying enigmatically of Mary Hattam, 'When I pray, I pray for her.'

Sir Roderic Chamberlain, *The Stuart Affair*.

21 December, 1914

Robert Upton and Charles Gribben, labourers in Jarrow, north-east England, had a peculiar ménage. They shared their housekeeper, a Mrs Burdon. She would sleep with Gribben the first part of the week before moving to the bed of Upton. This arrangement worked satisfactorily with the friends who were both heavy drinkers. It came to an end early in December 1914 when Mrs Burdon said she had tired of the favours of both men and was leaving the district to go and live with a third man, Jack Bloy.

Upton was quite unable to accept this and swore that she would, in future, have neither Bloy nor his old friend Gribben. Matters then seem to have calmed down because on 20 December, Upton, his son Joe, and Gribben went out drinking together. In the early hours of 21 December Joe awoke to find his father attacking Gribben with a razor. He was unable to prevent his father killing his friend. Upton then cut his own throat with the razor, saying to the police who had been called, 'I have killed the bastard, I done it, let me die.'

He was found guilty of murder at Durham Assizes and was hanged on 24 March 1915 by John Ellis.

22 December, 1986

On 22 December 1986 Sandra Lindsay was captured by the Philadelphia serial killer Gary Heidnik. He hanged her, dangling by her wrist from an overhead beam in his cellar at 3520 North Marshall Street, and she choked to death on a lump of bread pushed down her throat. Other victims included Deborah Dudley, whom he captured on 18 January 1987 and electrocuted by putting a live wire into the water pit in which he was keeping her.

Heidnik, who had an IQ of between 130 and 148, was financially astute, accumulating a fortune of more than half a million dollars. He elected however to live in a slum in the black part of Phildelphia and his victims were generally severely retarded black women. From his home he founded the United Church for Ministers of God which was apparently not wholly fraudulent but, apart from his interests in religion and the stock market, he devoted much of his time to pornography and prostitutes.

He had, it was claimed, an idea to begin a baby-farm in his cellar and he hunted girls who would bear his children. He killed two and tortured the others, keeping them shackled and chained and feeding them on a mixture of dog meat and the flesh of his victims. One of the women, Josefina Rivera, whom he captured on 29 November 1986, managed to escape and took the police to the church/torture house.

Heidnik was condemned to die in the electric chair.

Ken Englade, *Cellar of Horror*; Richard and Molly Whittington-Egan, *The Murder Almanac*.

23 December, 1995

The bodies of 16 members of a doomsday cult, the Swiss-based Order of the Solar Temple, were found shot, drugged, or asphyxiated near the village of St Pierre de Cherennes, 20 miles south-west of Grenoble on 23 December 1995. Amongst the dead, which included a number of children, were Edith Vuarnet, the wife of a French sunglasses manufacturer and a French policeman and his two daughters.

The charred bodies were found in a star formation in the embers of a huge bonfire. The police found notes from four of the victims saying they wished to see another world. Members, many of whom are from the professional classes, believe that the world will end in flames and that the way into the afterworld is to die by burning. Many of the victims had taken drugs and some faces were covered with plastic bags. There were calls for the Order to be banned in France but the authorities said there was little that could be done to prevent members of cults from killing again.

This was not the first mass death concerned with the cult. In October 1994 Swiss authorities discovered the bodies of 48 people in a farm and three chalets. They, too, had been burned. Five more bodies were found in a house belonging to a cult leader in Morin Heights, Quebec.

The Order, which has its roots in various centuries-old secret Roman Catholic Societies, has members from as far away as Australia. In April 1996 a Swiss judge leading the inquiry into the 1994 murders said that all but 15 victims had been murdered. There was a concurrent inquiry into whether the cult had infiltrated the publicly owned utility Hydro-Quebec in Canada. Michel Cote, a former employee, claimed in a wrongful dismissal suit that promotion depended on membership of the Order and that he had been sacked after refusing to join the cult.

24 December, 1930

Just after midday on 24 December 1930 Olive Wise, who lived in east London, told a neighbour, 'I have done the baby in, I have gassed him.' She had put her nine-month-old son Reginald in the gas oven. At the time she had been in severe financial trouble. She had been married in June 1916 but after her husband had left for service in the Far East she had, on and off, been associating with an Alfred John Wheatley and he was Reginald's father. A report in the papers had said she had been deserted but 'A Watcher' helpfully wrote to the police saying she had been divorced by her husband on the grounds of her adultery.

On 13 January 1931 she was found guilty of murder with a strong recommendation by the jury for mercy. Now a jury of matrons was empannelled to decide whether she was *enceinte*. There was not much doubt since she was eight months' pregnant at the time and they returned a verdict of 'about to become a mother'. This ensured there would be a stay of execution of the capital sentence until after the birth of the child. In the event she was reprieved.

The case was the first time since women jurors were allowed to sit that a jury of matrons had been required. Before then, when a woman convicted of murder claimed she was pregnant, married women amongst the spectators in court, and cleaners who might be in the building, were collected to form a jury of matrons.

After her release from prison Olive Wise took up again with Alfred Wheatley but the relationship was not a success. On 26 July 1933 he went into the police station at Lea Bridge Road, London, to say that his wife Olive and his two-and-a-half-year-old daughter were missing. She had left after a quarrel on 25 July, taking the child with her. He had traced them to the Central Homes, Union Road where they had been handed back to him but on their way back home she had, once more, gone off with her daughter.

The police noted that there appeared to be no suspicious circumstances but in view of the previous history of Mrs Wise made inquiries into the safety of the child.

25 December, 1994

On Christmas Day 1994, Phillip Manning, obsessed with his ex-wife Margaret Whitcombe, shot and stabbed her. He had only been on parole for two months following a previous attack on her. For that attempted murder he had been sentenced to four and a half years, serving two before being paroled.

Armed with a sawn-off shotgun, a butcher's knife and a pool cue, he had lain in wait in her garden in Abertilley, Gwent for her return with her new boyfriend, Neil Jones.

As Mrs Whitcombe went to open the front door Manning charged at Jones with the butcher's knife. He was hit several times on the left arm before being struck on the head. He needed plastic surgery and a plate inserted into his skull.

Mrs Whitcombe ran screaming indoors. Manning chased after her and shot her in the jaw. She died, almost immediately, choking on her own blood. Her young son Daniel was upstairs and he ran from the house into the arms of his elder brother Christopher who was himself just arriving home. Both were met by Manning who told them, 'I've killed them all.'

Manning was arrested in early January in a London pub. He had a nail bomb strapped to his body and was threatening to blow himself up. 'I didn't say anything to her. I just pointed the gun and pulled the trigger,' he told the police. His obsession with his ex-wife had developed after their 20-year marriage broke down.

'This is a tragic case of a man with a single flaw – he was obsessed with his wife,' said Mr Patrick Harrington QC, defending. 'He just wanted his old life back. He did not go to the house with any intention to kill his ex-wife. He only wanted to talk with her. He expected to see Margaret alone that night but instead he saw her with a new man. That was too much for him.'

Sentencing Manning at Cardiff Crown Court, the judge Mr Justice Jowitt said there should be no question of releasing him whilst there was a risk of him forming an emotional relationship.

26 December, 1994

The body of 27-year-old Dr Joan Francisco was found in her flat in St John's Wood, London, on Boxing Day 1994. The gynaecologist and obstetrician had been strangled with a vacuum cleaner cord.

In October 1995 Detective Inspector Michael Bennett told a coroner's inquest that 'I am a hundred per cent confident that I know who the killer is and so is everyone who has worked on the case.'

A search had been conducted of the man's flat and had uncovered a tape recorder with a sucker attachment that helped to relay a conversation through a window and a device to help the man find his way in the dark.

There were suggestions that the man was the same one who had been fined £10,000 for forging Dr Francisco's signature on a mortgage application but Mr Bennett denied this, saying that the man he suspected was a former boyfriend with whom she had parted when she went to university. Some six years earlier the police had been called when he had broken in through patio doors. The man had given a false alibi during the inquiries and on a second visit to the police station had refused to answer questions.

At first the Crown Prosecution Service refused to prosecute Joan's former boyfriend, Tony Diedrick, blaming a lack of evidence. In 1988 the Francisco family then sued Diedrick in the civil courts where the burden of proof is not so great. Even after they won the case the CPS still declined to prosecute. In fact the evidence was substantial. A sophisticated DNA test showed that there was his blood on the tee-shirt she had been wearing when she was killed. He was found guilty at the Old Bailey in October 1999.

27 December, 1985

Jacques Perrot, at whose wedding Laurent Fabius, the one time Socialist prime minister of France, had been the best man, was found shot dead on the landing of a block of flats in the fashionable 16th arrondissement in Paris on 27 December 1985.

Four and a half years later, at the trial of Marie-Elisabeth Cons-Boutboul, a 69-year-old disbarred lawyer, the prosecution alleged that the killing had been over the custody of Perrot's young son. In a complicated series of events Cons-Boutboul had been married to Robert Boutboul, a Tunisian Jew with property connections. When they split up she told their young daughter, Darie, her father was dead and that he had been killed in an air crash.

Perrot married Darie, then France's best woman jockey. They later became estranged and she refused him access to their child.

On the night of his death, said the prosecution, Perrot was due to have dinner with Mme Cons-Boutboul to discuss arrangements for the child but she cancelled the engagement. She denied there was ever any such appointment.

In 1989 the body of Bruno Dassac, a known French criminal, was found in the Channel near Le Havre. He had been shot in the head. He had boasted of the Perrot hit and claimed £15,000 had been transferred to his account by Mme Cons-Boutboul. Isauro Figuier, a prosecution witness, said he had introduced Dassac to Mme Cons-Boutboul when she said she wanted someone to give Perrot a beating. Mme Cons-Boutboul was charged with complicity in Dassac's killing but was acquitted.

The evidence against Mme Cons-Boutboul in the Perrot case was tenuous. No gun used in the killing was ever found. It was suggested by his friends that Perrot had discovered that his mother-in-law had been disbarred after being convicted of embezzling money from one of her clients, a Catholic charity. It was also thought that he was trying to use this as a lever to obtain access to his son. On 24 March 1993 Mme Cons-Boutboul was found guilty of ordering the murder of her son-in-law and sentenced to 15 years' imprisonment.

28 December, 1957

Seventeen-year-old Isabelle Cooke was murdered on Saturday, 28 December 1957 near her home at 5 Carrick Drive in the Glasgow suburb of Mount Vernon. About 7.15 pm she left to go with a friend, Douglas Bryden, to a dance in Uddingston. She had arranged to meet him at a bus stop in the village but she did not appear and Bryden waited in vain for three-quarters of an hour. To catch the bus to Uddingston she had to walk along a path across the railway line and about 7.30 pm a Mrs Gardiner, who lived in Hamilton Road near the path, heard a cry which she described as someone in fear and not a male voice. Her dog began to bark and she heard no more cries.

Isabelle's parents, who had been out for the afternoon, were not worried when they returned and found her not at home. They knew where she was going and with whom but when she had not returned by shortly after midnight they went out and looked up and down the path. Then Mr Cooke drove his car along the road in case she had missed a bus and was walking. By the next morning when she had not reappeared and it was apparent she had not stayed overnight with friends a full-scale search was organised.

That day the police found a cosmetic pouch under a railway bridge in Mount Vernon Avenue. The Cookes recognised it as belonging to Isabelle. Over the next two weeks searchers found various items of her clothing until finally her body was found buried in a newly ploughed field on the nearby farm of Burntbroom on 16 January 1958.

There was another killing in the neighbourhood when on New Year's Day the Smart family – Peter and Doris and their 11-year-old son Michael – were killed in their home at 38 Sheepbrun Road, Uddingston. Their bodies were discovered on 6 January. They were the last victims of Peter Manuel although another couple, John McMunn and his wife, were lucky to escape. On 4 January McMunn woke to find a man at his bedroom door. He called out to his wife that she should get the – non-existent – gun and the man fled. At 6.45 am on 14 January 1958 Manuel was arrested at his parents' home in Birkenshaw. He had been asleep on a folding chair in the living room. At 11.10 that night he was charged with the Smart murders on 1 January 1958.

Manuel's father had also been arrested and charged with receiving. Now Manuel tried to bargain with the police saying he would make a statement if his father was released. He was told that this was not an acceptable offer and he then wrote two letters offering to assist in clearing up murders. During the evening he showed the police where Isabelle Cooke's body was buried. At 4.15 am he began to write his confession. It took him two hours. Over the next three days he showed the police where he had disposed of a gun used in other killings and a piece of iron he said he had used to batter Anne Knielands, an earlier victim.

Manuel's killing spree had begun on 2 January 1956 when Anne Knielands, an 18-year-old girl, was killed. Her body had been found two days later. Although her clothing had been torn there was no indication of sexual interference. Semen stains were found indicating her killer had achieved an orgasm through his violence. Peter Manuel, a known local criminal with convictions for sex offences and burglary, was interviewed but provided an alibi. Tests of his clothes proved negative and he claimed he had given away a maroon jacket and pair of grey flannel trousers he was known to have had two months previously.

On 17 September 1956 the bodies of Marion and Vivienne Watt and Margaret Brown were found by their daily help, Helen Collison. They had been shot at pointblank range. Again Manuel was questioned to no effect. William Watt, Marion's husband, was charged with the murders and released after two months in Barlinnie. Peter Manuel had told Watt's solicitor that he had information which would help him and later named a criminal whom he said had done the killings. It would not be the end of Watt's ordeal. In Scotland a special defence is available of impeachment, that is naming a person who committed the crime of which the defendant is accused. During his trial Manuel, after he had dismissed his counsel, impeached William Watt.

Manuel was convicted on 26 May 1958 of seven murders; Isabelle Cooke, the Watt family and the Smarts. He was acquitted on the direction of the judge of the murder of Anne Knielands. He was hanged at Barlinnie on 11 July 1958.

Manuel had been born in Manhattan on 15 March

1927 and five years later the family returned to Scotland. His first court appearance was in October 1939 when he was put on probation for breaking and entering. There followed a series of convictions for small offences until in 1942 he was convicted of robbery and indecent assault. In 1946 he was sentenced to 12 months' imprisonment for 15 offences of housebreaking and whilst he was serving that sentence he received eight years for a rape committed prior to his arrest. He was released in 1953 and became engaged the next year to a bus conductress whom he treated well until he substituted a cheaper ring for the engagement present he had bought her and then sent her an anonymous note to say that his real father had been executed in America and that he had spied in Russia for the British Secret Service. She broke off the engagement and, on the day he had been due to marry, 30 July, he successfully defended himself before the Airdrie Sheriff's Court on a charge of indecent assault.

Prior to his trial Manuel was examined with a view to his fitness to plead and whether a defence of insanity could be mounted. He is reputed to have put a stop to this, saying to his representatives that he 'wanted nae mair o' that insanity business'.

After Manuel was hanged a coroner's jury found that he had killed Sydney Dunn on 8 December 1957. The Newcastle taxi driver had been found on the moors at Edmondbyers, County Durham. His throat had been cut and he had also been shot in the head. According to an article in the *Sunday Pictorial* shortly before his execution Manuel confessed to three more murders – Ellen 'English Nellie' Petrie, stabbed in Glasgow on 15 June 1956; Anne Steele, a 55-year-old spinster battered to death in Glasgow on 11 January 1956; and another prostitute, Helen 'Red Helen' Carlin, strangled in Pimlico, London in September 1954.

Murder Casebook No 26. *Glasgow's Multiple Killer*; John Gray Wilson, *The Trial of Peter Manuel*.

29 December, 1992

Millionaire David Martin disappeared from his home at Naphill, Bedfordshire on 29 December 1992. When his fiancée Kate Turnor failed to speak to him on the telephone she travelled from Lincolnshire to his home. The lights were on and there was half a glass of wine in his workroom. There were no signs of a struggle.

One theory was that he might have gone to Australia for a midwinter break but Mrs Turnor believed he had been abducted. She made a plea for his release. Almost certainly by this time he was dead.

Some days later Edward Finch, Mrs Turnor's teenage son, found a trail of blood in the workshop. The police had not noticed it on their first visit. The blood matched Mr Martin's and bloody footprints in the garage were linked to his business partner, Colin James. Mr Martin had sold one business in 1990 for £1.5 million and started in partnership with Colin James in the helicopter business. The venture was not a success and Martin told Mrs Turnor he believed that James was stealing from him. James claimed that two of the helicopters had been stolen and there were difficulties in obtaining the money from the insurance companies.

James's defence was that Martin had been seen in Slough after his disappearance. The prosecution's case was that he had killed his partner and then driven Martin's car to London to make it look as though he had gone to stay in his flat there. What James did not know was that the flat was uninhabitable.

'I am quite satisfied that the reason for this murder was that you were ripping off Martin,' said Mr Justice Popplewell sentencing James to life imprisonment.

The case is another in the growing list where convictions have been obtained even though no body has been found.

30 December, 1921

On Friday, 30 December 1921 the body of pretty 12-year-old Alma Tirtschke was found in the dead-end Gun Alley in Melbourne, Australia, part of a complex then known as the Eastern Market, a ragbag of cheap shops, bars and curtained doorways which led to brothels. The girl had been raped and her body had been washed and the police believed that this had been done to remove clues as to the killer's identity.

Along with his brother, Stanley, Colin Campbell Ross was the owner of a wine bar just over a hundred yards from where the naked body of the child was found. The floor of his wine bar had been recently scrubbed but, although he was one of the first to be questioned about the killing, Ross seems to have been unconcerned. He gave the detectives details of an alibi saying he had been with a friend, Gladys Wain, and that after he had shut his bar he had seen her to her home before catching the train at Spencer Street station to his own home.

This was one of those cases in which the police relied heavily on the evidence of known criminals and people with a grudge against Ross. They were later to share in the A£1,250 reward put up by the Victoria Government and the *Melbourne Herald*. Ivy Matthews, who had been questioned previously, decided on 9 January that Ross had confessed to her and that she had seen a girl, whom she believed to be the victim, peeping out of a cubicle in the wine bar. She, Matthews, had been given notice by Ross three weeks earlier. Another witness was a prostitute, Olive Maddox, who also said she had seen Alma in the wine bar and that Ivy Matthews had told her to tell the police.

Whilst on remand, Ross was said by Sidney Harding, a cellmate, to have confessed to the crime, a confession overheard by another prisoner who also gave evidence.

The witnesses were bitterly attacked by the defence who accused them of giving evidence in the hope that a conviction of Ross would bring them the reward money. In his alleged confession to Harding, Ross had said he had given the girl three glasses of wine but no alcohol was found in her stomach. Ivy Matthews said he had told her he got 'fooling about with her and had strangled her in his passion', adding 'I could have taken a knife and slashed her up, and myself too, because she led me on to do it'. Harding's version was that Ross had said, 'At six o'clock the girl was still asleep in the cubicle, and I could not resist the temptation.' Afterwards the girl called out and he went in to silence her and must have choked her. The so-called confessions by Ross to Matthews and to Harding differed in very substantial ways.

There was no forensic evidence except for some hairs similar to those of the girl's attached to a blanket. The forensic expert, Dr Charles Taylor, demonstrated the individual qualities of hair – something now no longer regarded as an exact science – matched. There were no bloodstains on the blanket nor on the floor of the bar. There was evidence too that Ross suffered from venereal disease, but there was no medical evidence to show a transfer of the disease to the child.

Ross's trial, which began on 20 February, lasted five days. It was carried out in an atmosphere of almost total public hostility towards Ross but the jury took over 24 hours to find him guilty. 'My life has been sworn away by desperate people. If I am hanged, I will be hanged as an innocent man,' he told the court.

As so often is the case, after the trial some witnesses came forward to support his story. One man said that he had been in the bar and the child could not have been on the premises without being seen by him. Another, a taxi driver, said he had heard a child scream. He had looked for the source but although he could not find it he was sure that the cry had not come from Ross's wine bar. The Court of Appeal refused to hear the witnesses, and although Ross intended to petition the Privy Council in

England he was executed before he could do so.

To his death Ross continued to protest his innocence, saying he had been framed by the Melbourne police. His detractors point out that he had originally told the police he had seen the girl when she was loitering in the doorway of Madame Ghurka, a fortune-teller. One story told against him is that, after his death, an acquaintance said that Ross had told him he 'preferred them without feathers', a reference to the lack of pubic hair amongst very young girls.

However, shortly before he was hanged Ross received a letter:

> You have been condemned for a crime which you have never committed, and are to suffer for another's fault . . . My dear Ross, if it is any satisfaction for you to know it, believe me that you die but once, but he will continue to die for the rest of his life. Honoured and fawned upon by those who know him, the smile on his lips hides the canker eating into his soul. Day and night his life is a hell without the hope of reprieve. Gladly would he take your place on Monday next if he had himself alone to consider. His reason, then, briefly stated is this: A devoted and loving mother is ill – a shock would be fatal. Three loving married sisters whose whole life would be wrecked, to say nothing of brothers who have been accustomed to take him as a pattern . . . It is too painful for him to go into the details of the crime. It is simply a Jekyll and Hyde existence . . . By a freak of nature he was not made as other men . . . This girl was not the first . . . With a procuress all things are possible . . . In this case there was no intention of murder – the victim unexpectly collapsed. The hands of the woman, in her frenzy, did the rest.

> May it be some satisfaction to yourself, your devoted mother, and the members of your family to know that at least one of the legion of the damned, who is the cause of your death, is suffering the

pangs of hell. He may not ask your forgiveness or sympathy, but he asks your understanding.

The letter bore the postmark of a small country town. The writer was never traced.

After his death Ross was championed by his junior barrister, the former journalist T. C. Brennan, who explains the remark by saying that 'never seen' meant never spoken to. Until his death in January 1944 at the age of 74 he believed evidence would be forthcoming which would clear Ross.

The reward money was shared out between the witnesses with Ivy Matthews receiving £350 and Harding £200. Madame Ghurka, whose real name was Julia Gibson, received £25 although it is not clear how she helped the case.

In 1963 Ivy Matthews, then known as Irene Cholet, died of a heart attack four days before she was due in court to answer charges relating to abortions. It was thought she was the last of the surviving witnesses.

T. C. Brennan, *The Gun Alley Tragedy*; Vince Kelly, *The Charge is Murder*; Alan Sharpe, *Crimes that Shocked Australia*.

31 December, 1948

In Andover, Hampshire on 31 December 1948, 38-year-old William Gray, an unhappily married man, shot and killed his wife, Una. He had planned the killing some days previously, discussing it with a friend who had tried unsuccessfully to dissuade him. He had made a down-payment on a gun and on 29 December he paid the balance and bought cartridges.

At the time Gray's wife was staying with her mother

and as she left the house with three friends Gray came behind them, called, 'Is that you, Una?' and then 'Stand clear!' to the others. He then shot his wife.

Later in the day he was found lying on a bank beside the road. He had blown part of his face away with the gun. On 16 March 1949, at Winchester Assizes, he pleaded guilty to his wife's murder and was condemned to death.

On 3 April he was reprieved in unusual circumstances. The injuries he had sustained when he shot himself were such that he could not physically be hanged. His jaw was now so brittle that the noose would have been likely to break it and so slip over his head. His sentence was commuted to one of life imprisonment.

This was not the only time when a man had been saved from the gallows because of a physical defect which prevented his being hanged properly. One man, convicted of shooting a gamekeeper, suffered from torticollis and the resulting deformity of the neck would have caused unnecessary suffering in the days when hanging resulted in strangulation. He was indeed fortunate: some time later another man confessed to the murder.

Bibliography

Abbott, J. *In the Belly of the Beast* (1981) New York, Random House
Adam, H. L. (ed) *The Trial of George Chapman* (1930) London, William Hodge
——*Murder by Persons Unknown* (1931) London, Collins
Adams, J. *Double Idemnity* (1994) London, Headline
Adamson, I. *The Great Detective* (1966) London, Frederick Muller
Austin, J. *Hollywood's Unsolved Mysteries* (1970), New York, Ace Publishing
Ayling, J. with T. Barnao and N. Lipson *Nothing But the Truth* (1993) Chippendale, Pan Macmillan
Beadle, W. *Wrongly Hanged?* (1995) London, Wat Tyler Books
Beltrami, J. *A Deadly Innocence* (1989) Edinburgh, Mainstream
Bennett, B. *Some Don't Hang* (1973) Cape Town, Howard Timmins
Bergreen, L. *Capone* (1994) London, Macmillan
Bland, J. *The Book of Executions* (1993) London, Warner
——*True Crime Diary* (1986) London, Futura
——*True Crime Diary Volume 2* (1989) London, Futura
Bogdanovich, P. *Killing the Unicorn* (1984) New York, William Morrow
Boot, A. *Psychic Murder Hunters* (1994) London, Headline
Borowitz, A. 'The Judge's Black Cadillac' in *The Vintage Car Murders* (ed Jonathan Goodman) (1988) London, Allison & Busby
Brennan, T.C. *The Gun Alley Tragedy* (1923) Melbourne, Gordon & Gotch
Bresler, F. *Lord Goddard* (1977) London, Harrap
——*Reprieve* (1965) London, Harrap
Brown, M. (ed) *Australian Crime* (1993) Sydney, Lansdowne
Browne, D.G. *Sir Travers Humphreys* (1960) London, Harrap
——and T. Tullett *Sir Bernard Spilsbury, His Life and Cases* (1951) London, Harrap
Burn, G. *Somebody's Husband, Somebody's Son* (1984) London, Heinemann
Burnside, S. and A. Cairns *Deadly Innocence* (1995) New York, Warner Books

Butler, I. *Murderers' England* (1973) London, Robert Hale
——*Murderers' London* (1973) London, Robert Hale
Campbell, D. *That was Business, This is Personal* (1990) London, Secker & Warburg
Canning, J. (ed) *Unsolved Murders and Mysteries* (1987) London, Futura
Capstick, J. *Given in Evidence* (1960) London, John Long
Cecil, H. *The Trial of Walter Rowland* (1975) Newton Abbot, David & Charles
Chamberlain, R. *The Stuart Affair* (1973) London, Robert Hale
Cherrill, F. *Cherrill of the Yard* (1953) London, Harrap
Church, R. *Murder in East Anglia* (1987) London, Robert Hale
——*Well Done, Boys* (1996) London, Constable
Clegg, E. *Return Your Verdict* (1965) Melbourne, Angus & Robertson
Cohen, D. *Great Unsolved Crimes* (1988) New York, Dodd, Mead & Company
Cornish, G. *Cornish of the 'Yard'* (1935) London, The Bodley Head
Cummings, J. and E. Volkman *Mobster* (1991) London, Futura
Deeley, P. *The Manhunters* (1970) London, Hodder & Stoughton
Dew, W. *I Caught Crippen* (1938) London, Blackie
Dilnot, G. (ed) *The Trial of Herbert John Bennett* – Famous Trials series (1928) London, Geoffrey Bles
Dubro, J. *Mob Rule* (1985) Toronto, Macmillan
——and R. F. Rowland *King of the Mob* (1987) Markham, Penguin
Du Rose, J. *Murder Was My Business* (1971) London, W H Allen
Englade, K. *Cellar of Horror* (1989) London, Angus & Robertson
Fabian, R. *Fabian of the Yard* (1955) London, Heirloom Modern World Library
——*London After Dark* (1954) London, The Naldrett Press
Farran, R. *Operation Tombola* (1960) London, Collins
Felstead, S. T. *Sir Richard Muir: The Memoirs of a Public Prosecutor* (1927) London, The Bodley Head
Fielding, S. *The Hangman's Record, Volume One 1868–1899* (1994) Beckenham, Chancery House Press
——*The Hangman's Record, Volume Two 1900–1929* (1995) Beckenham, Chancery House Press
Foot, P. *Murder at the Farm* (1996) London, Sidgwick & Jackson
Frankos, D. with W. Hoffman and L. Headley *Contract Killer* (1993) London, Warner Books
Fraser, F. and J. Morton *Mad Frank* (1994) London, Little, Brown
Fried, A. *The Rise and Fall of the Jewish Gangster* (1980) New York, Holt, Rinehard & Winston
Furneaux, R. *Famous Criminal Cases 6* (1960) London, Odhams Press
Gifford, Lord *The Broadwater Farm Inquiry* (1986) London, Karia Press
Gilmore, J. *Severed* (1995) London, Warner Books
Goodman, J. *Acts of Murder* (1986) London, Harrap

——(ed) *Masterpieces of Murder* (1992) London, Robson Publishing

——*Modern Murder File* (1995) London, Mandarin

Greenwall, H. *They Were Murdered in France* (1957) London, Jarrolds

Gurr, T. and H. H. Cox *Famous Australian Crimes* (1957) London, Frederick Muller

Harris, N. *Famous Crimes* (1933) Los Angeles, Arthur Vernon Agency

Harris, P. *The Garvie Trial* (1969) Glasgow, Impulse Books

Harrison, R. *Criminal Calendar* (1951) London, Jarrolds

Hastings, P. *Cases in Court* (1948) London, Heinemann

Heppenstall, R. *Bluebeard and After* (1972) London, Peter Owen

Higgins, R. *In the Name of the Law* (1958) London, John Long

Horn, T. *Life of Tom Horn: Government Scout and Interpreter, Written by Himself* (1964) University of Oklahoma Press

Hugget, R. and P. Berry *Daughters of Cain* (1956) London, Allen and Unwin

Humphreys, T. *Criminal Days* (1946) London, Hodder & Stoughton

Hyde, H. M. *Norman Birkett* (1964) London, Hamish Hamilton

Jackson, R. *Francis Camps* (1983) London, Panther

Jones, E. *The Last Two to Hang* (1966) London, Macmillan

Karp, C. *When Justice Fails* (1991) Toronto, McClelland & Stewart

Kelly, V. *The Charge is Murder* (1965) Adelaide, Rigby Ltd

Kennedy, L. *A Presumption of Innocence* (1976) London, Gollancz

Knight, R. *Black Knight* (1990) London, Century

Knowlton, J. and M. Newton *Daddy Was the Black Dahlia Killer* (1995) New York, Pocket Books

Knox, B. *Court of Murder* (1968) London, John Long

Kobler, J. *Capone* (1972) New York, Fawcett Publications Inc

Kray, Reggie *Villains We Have Known* (1993) Leeds, N K Publications

Kray, Reggie and Ronnie *Our Story* (1988) London, Pan

Lane, B. *The Encyclopaedia of Forensic Science* (1992) London, Headline

——and W. Gregg *The Encyclopedia of Serial Killers* (1992) London, Headline

——*The New Encyclopedia of Serial Killers* (1996) London, Headline

Leopold, N. *Life Plus 99 Years* (1958) New York, Doubleday

Lewis, D. and P. Hughman *Most Unnatural: An Inquiry into the Stafford Case* (1971) London, Penguin

Leyton, E. *Hunting Humans* (1989) Harmondsworth, Penguin

Linedecker, C. L. *The Man Who Killed Boys* (1980) New York, St Martin's Press

Lloyd, G. *The Part and Parcel Murders* (1993) London, Robert Hale

Lucas, N. *Britain's Gangland* (1969) London, Pan Books

Maas, P. *The Valachi Papers* (1970) St Albans, Panther

Marjoribanks, E. *The Life of Sir Edward Marshall Hall* (1926) London, Gollancz

Marshall, J. *The True Story of the Ollie Murder* (1988) Lewes, Seagull Books

Marshall Cavendish *Murder Casebook No 23 – The Paperboy Killing*, London
——*Murder Casebook No 26 – Glasgow's Multiple Killer*, London
——*Murder Casebook No 89 – The Lonely Head-Hunter*, London
——*Murder Casebook No 135 – Billionaire Boys' Club Murders*, London
McClement, F. *The Strange Case of Ambrose Small* (1974) Toronto, McClelland & Stewart
McConnell, B. *Found Naked and Dead* (1974) London, NEL
Meehan, P. *Innocent Villain* (1978) London, Pan Books
Millen, E. *Specialist in Crime* (1972) London, Harrap
Milner, E. R. *The Lives and Times of Bonnie & Clyde* (1996) Southern Illinois University Press
Morris, T and L. Blom-Cooper *A Calendar of Murder* (1964) London, Michael Joseph
Morn, F. *The Eye That Never Sleeps* (1982) Indiana University Press
Morton, J. *Gangland* (1992) London, Little, Brown
——*Gangland Volume 2* (1994) London, Little, Brown
——*Supergrasses and Informers* (1995) London, Little, Brown
Murdoch, D. *Disappearances* (1972) Toronto, Doubleday
Murray, G. 'The Ragged Stranger' in *The Chicago Crime Book* (1968) London, Souvenir Press
Narborough, F. *Murder on my Mind* (1959) London, Alan Wingate
Napley, D. *Not Without Prejudice* (1982) London, Harrap
Nash, J. R. *Bloodletters and Badmen, A Narrative Encyclopedia of American Criminals from the Pilgrims to the Present* (1973) New York, M Evans
——*Murder, America* (1981) London, Harrap
——*World Encyclopedia of 20th Century Murder* (1992) London, Headline
——*World Encyclopedia of Organised Crime* (1993) London, Headline
Normanton, H. (ed) *Famous British Trials: the Trial of Norman Thorne* (1992) London, Geoffrey Bles
O'Brien, D. *Two of a Kind* (1985) New York, NAL
Odell, R. *Landmarks in 20th Century Murder* (1995) London, Headline
O'Malley, M. *Gross Misconduct* (1988) Toronto, Penguin
Parker, R. *Rough Justice* (1981) London, Sphere
Pasley, F. D. *Al Capone* (1966) London, Faber & Faber
Pearson, J. *The Profession of Violence* (1985) London, Grafton
Prone, T. *Irish Murders* (1992) Swords, Poolbeg
Read, L. and J. Morton *Nipper* (1991) London, Macdonald
Robey, E. *The Jester and the Court* (1976) London, William Kimber
Robinson, J. *The Laundrymen* (1994) London, Simon & Schuster
Roemer, W. F. *The Enforcer* (1994) New York, Ballantine
Rule, A. *The Stranger Beside Me* (1994) London, Warner Books

Rumbelow, D. *The Complete Jack the Ripper* (1987) London, W H Allen

Salerno, J. and S. J. Rivele *The Plumber* (1991) New York, Knightsbridge Publishing Company

Saunders, G. *Casebook of the Bizarre* (1991) Edinburgh, John Donald

Schoenberg, R. *Mr Capone* (1995) London, Robson Books

Schwartz, T. *The Hillside Strangler* (1981) New York, Doubleday

Scott, J. *Caught in Court* (1989) London, André Deutsch

Sereny, G. *The Case of Mary Bell* (1972) London, Eyre Methuen

Sharpe, A. *Crimes that Shocked Australia* (1987) Crows Nest NSW, Atrand

Shew, E. S. *A Companion to Murder* (1961) New York, Alfred Knopf

——*A Second Companion to Murder* (1962) New York, Alfred Knopf

Sifakis, C. *The Encyclopedia of American Crime* (1982) New York, Facts on File

——*The Mafia File* (1988) Wellingborough, Equation

Simpson, K. *Forty Years of Murder* (1978) London, Harrap

Skelton, D. *A Time to Kill* (1995) Edinburgh, Mainstream

——and L. Brownlie *Frightener* (1992) Edinburgh, Mainstream

Smith, S. *Mostly Murder* (1984) London, Panther

Stoddart, C. N. *Bible John* (1980) Edinburgh, Paul Harris Publishing

Stockman, R. *The Hangman's Diary* (1993) London, Headline

Stone, I. *Clarence Darrow for the Defence* (1941) New York, Doubleday

Sullivan, T. and P. T. Maiken *Killer Clown* (1983) New York, Grosset & Dunlap

Symons, J. *A Reasonable Doubt* (1966) London, The Cresset Press

Tate, T. and R. Wyre *Murder Squad* (1992) London, Thames Mandarin

Taylor, B. and S. Knight *Perfect Murder* (1988) London, Grafton

Teresa, V. and T.C. Renner *My Life in the Mafia* (1973) London, Hart-Davis, MacGibbon

Thomas, D. with R. Grant *Seek out the Guilty* (1969) London, John Long

Thorwald, J. *The Marks of Cain* (1965) London, Thames & Hudson

Thurlow, D. *The Essex Triangle* (1990) London, Robert Hale

Treherne, J. *The Strange History of Bonnie and Clyde* (1984) London, Jonathan Cape

Tullett, T. *No Answer from Foxtrot Eleven* (1967) London, Michael Joseph

Wambaugh, J. *The Blooding* (1989) New York, William Morrow

Warner Hooke, N. and G. Thomas *Marshall Hall* (1960) London, Arthur Barker

Watkins, L. *The Sleepwalk Killers* (1976) London, Everest Books

Wensley, F. *Detective Days* (1931) London, Cassell

Whittington-Egan, R. and M. *The Murder Almanac* (1992) Glasgow, Neil Wilson Publishing

——*The Bedside Book of Murder* (1988) Newton Abbot, David & Charles Publishers

Wilkinson, L. *Behind the Face of Crime* (1967) London, Muller

Williams, P. *The General* (1995) Dublin, The O'Brien Press

Wilson, C. *Written in Blood* (1989) Wellingborough, Equation

Wilson, G. and D. Harnson *Inquest: Helen Smith and the Whole Truth* (1983) London, Methuen

Wilson, J. G. *The Trial of Peter Manuel* (1959) London, Secker & Warburg

Woffinden, B. *Miscarriages of Justice* (1987) London, Hodder & Stoughton

Wolf, M. J. and K. Mader *Fallen Angels* (1989) New York, Ballantine Books

——*L A Crime* (1989) Wellingborough, Equation

Yallop, D. *Deliver Us From Evil* (1980) London, Macdonald

Index